Combat and Morale in the North African Campaign

Military professionals and theorists have long understood the relevance of morale in war. Montgomery, the victor at El Alamein, said, following the battle, that 'the more fighting I see, the more I am convinced that the big thing in war is morale'. Jonathan Fennell, in examining the North African campaign through the lens of morale, challenges conventional explanations for Allied success in one of the most important and controversial campaigns in British and Commonwealth history. He introduces new sources, notably censorship summaries of soldiers' mail, and an innovative methodology that assesses troop morale not only on the evidence of personal observations and official reports but also on contemporaneously recorded rates of psychological breakdown, sickness, desertion and surrender. He shows for the first time that a major morale crisis and stunning recovery decisively affected Eighth Army's performance during the critical battles on the Gazala and El Alamein lines in 1942.

JONATHAN FENNELL is Lecturer in Defence Studies with King's College London, at the Airmen's Command Squadron, Royal Air Force, Halton.

Cambridge Military Histories

Edited by

HEW STRACHAN
Chichele Professor of the History of War, University of Oxford and
Fellow of All Souls College, Oxford

GEOFFREY WAWRO
Major General Olinto Mark Barsanti Professor of Military History, and
Director, Center for the Study of Military History, University of North
Texas

The aim of this new series is to publish outstanding works of research on warfare
throughout the ages and throughout the world. Books in the series will take a broad
approach to military history, examining war in all its military, strategic, political
and economic aspects. The series is intended to complement Studies in the Social
and Cultural History of Modern Warfare by focusing on the 'hard' military history
of armies, tactics, strategy and warfare. Books in the series will consist mainly of
single author works – academically vigorous and groundbreaking – which will be
accessible to both academics and the interested general reader.

A list of titles in the series can be found at:

www.cambridge.org/militaryhistories

Combat and Morale in the North African Campaign

The Eighth Army and the Path to El Alamein

Jonathan Fennell

CAMBRIDGE
UNIVERSITY PRESS

CAMBRIDGE
UNIVERSITY PRESS

The Edinburgh Building, Cambridge CB2 8RU, UK

Published in the United States of America by Cambridge University Press, New York

Cambridge University Press is part of the University of Cambridge.

It furthers the University's mission by disseminating knowledge in the pursuit of
education, learning and research at the highest international levels of excellence.

www.cambridge.org
Information on this title: www.cambridge.org/9781107681651

© Jonathan Fennell 2011

First published 2011
First paperback edition 2013

A catalogue record for this publication is available from the British Library

Library of Congress Cataloguing in Publication data
Fennell, Jonathan, 1979–
Combat and morale in the North African campaign : the Eighth Army and the
path to El Alamein / Jonathan Fennell.
      p.   cm. – (Cambridge military histories)
ISBN 978-0-521-19270-5 (hardback)
1. World War, 1939–1945 – Campaigns – Africa, North.   2. El Alamein, Battle
of, Egypt, 1942.   3. Great Britain. Army. Army, Eighth.   4. World War,
1939–1945 – Psychological aspects.   5. Morale.   6. Combat – Psychological
aspects.   7. Psychology, Military.   I. Title.
D766.82.F46   2010
940.54´2321–dc22

                                                                2010030395

ISBN 978-0-521-19270-5 Hardback
ISBN 978-1-107-68165-1 Paperback

Contents

Illustrations

Figures

Maps

Tables

Acknowledgements

I was sitting at a desk in the Australian War Memorial in Canberra when I was handed the first file of a series of documents that in many ways forms the spine of the research on which this book is based. I had the official censorship summaries of the soldiers' mail for Middle East Command in my hands. Because there are no copies of these files in UK archives, as far as I know I was the first historian tracing the morale of British soldiers in the desert to have the opportunity to study them.

The journey that brought me to this exciting moment and the work of writing this book have been assisted by many people, not all of whom I can mention here.

Above all, I cannot thank Professor Hew Strachan enough for his continuous help and guidance and for all the support and encouragement he has given me, not only as a research student under his supervision at Oxford but also through the long germination of this book and in my lecturing career.

I owe a special debt of gratitude to Dr Peter Stanley, who kindly pointed me in the right direction in the archives in Australia and also lent me a 'moveable archive' of material that he had used for his book *Alamein: The Australian Story*.

I also thank Professor Peter Dennis, Dr Ian McGibbon and John Crawford, who all took the time to meet me in Australia and New Zealand and discuss matters relating to their countries' forces in the desert.

I also owe a debt of gratitude to Dr Niall Barr for discussing my research with me and lending me material from his own work on *Pendulum of War*. I would like to thank Professor Gary Sheffield for contributing to the direction of this book and Dr Jeremy Crang and Dr Ben Shephard for taking the time to talk to me and pointing out many avenues of research I could follow.

Dr Declan Downey and Dr William Mulligan, who took me under their wings at University College Dublin as an undergraduate, have never failed to support and advise me over the years. My college supervisor at Pembroke College, Oxford, Dr Adrian Gregory, always added insights to the direction of my research.

Michael Watson, Chloe Howell, Joanna Breeze, Angela Turnbull and Hannah Ellis-Jones at Cambridge University Press could not have been more supportive in helping me finish off this book while juggling the commitments of beginning an academic career.

My colleagues at King's College London, the Royal Air Force College at Cranwell, the Airmen's Command Squadron at Halton, and in particular Dr Joel Hayward, have been very understanding and supportive and have facilitated me in every way possible during the final stages of completing the manuscript for this book.

Furthermore, without the patient help and guidance of many librarians and archivists this book could never have been completed. Special thanks are due to all those who helped and guided me at the National Archives, the Imperial War Museum, the Liddell Hart Centre for Military Archives, the Australian War Memorial, Archives Australia, the National Archives of New Zealand, the Alexander Turnbull Library and the South African Military Archives Depot.

I am grateful to Miranda Kaufmann for lending me Hugh Mainwaring's unpublished memoirs and Alexander Leithead for reading through a draft of the unfinished manuscript.

I would also like to thank my Anna, who has brought so much happiness and love into my life, and who has provided unending support during the critical phases of this project.

Finally I would like to thank my mother and father. They have offered unbelievable love and support throughout the process of writing this book and proof-read uncountable drafts. I cannot imagine having better or more wonderful parents.

Abbreviations

AA	Anti-aircraft
AAMC	Australian Army Medical Corps
ABCA	Army Bureau of Current Affairs
ACS	Army Council Secretariat
ADH	Assistant Director of Hygiene
ADMS	Assistant Director of Medical Services
AEC	Army Education Corps
AES	Army Education Scheme
AFV	Armoured fighting vehicle
AG	Adjutant-General
AIF	Australian Imperial Force
AIR	Records of the Air Ministry
ANZ	Archives New Zealand
ATk.	Anti-tank
AWM	Australian War Memorial
AWOL	Absent without leave
BAR	Browning automatic rifle
BBC	British Broadcasting Corporation
BEF	British Expeditionary Force
BLM	Bernard Law Montgomery
Bn	Battalion
CAB	Records of the Cabinet Office
CCS	Casualty Clearing Station
CGS	Chief of the General Staff
CIGS	Chief of the Imperial General Staff
C-in-C	Commander-in-Chief
CO	Commanding Officer
Col.	Colonel
Coys.	Companies
DAG	Deputy Adjutant-General
DCIGS	Deputy Chief of the Imperial General Staff

DCS	Deputy Chief of Staff
DDMS	Deputy Director Medical Services
DGAMS	Director-General of the Army Medical Service
DGAW&E	Director-General of Army Welfare and Education
Div Docs	Divisional Documents
DMI	Directorate of Military Intelligence
DMO	Directorate of Military Organisation
DMT	Director of Military Training
DSO	Distinguished Service Order
DSP	Directorate of Selection of Personnel
ECAC	Executive Committee of the Army Council
ENSA	Entertainments National Service Association
FO	Records of the Foreign Office
FSR	Field Service Regulations
FSS	Field Security Section
Gds.	Guards
Gdsm.	Guardsman
GHQ	General Headquarters
GOC	General Officer Commanding
GOC-in-C	General Officer Commanding-in-Chief
GSO	General Staff Officer
HO	Records of the Home Office
HW	Records of Government Communications Headquarters
INF	Records of the Central Office of Information
IO	Information Officer
IWM	Imperial War Museum
LAWO	Local Army Welfare Officer
LHCMA	Liddell Hart Centre for Military Archives
Lieut.	Lieutenant
ME	Middle East
MEF	Middle Eastern Forces
MEFCWS	Middle East Field Censorship Weekly Summary
MEMCFS	Middle East Military Censorship Fortnightly Summary
MEMCWS	Middle East Military Censorship Weekly Summary
METM	Middle East Training Memorandum
MG	Machine gun

MO	Medical Officer
NA	National Archives
n/a	Not available
NAA	National Archives of Australia
NAAFI	Navy, Army and Air Force Institutes
NCO	Non-Commissioned Officer
n.d.	Not dated
NOSU	New Officer Selection Unit
NYD(N)	Not yet diagnosed (nervous)
NZ	New Zealand
NZEF	New Zealand Expeditionary Force
OCTUs	Officer Corps Training Units
OR	Other rank
PIN	Records of the Ministry of Pensions
POW	Prisoner(s) of war
PREM	Records of the Prime Minister's Office
QMG	Quartermaster-General
RA	Royal Artillery
RAA	Royal Australian Artillery
RAC	Royal Armoured Corps
RAF	Royal Air Force
RAMC	Royal Army Medical Corps
RE	Royal Engineers
RMO	Regimental Medical Officer
RN	Royal Navy
RO	Routine order
RSM	Regimental Sergeant Major
RTR	Royal Tank Regiment
S-of-S	Secretary of State
SAMAD	South African Military Archives Depot
SAMC	South African Medical Corps
SSAFA	Soldiers', Sailors' and Airmen's Families Association
UDF	Union Defence Force
UWH	Union War Histories
VCIGS	Vice Chief of the Imperial General Staff
WDF	Western Desert Force
WO	Records of the War Office
WOSBs	War Office Selection Boards
WR	War Records

Maps

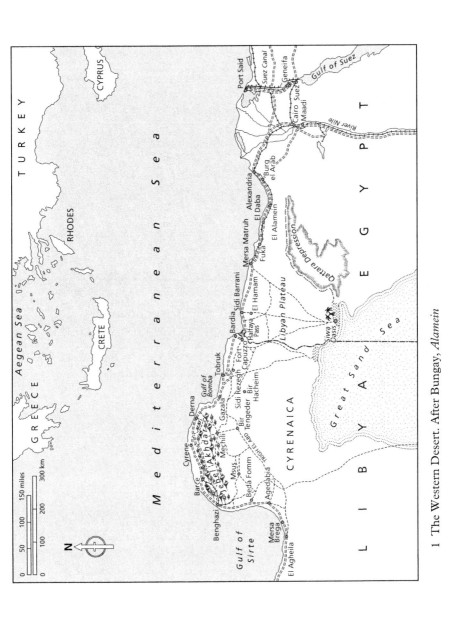

1 The Western Desert. After Bungay, *Alamein*

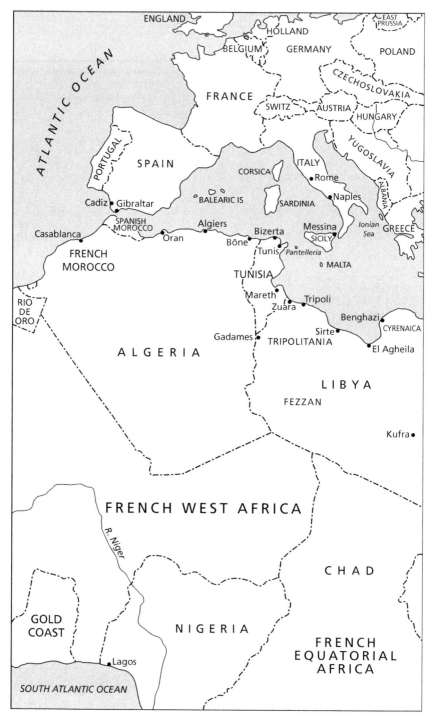

2 The Middle East theatre of war. Kitchen, *Rommel's Desert War*

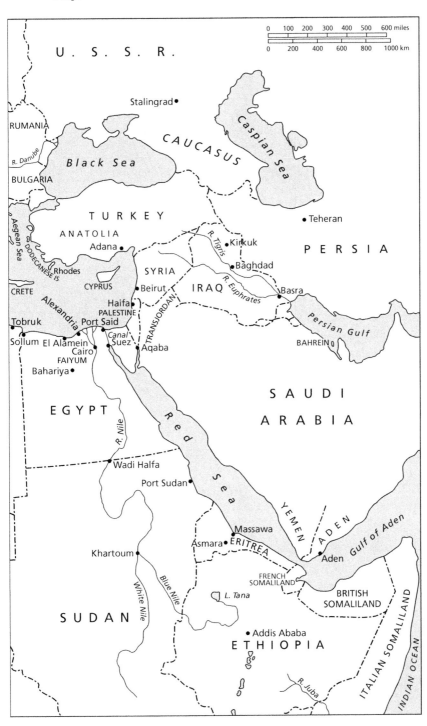

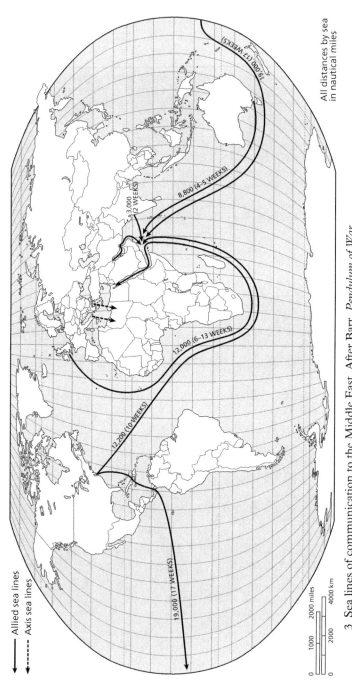

— Allied sea lines
---- Axis sea lines

19,000 (17 WEEKS)

12,200 (10 WEEKS)

12,000 (6–13 WEEKS)

3,000 (2 WEEKS)

8,800 (4–5 WEEKS)

19,000 (17 WEEKS)

All distances by sea
in nautical miles

0   1000   2000 miles
0   2000   4000 km

3 Sea lines of communication to the Middle East. After Barr, *Pendulum of War*

Introduction

> We have come through another great war and its reality is already cloaked in the mists of peace. In the course of that war we learned anew that man is supreme, that it is the soldier who fights who wins battles, that fighting means using a weapon, and that it is the heart of man which controls this use.
>
> (S. L. A. Marshall)[1]

On 20 October 1942, three days before the start of the battle of El Alamein, General Georg Stumme, in temporary command of the German and Italian *Panzerarmee Afrika*, informed his commanders that 'the enemy is by no means certain of victory. We must increase that uncertainty every day ... The feeling of complete moral superiority over the enemy must be awakened and fostered in every soldier, from the highest commander to the youngest man ... From this moral superiority comes coolness, confidence, self-reliance and an unshakeable will to fight. This is the secret to every victory.'[2]

In such words Stumme articulated his firm belief that morale was the key factor that would decide the upcoming battle of El Alamein. Sir Bernard Law Montgomery, Stumme's opponent at El Alamein, believed that morale was equally significant. He wrote after the battle that 'the more fighting I see, the more I am convinced that the big thing in war is morale'.[3] It is vital, therefore, he said, 'that we make a study of this subject'.[4] This book bases its analysis on this rationale, that war should be studied through the lens of morale. It considers the relationship

---

[1] S. L. A. Marshall, *Men against Fire: The Problem of Battle Command in Future War* (Gloucester, 1978), p. 23.

[2] Australian War Memorial (AWM) 54 492/4/77 Stumme to Lower Formations, 20 October 1942, German–Italian Forces in Africa, September to October 1942, Translation of Appendices to Panzerarmee Afrika War Diary. Quoted in Niall Barr, *Pendulum of War: The Three Battles of El Alamein* (London, 2005), pp. 305–6.

[3] National Archives (NA) War Office File (WO) 277/16 Lieut.-Col. J. H. A. Sparrow, 'The Second World War 1939–1945, Army Morale', p. 2.

[4] Imperial War Museum (IWM) 99/1/2 Maj.-Gen. Raymond Briggs, 'Exercise Evolution', p. 40.

between morale and combat performance, explores the issues that affected the morale of Eighth Army and addresses the question of whether morale was a key factor in deciding the outcome of the battle of El Alamein.

Throughout history, soldiers, military theorists and historians have identified morale as an important factor in combat performance. Four hundred years before Christ, Xenophon argued that 'in action, the sustaining of morale was an imperative',[5] and when morale was high 'action must be sought'.[6] In the sixteenth century, Machiavelli commented that 'if an army is to win the day it is essential to give it confidence so as to make it feel sure that it must win, whatever happens'.[7] Napoleon had his dictum that the moral outweighs the material by three to one.[8] Clausewitz argued that moral elements were 'among the most important in war',[9] while du Picq wrote that 'nothing can wisely be described in an army ... without exact knowledge of the fundamental instrument, man, and his state of mind, his morale'.[10] Foch's famous formula 'Victory = Will' was 'representative of opinion among military professionals throughout Europe' at the time of the First World War.[11] Liddell Hart argued, between the wars, for 'the predominance of moral factors in all military decisions'. On them, he argued, 'constantly turns the issue of war and battle. And in the history of war they form the more constant factors, changing only in degree, whereas the physical factors are fundamentally different in almost every war and every situation.'[12] Referring to the Second World War, Patton claimed that 80 per cent of a commander's role was 'to arouse morale in his men'.[13] Even today, General Sir Rupert Smith argues that 'the will to win is the paramount factor in any battle' and that 'we call this will morale'.[14]

[5] Godfrey Hutchinson, *Xenophon and the Art of Command* (London, 2000), p. 60.
[6] Ibid., p. 191.   [7] Niccolò Machiavelli, *The Discourses* (London, 1998), pp. 493–4.
[8] Letter from Napoleon to his brother Joseph advising him on how to rule Spain, 27 August 1808. Quoted in Trevor N. Dupuy, 'Theory of Combat', in Franklin D. Margiotta (ed.), *Brassey's Encyclopaedia of Military History and Biography* (London, 1994), p. 967.
[9] Carl von Clausewitz, *On War* (London, 1993), p. 216. First published in German in 1831.
[10] Col. Ardant du Picq, 'Battle Studies: Ancient and Modern Battle', in *Roots of Strategy, Book Two: Three Military Classics* (Mechanicsburg, PA, 1987), p. 65.
[11] David Englander, 'Mutinies and Military Morale', in Hew Strachan (ed.), *The Oxford Illustrated History of the First World War* (Oxford, 1998), p. 191.
[12] B. H. Liddell Hart, *The Decisive Wars of History: A Study in Strategy* (London, 1929), p. 3.
[13] Rick Atkinson, *An Army at Dawn: The War in North Africa, 1942–1943* (London, 2003), p. 138.
[14] General Sir Rupert Smith, *The Utility of Force: The Art of War in the Modern World* (London, 2005), p. 241.

Historians have not studied morale to the extent that might be expected from the significance accorded it in such statements. Morale is a nebulous and difficult to define concept. It is not obviously amenable to quantification. General Sir Ronald Adam, the Adjutant-General of the British Army, who set up the War Office Morale Committee in March 1942, said that morale could only be 'painted with the impressionistic brush of a Turner and not with the microscopic detail of a Canaletto'.[15] Without a clear and reliable definition of morale, or an accepted approach to quantify or 'measure' morale, it is extremely difficult to make connections between military outcomes and morale. Historians have, therefore, and perhaps quite wisely, concentrated on more quantifiable subjects such as technology, economics, logistics, fire and manoeuvre to explain the outcomes of battles and wars.

Published work on morale is consequentially quite limited. Most of the literature on morale has focused on the 'apocalyptic' struggles of 'total war' in the twentieth century. Beginning with John Baynes's *Morale: A Study of Men and Courage*, scholars have tried to explain how soldiers continued fighting for four terrible years in the dreadful conditions of the trenches in the First World War.[16] These authors have concentrated in particular on the French mutinies of 1917, the British Étaples mutiny of the same year and the German collapse at the end of 1918. Their works have clearly highlighted a connection between morale and combat performance, although one that, more often than not, (Alexander Watson's *Enduring the Great War* being an exception) is based mainly on personal accounts.[17]

Literature on morale in the Second World War has focused largely on the eastern front and Pacific theatres of operations. Much of this literature has concentrated on the ideological issues that can both build morale and

---

[15] NA WO 259/44 'Army Morale': Paper by Adjutant-General, May 1944.

[16] John Baynes, *Morale: A Study of Men and Courage* (London, 1967); Tony Ashworth, *Trench Warfare: The Live and Let Live System* (London, 1980); Hugh Cecil and Peter H. Liddle, *Facing Armageddon: The First World War Experienced* (London, 1996); John Horne (ed.), *State, Society and Mobilization in Europe during the First World War* (London, 1997); David Englander, 'Soldiering and Identity: Reflections on the Great War', *War in History*, 1(3), (1994); G. D. Sheffield, *Leadership in the Trenches: Officer–Man Relations, Morale and Discipline in the British Army in the Era of the First World War* (London, 2000); Alexander Watson, *Enduring the Great War: Combat, Morale and Collapse in the German and British Armies, 1914–1918* (Cambridge, 2008).

[17] Leonard V. Smith, *Between Mutiny and Obedience: The Case of the French Fifth Infantry Division during World War I* (Princeton, 1994); Wilhelm Deist, 'The Military Collapse of the German Empire: The Reality Behind the Stab-in-the-Back Myth', *War in History*, 3(2), (1996); David Englander, 'Mutinies and Military Morale', in Strachan (ed.), *The Oxford Illustrated History of the First World War*; Douglas Gill and Gloden Dallas, 'Mutiny at Étaples Base in 1917', in *Past and Present*, 69 (November 1975).

also lead to a barbarisation of warfare in combat between different cultures. These works put forward strong arguments to support the view that morale (sustained by e.g. the primary group, ideology, discipline or training) and combat performance are intimately related. However, again, these studies are mainly dependent on personal sources for their analysis of morale.[18]

Historians of the British Army in the Second World War and of Eighth Army in the North African campaign have mostly also steered clear of morale, although some have acknowledged that morale played an indefinable role in defeat and victory.[19] Instead, the largest body of literature on North Africa has addressed the issue of leadership.[20] The qualities and deficiencies of Field Marshal Montgomery, Field Marshal Sir Claude Auchinleck and Field Marshal Erwin Rommel have been tirelessly debated decade after decade since the cessation of hostilities. More recently, a number of new books have been published, focusing on the operational history of the campaign. Niall Barr's *Pendulum of War*, Peter Stanley and Mark Johnston's *Alamein: The Australian Story*, and Martin Kitchen's *Rommel's Desert War* stand out as excellent narratives that base their analysis firmly on extensive study of the primary sources. These works have pointed to the fact that morale played a role in determining

---

[18] See for example, Paul Addison and Angus Calder (eds.), *Time to Kill: The Soldier's Experience of War in the West 1939–1945* (London, 1997); John Ellis, *The Sharp End: The Fighting Man in World War II* (London, 1993; first published 1980); Omer Bartov, *The Eastern Front, 1941–45: German Troops and the Barbarisation of Warfare* (Oxford, 1985); Omer Bartov, *Hitler's Army: Soldiers, Nazis, and War in the Third Reich* (Oxford, 1992); John W. Dower, *War without Mercy: Race and Power in the Pacific War* (London, 1986); Gerald F. Linderman, *The World within War: American Combat Experience in World War II* (London, 1997); Sam C. Sarkessian (ed.), *Combat Effectiveness: Cohesion, Stress, and the Volunteer Military* (London, 1980); Catherine Merridale, *Ivan's War: The Red Army 1939–45* (London, 2005); Catherine Merridale, 'Culture, Ideology and Combat in the Red Army, 1939–45', *Journal of Contemporary History*, 41(2) (2006); Mark Johnston, *Australian Soldiers and Their Adversaries in World War II* (Cambridge, 2000); Hew Strachan, 'Training, Morale and Modern War', *Journal of Contemporary History*, 41(2) (2006).

[19] Barr, *Pendulum of War*, p. xxxix; Mark Johnston and Peter Stanley, *Alamein: The Australian Story* (Oxford, 2002), p. 270; Michael Carver, *Tobruk* (London, 1964), p. 262.

[20] See for example, Correlli Barnett, *The Desert Generals* (London, 1983; first published 1960. In the 1983 (2nd) edition Barnett addressed further some issues he had touched on in the first edition); Michael Carver, *Dilemmas of the Desert War: A New Look at the Libyan Campaign 1940–1942* (London, 1986); John Connell, *Auchinleck: A Biography of Field-Marshal Sir Claude Auchinleck* (London, 1959); Nigel Hamilton, *The Full Monty: Montgomery of Alamein 1887–1942* (London, 2002); Barrie Pitt, *The Crucible of War: Wavell's Command: The Definitive History of the Desert War*, vol. I (London, 2001; first published 1980); Barrie Pitt, *The Crucible of War: Auchinleck's Command: The Definitive History of the Desert War*, vol. II (London, 2001; first published 1980); Barrie Pitt, *The Crucible of War: Montgomery and Alamein: The Definitive History of the Desert War*, vol. III (London, 2001; first published 1982); Desmond Young, *Rommel* (London, 1950).

combat performance in the desert, without fully addressing the issue and its significance.[21]

There can be no doubt that the vast body of literature published on El Alamein has been due, in many ways, to the fact that the battle holds a special place in the British imagination. It was at El Alamein that British and Empire forces first defeated the Germans on land in the Second World War. Eighth Army was a remarkably heterogeneous force (with British, Australian, New Zealand, South African, Indian, Greek, French, Cypriot and even a few American soldiers) that represented, to a large extent, the strength of the Empire fighting together in pursuit of a common cause. Churchill remarked that it 'may almost be said, "before Alamein we never had a victory. After Alamein we never had a defeat."'[22] The battle saved the reputation of the British Army. It also created the myth of the Eighth Army and Montgomery.[23]

After the victory, the British and American press gave the battle saturation coverage. With nearly one hundred Allied war correspondents in the desert, including Alan Moorehead and Chester Wilmot, the struggle was well covered and commanded a mass following in the home countries.[24] Within months, the Allied publics could watch the events that had unfolded, on the big screen. Released in March 1943, *Desert Victory* became the biggest box-office success of all British war documentaries, grossing an impressive £77,250 in the first twelve months, against production costs of £5,793. Its director, David MacDonald, won an Oscar.[25]

It is perhaps no wonder that El Alamein has become so famous, considering the commander who brought the victory. Montgomery was, with the possible exception of Kitchener, Britain's first 'celebrity' general of the twentieth century. Where other more austere, traditional generals, such as Field Marshal Archibald Lord Wavell and Auchinleck, shunned the limelight, Montgomery actively embraced it and reaped the rewards. Following the war, Montgomery became a national symbol and remained in the public focus for as long as he lived, if for no other reason than he was consistently controversial. He was relentlessly self-aggrandising and obnoxiously insistent on his own infallibility. Nevertheless, 'Monty' became a tabloid hero. 'He was the people's soldier.'[26]

---

[21] Barr, *Pendulum of War*; Johnston and Stanley, *Alamein;* Martin Kitchen, *Rommel's Desert War: Waging World War II in North Africa, 1941–1943* (Cambridge, 2009). This is entirely understandable, as these works set out to describe the operational history of the El Alamein campaign rather than deal with thematic issues such as morale.

[22] Winston Churchill, *The Second World War* (London, 2002), p. 630. This abridged version of the book was first published in 1959.

[23] Stephen Bungay, *Alamein* (London, 2002), pp. 214–5.   [24] Ibid.

[25] Ibid., p. 216.   [26] Ibid.

Montgomery consistently praised and defended his troops and actively and consciously created Eighth Army's image. In a message to his men, on 8 April 1943, he said, 'I doubt if our Empire has ever possessed such a magnificent fighting machine as the Eighth Army; you have made its name a household word all over the world.'[27] Following the defeat of Germany, Montgomery described the morale of his troops during the war as 'second to none'.[28] In 1983, Correlli Barnett insisted that it was Montgomery's vanity that encouraged him to keep on embellishing his own myth as well as that of the Eighth Army.[29] Nevertheless, the image of the Eighth Army as an elite force with high morale and battle motivation survives today.[30]

This image, created by Montgomery during the war to bolster the confidence of his own troops, tells only a small part of the story. On taking over command of Eighth Army, on 13 August 1942, Montgomery found an army morally shaken, lacking in confidence and potentially on the verge of losing Egypt, the Suez Canal and the oil reserves of the Middle East. 'Early in August, 1942', Montgomery noted in his diary, 'the Eighth Army was in a bad state; the troops had their tails right down and there was no confidence in the higher command. It was clear that ROMMEL was preparing further attacks and the troops were looking over their shoulders for rear lines to which to withdraw ... The whole "atmosphere" was wrong. The condition of Eighth Army ... was almost unbelievable.'[31] Montgomery, who was not, perhaps, the most objective of commentators, would later argue that it was his ability to revive the morale of Eighth Army, in the days leading up to the battles of Alam Halfa and El Alamein, that secured victory for the British forces in the desert and proved the turning point of the war.[32]

The desert war provides an ideal case study to examine the relationship between morale and combat performance and to explore the factors that affect morale. Montgomery's version of events at El Alamein placed morale at the centre of the story. Indeed, if morale is 'the big thing in war', then it rightfully should be placed at the centre of explanations for

[27] IWM Misc 74 (1110) Eighth Army, Personal Message from the Army Commander to be read out to all troops. B. L. Montgomery, General Eighth Army, 8 April 1943.

[28] Bernard Law Montgomery, *The Memoirs of Field Marshal Montgomery of Alamein* (London, 1958), p. xi.

[29] Barnett, *The Desert Generals*, p. 312.

[30] Robin Neillands, *Eighth Army: From the Western Desert to the Alps, 1939–1945* (London, 2004), p. xxv.

[31] IWM Papers of Field Marshal Bernard Law Montgomery (BLM) 27 Diary Notes, 12 August to 23 October 1942.

[32] Montgomery, *Memoirs*, pp. 112–16.

military outcomes. This book, therefore, deals directly with the role of morale at El Alamein.

The approach taken to researching morale incorporates a number of strands. In the first instance, the book tackles the problem of over reliance on personal records and reminiscences in the study of morale by making greater use of official sources. Many of these have been mostly unexplored in work on the desert war, particularly the weekly and fortnightly censorship summaries of the soldiers' mail. About one letter in every thirteen or fourteen sent by the soldiers in the desert was examined by the army authorities to assess the troops' morale and the issues that were affecting it. These summaries described in detail the state of morale of the constituent parts and nationalities of Middle East Command, as well as the causes of good or bad morale. Many of them are to be found in the Australian War Memorial in Canberra and the rest in Wellington, at Archives New Zealand. The portions of the summaries that deal with Australian morale have been used by Mark Johnston and Peter Stanley in their works on the Australian experience during the Second World War. The New Zealand Official Histories and John McLeod, in *Myth and Reality: The New Zealand Soldier in World War II*, used the parts referring to New Zealand morale.[33] The sections referring to British and South African morale, as far as the author is aware, have never before been used.

The summaries covered morale as widely and deeply as possible and only expressed views that represented a considerable body of opinion among the troops in the desert, not isolated instances of over-exuberance or ill temper.[34] When evaluating the historical value of these official sources, however, due attention should be given to the fact that they are based on soldiers' letters. The soldiers of Eighth Army, like soldiers in most armies, would have tried to 'minimise the dangers and discomforts of war in [their] letters to loved ones'.[35] A report on the 'Assessment of Morale by Statistical Methods', carried out during the war, noted that 'in correspondence topics of great importance which are disturbing may well be suppressed, because of fear of upsetting the correspondent or unwillingness to disclose opinions to the censor. There is likely to be little

---

[33] Mark Johnston, *At the Front Line: Experiences of Australian Soldiers in World War II* (Cambridge, 1996); Johnston, *Australian Soldiers and Their Adversaries in World War II*; Johnston and Stanley, *Alamein*; J. L. Scoullar, *Battle for Egypt: The Summer of 1942. Official History of New Zealand in the Second World War 1939–1945* (Wellington, 1955); John McLeod, *Myth and Reality: The New Zealand Soldier in World War II* (Auckland, 1986).

[34] AWM 54 883/2/97 Middle East Field Censorship Weekly Summary (MEFCWS), no. I (12 to 18 November 1941), p. 1.

[35] Myles Hildyard, *It Is Bliss Here: Letters Home 1939–1945* (London 2005), p. 14; ANZ WAII/1/DA508/1 vol. 1, MEFCWS, no. XXXV (8 to 14 July 1942), p. 1.

mention of long standing troubles, however much they may concern the writer.'[36] To that extent the letters written by the troops of Eighth Army can portray a more positive picture of morale than actually existed. Reported instances of poor morale are, therefore, all the more striking.

To give an example of the extent of investigation that went into the formulation of these summaries, the 1st and 2nd New Zealand field censorship sections examined approximately 33,855 letters out of a total of 454,320 sent in April, May and June 1942.[37] From letters such as these, the censors summarised, on a weekly basis, and, from 7 October 1942, fortnightly, the main factors relating to morale, and passed them on to divisional, corps, army and command headquarters. Each summary was quite detailed, being, on average, about twenty typed pages long. Those used in this book cover the period from 3 July 1941 to 15 December 1942, involving, in all, some seventy weekly summaries from the component parts of Middle East Command.[38] The use of these sources allows this study to describe and assess morale in a way heretofore impossible. Every quarter, the Commander-in-Chief in the desert was obliged to write a report, compiled from these summaries and material available at divisional and brigade headquarters, on the state of morale of his troops. All these reports were subsequently passed on to London for inclusion in the War Office quarterly morale reports begun by the Adjutant-General, Ronald Adam, in February 1942 for his newly devised Morale Committee.[39] These, less detailed, official appraisals of morale are also included in this analysis. Official and other documents from the South African Military Archives Depot in Pretoria (many of which are not available in the UK) are also used.

The second main strand of the approach to researching morale taken in this book addresses the conceptualisation and assessment of morale. Morale is a complex term that can be defined in many different ways. Lieutenant-Colonel J. H. A. Sparrow, the compiler of the army morale reports during the Second World War and later Warden of All Souls

---

[36] NA WO 193/453 Assessment of Morale by Statistical Methods (Report by IS2), n.d. but probably 1942 or 1943.

[37] ANZ WAII/1/DA 302/15/1–31 History 1 and 2 NZ Field Censor Sections, p. 35.

[38] The summaries did not address the morale of Indian units; virtually all of the censorship reports that dealt with Indian morale were destroyed. See Gerald Douds, '"Matters of Honour": Indian Troops in the North African and Italian Theatres', in Addison and Calder (eds.), *Time to Kill*, p. 121. The censorship summaries for 3 to 9 September and 10 to 16 December 1941 were not available in the archives.

[39] NA WO 193/453 Morale Committee Papers, 25 February 1942 to 25 October 1945, 'Assessment of Morale by Statistical Methods (Report by IS2). These morale reports were also based on intelligence reports from the Ministry of Intelligence, censorship reports on letters of complaint and enquiry received by the BBC and the *News of the World*, letters to the War Office and courts martial statistics.

College, Oxford, defined morale as the 'attitude of the soldier towards his own employment'.[40] It comprised, according to Sparrow, 'all those things' which made 'the soldier more, or less, keen to carry out his job of soldiering, and readier, or less ready, to endure the hardships, discomforts, and dangers that it entails'.[41] Montgomery defined morale, in a paper he wrote on the subject in April 1946, as 'endurance and courage in supporting fatigue and danger . . . the quality which makes men go forward in an attack and hold their ground in defence. It is the quality without which no war can be won.'[42] Morale, according to these definitions, is not just a feeling or emotion, but is more like an overall causative influence on a soldier's conduct; some psychologists use the term 'motivation' in similar contexts.[43]

Sparrow's and Montgomery's definitions get to the heart of the concept of morale. Sparrow referred to morale as 'keenness' or 'readiness' to carry out a 'job' or action. Montgomery defined morale as 'courage' or 'a quality' which makes soldiers 'go forward' or 'hold their ground', or to put it another way, act in an institutionally required manner. Morale, therefore, can be defined as the willingness of an individual or group to prepare for and engage in an action required by an authority or institution; this willingness may be engendered by a positive desire for action and/ or by the discipline to accept orders to take such action. The degree of morale of an individual or army relates to the extent of their desire or discipline to act, or their determination to see an action through. This is the broad approach to the conceptualisation of morale that is taken in this book.

The problem of how to 'measure' morale is also a major hurdle for historians. Commanders, the War Office and military psychologists and psychiatrists assessed morale not only through the actual fighting behaviour of the troops or their stated 'willingness' to engage with the enemy, as evidenced for instance in the censorship summaries, but by means of a complex web of other factors.[44] These factors can be categorised as follows:

• rates of desertion, sickness, surrender and breakdown among the troops
• the troops' perceptions of their weapons and military hardware as compared with those of the enemy

---

[40] NA WO 277/16 Sparrow, 'Army Morale', p. 1.   [41] Ibid., p. 3.
[42] IWM 99/1/2 Maj.-Gen. Raymond Briggs Papers, Paper by Field Marshal Montgomery, 'Morale in Battle: Analysis, 30 April 1946', p. 43.
[43] Douglas A. Bernstein, Alison Clarke-Stewart, Edward J. Roy, Christopher D. Wickens, *Psychology* (Boston, 1997). p. 337.
[44] NA WO 193/453 Assessment of Morale by Statistical Methods (Report by IS2), n.d. but probably 1942 or 1943.

- the quality of both ordinary recruits and officers and how they were allocated to duties
- supplies of food and water, and other issues relating to leave and the terrain in which a campaign was waged
- news from and contact with home and loved ones, and how this was managed by the army
- welfare provisions for mitigating the discomfort and boredom of army life
- the troops' belief in the cause for which they were fighting and how this was inculcated in them by the army
- the quality of leadership and command
- the troops' experiences of victory and defeat
- the training and disciplining of the troops
- the troops' level of integration within their immediate group
- casualty rates.

Some of these factors are primarily outcomes or correlates of morale; desertion and surrender rates easily fall into this category. Others, however, are influencers or determinants of morale; weapons, quality of manpower and the desert environment would fall into this category. Each factor is explored, using the available primary and secondary sources, thus generating a multidimensional contextualisation of morale that not only recognises and gives expression to morale's complexity but also takes account of the many factors that sustain or undermine morale or are correlates of good or bad morale.

Some factors (such as desertion, surrender, sickness and breakdown rates) are amenable to quantitative analysis and comparisons. Where such analysis on official records is possible, it is presented here. More well established qualitative procedures for assessing troop morale, such as the examination and interpretation of recorded perceptions of the troops themselves, their commanders and the War Office, are also presented. This overall integration of quantitative and qualitative analyses of the many factors that are associated with morale introduces, it is suggested, a methodological innovation in the study of the British Army during the Second World War. The detailed picture of morale that emerges is then compared with Eighth Army's known battlefield performance in the desert. This allows the development of a clear and supportable narrative plotting the relationship between morale and combat performance.

This book aims, as Archibald Wavell advised Staff College candidates in the 1930s, 'to study the human side of military history'. Wavell said that 'to learn that Napoleon in 1796 with 20,000 men beat combined forces of 30,000 by something called "economy of force" or "operating on interior lines" is a mere waste of time'. Instead he encouraged his students to 'understand how a young, unknown man inspired a half-starved, ragged, rather Bolshie crowd; how he filled their bellies; how he out-marched, outwitted, out-bluffed and defeated men who had studied war all their lives and waged it according to the textbooks of the time'.

Then, he said, 'you will have learnt something worth knowing'.[45]

---

[45] Pitt, *Wavell's Command*, p. 4.

1　Morale crisis and recovery

> The War is going to be won or lost on morale. We are too apt to leave the problem alone. Morale is a psychological problem like sex, and therefore the Britisher is almost ashamed to talk about it.
>
> (General Ronald Adam, the Adjutant-General of the British Army, February 1942)[1]

The defeats suffered by the British Army during the first three years of the war, in France, the Far East and North Africa, raised serious questions about the morale of the British and Commonwealth citizen army. Large portions of the British Expeditionary Force (BEF) surrendered in France, while Singapore and Tobruk are names that have become synonymous with humiliation and capitulation. Historians have quite rightly contrasted the zeal and determination of German and Japanese troops with the apparent absence of these qualities among their British and Commonwealth foes.[2]

Ronald Adam, the Adjutant-General of the British Army, believed that defeats, such as the loss of Malaya and Hong Kong and the withdrawal in Burma at the beginning of 1942, had all been 'due to the low morale of our troops'. He considered the issue so crucial and the extent of the problem to be of such concern, that, in February 1942, he proposed the creation of a Morale Committee to the Executive Committee of the Army Council (ECAC).[3] It was apparent to Adam that no authority either inside or outside the War Office was responsible for

(a) surveying and analysing the state of the morale of the Army as a whole and the factors particularly affecting it at any time;

---

[1] NA WO 259/62 Note by AG for consideration by the Executive Committee of the Army Council (ECAC) at their forty-eighth meeting to be held on 27 February 1942.

[2] David French, *Raising Churchill's Army: The British Army and the War against Germany 1919–1945* (Oxford, 2000), pp. 1–3.

[3] NA WO 193/453 Executive Committee of the Army Council. 'Morale in the Army', Note by AG for consideration by the ECAC at their forty-eighth meeting to be held on 27 February 1942, 25 February 1942.

(b) considering what measures should be taken from time to time for the express purpose of improving the state of morale generally;

(c) judging proposed changes in army administration, regulations, etc., in the light of their probable repercussion on morale.[4]

The Morale Committee came into being in March 1942, its terms of reference 'to discuss, monthly, questions of morale arising from reports received from all sources, contained in the Adjutant-General's quarterly report, or brought before them by a member of the committee, and to co-ordinate action'.[5] Adam believed that the committee would 'serve a useful purpose in not only reviewing the causes adversely affecting Army Morale, but in planning ahead to counteract and guard against such adverse influences' in the future.[6]

The setting up of the Morale Committee reflected three strands of thinking on the part of Adam and the War Office. First of all, the very existence of a morale committee signified a realisation that morale was fundamentally crucial to success in modern war. Second, it demonstrated that the War Office thought that there was a problem with British morale. Third, the committee represented a concerted effort by Adam and the War Office to achieve cross-directorate coordination in dealing with morale, so that, as Adam himself said, 'quick action could be taken by those responsible in the various fields'.[7]

Scholarship on the British Army in the Second World War has acknowledged the limitations of a citizen army with questionable morale fighting in a modern industrial war. Recent literature has emphasised that the British and Commonwealth war effort was hampered by the considerable length of time it took for a citizen army to gain the necessary skills and experience to fight and win a war with Germany and Japan. What was learnt in the defeats in France, the Far East and North Africa was vital to the success of the Normandy landings and eventual victory in Northwest Europe.[8]

Another vein of literature, characterised by the works of Stephen Ashley Hart and David French, has argued that the British and Commonwealth

---

[4] NA WO 277/16 Sparrow, 'Army Morale', p. 5.

[5] Ibid., p. 24; WO 193/453 Note by AG for consideration by the ECAC at their forty-ninth meeting on 6 March 1942.

[6] NA WO 193/453 Executive Committee of the Army Council. Minutes of the forty-eighth meeting held on 27 February 1942.

[7] Liddell Hart Centre for Military Archives (LHCMA) Adam 3/13 Narrative covering aspects of work as AG, WWII, chap. 5, Morale and Discipline.

[8] Timothy Harrison Place, *Military Training in the British Army, 1940–1944: From Dunkirk to D-Day* (London, 2000); Douglas Porch, *Hitler's Mediterranean Gamble: The North African and the Mediterranean Campaigns in World War II* (London, 2004); Rick Atkinson, *An Army at Dawn: The War in North Africa, 1942–1943* (London, 2003).

citizen army proved much more militarily effective than has often been suggested.[9] However, both works acknowledge morale difficulties in the British Army during the Second World War. French, in particular, has pointed out that one of the main lessons learned by the British, following Dunkirk, was that morale had been a key factor in the defeat. In fact, both French and Ashley Hart have highlighted the fact that operations and tactics following Dunkirk were specifically designed to take the 'questionable' morale of the citizen army into account. In this way, they fundamentally agreed with Adam in connecting British combat performance with morale.

However, French has also argued that too much has been made of 'the apparently poor morale of the British army'. Historians, he has written, have too often been 'willing to generalize about poor morale from an excessively narrow range of evidence'.[10] Indeed, the lack of an adequate methodology to study and assess morale has made it a very difficult issue to address and it has proved close to impossible to plot relationships between morale and outcomes on the battlefield.

The lack of an adequate approach to studying morale has had similar implications for scholarship on the desert war. Following the cessation of hostilities in May 1945, numerous personal histories and memoirs were published by the men who had fought in the Middle East. Reputations were on the line to be won or lost and in many cases the crisis years of 1941 and 1942 took centre stage. The calamitous defeats at El Algheila, Tobruk and Gazala all required explanation. Among those who fought in the desert, Major-General Sir Francis de Guingand, Lieutenant-General Sir Brian Horrocks, Montgomery and Field Marshal Sir Harold Alexander had all published memoirs by the beginning of the 1960s.[11] These memoirs stressed the significance of a morale crisis in the summer months of 1942. Montgomery's arrival, in August 1942, was hailed as the catalyst for the revival of morale that led to the victories at Alam Halfa and El Alamein in September, October and November 1942.

During the late 1950s and 1960s, a number of works were published revising the commanders' accounts of what had happened in the desert.[12] These painted a very different picture of the events that had unfolded.

---

[9] Stephen Ashley Hart, *Colossal Cracks: Montgomery's 21ˢᵗ Army Group in Northwest Europe, 1944–45* (Westport, CN, 2000); French, *Raising Churchill's Army*.

[10] French, *Raising Churchill's Army*, p. 122.

[11] Montgomery, *Memoirs*; Brian Horrocks, *A Full Life* (London, 1960); Maj.-Gen. Sir F. de Guingand, *Operation Victory* (London, 1947); John North (ed.), *Field-Marshal Earl Alexander of Tunis: The Alexander Memoirs, 1940–1945* (London, 1962).

[12] Barnett, *The Desert Generals*; Connell, *Auchinleck*; C. E. Lucas Phillips, Alamein (London, 1962); Michael Carver, *El Alamein* (London, 1962); Carver, *Tobruk*.

John Connell's biography of Auchinleck and Corelli Barnett's *The Desert Generals* sought, in particular, to reinstate Auchinleck's reputation and query Montgomery's self-proclaimed image as the 'messiah' of Eighth Army. They downplayed the idea that there was a morale crisis when Montgomery assumed command in August 1942, perhaps because the reality of such a crisis might question Auchinleck's contribution to Eighth Army. Thus, the issue of morale was relegated to the periphery of the debate.

Since then, Nigel Hamilton has tried to counter these revisionist works in a number of biographical books concentrating on Montgomery's life and military achievements.[13] Hamilton stressed Montgomery's fundamental belief in the relevance and importance of morale and attributed much of the success of August, September and October 1942 to Montgomery's stirring arrival on the scene. However, Hamilton based most of his arguments on the memoirs and recollections of those who had fought in the desert. In fact, much of the published work on the desert war has failed to base itself fully on the official records that, in the British case, came into the public domain in 1995.[14] The notable exceptions have been *Pendulum of War* by Niall Barr, *Alamein, The Australian Story* by Mark Johnston and Peter Stanley and *Rommel's Desert War* by Martin Kitchen.[15]

This book, like those of Johnston and Stanley, Barr, and Kitchen, bases its analysis on the official records. Chapter 1 first provides a brief outline of the ebb and flow of battle over the relevant months of the North African campaign; battle maps are included in the Appendix. It then addresses the 'myth' of a morale crisis in the summer of 1942. Quantitative analyses of sickness, battle exhaustion, POW and desertion rates, key indicators of the state of troops' morale, are presented together with a qualitative consideration of personal and official perceptions of morale. This provides an opening assessment of the extent to which morale was a key element in Eighth Army's combat performance in the run-up to the battle of El Alamein in October 1942.

The desert war began in September 1940 when Benito Mussolini, The Italian Duce, ordered his Tenth Army, under Marshal Rodolfo Graziani, to invade Egypt. Graziani advanced sixty miles into Egyptian territory, halted,

---

[13] Nigel Hamilton, *Monty: The Making of a General 1887–1942* (London, 1982); Nigel Hamilton, *Master of the Battlefield: Monty's War Years 1942–1944* (London, 1983); Nigel Hamilton, *Monty: The Man behind the Legend* (London, 1988); Hamilton, *The Full Monty*.

[14] John Latimer, *Alamein* (London, 2002); Bungay, *Alamein*; Richard Doherty, *The Sound of History: El Alamein, 1942* (London, 2002).

[15] Barr, *Pendulum of War*; Johnston and Stanley, *Alamein*; Kitchen, *Rommel's Desert War*.

and ordered his forces to construct a number of bases to prepare for further operations. Tenth Army remained in Egypt for three months before the Western Desert Force (WDF), made up of British, Australian and Indian troops, launched a counteroffensive, Operation Compass, in December 1940. The WDF, made up of 36,000 troops, opposed an army of 200,000 Italians. Led by Generals Archibald Wavell and Sir Richard O'Connor, the WDF advanced 500 miles in the space of two months and totally destroyed a force of ten Italian divisions, for a loss of 500 killed, 1,373 wounded, and 55 missing. Around 130,000 prisoners were taken; 180 medium and more than 200 light tanks and 845 guns were captured.[16]

The WDF was largely made up of regular seasoned troops,[17] whom General O'Connor described as going into battle 'in very good heart'.[18] The war against the Italians, in 1940/41, was the only campaign of the Second World War in which the interwar Regular Army fought alone, unhindered by significant numbers of territorial, conscript or volunteer troops.[19] Many of these men had been stationed in Palestine since 1936, suppressing the Arab rebellion. Others had been posted on the northwest frontier of India in the 1930s.[20] The 7th Armoured Division had been in the Middle East since the 1938 Munich crisis.[21] Accustomed to their surroundings and well trained, they were prepared mentally and physically for the trials of fighting in the desert. As professionals, many of the 7th Armoured Division hankered to put years of training into practice.[22]

By comparison, as a report written on the lessons learned from Operation Compass stressed, the quality of the Italian Tenth Army left much to be desired. The report pointed out that 'the operations ... have been conducted against an enemy who, with very few exceptions, has proved himself to be generally lacking in soldierly qualities as we understand them, who has displayed little courage, initiative or determination, and who, as soon as he suffers reverses, quickly gives way to demoralization'.[23]

---

[16] Pitt, *Wavell's Command*, p. 190.

[17] Barnett, *The Desert Generals*, p. 27; Pitt, *Wavell's Command*, p. 9.

[18] Barnett, *The Desert Generals*, p. 35.

[19] John Bierman and Colin Smith, *Alamein: War without Hate* (London, 2003), p. 29. There were a few Territorials and conscripts involved to fill up the establishment. The BEF in France in May 1940 had five territorial infantry divisions.

[20] Pitt, *Wavell's Command*, p. 9.   [21] Bierman and Smith, *Alamein*, p. 29.

[22] Ibid.; Pitt, *Wavell's Command*, p. 86.

[23] NA WO 201/352 Report on Lessons of Operations in the Western Desert, December 1940. For a revisionist view on Italian morale and combat effectiveness in the Second World War see Brian R. Sullivan, 'The Italian Soldier in Combat, June 1940–September 1943: Myths, Realities and Explanations' in Addison and Calder (eds.), *Time to Kill*, pp. 177–205.

Following the Italian rout, many of Wavell's and O'Connor's forces were sent to Greece to counter the developing German advance through the Balkans. From that time on, the make-up of the desert army in North Africa fundamentally changed. It became a mixture of regular, territorial, volunteer and conscript soldiers. The new citizen army that gradually formed was comprised of men who had little to no interest in the affairs of the world[24] and, like most citizen armies, no wish to be soldiers.[25]

They were the 'hostilities only' soldiers – civilians who had either joined the Territorial Army before the war and spent some of their weekends and two weeks every summer in keen but amateur military endeavour, or who had been called up under the National Service regulations and subjected to hastily organised training in little but the basic elements of their new craft.[26]

By the end of July 1941, 200,000 of these new troops had arrived on Egyptian soil. These soldiers were not of the same calibre as those who had so decisively defeated the Italians.[27]

On 11 January 1941, Adolf Hitler, in response to the Italian disasters in North Africa, issued Directive 22, committing Germany to aiding Italy in the desert. The German 5th Light Division and 15th Panzer Division were sent to the theatre to create the *Afrika Korps* under the command of General Erwin Rommel. The Germans did not waste time and, in March and April 1941, the British forces stationed at El Agheila, west of Tobruk, were driven out of Cyrenaica, and the rout of the Italian Army was reversed. Poorly trained and lacking in experience, the newly created citizen army succumbed to the battle-hardened troops of the *Afrika Korps*, many of whom had taken part in the invasions of Poland, Belgium and France. According to Correlli Barnett, the 'superiority of German skill, training and anti-tank artillery [told] in a way devastating to the morale of British troops'.[28] J. H. Witte, a gunner with the 160th Light Anti-Aircraft (AA) Battery Royal Artillery (RA), described the retreat from El Agheila as a 'demoralizing' and 'ugly rout with panic spreading like a bush fire'.[29] Len Tutt, a gunner with the 104th Royal Horse Artillery, referred to it as 'the most demoralising phase of all [his] war service'.[30]

Wavell, under considerable pressure from Prime Minister Winston Churchill, launched two counteroffensives, codenamed 'Brevity' and

---

[24] NA WO 32/9735 'ABCA, Current Affairs in the Army. The Outline of a New Plan', 21 July 1941, p. 2.
[25] Richard Holmes, *Acts of War: The Behaviour of Men in Battle* (London, 2004), p. 81.
[26] Pitt, *Auchinleck's Command*, p. 5.
[27] Harrison Place, *Military Training in the British Army*, p. 3.
[28] Barnett, *The Desert Generals*, p. 149.
[29] IWM 87/12/1 J. H. Witte, 'The One That Didn't Get Away', p. 100.
[30] IWM 85/35/1 L. E. Tutt, 'Gentlemen Soldiers', pp. 110–11.

'Battleaxe', in May and June 1941. Both failed to drive the Axis forces out of Cyrenaica or relieve the now besieged town of Tobruk. By July, a disgruntled Churchill replaced Wavell with General Claude Auchinleck. The new Commander-in-Chief Middle Eastern Forces (C-in-C MEF) was faced immediately with pressure from Churchill to open a fresh offensive.

Massive reinforcements poured into the Middle East in the second half of 1941, and, with the Wehrmacht fully committed in Russia, Auchinleck launched the newly created Eighth Army into battle on 18 November 1941. The field censorship summary for 12 to 18 November stated that 'on the eve of the great Libyan offensive ... the morale of the MEF has never been so high in the 26 months of war as at the present time ... The men's belief in success is based on faith in their commanders, the excellence and quantity of the material at their disposal, the increased amount of air support, and the certainty that, man for man, they are better than the enemy.'[31]

The Crusader offensive constituted the first large-scale engagement in the desert war, an engagement that Eighth Army came very close to losing. During the battle, Auchinleck was forced to remove Lieutenant-General Sir Alan Cunningham, his Commander Eighth Army, and replace him with Lieutenant-General Sir Neil Ritchie. At this stage of the desert war, decisions at the highest level were being made with reference to their potential effects on morale.[32] Auchinleck viewed Cunningham's dismissal as

A very serious step. It might have adversely affected the morale of the Eighth Army very greatly. It would certainly encourage the enemy, who would count the removal as a confession of defeat. It would lower our prestige and morale everywhere, not only in Egypt, because it was a confession of failure. Therefore it was a difficult decision.[33]

He was however, a little later, able to explain the appointment of Ritchie in Cunningham's place by the rationale that the army was 'morally shaken and therefore needed a strong, unflustered, self-confident commander. Ritchie seemed therefore on all counts just the man.'[34]

The narrow victory at Crusader was won at the cost of overstretching Eighth Army.[35] Nevertheless, Tobruk was relieved and the Axis forces were once more driven out of Cyrenaica. Many of the units engaged in the battle attributed Eighth Army's success to the morale of the troops. A 2nd New Zealand Division report noted that the first lesson from the operation

---

[31] AWM 54 883/2/97 MEFCWS, no. I (12 to 18 November 1941), p. 1.
[32] French, *Raising Churchill's Army*, p. 242.   [33] Barnett, *The Desert Generals*, pp. 116–7.
[34] Ibid., pp. 123–4.   [35] John Keegan, *The Second World War* (London, 1997), pp. 275–6.

had been that 'there is a time in all battles when the men on both sides are exhausted. It is the man who can hold on longest and who fights with the greatest determination who will win.'[36] Another report, by Sir Giffard Le Quesne Martel, who was commander of the Royal Armoured Corps, stated that in spite of the fact that the enemy 'started far superior to [Eighth Army] in numbers and equipment, except for [Eighth Army's] superiority in numbers of tanks ... the bravery of the troops was magnificent throughout. The armoured forces ... had practically no letup for the whole period. They faced superior gun power, and overcame it, although they had heavy losses in consequence. Everyone remarked on their fighting qualities and grim determination.'[37]

The German situation reports blamed the Axis defeat squarely on the morale of the Italian troops. By 15 December 1941, after 'four weeks of heavy, uninterrupted and costly fighting', the daily report recounted that 'a decrease in the fighting spirit of the [Italian] troops is clearly evident'.[38] By 16 December, an appreciation of the situation described a 'further decline in the fighting spirit of the Italian troops'. It was to be expected that, 'owing to the non arrival of supplies and reinforcements, the morale [of the Italians] would sink lower, if the enemy continued his attacks'.[39] The Commander-in-Chief's daily report for the same day reported that 'the uninterrupted attempt of the enemy to bring about the envelopment of our flank, the penetration of the Gazala position, and the decline of the fighting spirit of the troops were making it necessary to withdraw the front during the night'.[40] The battle report for the *Panzergruppe Afrika*, on 20 December 1941, pointed out that thousands of Italian soldiers were 'singly and in groups without a leader, on vehicles and on foot ... streaming back' towards the rear. So serious was this crisis that 'steps' had to be 'taken to collect these stragglers and to end the unauthorised rearward trend'.[41] Rommel blamed his inability to hold on to Tripolitania and obey the Duce's orders to fight to the last man on the effects of five weeks'

[36] ANZ WAII/2 Accession W3281, Box 1, 101b part 1, The New Zealand Division in Cyrenaica and Lessons of the Campaign, part 1, Narrative and Lessons, p. 26.

[37] NA WO 201/2870 General Martel's Report on His Visit to the Middle East, 26 January 1942.

[38] South African Military Archives Depot (SAMAD) Union War Histories (UWH), Foreign Documents, Box 184, Battle Report Panzerarmee Afrika, Translation no. 6(a), Daily Report, 15 December 1941, p. 72.

[39] SAMAD UWH, Foreign Documents, Box 184, Battle Report Panzerarmee Afrika, Translation no. 6(a), Appreciation of the Situation, 16 December 1941, p. 73.

[40] SAMAD UWH, Published Books, Box 368, Schlachtbericht (Daily Report) 16 December 1941.

[41] SAMAD UWH, Foreign Documents, Box 184, Battle Report Panzerarmee Afrika, Translation no. 6(a), Orders and Reports, 20 December 1941, p. 91.

'uninterrupted fighting'. He argued that the 'fighting efficiency of the Italian formations has suffered to such an extent that they are no longer able to hold an enemy attack'.[42]

Unsurprisingly, the German war diaries did not blame defeat on their own soldiers. Nevertheless, a 2nd New Zealand Division report after the battle highlighted the fact that 'as the campaign progressed the morale of the German infantry fell'. It is certain, the report continued, that German morale 'is not proof against heavy pressure and it has again been demonstrated that although the German is a hard fighter he is not a tough one'.[43]

A brief period of recuperation followed Crusader. Rommel believed that if it was 'possible to reorganise the Italian formations' and to 'stiffen their morale', then he would 'be able to call a final halt to the advancing enemy'.[44] Rommel was able to do just that, while, correspondingly, British morale faded. The censorship summaries identified a weariness and frustration among the troops of Eighth Army following Crusader. The battle had been built up in the soldiers' minds as the climax of the desert war. Since July 1941, many soldiers had anticipated victory and a return home by Christmas or at least early in the New Year.[45] One soldier wrote, 'I'm afraid I was rather too optimistic about meeting you again by the end of the year, but still I think Jerry surprised practically everybody by his toughness out here.'[46] Private R. L. Crimp of the 2nd Battalion the Rifle Brigade wrote in his diary that 'there seems little pep or punch left now, only fumbling and stumbling in anti-climax after our hectic chase across Cyrenaica ... the truth is that we're at the end of our tether, psychologically as well as geographically, and pretty skint as regards numbers'.[47]

The pursuit by Eighth Army of the defeated Axis forces was strangely ineffective. The ease with which the *Panzergruppe* completed each

---

[42] SAMAD UWH, Foreign Documents, Box 184, Battle Report Panzerarmee Afrika, Translation no. 6(a), Message from Rommel C-in-C, Panzergruppe to German General HQ, Italian Armed Forces, Rome (for translation to the Duce), 22 December 1941, p. 96.

[43] ANZ WAII/2 Accession W3281, Box 1, 101b part 1, The New Zealand Division in Cyrenaica and Lessons of the Campaign, part 1, Narrative and Lessons, p. 1.

[44] SAMAD UWH, Foreign Documents, Box 184, Battle Report Panzerarmee Afrika, Translation no. 6(a), Message from Rommel, C-in-C, Panzergruppe, to German General HQ, Italian Armed Forces, Rome (for translation to the Duce), 22 December 1941, p. 96.

[45] AWM 54 883/2/97 British Troops in Egypt, no. 92 Field Censorship Report Week Ending 31 July 1941, p. 1.

[46] AWM 54 883/2/97 MEFCWS, no. VI. (17 to 23 December 1941), p. 1.

[47] IWM 96/50/1 and PP/MCR/245, R. L. Crimp, 'The Overseas Tour of a Conscript Rifleman (the Diary of a Desert Rat), A Four Years Diary, The Western Desert and Tunisia, 1 June 1941 to 12 May 1943', p. 92.

appointed stage of the retreat caused the morale of the Axis troops to rise while the men of Eighth Army watched their efforts fizzle out in futile pushes and proddings which were timidly abandoned in the face of perfunctory opposition.[48] Axis morale bounced back swiftly, just as Rommel hoped it would. General Ugo Cavallero, the Italian Commando Supremo, wrote in his diary that 'Rommel has expressed his surprise and his satisfaction regarding the aggressive offensive spirit the Italians have displayed so short a time after their withdrawal.'[49]

At the end of January, Rommel, taking advantage of this morale resurgence, launched a counteroffensive. The parallels with what had happened in March 1941 were striking. Rommel, once again, was faced with newly arrived and inexperienced units who were tasked with relieving the worn-out formations that had fought during Crusader. The 1st Armoured Division proved completely incapable of dealing with Rommel's rapid offensive and caustic remarks about 'that yearly event ... the Benghazi Handicap' became the order of the day.[50] At the same time the censorship summaries reported 'numerous accounts' where the morale of the 'new armoured' division was criticised as being 'poor'.[51]

By 4 February, the British forces had been driven back as far as Gazala, thirty miles west of Tobruk. The censorship summary for mid-February pointed out that there was 'no denying the fact that the tone of correspondence from British troops in the forward areas was lower than it ha[d] ever been in the last three months, and reflected the general disappointment of all ranks over our hurried withdrawal'.[52] The morale report for the same period, one of a series designed to inform and help Adam's Morale Committee, identified a tendency among troops to 'criticise the war effort and general conduct of operations'. The report noted that one censorship section had stated, in mid-March, that 45 per cent of the letters examined complained of being 'browned off'.[53]

In the hiatus following the Axis advance, the morale of Eighth Army improved considerably as both sides prepared for further offensive operations.[54] By May 1942, Auchinleck was ready to launch a rejuvenated

[48] SAMAD UWH, Published Books, Box 368, See-Saw in the Desert, Retreats and Recoveries, The Desert Ebb and Flow, handwritten note.
[49] SAMAD UWH Foreign Documents Box 205, Cavallero's Diary, 'Commando Supremo', 2 November 1941 to 31 March 1942, p. 77.
[50] AWM 54 883/2/97 MEFCWS, no. XIII (4 to 10 February 1942), p. 1.
[51] AWM 54 883/2/97 MEFCWS, no. XVI (26 February to 4 March 1942), p. 1.
[52] AWM 54 883/2/97 MEFCWS, no. XIV (11 to 17 February 1942), p. 1.
[53] NA WO 163/51 Morale Report, December 1941 to April 1942.
[54] AWM 54 883/2/97 MEFCWS, no. XXVI (6 to 12 May 1942), p. 1; AWM 54 883/2/97 MEFCWS, no. XXVII (13 to 19 May 1942), p. 1; AWM 54 883/2/97 MEFCWS, no. XXVIII (20 to 26 May 1942), p. 1.

Eighth Army on another attack against the newly named *Panzerarmee Afrika*.[55] However, on the night of 26/27 May, he was forestalled by Rommel, who advanced on Eighth Army at the Gazala line. The *Panzerarmee* attacked a materially superior Eighth Army. It possessed 330 German and 230 obsolete Italian tanks, 560 in all. Eighth Army had 850 tanks and also had a numerical superiority of three to two in guns. In spite of this advantage, Eighth Army was forced to retreat from the Gazala line on 14 June. It retreated eastward, in what the troops christened the 'Gazala gallop', to a defensive position at Mersa Matruh. Tobruk was once again invested by the Axis forces.[56]

Auchinleck decided, controversially, to hold on to Tobruk. Churchill wrote to him on 14 June, offering his support. 'Your decision to fight it out to the end', he wrote, is 'most cordially endorsed. We shall sustain you whatever the result. Retreat would be fatal. This is a business not only of armour but of will-power. God bless you all.'[57] Nevertheless, on 21 June, *Panzerarmee Afrika* captured Tobruk. The shock was felt throughout the British Empire and prompted Churchill to utter his famous words 'defeat is one thing; disgrace is another'.[58] He described the surrender of Tobruk as reflecting poorly on the morale of the British Army; 'If this was typical of the morale of the Desert Army', he declaimed, 'no measure could be put upon the disasters which impended in North-East Africa.'[59] Auchinleck, for the second time, was forced to remove his army commander, and, on 25 June, assumed command of Eighth Army himself along with his position as Commander-in-Chief Middle Eastern Forces.

This period represented a low point for the British Army's morale during the Second World War.[60] Greece had been abandoned. On 15 February, at Singapore, 85,000 men had surrendered to inferior numbers of Japanese.[61] On 7 March, Rangoon, the capital of Burma, also fell to the Japanese.

The line at Mersa Matruh did not hold for long and Eighth Army raced its pursuer back towards the defensive line at El Alamein. It reached it on 30 June 1942. The field censorship summary for the period covering the

---

[55] AWM 54 883/2/97 MEFCWS, no. XXVIII (20 to 26 May 1942), p. 1.

[56] Bungay, *Alamein*, p. 23.

[57] NA WO 236/1 *Egyptian Gazette*, Sunday October 29 1950. 'The Hinge of Fate', XV, The Battle for Tobruk.

[58] Churchill, *The Second World War*, p. 565.

[59] Ibid. There were of course other reasons for the fall of Tobruk. The town's defences had been left to decay and were no longer in a state comparable to that of 1941. However, it was the issue of morale that Churchill found of most concern.

[60] David Fraser, *And We Shall Shock Them: The British Army in the Second World War* (London 1999), pp. 104–5.

[61] Churchill, *The Second World War*, p. 565.

Illustration 1 An RAF Lysander flies over a convoy of lorries during the
retreat into Egypt, 26 June 1942. The shock of losing Tobruk prompted
one of Churchill's most cutting remarks about the British armed forces:
'Defeat is one thing; disgrace is another.'

fall of Tobruk and the hasty retreat from the Gazala line pointed out that
'the high morale of the troops had suffered a set back, chiefly due to utter
physical exhaustion combined with the realisation of the horror of battle
and the loss of comrades ... optimism regarding an early finish to the
campaign has been tempered by the stiff opposition encountered'.[62] By
the start of July, the reports stated that 'the withdrawal into Egypt has
provoked expressions of very bitter disappointment from all ranks of the
Eighth Army, accompanied by admissions of weariness and fatigue'.[63]
A XXX Corps intelligence summary for 1 July described how 'indiscreet

[62] ANZ WAII/1/DA508/1 vol. 1, MEFCWS, no. XXXII (17 to 23 June 1942), p. 1.
[63] ANZ WAII/1/DA508/1 vol. 1, Middle East Military Censorship Weekly Summary
(MEMCWS), no. XXXIV (1 to 7 July 1942), p. 1.

and defeatist talk' was rife among the disorganised units streaming back towards Alexandria.[64]

An officer, weighing up the position at El Alamein, wrote on 2 July 1942, 'this disaster goes on and on and now it has raised a sort of impetus which takes a lot of stopping. For no good cause chaps sort of say "where do we retreat to next?" That sort of spirit is quite inevitable but very very difficult to compete with. If we do not succeed in stopping the brutes that mental aspect will be at least 50% responsible.'[65] The correspondent Alan Moorehead, driving out into the desert in the summer of 1942 to assess the situation for himself, noted in his diary how he was greeted by the sight of 'exhausted and sleeping men' pouring eastwards. No one had any idea what was going on, least of all the soldiers. Moorehead conceded that German 'morale was higher than ours in the Middle East'.[66]

At the start of July, Rommel launched his first offensive on the El Alamein line. Crucially, Eighth Army repelled the attack. Egypt was temporarily saved. The German soldiers, by this time, as the *Afrika Korps* war diary confirms, were even more exhausted than their British counterparts.[67] Moorehead pointed out how they 'were wearied to the point where they had no more reserves either of body or of willpower, where all the goading and enticement could make no difference, where they were compelled to stop and sleep'.[68]

Comparatively, by the second week of July, Eighth Army's morale showed some signs of a limited improvement, as the arrival of new and better equipment, the improved air support provided by the Royal Air Force (RAF) and Auchinleck's efforts to take control of the situation paid dividends.[69] By the third week of July the censorship summaries were reporting on the 'high morale prevailing among all ranks' of Eighth Army.[70] Auchinleck, therefore, looking to capitalise on this mini revival and aiming to take advantage of the over-stretched state of the *Panzerarmee*, launched successive offensives along the El Alamein line. None of these offensives,

[64] NA WO 169/4035 XXX Corps Intelligence Summary, 1 July 1942, War Diary XXX Corps G Branch.

[65] ANZ WAII/1/DA508/1 vol. 1, MEMCWS, no. XXXIV (1 to 7 July 1942), p. 1.

[66] Alan Moorehead, *African Trilogy: The Desert War 1940–1943* (London, 2000), p. 413. First published in London in 1944 under the title *African Trilogy: Comprising Mediterranean Front, A Year of Battle, The End.*

[67] SAMAD UWH, Draft Narratives, Box 316, War Diary of the German Africa Corps, 2 and 3 July 1942.

[68] Moorehead, *African Trilogy*, pp. 389–90.

[69] ANZ WAII/1/DA508/1 vol. 1, MEFCWS, no. XXXV (8 to 14 July 1942), p. 22; See Chapter 2 for a discussion of the effect of technology on troop morale and Chapter 7 for a discussion of the impact of command on troop morale.

[70] ANZ WAII/1/DA508/1 vol. 1, MEFCWS, no. XXXVI (15 to 21 July 1942), p. 1.

however, provided a decisive breakthrough. By the end of July, he called off the attacks due to high casualties and a lack of success. It may be that the reported morale improvement had been illusory, perhaps based on what the censors referred to as the 'troops' anxiety to allay all tension and doubts at home' by pointing out that 'all was well and there was very little to worry about'.[71] In any event, it was definitely short-lived; by the end of the month the censors were reporting an increased amount of 'individual cases of depression'.[72] Many of the troops were 'beginning to lose interest in the war, to some in fact the reason for the war itself has become dimmed'.[73] The censorship report for the period 5 to 11 August stated that the soldiers' mail had shown a 'spate of grouses and an increase in the number of writers who stated they were "browned off" . . . there were little or no traces of the offensive spirit, and an almost complete absence of any reference to forcing the enemy to give up the ground gained in the last two months'.[74] Such negative references were given all the more colour when compared with the usual positive picture the censors portrayed of the fighting troops' morale.[75]

By this stage, Churchill had lost faith in Auchinleck. On 13 August 1942, after flying out to the Middle East to assess the situation, he replaced Auchinleck, as Commander Eighth Army, with Bernard Montgomery. Auchinleck was also removed as Commander-in-Chief Middle Eastern Forces and was replaced by Harold Alexander. Montgomery and Alexander contributed to a dramatic improvement in the morale of the troops. The censorship summary for 19 to 25 August reported that 'a breath of fresh, invigorating air has swept through British Troops in Egypt, and the mail has altered in tone almost overnight. Renewed optimism and confidence were everywhere apparent, and the old aggressive spirit . . . is in the process of being recovered.'[76]

On 30 August, Rommel once more attacked, this time along the Alam Halfa ridge. Eighth Army successfully repelled the Axis thrust towards Alexandria and the tide began to turn in the desert war. Montgomery now put all his energy into preparing Eighth Army for its own offensive.

In the run up to the battle of El Alamein in October 1942 the morale of the troops recovered and grew as the effect of the new commanders, the victory at Alam Halfa and the ever increasing amounts of new weaponry told on the troops. Lieutenant-General Leslie Morshead, the commander

[71] ANZ WAII/1/DA508/1 vol. 1, MEFCWS, no. XXXV (8 to 14 July 1942), p. 1.
[72] ANZ WAII/1/DA508/1 vol. 1, MEFCWS, no. XXXVII (22 to 28 July 1942), p. 1.
[73] ANZ WAII/1/DA508/1 vol. 1 MEMCWS, no. XXXVIII (29 July to 4 August 1942), p. 2.
[74] ANZ WAII/1/DA508/1 vol. 1 MEMCWS, no. XXXIX (5 to 11 August 1942), p. 1.
[75] IWM BLM 57 Wimberley to Montgomery, 9 June 1953.
[76] ANZ WAII/1/DA508/1 vol. 3 MEMCWS, no. XLI (19 to 25 August 1942), p. 1.

of the Australian 9th Division, wrote that 'the men are full of determination and confidence. Going round them talking with them, and
addressing them I have witnessed an air of quiet and confident pur-
posefulness.'[77] The morale report for August to October 1942 pointed
out that

Morale reached its peak as a result of the Army Commander's message to his
troops on the eve of the offensive, and of the fact (commented on widely in the
mail) that all ranks, down the whole chain of command, were taken into confidence about the plan of attack. In the words of the censor 'the fact that the
G.O.C.-in-C., 8th Army, took the whole army into his confidence right down to
the last man and stated exactly what he hoped to do and how he was going to do it,
the belief that the plan was good, and the knowledge that the tools at their disposal
were more numerous and effective than they have ever been, brought the spirit
of the troops to a new high level and intensified their assurance and grim
determination ... On the evidence of this mail no army ever went to battle with
higher morale.[78]

On 23 October 1942, Montgomery unleashed the re-formed and
retrained Eighth Army at El Alamein. This time Eighth Army decisively
defeated the newly named *Deutsch–Italienische Panzerarmee*, and, by
4 November, Rommel's forces were in full retreat. By 13 November,
Tobruk was recaptured, and by 23 November, Rommel was once again
driven out of Cyrenaica to El Agheila. The Anglo–American invasion of
Morocco and Algeria (Operation Torch) was launched on 8 November.
By May 1943, the Eighth Army and British First Army, with the help of
the Americans, had captured Tunis, approximately 1,500 miles west of El
Alamein. The war in North Africa was over.

The months from October 1942 to May 1943 saw the destruction of
Axis forces at El Alamein (around 50,000 killed and captured)[79] and
Tunisia (around 250,000 captured).[80] By May 1943, more Axis soldiers
had surrendered at what the German soldiers called 'Tunisgrad' than the
Russians captured at Stalingrad.[81] A remarkable turnaround had taken
place.

The defeats that Eighth Army suffered in the summer of 1942 have been
attributed to many factors. Most historians have blamed inadequate
weapons, faulty leadership, and a deficient conceptual approach to warfare. Many have also acknowledged certain morale problems in the desert.

---

[77] AWM 3 DRL 2632 Items 1–4 Morshead to his wife (Bridgette) 23 October 1942.
[78] NA WO 193/453 Morale Report, August to October 1942.
[79] Bungay, *Alamein*, pp. 196–7.   [80] Atkinson, *An Army at Dawn*, p. 537.
[81] Bierman and Smith, *Alamein*, p. 407.

Michael Carver maintained that Eighth Army fought with less élan and determination at Gazala than in other battles.[82] Other historians have completely denied the existence of any morale difficulties in the summer of 1942. Jon Latimer, in *Alamein*, has described it as a 'legend' that 'Eighth Army was hopelessly dispirited' after their defeat at Gazala. In fact, 'few parts of the army had lost faith in themselves ... The army was not beaten or dispirited: it just wanted to be led to victory.'[83] Desmond Young in his biography of Field Marshal Erwin Rommel stressed that this 'legend is unfair to the Eighth Army: it is also contrary to the facts',[84] while Martin Kitchen described it as 'pure myth'.[85]

However, the evidence suggests that Eighth Army's defeats were due in many ways to poor morale. It is clear from the personal accounts, the censorship summaries and the official reports already adduced that morale was at the very least uncertain and unreliable during the summer of 1942. In addition to these more well established qualitative approaches to assessing the evidence regarding morale, there are also a number of quantifiable indicators and corollaries of morale whose presence indicated to commanders in the desert that there was a morale problem and that it was affecting combat performance. These were incidences of sickness, psychological breakdown, surrender and desertion. Where the evidence from these quantifiable sources coincides with the indications from the more qualitatively assessable sources, it is reasonable to conclude that they mutually reinforce one another.

According to the doctors, psychiatrists and commanders who fought in the desert, the incidence of sickness and psychological breakdown[86] in fighting units was one of the best indicators of morale problems in an army.[87] By the end of July 1942, sickness rates and incidences of NYD(N) (not yet diagnosed (nervous)) were causing serious concern in the Middle East. The medical situation report for July 1942 noted a 'considerable rise' in the number of men reporting sick that was 'most disquieting'.[88] The daily sickness rate had risen from 1.4 men per thousand in March (a monthly rate of 43.4 per thousand), before Rommel's successful offensive, to 2.39 per thousand in July (a monthly rate of 74.1 per thousand). It would rise even

---

[82] Carver, *Tobruk*, p. 262. Nigel Hamilton, Montgomery's biographer, has also stressed the relevance of morale problems in the desert. See *The Full Monty*, p. 529.

[83] Latimer, *Alamein*, pp. 97–8.   [84] Young, *Rommel*, p. 162.

[85] Kitchen, *Rommel's Desert War*, p. 287.

[86] Often referred to as NYD(N), anxiety neurosis or battle exhaustion.

[87] NA Cabinet Papers (CAB) 21/914, The Work of Army Psychiatrists in Relation to Morale, January 1944; Maj.-Gen. F. M. Richardson, *Fighting Spirit: A Study of Psychological Factors in War* (London, 1978); IWM BLM 49 Montgomery to Alan Brooke, 15 April 1943, p. 3.

[88] NA WO 177/324 Medical Situation Report, 24 July 1942.

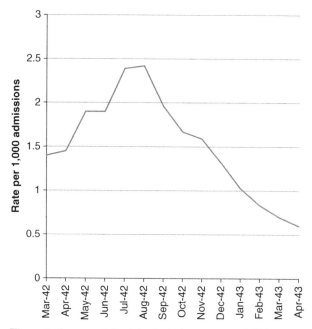

Figure 1 Average daily sick admissions rate per 1,000 to general hospitals and casualty clearing stations

further again to 2.42 per thousand in August 1942 (a monthly rate of 75 per thousand).[89] That is a 73 per cent increase from the beginning to the climax of Rommel's offensive. Such an increase in sickness rates undoubtedly had an effect on the fighting power of Eighth Army.[90] Although the increase could certainly be blamed to some extent on the effects of the African summer, the rise (and fall) is still remarkable (Figure 1).

The incidence of NYD(N), or anxiety neurosis, also proved disturbingly high. On 28 July 1942, Brigadier G. W. B. James, the Consultant Psychiatrist Eighth Army, reported that NYD(N)/exhaustion cases were forming 7 to 10 per cent of the total sick and battle casualties on the El Alamein line.[91] The situation had become so acute, according to Major H. B. Craigie of the Department of Army Psychiatry in the Middle East,

[89] NA WO 177/324 Monthly Report on Health Eighth Army, March, July, August 1942.
[90] Mark Harrison, *Medicine and Victory: British Military Medicine in the Second World War* (Oxford, 2004), p. 85.
[91] NA WO 177/324 Memo 'Sickness, Army Troops', by DDMS Eighth Army, 26 July 1942; Report on Tour of Eighth Army, 18 to 24 July 1942 by Consultant in Psychological Medicine (Brig. G. W. B. James), 28 July 1942.

that, by mid-1942, the three hospitals for mental cases in the Middle East were holding nearly 1,400 patients. More accommodation had to be obtained as they had been designed to take under 1,000 cases between them.[92] James was asked to visit the front lines and report on the problem. He found that the majority of cases sent back as NYD(N) were purely physical fatigue and approximately 90 per cent of men were fit to return to their units after three or four days rest, feeding and sleeping. He reported that, on the whole, the morale of the troops was 'very high'. However, it was clear that a number of the units involved in the fighting were 'physically very tired' and in need of rest. These were, in particular, the 2nd New Zealand Division, the 1st South African Division and the Guards Brigade. James suggested that the true NYD(N) figure was 1.9 per cent of the total sick and battle casualties and 'in view of the trying nature of operations since 27 May this figure cannot be considered unduly high'.[93]

However, James's positive appraisal of the situation must be considered in the light of two facts which suggest that there was a greater problem than he was indicating. First, James was employed by the army to ensure that a maximum number of soldiers were ready for combat. His loyalty was, therefore, first to the army and second to the troops. Second, James ignored the fact that fatigue was itself probably the greatest danger to morale.[94]

The British Field Service Regulations of 1929, in a passage that formed the bedrock of British offensive doctrine in the Second World War, pointed out that

Troops engaged in close fighting under conditions of modern war are soon affected by physical and moral exhaustion; recovery from the former is ensured by a few hours sleep and suitable food; but recovery from the latter is a longer process. If troops, as is probable, are to be engaged with the enemy for long periods of time, it is important that their moral qualities should not be reduced to a point at which comparatively speedy recovery is impossible. The individual soldier should, therefore, not be engaged to the point of exhaustion, except in pursuit.[95]

E. L. Cooper and A. J. M. Sinclair pointed out in a report on 'War Neurosis at Tobruk', written in 1941, that 'there is no doubt that exhaustion plays a

---

[92] NA CAB 21/914 Expert Committee on the Work of Psychologists and Psychiatrists in the Services, Note by Maj. H. B. Craigie of the Department of Army Psychiatry in the Middle East to Sir Stafford Cripps (Lord Privy Seal) on Psychiatric Cases in the Middle East, 21 July 1942.

[93] NA WO 177/324 Memo, 'Sickness, Army Troops', by DDMS Eighth Army, 26 July 1942; Report on Tour of Eighth Army, 18 to 24 July 1942 by Consultant in Psychological Medicine (Brig. G. W. B. James), 28 July 1942.

[94] Shelford Bidwell, *Modern Warfare: A Study of Men, Weapons and Theories* (London, 1973), p. 133.

[95] French, *Raising Churchill's Army*, p. 24.

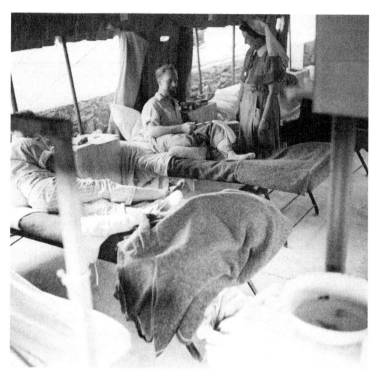

Illustration 2 A sister on her rounds chats with a soldier convalescing in a tented ward of a base hospital in the Middle East, April 1942. The rate of sickness in Eighth Army, a good indicator of morale problems in an army, increased by 73 per cent between March and August 1942.

part in the development of the majority of war neuroses'.[96] In July 1942, Major T. F. Main, a psychiatrist working with battle schools in Britain, noted that morale tended to wane during fatigue states.

At the Battle School certain facts about fatigue are clear. When fatigued men lost confidence in themselves, became apathetic and careless and lost their military conscience ... tactical planning became scrappy and bad. At these times battle discipline was apt to go to pieces in spite of all efforts and bad temper and selfishness – for food, cigarettes and seats – increased ... This change of attitude was commonly observed and led some to conclude that an officer should be judged primarily on his capacity at these times.[97]

---

[96] AWM 54 481/12/120 'War Neurosis at Tobruk', by E. L. Cooper and A. J. M. Sinclair, p. 10.
[97] NA WO 199/799 Note on 'suggestions for future investigation into morale during fatigue states, 21 July 1942, from T. F. Main, Major, RAMC, Psychiatrist, to MG Infantry GHQ, Home Forces.

Another report written later in the war suggested that there was 'evidence' that fatigue was 'the chief enemy of morale in the front line: in the words of an officer who commanded a battalion in Sicily and Italy, "fatigue lowers morale more than anything the enemy can do"'.[98]

As the war progressed, James ceased to refer to psychological casualties as 'anxiety neurosis' or 'NYD(N)'; instead he used the terminology 'battle exhaustion'.[99] As Terry Copp has pointed out, 'the large majority of individuals diagnosed as suffering from battle exhaustion exhibited what the psychiatrists described as acute fear reactions and acute and chronic anxiety manifested through uncontrollable tremors, a pronounced startle reaction to war-related sounds and a profound loss of self-confidence'.[100] In this sense, they were no different from NYD(N) casualties. British understanding of the treatment of psychological casualties was in its infancy in North Africa. James's effort to reclassify the large number of NYD(N) casualties in Eighth Army as exhaustion cases must be understood in this light. As front-line psychiatry developed during the war, psychiatrists increasingly understood that breakdown in battle was not caused solely by 'inadequate personalities' but as a result of the collapse of unit morale and/or of individual morale in specific battle situations. Stable personalities were just as likely to break down under stress in battle as those with previous psychological problems.[101] James's belief that the true NYD(N) figure was 1.9 per cent reflects the thinking of British psychiatrists at the time, who were focused on the psychological issue of selection and the removal of 'misfits' from the battle environment, rather than on the psychological implication of battle stress on stable individuals.

The 2nd New Zealand Division was one of the units James identified as being particularly worn out. It only entered battle, after a number of months of rest and training, on 25 June, while many of the British and South African units had been serving in the desert for anything from six to fifteen months. In the two months of fighting between July and August 1942, the 2nd New Zealand Division had 489 cases of NYD(N) admitted to hospital. The four rifle companies of a 1942 infantry battalion were made up of 496 men.[102] In the space of two months, therefore,

[98] NA WO 193/453 Draft Morale Report: Overseas Commands: November 1943 to January 1944.

[99] Terry Copp and Bill McAndrew, *Battle Exhaustion: Soldiers and Psychiatrists in the Canadian Army, 1939–1945* (London, 1990), p. 47.

[100] Terry Copp, ' "If this war isn't over, And pretty damn soon, There'll be nobody left, In this old platoon …": First Canadian Army, February–March 1945', in Addison and Calder (eds.), *Time to Kill*, p. 149.

[101] Copp and McAndrew, *Battle Exhaustion*, pp. 5, 23, 46.

[102] IWM TM 30–410 *Technical Manual, Handbook on the British Army with Supplements on the Royal Air Force and Civilian Defence Organizations* (Washington, 1943), p. 25.

they lost the equivalent of the fighting part of one whole infantry battalion to battle exhaustion.

A further analysis of these figures shows that there were 16 exhaustion and neurosis casualties per 100 battle casualties in July, rising to 28 such cases per 100 battle casualties in August 1942.[103] The August figures, in particular, are significantly higher than the average figures for all combatants and all theatres in the Second World War (between 10 and 15 per cent).[104] They also compare unfavourably with the other campaigns in the desert. The campaign against the Italians (December 1940 to March 1941) produced less than 200 psychological cases for all services (around 10 per cent of battle casualties).[105] During 1941, James reported that one in every six battle casualties (16.66 per cent) was psychiatric.[106]

The commander of the 28th New Zealand (Maori) Battalion retrospectively described the situation in December 1942. He pointed out that morale had been 'severely shaken' during the July battles 'by some disastrous engagements and the heavy loss of men and officers including the CO'.

Things with the 8th Army were not bright then. The night I reached the front a rather disastrous attack was launched by the N. Z. followed a few days later by another, the two for a time making an awful hole in the Div. and not making people very bright. In my own show I had taken over a Bn. which had earned the greatest reputation I suppose of any this century, certainly any this war. I found to my surprise that the feeling or spirits of the officers as well as the men was anything but up to their standard. Even in our darkest days in Crete I had never seen them like this. No one outside the show realised this (although long afterwards I told the Brigadier).[107]

A report on the morale of South African troops in the Middle East, written on 8 August 1942, pointed to similar problems. The report stated that South African morale was 'defective in that there is a large wastage of manpower owing to neurotic illness' and the various ways in which men got 'themselves out of the fighting line, due to a loss of will to fight'.[108]

By July 1942, a general feeling was developing in the desert that Eighth Army's reverses were 'due to all the chaps being so dud up with being out here so long'.[109] James had identified the 1st South African Division as

---

[103] ANZ WAII/8/Part 2/BBB Freyberg Papers, Morale.
[104] Ellis, *The Sharp End*, p. 246.
[105] F. Crew (ed.), *History of the Second World War: United Kingdom Medical Services – Army Medical Services*, vol. I, *Campaigns* (London, 1957), p. 464.
[106] Crew, *History of the Second World War*, table J, p. 491.
[107] ANZ WAII/1/DA508/1 vol. 4, Middle East Military Censorship Fortnightly Summary (MEMCFS), no. LII (2 to 15 December 1942), p. 1.
[108] SAMAD Divisional Documents (Div Docs), Gp 1, Box 1, Memorandum on Morale of SA Troops in ME, 8 August 1942, p. 9.
[109] ANZ WAII/1/DA508/1 vol. 1, MEFCWS, no. XXXIV (1 to 7 July 1942), p. 7.

being one of the units 'tired out' from the summer fighting. The censorship summary for 22 to 28 July noted that 'correspondence from Union Defence Force personnel indicated that the forward units are undoubtedly feeling the strain of eight months continuous desert service'. One South African wrote, 'how much longer will we be kept in action. It's been continuous strain and suspense for a few months now, and I'm so horribly tired of it. It's a year now since I saw anything but desert and planes and bombings and guns and all the rest of this unnatural life. Everyone is "run down" to the point of mental and physical collapse – almost.'[110]

The censorship summary for 12 to 18 August pointed out that the 1st South African Division was still exhausted. One man wrote, 'why is it that all other troops are only kept in the front line for two or three months and then pulled out and given a rest. Here we have been 10 solid months in the front line and are still there ... slowly the boys are cracking up, one by one.' An officer wrote that 'the first Brigade is still in the line, which means that for nearly two years they have been practically continuously in the forefront of the business up here, and have taken part in every push (or otherwise) in this theatre of war, since the Union took an active interest in the war. They are still going on and really expect to do so until either wiped out or the war ends.'[111]

The 1st South African Division suffered 40 cases of NYD(N) in the three months from April to June 1942. This was a rate of 12.2 cases per one hundred battle casualties.[112] However, the South Africans suffered sixty-nine cases of NYD(N) in the month of July alone.[113] As almost all of 2nd South African Division was captured at Tobruk,[114] it is likely that 1st South African division made up the majority of these psychological casualties. If this was the case, then the rate of psychological casualties to battle casualties in 1st South African Division could have been as high as 25.5 per cent.[115]

The incidence of battle exhaustion among armoured formations was also of concern. A report on 'Casualties in Armoured Fighting Vehicles', released in July 1942, pointed out that the number of exhaustion cases admitted to hospital, in June 1942, was 'between three and four times the

---

[110] ANZ WAII/1/DA508/1 vol. 1, MEMCWS, no. XXXVII (22 to 28 July 1942), p. 13.
[111] ANZ WAII/1/DA508/1 vol. 1, MEMCWS, no. XL (12 to 18 August 1942), p. 14.
[112] SAMAD Div Docs, Gp 1, Box 6, Ops Reports and Lessons April to July 1942. Work Done by Medical Services during the Quarter Ending on 30 June 1942.
[113] NA WO 177/324 Monthly Statistical Report on Health Eighth Army, July 1942.
[114] I. S. O. Playfair *et al.*, *The Mediterranean and the Middle East*, vol. III, *British Fortunes Reach their Lowest Ebb. History of the Second World War* (London, 1960), p. 274; SAMAD Deputy Chief of Staff (DCS) – Chief of the General Staff (CGS), Box 51, Units known to have been in Tobruk.
[115] NA WO 177/324 Monthly Statistical Report on Health Eighth Army, July 1942.

normal rate'. The report stated that 'while the number of cases in the R.A. and infantry' had approximately 'doubled in June', the incidence in the armoured formation had grown at a much higher rate.[116]

The New Zealander and South African instances referred to thus far amount to 598 cases. But Middle East Command recorded 9,000 cases of combat neurosis in 1942.[117] The majority of these would have occurred among the British troops that made up between 40 and 70 per cent of Eighth Army's fighting units at different stages of 1942.[118] Nine thousand troops amounts to over half of the establishment of a full infantry division[119] and represents more than 133 per cent of the fighting portion of a front line infantry division.[120]

A number of investigations carried out during the war showed that desertion and absenteeism from units could also be regarded as very good indicators of morale.[121] Lieutenant-Colonel J. C. Penton undertook one such study on the British Army of the Rhine in 1944–5. Penton pointed out that, as the morale of the unit faltered, so did the morale of the individual and his reliability as a fighting man. There were two natural reactions to danger: fight was the response of the man well integrated in a fighting group; flight, that of the unintegrated. Thus, desertion would take place when group morale disappeared and individual morale sank to 'flight level' or 'desertion point'.[122] In his 'Study in the Psychology of Desertion and Absenteeism in Wartime, and Its Relation to the Problem of Morale', written in July 1946, Penton concluded that experience had shown that when the morale of the unit in war ceases to hold a soldier in his place, one of two reactions is likely: either the soldier will become obviously ill ('battle exhaustion') and will be treated as an invalid, or he will evade action by other means (usually desertion), whereupon he will be treated as a criminal.[123]

In 1942, the situation in the Middle East as regards desertion became so serious that the Commander-in-Chief, Claude Auchinleck, with the

---

[116] NA WO 222/65 Report on Casualties in Armoured Fighting Vehicles, Medical Research Section, GHQ, MEF, 20 July 1942; NA WO 177/127 Report of Factors Affecting Efficiency of Tank Crews, Medical Research Section, GHQ, MEF, 2 July 1942.

[117] Harrison, *Medicine and Victory*, p. 122.

[118] NA WO 163/51 The Army Council, Death Penalty in Relation to Offences Committed on Active Service, 11 August 1942; NA WO 201/444 Total Daily Strength and Casualties as at 0600 HRS 5 November 1942 Libya Period 6 – no. 13.

[119] IWM TM 30–410 *Handbook on the British Army*, p. 24.

[120] Bungay, *Alamein*, pp. 198–9.

[121] NA CAB 21/914 The Work of Army Psychiatrists in Relation to Morale, January 1944; Bidwell, *Modern Warfare*, p. 129.

[122] Quoted in Robert H. Ahrenfeldt, *Psychiatry in the British Army in the Second World War* (London, 1958), p. 204.

[123] Ahrenfeldt, *Psychiatry in the British Army*, p. 123.

unanimous agreement of his army commanders, forwarded to the War Office a recommendation for the reintroduction of the death penalty (which had been abolished in 1930) for 'desertion in the field' and for 'misbehaving in the face of the enemy in such a manner as to show cowardice'. Auchinleck first raised the issue in April 1942 after the disappointment of the German counteroffensive in early February. To back up his request, he recounted evidence that since April 1941 there had been 291 convictions for desertion and 19 convictions for cowardice in the Middle East.[124] Auchinleck, at the time, felt the situation was so serious that, while waiting for a response, he took matters into his own hands and ordered that senior officers were to 'take the strongest possible action against any individual of whatever rank who refuse[d] to conform to orders. If necessary in order to stop panic, there must be no hesitation in resorting to extreme measures, such as shooting an individual who cannot otherwise be stopped.'[125]

Following the fall of Tobruk and the retreat from the Gazala line, Auchinleck once again cabled London demanding the return of the death penalty. He provided more statistics to lend weight to his argument. He reported that 63 absentees had been apprehended at Matruh in a single day during the Knightsbridge fighting along the Gazala line in June 1942. During the twenty-seven days of battle ending 13 July 1942, 907 absentees had been reported to the Corps of Military Police, of whom 430 were subsequently apprehended. The total number of unapprehended British and colonial absentees was still 1,728 at the time of writing. The average monthly number of soldiers sentenced for desertion in the five months from February to June 1942 was 34. There were over 120 soldiers awaiting trial by courts martial in Cairo and in one high category unit (it is apparent that this was the Guards Brigade, one of the three units mentioned by James as being extremely worn out), 18 cases of desertion in the face of the enemy had been reported during the recent fighting.[126] He later amended this figure to 23 desertions during and immediately after the Knightsbridge fighting. 'In view of the high quality personnel of this unit', Auchinleck found this figure 'most striking'.[127]

The Guards Brigade had only had three weeks rest since the Crusader offensive at the end of 1941.[128] In the confused fighting around Tobruk,

[124] NA WO 32/15773 Auchinleck to the Under Secretary of State, the War Office, 7 April 1942.
[125] NA WO 201/538 Corbett to 8, 9 and 10 Armies, 24 May 1942.
[126] NA WO 32/15773 C-in-C Middle East to the War Office, 24 July 1942.
[127] NA WO 32/15773 C-in-C Middle East to the War Office, 9 August 1942.
[128] D. C. Quilter, *No Dishonourable Name: The 2nd and 3rd Battalions Coldstream Guards 1939–1946* (London, 1972), p. 142.

both the Coldstream and the Scots Guards suffered such debilitating casualties that they had to be formed into a composite battalion made up of two companies of the Scots Guards and two of the Coldstream Guards. The Coldstream Guards were left with 13 officers and 183 ordinary recruits, out of approximately 800 men, after fighting their way out of Tobruk at the end of June,[129] while, by 13 June, the Scots Guards had suffered 13 officer and about 300 ordinary recruit casualties.[130]

These units were so worn out by the end of July that the censorship summary for 5 to 11 August described the Guards' morale as the 'lowest' in the desert.[131] An officer wrote that

our hoped for rest after the Tobruk escape lasted 5 days only ... To our horror we got sent off into the blue as a composite Bn. with the Scots Guards ... someone very grand had assured us we were for the Delta and reforming, and we had no apology or explanation when we were sent forward again. We were assured that our relief was a matter of days (as opposed to weeks or hours). It all seemed quite unreal – We were then ordered south to another Division and informed that our relief was indefinitely postponed. Life seemed to hold nothing grimmer.[132]

The men felt no less aggrieved. 'I don't know what they are trying to do to this battalion, but all I can say is that it seems to me they are trying their best to exterminate it ... The men who came out [here] were nothing less than gibbering idiots for days after and I was as bad myself. We often wonder, is it worth while.' Another argued that 'if they put us back up to the front line half of the lads will go absent. It is definitely up to them to give us a decent rest out of this bloody sand after what we have been through. Eighteen months in the desert is no place for anybody. They can surely spare us – one battalion under half strength.' Yet another remonstrated that it was 'always the same men' who did all the fighting, until 'worn out by the desert and the strain of battle, they crack'.[133]

This situation was made all the more striking by the fact that the censorship summaries had reported the morale of the Scots Guards to be 'outstanding' in March 1942.[134] The summary for 12 to 18 March had stated that the 'spirit of the Guards Brigade' was such that 'no Rommel' could 'break' it.[135] Nevertheless, five months later, the censorship summary for 12 to 18 August pointed out that 'this unit has been hard hit in the course of the last two months, and personnel are generally showing

[129] David Erskine, *The Scots Guards, 1919–1955* (London, 1956), p. 106.
[130] Ibid., p. 105.
[131] ANZ WAII/1/DA508/1 vol. 1, MEFCWS, no. XXXIX (5 to 11 August 1942), p. 4.
[132] Ibid.   [133] Ibid.
[134] AWM 54 883/2/97 MEFCWS, no. XX (25 to 31 March 1942), p. 1.
[135] AWM 54 883/2/97 MEFCWS, no. XVIII (12 to 18 March 1942), p. 1.

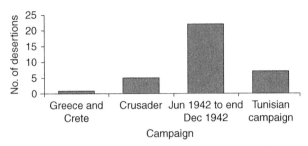

Figure 2 2nd New Zealand Division desertion statistics

poor morale'. One Guardsman wrote 'I don't think we shall be here long before we get moved up again but a lot of lads will not go up again. Most of them are going to go absent and I do not blame them.' Another Guardsman wrote 'honestly speaking ... there are times when you would wonder if it would not be better to be a prisoner of war rather than soldier on in this country, especially after being well over 18 months in the desert without a really decent break. They've ruined one of the best brigades out here by keeping them at it too long, whereas if we got a break now and again we would still have been as good as when we first went into action.'[136]

Many of the commanders in the desert, including Lieutenant-General Bernard Freyberg, the commander of 2nd New Zealand Division, saw desertion as a clear indicator of low morale within units.[137] As Figure 2 demonstrates, the 2nd New Zealand Division suffered twenty-two desertions between June and December 1942. The vast majority of these undoubtedly occurred during July and August, after the morale-damaging casualties of the July battles.

Other statistics for courts martial convictions in British overseas commands in 1941 and 1942 show that there was a peak immediately following July 1942, a time when there was no major action other than that taking place in the desert (Figure 3).

So severe was the problem of desertion among South African units that in April 1942 the Union Defence Force requested the establishment of a permanent court martial in the South African base depot to deal with the number of cases.[138] Another report on 'Illegal Absentees', written in August 1942, stated that 'numerous cases of AWOL [absence without

[136] ANZ WAII/1/DA508/1 vol. 1, MEMCWS, no. XL (12 to 18 August 1942), p. 5.
[137] ANZ WAII/8/Part 2/ BBB Freyberg Papers, Morale, 'Note on Morale', written 1945.
[138] SAMAD Div Docs Box 119 UDF Admin HQ MEF to GOC 1st and 2nd SA Divs, 'President: Permanent Court Martial', 29 April 1942.

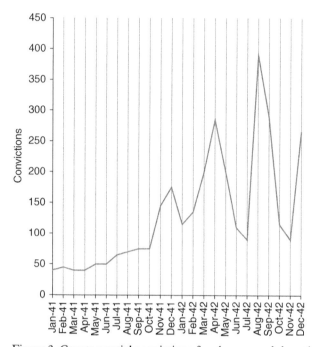

Figure 3 Courts martial convictions for absence and desertion overseas commands, 1941–1942

leave] from the front line have been reported of late'.[139] A report on 'Desertion and Absence Without Leave from the Front Line', written later in the same month by Major-General Dan Pienaar, the commander of 1st South African Division, stated that 'despite the fact that numerous cases of Desertion and AWOL from the forward areas have been disposed of by Courts Martial, this offence continues to be committed. It can, therefore, only be assumed that the sentences imposed by Courts have not been sufficiently severe to act as a deterrent to others ... As from receipt hereof, the proceedings of all Courts Martial will be promulgated on parade, provided this can be done.'[140]

A further indicator of morale problems in Eighth Army was the surrender rate. In July, Auchinleck presented statistics to the War Office to support

---

[139] SAMAD Div Docs Box 119 UDF Adm HQ MEF to Comd. SA Base, 'Illegal Absentees', 8 August 1942.

[140] SAMAD Div Docs Box 119 'Desertion and Absence without Leave from Front Lines', Main HQ 1 SA Div, 23 August 1942.

his request for a reintroduction of the death penalty for offences committed on active service. These figures showed an alarming ratio of 'missing' to overall casualties. Between the beginning of Rommel's offensive at the end of May and late July, Eighth Army lost 1,700 killed and 6,000 wounded, but had 57,000 categorised as missing, 'of whom the great majority must be assumed to be prisoners of war'.[141]

Those categorised as 'missing' included dead and wounded who were left on that part of the battlefield controlled by the enemy, but they also included those who had surrendered to the enemy. It is almost impossible to ascertain how many 'missing' troops were actually killed, or even mistakenly identified as 'missing' in the confusion that permeated Eighth Army in June and July 1942. The official history does not shed any light on the matter. Nevertheless, it has to be assumed, as the Army Council did, that the great majority of those categorised as missing were soldiers taken prisoner. Casualty statistics for other battles in the Middle East suggest that around 85 to 98 per cent of those identified as missing tended to be prisoners.[142] It would be invidious to apply any arbitrary percentage to the 'missing' figures in order to generate a surrender rate, so the 'missing' rates will be quoted as 'missing/surrender' rates with the clear understanding that they approximate very closely to the real surrender rates.

If this approach is used, it can be seen that, using Auchinleck's figures, there was a missing/surrender rate of around 88 per cent of casualties during the summer fighting. Both Adam and Sir James (P. J.) Grigg, the Secretary of State for War, believed that such figures did indeed 'lend colour to the suggestion that the British soldier is inclined to surrender rather than to fight it out', and therefore agreed to reopen the death penalty issue as demanded by Auchinleck.[143] Ten days later, the Army Council concluded that 'the capitulation at Singapore, the fall of Tobruk and the large proportion of unwounded prisoners in the operations in Cyrenaica, are pointers to a condition existing in the Army which does not appear to accord with its old traditions'.[144]

The censorship summaries for this period support this contention. The summary for 8 to 14 July reported that 'some officers ... were rather

[141] NA WO 32/15773 The Army Council, Death Penalty in Relation to Offences Committed on Active Duty, 31 July 1942, p. 1.
[142] AWM 3DRL 2632 6/18 Summary of AIF Battle Casualties, 2 May 1942; AWM 54 171/2/32 Casualties 9th Division Western Desert 1941–2; NA WO 201/2834 HQ Middle East Casualty Statistics; NA WO 32/10810 AG Stats, 18 January 1950.
[143] NA WO 163/89 ECAC, The Death Penalty for Offences Committed on Active Service, 21 July 1942.
[144] NA WO 32/15773, The Army Council, 'Death Penalty in Relation to Offences Committed on Active Duty', 31 July 1942, p. 3.

Illustration 3 British prisoners captured by the Germans during the siege of Tobruk, 1942. Rates of missing/surrendered were so high during the summer battles of 1942 that Auchinleck asked the War Office to reinstate the death penalty for cowardice and desertion in the field.

concerned regarding the spiritless attitude of some of the troops'. One officer stated that 'the one thing that rather depresses me [is] what I have seen and heard . . . of the Tommy . . . I don't know how we have continued to produce such an entirely spiritless attitude . . . It leaves officers like myself with the rather unpleasant job of making them fight if they won't be persuaded into it.' Another officer pointed out that there was 'too much hands-upping' in the desert.[145]

The 'hot spot' casualty reports that arrived in the War Office in London to give initial estimates of attrition at the front also seemed to support Auchinleck's figures. By 4 August, Adam had some disturbing 'approximate' casualty figures to consider (Table 1). The offensive in the Middle East from 27 May to 4 August had cost 74,300 casualties, 62,900 of which were either prisoners or missing in action.

From these statistics, the rate of missing/surrendered to total casualties was 85 per cent. This is consistent with the figures Auchinleck provided in

[145] ANZ WAII/1/DA508/1 vol. 1, MEFCWS, no. XXXV (8 to 14 July 1942), p. 7.

Table 1 *'Hot spot' casualty figures 27 May to 4 August 1942*

	British	Dominion	Indian	Total
Killed and wounded	5,400	4,800	1,200	11,400
Missing	32,800	16,600	13,500	62,900
Total	38,200	21,400	14,700	74,300
% missing of total	84%	78%	92%	85%

Source: LHCMA, Adam Papers, Box 2, Notes on ACS. Paper Comparison of Casualties, Libya, AG Stats, 6 August 1942.

July.[146] The total number of POW and missing soldiers reported by the army during the Second World War amounted to 185,847; this was 32.6 per cent of total casualties. The statistics from the desert in the summer of 1942 are clearly out of line with the general picture and require explanation.[147]

Another set of estimated casualty figures presented to the Army Council on 11 August 1942, as it debated the issue of reintroducing the death penalty, illustrates beyond contention the seriousness of the missing/surrendered issue in the summer of 1942 (Table 2). A comparison between the Crusader offensive and the summer battles is particularly instructive (Figures 4 and 5). Missing/surrender rates during the summer battles were significantly higher than during Crusader and were also far higher than the German and Italian missing/surrender rates.

David French has argued that the high proportion of prisoners to killed and wounded in the North African battles of the summer of 1942 proved little about the morale of Eighth Army. He suggested that the high proportion of prisoners was probably inevitable as unarmoured troops had little option other than to surrender if they found themselves surrounded by enemy tanks and were bereft of anti-tank weapons. He pointed out that the Germans behaved in much the same manner as the Commonwealth forces in this respect.[148] The tactical picture at Gazala and during the July battles did indeed put units under extreme pressure. At Gazala, the British infantry brigades were deployed in dug-in 'boxes'

---

[146] NA WO 32/15773 The Army Council, 'Death Penalty in Relation to Offences Committed on Active Duty', 31 July 1942, p. 1.

[147] LHCMA, Adam Papers, Box 2, White Paper, *Strengths and Casualties of the Armed Forces and Auxiliary Services of the United Kingdom 1939 to 1945*, London, His Majesty's Stationery Office, p. 8.

[148] David French, 'Discipline and the Death Penalty in the British Army in the War against Germany during the Second World War', *Journal of Contemporary History*, 33(4) (October 1998), p. 541.

Table 2 *Comparisons of casualties, Crusader and summer campaigns*

	British	Dominion	Indian	Total	German	Italian	Total
November 1941–January 1942 (Crusader)							
Strength engaged	82,000	54,000	19,000	155,000	42,000	56,000	98,000
Killed and Wounded	4,700	4,200	1,000	9,900	11,500	13,500	25,000
Missing	2,500	4,700	300	7,500	10,500	26,000	36,500
Total	7,200	8,900	1,300	17,400	22,000	39,500	61,500
% Killed and Wounded	6%	8%	5%	6%	27%	24%	25%
% missing	3%	9%	2%	5%	25%	47%	37%
Total	9%	17%	7%	11%	52%	71%	62%
% missing to total casualties	35%	53%	23%	43%	48%	66%	60%
27 May 1942–24 July 1942 (summer) including Tobruk							
Strength engaged	80,000	63,000	48,000	191,000	50,000	35,000	85,000
Killed and Wounded	5,000	3,400	600	9,000	21,600	4,000	25,000
Missing	31,000	15,300	13,000	59,300	2,100	6,000	8,100
Total	36,000	18,700	13,600	68,300	23,700	10,000	33,700
% Killed and Wounded	6%	5%	1%	5%	43%	11%	30%
% missing	39%	24%	27%	31%	4%	17%	10%
Total	45%	29%	28%	36%	47%	28%	40%
% missing to total casualties	86%	81%	95%	87%	9%	60%	24%
27 May 1942–24 July 1942 (summer) excluding Tobruk							
Strength engaged	66,000	51,100	48,000	162,600			
Killed and Wounded	5,000	3,400	600	9,000			
Missing	17,000	3,400	10,500	30,900			
Total	22,000	6,800	11,100	39,900			
% Killed and Wounded	7.5%	6.5%	1.5%	5.5%			
% missing	25.5%	6.5%	21.5%	19.5%			
Total	33%	13%	23%	25%			
% missing to total casualties, 4 August 1942	80%	50%	95%	80%			

Source: NA WO 163/51 The Army Council, Death Penalty in Relation to Offences Committed on Active Service, 11 August 1942.

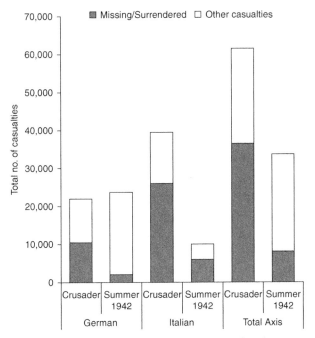

Figure 4 Axis proportion of missing/surrendered compared to total casualties, Crusader and summer campaigns

which, when attacked, could be easily surrounded if support in the form of British armour was not forthcoming. Once surrounded, the infantry and their supporting arms had little choice but to fight it out where they were or surrender. Infantry in dug in positions had, by definition, sent their transport away and thus had no real opportunity to break out and escape. In the July battles there were a number of occasions in which Anzac infantry pushed deep into the Axis defences in the expectation that they would be supported by British tanks. When the tanks did not turn up, again the infantry had little choice but to fight or surrender. These types of actions certainly contributed to a high surrender rate but it is debatable whether the surrender rate was entirely due to an impossible tactical situation or whether morale issues played a part.

Leslie Morshead, the commander of 9th Australian Division, certainly thought that morale had played a part in causing the problem. He believed that 'far too many unwounded prisoners' had been taken in the desert. He wrote, 'the modern term "in the bag" is too excusable, it is not harsh enough, and it seems to mitigate having failed to make a proper stand and

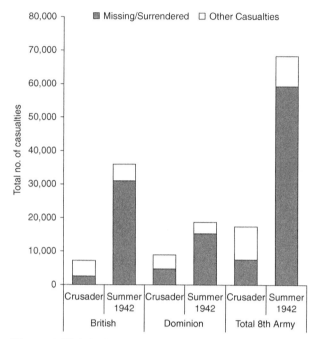

Figure 5 Eighth Army proportion of missing/surrendered compared to total casualties, Crusader and summer campaigns

even to having just merely surrendered. We must make it unfashionable. I have closely questioned escaped prisoners and I know what actually happened in some instances.'[149]

The figures for the different nationalities of Eighth Army at Gazala, Tobruk and during the July battles demonstrate that Eighth Army's experience in this regard was not monolithic. Around 82 per cent to 86 per cent of British troops were classified as missing/surrendered during these battles. The Australian figure was about 34 per cent, the New Zealand 42 per cent while the South African was 90 per cent.[150] It is clear that certain elements of Eighth Army were more likely to fight it out than others.

It must be accepted that, for some units surrounded in the open desert, continued resistance to German pressure would have been tantamount to

---

[149] AWM 3 DRL 2632 Morshead Papers, El Alamein, 10 October 1942.
[150] NA WO 32/10810 Battle casualties (exclusive of deaths from natural causes) incurred by forces under British Empire control as reported by "hot spot" cables from 3 September 1939 to 28 June 1946.

collective suicide. Such tactical explanations of Eighth Army's behaviour, however, do not justify statistics of missing/surrendered as high as 88 per cent for the whole of Eighth Army. If the matter was so easily explained then it would not have been of such concern to Auchinleck and his commanders. The German ratio of POW to total casualties during 'Crusader' was 69 per cent (the British rate was 42 per cent) according to the British official history.[151] Crusader, much like the battles on the Gazala line, involved periods of mobile warfare and static warfare, and, in a similar vein to Tobruk, large numbers of Axis prisoners were captured when Bardia and Halfaya fell to Eighth Army. At El Alamein, in October and November 1942, German surrenders can best be estimated at 40 per cent of total casualties, while the Italians had a rate of 63 per cent (the rate for British and Commonwealth troops was 17 per cent).[152]

Eighth Army's high ratio of missing/surrendered to total casualties is, in fact, only comparable with that of the Italian forces that fought during Crusader in November/December 1941. Casualty statistics from the Crusader battle provided by the British Official History show that Italian elements of *Panzerarmee Afrika* suffered a POW rate of 84 per cent.[153] It is worth noting that the troops of Eighth Army had nothing but contempt for the Italian soldiers' willingness to surrender. To suggest that it was acceptable for British and Commonwealth soldiers to surrender at similar rates, whatever the tactical situation, while ridiculing the Italians, whose morale was, and still is, universally recognised to have been atrocious, is inconsistent.

Churchill was so concerned about the issue of surrender that he consulted P. J. Grigg, the Secretary of State for War, with a view to submitting to the War Cabinet proposals defining the conditions which must be satisfied before an officer in the field was justified in surrendering. He also wished to emphasise the obligation on all units to continue fighting as long as possible.[154]

---

[151] Derived from statistics quoted by Playfair, *The Mediterranean and Middle East*, vol. III, p. 97. Playfair's figures are approximately the same as those received by the War Office at the time. NA WO 163/51 Battle Casualties in Libya 18 November 1941 to 10 January 1942. These figures are somewhat higher than the figures presented thus far in this chapter, e.g. in Table 2.

[152] Derived from statistics quoted by Bungay, *Alamein*, pp. 196–7.

[153] Derived from statistics quoted by Playfair, *The Mediterranean and Middle East*, vol. III, p. 97. This figure is again somewhat higher than the figure presented in Table 2.

[154] NA WO 32/15773 ECAC, 'The Death Penalty for Offences Committed on Active Service', p. 2.

Ultimately, the issues of surrender and the death penalty were settled through political expediency. Grigg felt that

To justify a modification of the present law we should have to produce facts and figures as evidence that the British soldiers' morale in the face of the enemy is so uncertain as to make the most drastic steps necessary to prevent it breaking. Any such evidence would come as a profound shock to the British public and our allies and as a corresponding encouragement to our enemies ... if military efficiency were the sole consideration, I should be in favour, as are my military advisers, of the re-introduction of the death penalty for the offences in question. But the political aspects are, at any rate, in present circumstances, as important, if not more important, than the military.[155]

The statistics thus far presented suggest that Eighth Army did indeed suffer a morale problem in the summer of 1942. A similar analysis of statistics also points to the reality of a dramatic turnaround in morale that coincided with the arrival of Montgomery in the desert. At Alam Halfa and El Alamein the morale and confidence of Eighth Army was renewed and built upon. The success of Eighth Army in North Africa was driven by this morale turn-around. As Gary Sheffield has said 'the ultimate test of morale is willingness to engage in combat'.[156] At El Alamein, Eighth Army suffered 13,560 casualties. In all, 2,350 of its men were killed, another 8,950 servicemen were wounded and 2,260 were missing in action (most of whom were captured). In the words of Niall Barr, by the end of the battle, 'Eighth Army had virtually run out of formed infantry units that could still be used in the attack.'[157] Many of these units had suffered well over 50 per cent casualties among their front-line troops in the space of thirteen days.[158]

Although the exact number of NYD(N) casualties for El Alamein is unknown, it is generally accepted that the incidence of breakdown during the thirteen days of fighting was remarkably low, especially for an attri-tional infantry battle.[159] The monthly statistical reports on the health of Eighth Army for October and November 1942 stated that the inciden-ces of NYD(N) were much smaller during the El Alamein offensive than they had been in previous battles, the total number of cases for the two months combined being 209. The number for the July battles alone had been 557.[160]

---

[155] NA WO 32/15773 'Death Penalty for Offences Committed on Active Service'. Memorandum by the Secretary of State for War (P. J. Grigg), 12 June 1942.
[156] Sheffield, *Leadership in the Trenches*, p. 181.   [157] Barr, *Pendulum of War*, p. 397.
[158] See Chapter 8 for further discussion on casualty statistics in Eighth Army.
[159] Ben Shephard, *A War Of Nerves: Soldiers and Psychiatrists 1914–1994* (London, 2002), p. 217; Harrison, *Medicine and Victory*, p. 123.
[160] NA WO 177/324 Monthly Statistical Report on Health of Eighth Army, October and November 1942.

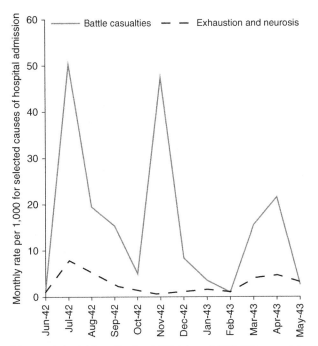

Figure 6 2nd New Zealand Division, NYD(N) casualties in relation to battle casualties, June 1942 to May 1943

The 2nd New Zealand Division suffered only fifty-seven instances of battle exhaustion at El Alamein. This represented a ratio of one to one hundred battle casualties, the lowest New Zealand ratio of the war (Figure 6).[161] The correlation between psychiatric casualties, stress and morale is clearly illustrated in these figures. In July and August the division was in a static position, exposed to the most tiring of conditions and a series of disastrous battles. Morale, as John McLeod has argued, sank slowly 'to what was its lowest ebb'.[162]

At El Alamein, however, after the morale recovery, exhaustion and neurosis casualties were virtually non-existent. The commander of the 28th New Zealand (Maori) Battalion recalled that, in the months leading up to El Alamein, once his unit 'snapped out of it and we got up reinforcements and then gave old Jerry a couple of good cracks, they never looked back. When we came out of the line I set to work on

[161] ANZ WAII/8/Part 2/BBB Freyberg Papers, Morale.
[162] McLeod, Myth and Reality: The New Zealand Soldier in World War II, p. 74.

discipline and training. No unit trained anything like as much as we did in that 6 weeks and when we went forward again many things had been achieved. No unit in the div. was ... in better heart ... My confidence was justified for in the days up till I was hit they were just grand.'[163]

The figures for NYD(N) for 1st South African Division point to a similar turnaround. The division suffered about 900 casualties at El Alamein;[164] during October and November 1942 the division suffered a total of 15 NYD(N) casualties.[165] That meant that the South Africans suffered a rate of perhaps 1.7 NYD(N) cases per 100 battle casualties at El Alamein. The rate during the summer battles could have been as high 25.5 cases per 100 battle casualties.[166]

The daily sick admission rate was also remarkably low. By November, the rate was 1.59 per 1,000 (a monthly rate of 47.7 per 1,000), a considerable drop from 2.42 in August (a monthly rate of 75 per 1,000). The report for November 1942 made it clear that the majority of the sick were non-divisional troops and not those involved in the fighting. Some time after El Alamein, in April 1943, Montgomery wrote to the Chief of the Imperial General Staff (CIGS) that 'the high morale of my soldiers is almost unbelievable ... they believe that this Army is invincible and can do nothing wrong ... A feature of this morale', he said, 'is the low sick rate.' Montgomery was able to report proudly that the daily rate of admissions to hospital was as low as 0.6 per 1,000 (a monthly rate of 18 per thousand).[167]

The incidence of surrender and desertion also dramatically decreased. At El Alamein, instances of missing/surrender made up only 17 per cent of casualties. This was a substantial reduction from the height of the crisis in the summer of 1942, when figures were around 88 per cent. Two days after the end of the battle, replying to an enquiry by the Secretary of State for War on the continuing need to consider the reintroduction of the death penalty, Alexander, Commander-in-Chief in the Middle East, was able to report that desertion and cowardice cases were 'decreasing and I think they will continue to do so.'[168]

[163] ANZ WAII/1/DA508/1 vol. 4, MEMCFS, no. LII (2 to 15 December 1942), p. 1.
[164] NA WO 201/2834 Eighth Army, Summary of Battle Casualties (excluding sick) for Major Operations in Egypt, Libya and Tunisia during the Period 2 July 1942 to 14 May 1943.
[165] NA WO 177/324 Monthly Statistical Report on Health of Eighth Army, October and November 1942.
[166] NA WO 177/324 Monthly Statistical Report on Health Eighth Army, July 1942.
[167] IWM BLM 49 Montgomery to Alan Brooke, 15 April 1943.
[168] NA WO 32/15773 Alexander to Sir James Grigg (Secretary of State for War), 6 November 1942.

Brigadier A. B. McPherson, the compiler of the army monograph on 'Discipline' produced after the war, pointed out that reports from the Middle East during 1942–3 showed that, as the tide turned in the Allies' favour, and repeated withdrawals and uncertainty gave way to advances and confidence in their leaders, especially in the Eighth Army, morale improved and crime as a whole decreased. This was particularly so among troops in the forward areas.[169]

It is clear that Eighth Army did experience a morale crisis in the desert. This is discernable in personal accounts, in the censorship summaries and in official reports. In addition, the sources confirm that the New Zealanders, South Africans and British[170] all suffered extremely high sickness, breakdown, POW and desertion rates in the summer of 1942 (problems that many commentators described as good indicators or corollaries of morale). Reference has been made to this crisis in the historiography of the North African campaign. However, such references have until now been based on anecdotal and personal accounts rather than on a thorough qualitative and quantitative appraisal of all the available sources.

Many of the units that fought in the desert understandably have not drawn attention to this morale crisis. The commanding officer of the 28th New Zealand (Maori) Battalion, already referred to, made it clear in his letter of December 1942 that 'I do not want any part of this letter disclosed to anyone . . . I would not like that news ever to get abroad about the boys, certainly not from me, and the Lord knows they have been through enough to warrant it.'[171] Neither the history of the Coldstream Guards nor that of the Scots Guards highlights the morale problems in the desert in the summer of 1942.[172]

Nevertheless, in spite of all the concerns about Eighth Army's morale, among the troops themselves, among their commanders, and in the War Office, it is clear that morale was revitalised leading up to the battle of El Alamein. The improvement in Eighth Army's performance on the battlefield coincided with this recovery in the morale of the troops. One fed the other.

[169] NA WO 277/7 Brigadier A. B. McPherson, *Army: Discipline* (The War Office, 1950), p. 46.

[170] Some of the evidence suggests that Indian units suffered similar problems.

[171] ANZ WAII/1/DA508/1 vol. 4, MEMCFS, no. LII (2 to 15 December 1942), p. 1.

[172] Quilter, *No Dishonourable Name*; Erskine, *The Scots Guards*, pp. 108–15.

2   Technology, firepower and morale

> From the moment that the overwhelming industrial capacity of the
> United States could make itself felt in any theatre of war, there was no
> longer any chance of ultimate victory in that theatre ... Tactical skill
> could only postpone the collapse, it could not avert the ultimate fate of ...
> [that] theatre.
>
> (Field Marshal Erwin Rommel)[1]

Literature on the Second World War is replete with references to
the economic and quantitative disadvantages suffered by Germany in
comparison to her enemies.[2] The unbending logic of numbers and economics, as many historians argue, precluded Germany from winning a
war against the future superpowers of the USA and USSR. John Keegan,
in *The Second World War*, argued that 'in the final enumeration of Hitler's
mistakes in waging the war, his decision to contest the issue with the
power of the American economy may well come to stand first'.[3] John
Ellis in *Brute Force* claimed that the decisive differentiator between
the Allied and Axis armies was the technological advantage enjoyed by
the Allies in the years following 1942.[4] The German war diaries from the
North African campaign leave no doubt that the *Afrika Korps'* own
commanders saw Allied technological and numerical superiority as the
cause of their defeat.[5]

Such commentary clearly advocates a deterministic view of history that
suggests that technology, weapons and numbers by themselves are the
decisive factors in deciding military outcomes. It also relegates factors

---

[1] John Ellis, *Brute Force: Allied Strategy and Tactics in the Second World War* (London, 1990),
p. 525.
[2] See for example, Ellis, *Brute Force*; John Keegan, *The Second World War* (London, 1997);
Richard Overy, *Why the Allies Won* (London, 1995); Adam Tooze, *The Wages of
Destruction: The Making and Breaking of the Nazi Economy* (London, 2006).
[3] Keegan, *The Second World War*, p. 178.   [4] Ellis, *Brute Force*, p. xvii.
[5] ANZ WAII/11/20 German–Italian Forces in Africa 23 October 1942 to 23 February 1943.
From German War Narrative, 2 November 1942.

such as morale to the sidelines when analysing the reasons for Allied victory in North Africa and in the Second World War in general.

In the years following 1945, the doctrine of technological determinacy gained credibility. The two major military powers to emerge from the war, the United States and the Soviet Union, both acknowledged that great advances had been made in weapons technology between 1939 and 1945 and that these developments had been crucial in achieving victory. As a result, they stockpiled vast quantities of highly destructive conventional and nuclear armaments in preparation for future conflicts. One of the more influential authors on the subject in the United States was S. L. A. Marshall. He contended that what was needed in battle was 'more and better fire'.[6] He argued that 'fundamentally fire wins wars and that every other aspect of operations is important only in the measure that it contributes to this grand object'.[7] His ideas became dogma in the US Army, and there was, as Hew Strachan has pointed out, a clear trajectory from the publication of *Men against Fire* to the performance of the US Army in the wars that followed, such as in Vietnam. But, notwithstanding the massive superiority in firepower enjoyed by the USA over the North Vietnamese in Southeast Asia, the morale of the US Army collapsed[8] and it lost the war.

Marshall's theories on firepower were, in fact, misapplied by the US Army. Marshall did not suggest that firepower could determine victory by itself, a fact that became apparent in Vietnam. Instead, he claimed that its significance lay in its relationship with the psychology of the fighting soldier.[9] 'Among fighting men', he contended, 'morale endures only so long as the chance remains that ultimately their weapons will deal greater death or fear of death to the enemy. When that chance dies, morale dies and defeat occurs.'[10] This statement encapsulates Marshall's contribution to a debate that had been running for a hundred years.

With the development of modern artillery and the machine gun in the middle of the nineteenth century, the battlefield changed forever. It appeared to many that the human factor in warfare would be made increasingly subservient to the science of ballistics and firepower.[11] However, in many ways, firepower produced the opposite effect. The

---

[6] Marshall, *Men against Fire*, p. 23.   [7] Ibid., pp. 66–7.

[8] Hew Strachan, 'Training, Morale and Modern War', *Journal of Contemporary History*, 41(2) (London, 2006), p. 225.

[9] Ibid., p. 217.   [10] Marshall, *Men against Fire*, p. 67.

[11] Michael Howard, 'Men against Fire: The Doctrine of the Offensive in 1914', in Peter Paret (ed.), *Makers of Modern Strategy from Machiavelli to the Nuclear Age* (Oxford, 1986), pp. 510–26.

unifying force of massed ranks of soldiers facing fire together was replaced with the need for dispersion to counteract the effects of machine guns and high explosives. Individuals, therefore, had to become more self-sufficient and their morale had to be more resilient to stand up to the increasingly 'lonely' battlefield. It was necessary, as a result, for armies to produce better trained and motivated soldiers, a requirement which became far more difficult as higher casualties resulting from more lethal weapons drove warfare towards the 'total' mobilisation of entire societies.

The terrible reality of modern weapons convinced many late-nineteenth- and early-twentieth-century military thinkers that the balance in warfare necessarily had to shift from the offensive to the defensive. Victory in the end, they believed, would likely belong to the side with the greater ability to absorb casualties. It therefore became strategically more advantageous to dig in and let the other side waste itself in futile offensives against well-prepared positions.[12] It followed from this belief that morale would necessarily play a diminished role in warfare, as it took less courage to sit in a trench and fire machine guns than it did to advance across the fire-swept zone.

Nevertheless, there were still good practical arguments for the offensive in modern war. Although the attack could prove costly in casualties, over a long period of attritional warfare casualties could often mount just as high. Helmuth von Moltke, the Prussian Chief of the General Staff between 1857 and 1888, refused to abandon the concept of the offensive war. Germany, surrounded by potential enemies on all sides, could not afford to resort to wars of attrition to settle its differences with a hostile France or Russia.

According to Moltke, offensive warfare required improvisation and speed in making and executing decisions rather than lengthy searches for ideal solutions. He therefore, like Clausewitz, emphasized moral factors in war and the need for independent action by local commanders.[13] The experience of the Russo–Japanese War of 1905 reinforced this notion that élan, or 'will', was still a decisive element in military success. It became clear to military practitioners and theorists, as Michael Howard has argued, that 'the truly important element in modern warfare was not technology but morale; and the morale, not of the army alone, but of the nation from which it was drawn'. Japanese offensives, although terribly costly, managed, not least through sheer determination, to overcome well-entrenched Russian positions at Port Arthur and Mukden. The offensive could still triumph.[14]

---

[12] Ibid., pp. 510–11.
[13] Daniel J. Hughes, *Moltke on the Art of War: Selected Writings* (Novato, CA, 1993), pp. 5–6.
[14] Howard, 'Men against Fire', in Paret (ed.), *Makers of Modern Strategy*, p. 519.

The First World War, however, produced a number of different viewpoints on the relevance of morale in modern war. In the case of Britain, the general attitude was that morale had not been the crucial factor in victory. The perceived lack of a decisive military defeat of Germany convinced writers such as Liddell Hart that Britain had prevailed in the end due to her technological and numerical superiority at sea. The British fleet had blockaded Germany into submission.[15] In other words, the monumental human effort on the western front had not been the decisive factor.

In so far as there were lessons to be learned from the battlefield, technological advances, such as the development of the tank and improved coordination and accuracy in artillery, had restored the desired mobility to warfare. The solutions to overcoming the problems presented by modern firepower were technological, not human. David French has argued in *Raising Churchill's Army* that the British Army between the wars developed a combined arms doctrine designed to employ a minimum of manpower and a maximum of machinery. In his words, 'post-war doctrine abandoned a search for a "human solution" to the conundrum of how to combine firepower, manoeuvrability, and surprise and enthusiastically embraced a technological solution'.[16] By the early 1920s, the General Staff accepted that 'a relatively small but highly professional army, equipped with the most modern weapons, offered them the best way of avoiding a repetition of the stalemate and high casualties of the Western Front and the collapse of morale that it threatened'.[17] In 1927, the Chief of the Imperial General Staff, George Milne, concluded that 'in the war of the future we cannot depend on the man-power that we had in the last great war, nor will any nation stand the losses we went through again for another 100 years'.[18] Although the General Staff never lost sight of the possibility that they might have to raise another national army in the future, their 'ideal in the 1920s and for much of the 1930s was to establish a small, highly mechanized professional army'.[19]

The Germans, on the other hand, derived very different lessons from the First World War. The 'stab in the back' theory propounded by ardent nationalists, such as Hitler, ensured that morale played a far more central role in explaining success and defeat on the battlefield.[20]

---

[15] B. H. Liddell Hart, *A History of the World War, 1914–1918* (London, 1934), pp. 587–9.

[16] French, *Raising Churchill's Army*, p. 276.   [17] Ibid., p. 15.

[18] NA WO 279/57 Report on the Staff Conference held at the Staff College Camberley, 17 to 20 January 1927.

[19] French, *Raising Churchill's Army*, p. 15.

[20] NA WO 193/456 Notes on Memorandum prepared by the Committee for National Morale, New York, 20 June, 1941. 'German Psychological Warfare'.

It was a collapse in home morale that had caused defeat while concurrently it was the high morale of the German troops on the western front that had prevented military defeat in the face of overwhelming Allied numerical and technological superiority.[21] Whereas Britain had focused on technological solutions to overcome the stalemate on the western front, Ludendorff and Hindenburg looked to maximise the output of their human resources. Where Britain developed tanks, Germany developed storm troopers. Germany aimed at empowering the individual soldier through training and political education to achieve its desired outcomes. 'In this war, which is apparently dominated by science and numbers', ran the report of the 1st Army on its experiences on the Somme, 'individual will-power is nevertheless the ultimate deciding factor.'[22]

During the interwar years, the German Army concentrated on training its manpower and leaders for a future war. As James Corum has pointed out, 'thanks to the Reichswehr's excellent training program' a typical German Army captain or major in 1940 would have been better trained 'than the average British or French general'.[23] German doctrine also stressed the need for movement, speed and shock in the attack.[24] The combined arms doctrine of the German interwar army was designed to amass 'sufficient firepower and shock against the enemy' to allow 'the infantry to break through deeply and to break the enemy resistance decisively'.[25] Thus, the *Reichswehr* applied the morale and psychological lessons derived from the First World War to its use of the new technologies developed throughout the 1920s and 1930s.

The impact of German methods on French morale in the summer of 1940 proved German doctrine to be correct. Ellis concluded that 'it was not so much the physical effect of German guns and planes' that so incapacitated the Allies in France as their 'impact on morale'. The troops were not paralysed by the actual losses amongst men and equipment but 'by the fear of what bullets, shells and bombs might do'. Men simply, in Ellis's words, 'panicked and quit perfectly tenable positions, roads became hopelessly blocked as vehicles were abandoned and march discipline evaporated, and communications broke down ... A hundred

---

[21] Liddell Hart, *A History of the World War*, epilogue.
[22] Strachan, 'Training, Morale and Modern War', *Journal of Contemporary History*, 41(2) (London, 2006), p. 220.
[23] James S. Corum, *The Roots of Blitzkrieg* (Lawrence, KS, 1992), p. 205.
[24] Bruce Condell and David T. Zabecki, *On the German Art of War: Truppenführung* (London, 2001), p. 88.
[25] Ibid., p. 92.

such failures quickly bred a thousand more, and these in turn gave rise to defeatism, despair and a fixed conviction that the enemy was invincible.'[26]

Rommel recorded similar sentiments during the fighting in France. He was struck by the role firepower played in undermining the enemy's morale. 'I have found again and again that in encounter actions, the day goes to the side that is the first to plaster his opponents with fire. The man who lies low and awaits developments usually comes off second best.' Rommel discovered that opening fire on anti-tank positions 'early' was so effective that 'in most cases' the enemy was 'completely unable to get into action or else g[a]ve up his position' without a fight.[27]

By July 1940, it had become abundantly clear to the War Office that the Germans deliberately attacked morale. The Army Training Memorandum, 'Morale and Fighting Efficiency' described how 'mere individual determination to refuse to succumb to "frightfulness"' was not enough. Only 'a corporate sense of discipline' would 'maintain the fighting value of a unit or sub-unit under the strain of the technique of demoralization as now practised by the German Army and Air Force'.[28] By February 1941, the War Office's 'Periodic Notes on the German Army' highlighted that German tactics focused on speed and surprise in battle, 'on the need for concentration of all means, moral, physical and material, at the decisive place and time'.[29] The methods of 'lightning' warfare were as much an attack on the morale qualities of the enemy as they were on his physical attributes. 'By continuous raids and the use of loudspeakers before the attack and by the noise of whistling bombs, loud explosions and the lavish employment of grenades, the German hopes to destroy the morale of his opponents, particularly of those in the forward defences.'[30] German artillery was taught to shoot first and correct later, believing, as Rommel did, that the shock of getting their own artillery active before their enemies was a crucial factor in success.[31] Other sources offered similar insights. An article in the *British Medical Journal*, on 4 April 1942, said that morale, 'built by whatever means, is considered by the German Leaders to be at least as important as weapons. This is all the

---

[26] Ellis, *Brute Force*, pp. 12–13; see also Mark Connelly and Walter Miller, 'The BEF and the Issue of Surrender on the Western Front in 1940', *War in History*, 11(4), (2004), and Glyn Prysor, 'The "Fifth Column" and the British Experience of Retreat, 1940', *War in History*, 12(4), (2005).

[27] B. H. Liddell Hart (ed.), *The Rommel Papers* (New York, 1953), p. 7.

[28] NA WO 277/7 McPherson, 'Army: Discipline', pp. 6–7.

[29] SAMAD Div Docs, Gp 1, Box 49, 'Periodic Notes on the German Army' no 35, February 1941, p. 7. Note underlining added by this author.

[30] Ibid., p. 9.   [31] Ibid., p. 14.

more impressive when we consider how important they have proved weapons to be.'[32]

The relationship between technology and morale played a fundamental role in deciding defeat and victory in the desert as well. 'Middle East Training Pamphlet no. 10', which dealt with the lessons from the Cyrenaica campaign against the Italians in 1940/1941, pointed out that throughout the operation 'the attack displayed a marked superiority over defence'. The reason for this was the 'difference in morale, personnel and equipment between the two armies'.[33] Another report on the 'Lessons Learned from the Operations in the Western Desert' stated that the Italians had 'to a remarkable extent neglected to exploit a considerable numerical superiority' and had been 'content to employ [their] mobile forces in a purely defensive role'.[34] The reason for this defensive attitude was, according to the report, the poor morale of the Italian Army.

The superior weapons of the Western Desert Force (WDF) had a 'marked effect upon the morale' of the Italians, who found themselves 'confronted with a tank [the British 'I' tank (Matilda II)] virtually immune to all forms of fire'. Italian and Libyan troops were completely surprised by these weapons. 'Grenadiers were seen to rise from their trenches, hurl grenades at tanks, and become amazed, horrified and petrified when they observed that the tanks were impervious to such action.' 'Generally speaking', the report concluded, 'the enemy' became 'demoralized' and 'surrendered in large numbers.'[35]

Rainer Kriebel, a staff officer in the *Afrika Korps*, understood that the Italians 'felt very bitter about their very inferior equipment and armament'. The small range and the obsolete system of laying their guns meant that on many occasions Italian artillery units 'were shot to pieces by British batteries at long range before they could even open fire'. The calibre of the Italian anti-tank guns was insufficient; the Italian tanks were poorly armoured and armed; the Italian anti-aircraft artillery was obsolete. It was

[32] NA WO 193/423 *British Medical Journal*, 4 April 1942, Article reviewing a survey by the American Committee for National Morale, by R. D. Gillespie.

[33] NA WO 201/2586 'Middle East Training Pamphlet no. 10'. Lessons of Cyrenaica Campaign: training pamphlet, December 1940 to February 1941.

[34] NA WO 201/352 Operations in the Western Desert: Lessons Learned December 1940 to September 1941.

[35] NA WO 201/352 Operations in the Western Desert: Lessons Learned December 1940 to September 1941. Report on Capture by the 4th Indian Division of Enemy Positions at Nibeiwa ... Leading to the Capture of Sidi Barrani itself. 9, 10, 11 December 1940.

therefore, in Kriebel's words 'not surprising that the Italian troops felt that they were inferior to the British'.[36]

The nature of war in the desert highlighted differences in the quality of equipment. With little cover and almost limitless space, tanks and artillery played a central role almost unequalled in any other theatre in the Second World War. Technology therefore mattered very greatly in maintaining or inhibiting morale. Italian soldiers surrendered en masse when they realised that they did not have the equipment to destroy the British heavy tanks. At the same time, the morale of the WDF improved as it realised it was supported by weaponry that was far superior to anything the Italians had at their disposal.

The WDF's success over the Italians could be seen as the culmination of British interwar doctrinal development. A mainly regular force of seasoned troops,[37] whom Niall Barr has described as 'perhaps the finest-trained, if not the best-equipped, force that Britain possessed',[38] decisively defeated a much larger opponent by substituting manpower with machinery. In a situation where British forces were unquestionably better equipped than their opponents, this doctrine made exquisite sense. However, the force that defeated the Italians was very different from the army that fought subsequent battles in the desert. With the arrival of the German 5th Light Division in March 1941, the technological balance shifted quite sharply to the detriment of the WDF.

The defeats suffered by the WDF at El Agheila, and in Brevity and Battleaxe, were in many ways caused by the shock of confronting new and superior German firepower and tactics. The paralysing effects of this form of warfare, that had so shattered the French and British armies' morale in 1940, were witnessed once again in the desert. The problem, as Len Tutt, a gunner with the 104th Royal Horse Artillery, saw it, was that the forces left to face the German onslaught were 'criminally under equipped'.[39] The best of the British armour and infantry had been sent to Greece, leaving only worn-out tanks and salvaged Italian equipment for the forces that remained.

Auchinleck, who replaced Wavell following Battleaxe in July 1941, began immediately to build up a stockpile of armaments that he believed would enable the British to take on the *Afrika Korps* on something closer to an equal technological footing. By the end of October 1941, the newly

---

[36] SAMAD UWH, Foreign Documents, Box 203, History of the Campaign in North Africa, vol. 1 part 2, by Rainer Kriebel. Up to and including 23 November 1941, p. 59.

[37] Pitt, *Wavell's Command*, p. 9.   [38] Barr, *Pendulum of War*, p. 46.

[39] IWM 85/35/1 L. E. Tutt, 'Gentlemen Soldiers', pp. 110–11.

formed and newly named Eighth Army had swelled its arsenal with new weapons from Britain and America. Some 300 British cruiser tanks, 300 American Stuart tanks, 170 'I' tanks, 34,000 lorries, 600 field guns, 80 heavy and 160 light anti-aircraft guns, 200 anti-tank guns and 900 mortars had arrived in time for the planned Crusader offensive. Churchill sent a message to the troops on the eve of the attack, claiming that

for the first time British and Empire troops will meet the Germans with an ample supply of equipment in modern weapons of all kinds. The battle itself will affect the whole course of the war. Now is the time to strike the hardest blow yet struck for final victory, home and freedom. The Desert Army may add a page to history which will rank with Blenheim and Waterloo. The eyes of all nations are upon you. All our hearts are with you. May God uphold the right![40]

The censorship summaries reported that by 'the eve of the great Libyan offensive' the 'excellence and quantity of the material' and 'the increased amount of air support' had made a considerable difference to the morale of Eighth Army. In fact, they reported that 'the morale of the M.E.F. has never been so high'.[41] By the end of November, Eighth Army had more tanks and aircraft than had ever before been assembled in the Western Desert. The Germans and Italians together had, in their armoured divisions, about 390 tanks, including the inferior panzer Mark IIs but excluding the Italian light tanks.[42] The Germans had no operational reserves while the British had a sizable one and were expecting a further convoy of tanks to arrive soon.

In spite of these quantitative improvements, there remained qualitative deficiencies that hampered Eighth Army's combat performance. The Crusader tank, which constituted the next generation of British cruiser tanks and made up nearly half of Auchinleck's cruiser force, was, just like all of the British tanks in the desert, under armed. It possessed a two-pounder gun, an inferior weapon to the German 50 mm and 75 mm guns. In addition, all the British cruiser tanks remained notoriously prone to mechanical breakdown. The American Stuart, another new introduction to Eighth Army, was mechanically reliable and its 37 mm gun used capped ammunition which gave it greater penetration against the German armour. However, its fuel capacity was modest, which only allowed it a small radius of action. This was a disadvantage in the wide expanses of the desert, a problem which equally affected the laborious and heavy 'I' tanks.[43]

---

[40] Barnett, *The Desert Generals*, p. 93.
[41] AWM 54 883/2/97 MEFCWS, no. I (12 to 18 November 1941), p. 1.
[42] Playfair, *The Mediterranean and Middle East*, vol. III, p. 29.   [43] Ibid., pp. 27–30.

Auchinleck's and Cunningham's plan for Crusader was to meet Rommel's panzer forces in a climactic armoured engagement that would decide the fate of the desert war. Auchinleck reasoned that his numerical superiority would negate the qualitative advantages enjoyed by the German armour. Outnumbered as he was, Rommel declined the head-on encounter and contrived to defeat Eighth Army in detail. The decisive phase of the engagement played itself out around the airfield at Sidi Rezegh.

The flat ground meant there was nowhere to hide for the under-gunned British armour, resulting in heavy casualties. 'We all met Mr Death that day in Sidi Rezegh,' recounted one soldier. 'We were ... blown to pieces a bit at a time by the enemy and we could not do a thing about it.'[44] The main trouble appeared to Private R. L. Crimp of the 2nd Battalion Rifle Brigade, the 7th Armoured Division, as it did to many others, to be the disparity between British and German tanks.

We may have had the greater number, but most of them were ... lanky, light-weight, gangling cruisers, pretty fast, but mounted with feeble 2-pounder guns, no earthly good against the thicker armour and much more powerful 75-mm. armament of the German Panzers. How many crews have been wasted in useless tanks, not being able to retaliate against the longer-ranged enemy guns before having approached several hundred yards nearer their opponents over open desert and under fire? And only then with a mere 'pea-shooter'![45]

Four Victoria Crosses were awarded for the fighting at Sidi Rezegh. With the short effective range of the inferior British tank and anti-tank guns, the proneness of the cruisers to mechanical breakdown, and the short radius of action of the Stuarts, the British armour resorted to charging the enemy tanks and guns in the hope of knocking them out. Commanders such as Brigadier Jock Campbell had no alternative but to rely on more and more extreme ways to motivate tank men to take such risks. Campbell famously led his tanks into the attack in his open unprotected staff car. He believed, according to Jake Wardrop of the 5th Royal Tank Regiment, that 'tanks should charge no matter the odds'. Protests from the likes of Wardrop, who admitted to 'quite frankly' not being 'so strong for this charging business',[46] were met with the reply, 'that's what you are soldiers for – to die!' One officer summed up the situation very well when he said that 'most people were far more scared of Jock Campbell than they were of the enemy!'[47]

---

[44] Latimer, *Alamein*, p. 36.
[45] IWM 96/50/1 Crimp, 'The Overseas Tour of a Conscript Rifleman', p. 73.
[46] George Forty, *Tanks across the Desert: The War Diary of Jake Wardrop* (Stroud, 2003), pp. 33–4.
[47] Ibid., p. 29.

By 23 November, Eighth Army's losses were becoming critical. Reports suggested that so many of Cunningham's tanks had been knocked out that the enemy now possessed a numerical advantage of three to one. Cunningham called for Auchinleck to fly out to the desert to assess the situation for himself. He presented two options to his Commander-in-Chief, either to withdraw and hope to save Egypt and what remained of his tank force or to continue to fight on. Auchinleck chose to fight and issued his order to Cunningham. 'You will ... continue to attack the enemy relentlessly using all your resources even to the last tank.'[48] The Crusader battle at this stage had ceased to be a battle of material, it was now a battle of wills.

In spite of the crisis of 23 November, the Crusader offensive resulted in a victory for Eighth Army. Superficially this success appeared to vindicate the British doctrine of replacing manpower with technology. General Ettore Bastico, the Italian Commander-in-Chief North Africa, blamed defeat on 'the extraordinary superiority of the enemy in numbers of troops and equipment.'[49] Cavallero, the Italian Commando Supremo, similarly believed that technological and numerical shortcomings were responsible for the reverse. He wrote in his diary that 'one cannot possibly ask from the Italian soldier, however brave and heroic a fighter he is, to go into battle without suitable equipment'. The Italian divisions at present, he mourned, 'have no suitable weapon to deal with the British Mark 2 tank [the 'I' tank]; it is absolutely necessary to provide each division with an 88 type of gun to serve as an anti-tank weapon'.[50]

Rommel similarly blamed defeat to a large extent on the material advantages enjoyed by the British, and specifically on 'the extraordinarily strong enemy air superiority'.[51] The battle report for *Panzergruppe Afrika* on 20 December 1941 supported Rommel's claims.[52] However both Rommel's accounts and the *Panzergruppe's* own records ignore the fundamental relevance of air power in the desert – its effect on morale.

[48] Playfair, *The Mediterranean and Middle East*, vol. III, p. 52.
[49] SAMAD UWH, Foreign Documents, Box 184, Battle Report Panzerarmee Afrika, Translation no 6(a), Message to the troops from High Command Armed Forces, North Africa, 14 December 1941, p. 68.
[50] SAMAD UWH, Foreign Documents, Box 205, Cavallero's Diary, 'Commando Supremo,' 2 November 1941 to 31 March 1942, p. 20.
[51] SAMAD UWH, Foreign Documents, Box 184, Battle Report Panzerarmee Afrika, Translation no. 6(a), Message from Rommel C-in-C Panzergruppe to German General HQ, Italian Armed Forces, Rome (for translation for the Duce), 22 December 1941, p. 96.
[52] SAMAD UWH, Foreign Documents, Box 184, Battle Report Panzerarmee Afrika, Translation no. 6(a), Orders and Reports 20 December 1941, p. 91.

The Germans viewed bombardment from the air as much from the point of view of disintegration of enemy morale as from that of material destruction.[53] The German's main close air support weapon, the Stuka dive-bomber, was employed with morale effects in mind. Elements of the Stuka's attack, such as the use of sirens attached to the bottom of the dive-bomber, the extreme angle of their descent (70–80 degrees) and the low height at which they dropped their bombs (c. 500 feet),[54] played havoc with the psychology of the bombed soldier. Successive British reports, written during 1941 and on into 1942 and 1943, highlighted this fact. A report on the lessons learned in the Crete campaign in 1941 concluded that 'the dive bomber is most inaccurate [and] has an <u>unnecessary</u> detrimental effect on morale'.[55] Another report, written after the Crusader offensive, once again noted that 'dive bombing on an average does practically no damage' and that 'every effort should be made to educate gun detachments to this fact. They soon realise it after experience in action, but are apt to overestimate the potential of dive bombing before they have gained experience.'[56]

Aerial bombardment therefore, in both the German and British forces, was recognised as an important method of attacking the psychological armour of the enemy. A study on the morale effect of weapons, carried out in 1943 on a group of 300 wounded soldiers in North Africa, illustrates the point. From the sample, 176 soldiers experienced dive-bombing during the campaign. Of these soldiers, only 9 per cent suffered wounds. As a comparison, 60 per cent of those who had faced a German 88 mm had been wounded. Nevertheless, 40 per cent of those who had experienced dive-bombing attacks regarded the Stuka as their 'most disliked' weapon.[57] The report stated that the dive-bomber was 'disliked to an extent out of all proportion to its real effectiveness'.[58] Furthermore, 48 per cent of men disliked being bombed by dive-bombers more as time went on. This compared with 33 per cent of men whose dislike decreased. The findings pointed to a lack

---

[53] NA WO 193/423 *British Medical Journal*, 4 April 1942, Article reviewing a survey by the American Committee for National Morale, by R. D. Gillespie; AWM 54 526/6/19 The Crisis at El Alamein, 30 June to 4 July 1942, p. 58.

[54] SAMAD CGS, Gp 2, Box 651 'Tobruk, the Battle with the Dive Bomber', p. 2.

[55] SAMAD Div Docs, Box 248, 'Lessons From the Battle of Crete'.

[56] AWM 54 526/6/2 Libya, Day by Day, and the Battle for Egypt. Report on Withdrawal from Libya to El Alamein 27 May 1942 to 1 August 1942. Part 1, sec. 1, Libya (Advance to Agheila, 18 November 1941 to 12 January 1942). App. C: Notes by a Lt AA Bty Commander.

[57] NA WO 222/124 The Moral Effect of Weapons, Investigation into reactions of group of 300 wounded men in North Africa, 1943, p. 2.

[58] Ibid., p. 3.

of rationality among soldiers when faced with what the report called 'moral weapons'.[59]

The fundamental importance of air power to morale was highlighted in another report written on 'War Neurosis at Tobruk' by Lieutenant–Colonel E. L. Cooper and Captain A. J. M. Sinclair of the Australian Imperial Force (AIF). The report made it clear that during the first two months of the siege, while German planes ruled the skies, and 'when the severity of enemy air raids reached a maximum, there was almost a complete lack of aerial support from the RAF'. This absence of support from British planes 'for weeks at a time played a large part in the development of war neurosis in some men'.[60] The consequence of repeated experiences with the dive-bomber was that psychologists began to accept that 'a very high standard of morale and courage' was 'required to face enemy attack by Stukas and low flying fighters even if spaced over a long period of time'. It was all important, according to another report written on the 'Battle with the Dive-Bomber at Tobruk', that 'every man … must develop to the full the offensive spirit. Those not engaged in manning guns will fire rifles and light automatics. "Going to ground" when weapons are available must be forbidden.'[61] This type of 'active' defence was designed to prevent men from cowering in slit trenches consumed by fear. It was believed that if men fired back they would feel empowered and therefore their morale would be protected.[62] Battle schools in Britain and more realistic training in theatre were also designed to condition soldiers to the sounds of war and ideally prevent them from developing irrational fear syndromes caused by 'moral weapons'.[63]

The detrimental effects of dive-bombing on morale were exacerbated in the desert as a result of the experiences of many of the British and dominion troops in Greece and Crete before Crusader. On 13 October 1941, a month before the opening of the campaign, the Prime Minister of New Zealand, Peter Fraser, telegraphed Churchill about the upcoming offensive. 'In the light of our experience in Greece and particularly in Crete', he said, 'you will understand that we are naturally apprehensive lest our troops should again and for the third time be permitted to battle

---

[59] Ibid., p. 4.
[60] AWM 54 481/12/120 'War Neurosis at Tobruk' by E. L. Cooper, Lieut.-Col. and A. J. M. Sinclair, Capt., AAMC, AIF.
[61] SAMAD CGS, Gp 2, Box 651, 'Tobruk, the Battle with the Dive Bomber', p. 3.
[62] SAMAD CGS, Gp 2, Box 651, Report by the Senior Medical Officer at Tobruk on the Psychological Effects of Dive-Bombing on AA Personnel, Annex 'A', pp. 1–2.
[63] Training methods used to accustom soldiers to the battle environment are discussed in Chapter 7.

without adequate air support and in circumstances in which they are unable to defend themselves against unrestricted air attacks.' Fraser wanted assurances that 'the question of air support,' which the New Zealand government regarded as 'a vital factor', had been 'fully considered and appreciated by those responsible', and that a situation in which New Zealand men were called upon to fight 'without the necessary means of defence and offence' would 'not recur'.[64]

Churchill passed on his New Zealand counterpart's concerns to Auchinleck, in a telegram sent on 15 October, in which he also referred to the fact that Air Marshal Sir Arthur Tedder, Commander RAF Middle East Command, had been doubtful of his ability to provide the air cover demanded by Fraser. The next day the War Office once again telegraphed Auchinleck, this time assuring him that 250 Bofors anti-aircraft guns were being sent for use by Eighth Army. 'Never more', the telegram continued, 'must the army rely solely on aircraft for its protection against attacks from the air.'[65]

The Desert Air Force's performance during Crusader exceeded Tedder's expectations. This proved not only devastating to German and Italian morale but also a major factor in reinforcing the fighting spirit of Eighth Army. The censorship summary for the period 17 to 23 December 1941 concluded that the Royal Air Force's 'overwhelming superiority' and 'incessant activity' had created a 'tremendous impression' on the troops. 'All those who were concerned in the Crete campaign' agreed that 'the RAF have proved far more devastating than the Luftwaffe' ever had.[66] A New Zealand report, written after the battle, confirmed that 'the lack of RAF support "bogy" has been completely banished'. All ranks now 'speak in the highest terms of the work of the RAF'.[67] A South African report stated emphatically that 'air superiority gives ground troops a tremendous moral advantage'.[68]

The most positive element of the Crusader offensive for many of Eighth Army was the fact that they had defeated the *Panzergruppe* even though 'they had bigger guns and thicker tanks'.[69] The 'brave to the point of

---

[64] NA WO 259/38 Telegram from War Office to C-in-C Middle East despatched 15 October 1941.

[65] NA WO 259/38 Telegram from War Office to C-in-C Middle East despatched 16 October 1941.

[66] AWM 54 883/2/97 MEFCWS, no. VI (17 to 23 December 1941), p. 3.

[67] ANZ WAII/1/DA21.1/9/G4/12 part 1, HQ 2 NZ Div (G Branch) Security and Intelligence Reports, Security Report 30 December 1941 to 3 January 1942.

[68] SAMAD Div Docs, Box 62, 1 SA Div Operations Report Cyrenaica 18 November to 2 December 1941, 22 January 1942, p. 16.

[69] Forty, *Tanks Across the Desert*, p. 32.

foolhardiness'[70] actions of the Royal Armoured Corps and the effects on morale of RAF bombardment had in many ways painted over the cracks. If there were rumblings of dissatisfaction among the men of Eighth Army about British technology and weapons, the censorship summaries show that they were not widespread.

The shortened lines of communications and supply, following the Axis retreat in December 1941, allowed the German and Italian *Panzergruppe* quickly to regain its material strength. By mid-January, the Axis forces mustered 173 serviceable tanks at the front plus 300 serviceable aircraft. As Rainer Kriebel has pointed out, the rest period granted to the soldiers and the arrival of reinforcements in the beginning of January had a 'favourable influence on the fighting spirit of the Italian formations' that made up the major part of the *Panzergruppe*'s manpower.[71] The British were still recovering from their estimated 800 tank casualties during Crusader, while they retained about 280 serviceable aircraft.[72]

The remarkable counteroffensive launched by Rommel in late January 1942 was built on this morale regeneration. As in March 1941, the effects of the German tactics were as much psychological as physical. The censorship summaries emphasised 'the severe enemy dive bombing and machine gunning from the air'. References to RAF support completely disappeared, while some writers complained that there was 'not much hope of successfully tackling German tanks with 6 pdr. guns with tanks armed with 2 pdrs.'[73] One man with the 7th Field Squadron Royal Engineers described how 'dive bombing, dive machine gunning and shelling together with a shortage of food and water' had left his unit 'in a hell of a state'.[74] Robin Neillands has argued that the material damage caused by the retreat at the beginning of 1942 was not severe. What was of greater concern was its effect on the confidence of the men. A relatively modest 1,390 men were killed, wounded or missing during the retreat, while seventy-two tanks and forty field guns were lost. The worst aspect of this reverse was that, as Auchinleck wrote to Churchill, 'personnel of the Royal Armoured Corps [were] losing confidence in their equipment'.[75]

What was happening in the desert was the beginning of a process that would contribute greatly to the morale crisis in the summer of 1942. The inadequacies of British guns, such as the two-pounder, were forcing Eighth Army into a style of warfare that bred dispersion and mobility

[70] AWM 54 883/2/97 MEFCWS, no. VI. (17 to 23 December 1941), p. 5.
[71] SADMAD UWH, Foreign Documents, Box 203, Rainer Kriebel, History of the Campaign in North Africa, p. 116.
[72] Playfair, *The Mediterranean and Middle East*, vol. III, p. 140.
[73] AWM 54 883/2/97 MEFCWS, no. XV (18 to 25 February 1942), p. 1.   [74] Ibid.
[75] Neillands, *Eighth Army*, p. 118.

rather than concentration of firepower.[76] The two-pounder, which was the standard anti-tank and tank gun, was incapable of penetrating the 'face hardened' armour of the German Mark III and IV panzers beyond 500 yards. The German panzers were therefore able to engage the British armour and anti-tank guns at a safe distance using their superior 50 mm and 75 mm guns. The Mark III, for example, could engage British tanks and anti-tank units up to 1,000 yards away with its 50 mm gun.[77]

The inferior penetration of the two-pounder anti-tank gun left the infantry without adequate protection from tanks, the decisive arm in desert warfare. The infantry therefore demanded that it be protected by tanks and twenty-five-pounder batteries, in addition to the ineffective anti-tank guns. In fact, during Crusader, the twenty-five-pounder 'proved to be the best destroyer of [German] tanks'.[78] These require-ments encouraged the commanders of Eighth Army to split their forma-tions into brigade groups and Jock columns made up of units of infantry, armour and artillery. Shelford Bidwell has argued that the most serious consequence of this policy was the 'fragmentation and decentralisation of the British field artillery, acknowledged by the Germans to be their most dangerous and efficient opponent'. The divisional commanders were deprived of the 'most flexible source of fire power in their armoury, seventy or more guns concentrated on a single target'.[79]

The need to create mobile self-sufficient units created a vicious circle. For morale reasons, the infantry demanded protection from tanks and artillery. This forced Eighth Army to disperse its firepower as equally as possible among its constituent units. This meant that Eighth Army did not possess enough concentrated firepower to meet the newly named *Panzerarmee* head on. This, in turn, created morale problems as units lost confidence in their ability to fight the enemy with equal weapons on equal terms.[80] In marked contrast, the Germans proved masters at concentrating their forces at the decisive point and in defeating Eighth Army in detail.

The problem was exacerbated by the fact that German panzers were equipped with dual purpose guns capable of firing armour piercing and high explosive rounds. They could act both as tank killers and mobile artillery. More often than not, German panzers would sit out of range of

---

[76] NA WO 201/357 Operation 'Battleaxe', Lessons of the Campaign, June to November 1941. Lessons from Recent Operations, 7th Armoured Division.

[77] Barr, *Pendulum of War*, p. 59.

[78] NA WO 201/527 HQ Eighth Army MEF, Role of Armoured Formations (n.d. but clearly written after Crusader).

[79] Shelford Bidwell and Dominick Graham, *Firepower: British Army Weapons and Theories of War 1904–1945* (London, 1982), p. 225.

[80] Ibid., pp. 221–47.

Illustration 4 Troops are shown the effects of anti-tank rounds on a knocked-out German Mark IV tank, March 1942. Many of Eighth Army's soldiers had little confidence in the hitting power of the two-pounder gun. Demonstrations like this, which showed troops evidence of the ability of the gun to penetrate German armour, played an important role in building Eighth Army's belief in its weaponry.

Eighth Army's anti-tank gun detachments and knock them out using high explosive and machine gun fire. Eighth Army had to rely on twenty-five-pounders or medium artillery to provide such support as British tanks only fired armour-piercing shot. Needless to say, twenty-five-pounder guns were not as mobile as tanks. German units were, therefore, always able to amass more firepower, quicker than the British, by using their tanks' high explosive rounds in addition to the artillery's. The *Panzerarmee* also had the use of aerial artillery through their Stuka dive-bombers, a luxury Eighth Army would not enjoy until autumn 1942.

With the superior firepower afforded to the *Panzerarmee* in the desert by the Mark III and IV panzers and the Stuka dive-bombers, the Axis forces were almost always able to 'plaster the enemy with fire' before the British forces could retaliate.[81] This gave the *Panzerarmee* a massive morale advantage over Eighth Army, just as it had given the Wehrmacht a great advantage over the BEF and French armies in 1940. The fact that British units were incapable of mustering enough firepower to deal with German attacks led to morale difficulties as units lost confidence in their weapons and in their ability to defeat the enemy.[82]

By late May 1942, Auchinleck had significantly re-equipped and reorganised his retreating army. New armour swelled Eighth Army's arsenal to 850 tanks, whereas the Germans possessed only 330 and the Italians 230, 560 in all. New guns provided Eighth Army with a three to two advantage over the *Panzerarmee*.[83] The Axis forces did have a substantial advantage in the sphere of serviceable aircraft. They possessed 497 aircraft in the desert while the Desert Air Force had only 190. The Axis also had a superiority in aircraft for the whole Mediterranean theatre of about 1,000 compared to 739.[84] So, while the Allies had a significant advantage in terms of numbers on the ground, the Axis had an advantage in the air, a form of warfare viewed by both sides as a significant 'morale weapon'.

The quality of some of the equipment sent to Eighth Army also began to improve. The arrival of the Grant tank from America, plus the introduction of the new British six-pounder anti-tank gun, narrowed the gap in capabilities between the two sides. The Grant tank was a significant improvement on all British armour previously seen in the desert. It possessed a 75 mm gun in a sponson at one side capable of firing both high explosive and armour-piercing shot. It was heavily armoured, reasonably fast and very reliable. The Grant also possessed a 37 mm gun similar to that of the Stuart in the turret.[85] For the first time, Eighth Army had a tank that could reasonably be expected to take on the German panzers on an equal footing. For 'strong psychological reasons', it was decided to give every regiment a quota of these new and powerful Grants.[86] Thus the 242 Grant tanks available to Eighth Army were spread among the armoured regiments as evenly as possible instead of concentrating them together as a powerful strike force. A further complication was caused by the fact that some regiments had barely received all of their Grants by the time the German offensive began.

---

[81] NA WO 202/33 Notes on Desert Warfare compiled by Capt. E. E. Tomkins, Intelligence Corps, and Capt. C. J. Fitzgerald, Recce Corps, for the French, 26 December 1941.
[82] Bidwell and Graham, *Firepower*, pp. 221–47.
[83] Barr, *Pendulum of War*, p. 13; Bungay, *Alamein*, p. 23.
[84] Playfair, *The Mediterranean and Middle East*, vol. III, pp. 220–1.
[85] Ibid., pp. 214–15.   [86] Ibid., p. 215.

Similarly, only 112 of the new six-pounder anti-tank guns arrived in the desert by the time of the *Panzerarmee*'s attack.[87] By 26 May, XXX Corps had approximately 40 per cent of its establishment.[88] This meant that many of the anti-tank batteries that were to participate in the battle were still armed with two-pounder guns and many of the infantry and motor battalions that were due to receive two-pounders (once they had been replaced by six-pounders in the anti-tank regiments) had not received their anti-tank guns at all. While Eighth Army was on paper better equipped than ever before, many of the units designated to receive new weapons were not fully trained to use them and consequently did not have the time to develop confidence in their new equipment.

Nevertheless, in spite of the imperfect integration of these new weapons into the organisation of Eighth Army, correspondence from British troops engaged in the opening phases of the Gazala battle provided 'ample proof' that their fighting spirit had 'been enhanced'. The censorship summaries show that the improvement in British armament had caused 'much general satisfaction' and had contributed 'in no small measure' to a morale improvement. By early June, the general attitude was 'now that we're decently armed and able to fight on equal terms, we're on top of the world', and 'some of this Yankee stuff is the real goods'.[89] Intelligence summaries gathered from South African troops in Eighth Army reported that the 'sufficiency and quality of their equipment' had provided them with a 'flaming burst of enthusiasm to be at grips with the enemy'.[90] One British tank man described his new Grant tank as 'super, the finest thing [he] had ever seen'.[91]

The buoyant mood of Eighth Army did not last long into the Gazala campaign. It quickly became apparent to the troops that their new equipment did not guarantee them the easy victory they expected. The censorship summary for the week 17 to 23 June reported that the mail 'did show that the high morale of the troops had suffered a set back'. The typical view that 'we think it is in the bag' had given way to 'the end of this lot seems to be as far away as ever'. Praise of equipment, 'a noticeable feature in the opening stages of the operations, was less marked and there were references to the superior armament of the enemy'. Although tribute was often paid to the amount of punishment the new American tanks could take

---

[87] Ibid.
[88] SAMAD UWH, Box 322, The German Assault on the Gazala Position and the Fall of Tobruk, 26 May 1942 to 21 June 1942, book 1, Brig. C. J. C. Molony, p. 14.
[89] AWM 54 883/2/97 MEFCWS, no. XXXI (10 to 16 June 1942), p. 1.
[90] SAMAD CGS (War) Box 248, Summary of 'I' Summaries for CGS, Middle East Military Censorship Weekly Summary: 2 to 9 June 1942.
[91] Forty, *Tanks Across the Desert*, p. 43.

without being put out of action, the general consensus was that 'Jerry has worked one on us again ... give us tanks, Winston'.[92] Furthermore, as the campaign continued, more and more soldiers named the 'primary cause of the debacle' once again as a 'lack of air support'.[93]

The effects of the *Panzerarmee*'s concentration of firepower on British morale was described by one NCO, who wrote,

[I] have seen enough in the last two weeks to become a most ardent pacifist. The other campaign was a child's game compared to this. We are all in a state known as 'bomb happy' – the effect of continuous shelling, bombing, and straffing, they even keep it up during the night which isn't funny. It's a lousy feeling to wake up with tracer bullets buzzing around one; 'fraid I feel rather shaky ... I've seen and known the filthiest sights here.[94]

Robin Dunn, a tank commander in the Second Armoured Brigade, recalled, 'when I am asked why the great tank battle on June 12th was lost I say because the enemy had higher morale, and ... our tank crews were fighting an enemy better equipped than themselves, in tanks better armoured and more important with longer range guns'. Dunn recounted how 'this inequality was too much for even the finest units' to bear. 'The first time they met the Germans they would go in with tremendous dash and courage, and very few of them would come out. One by one the morale of these proud regiments was broken ... It was more than flesh and blood and nerves could stand always to be asked to fight at such fearful odds.'[95] Lieutenant-General William 'Strafer' Gott, the commander of XIII Corps, noted, in a report he wrote on the operations, that 'in the first onslaught on May 26/27, armoured regiments had very heavy casualties, and it follows one cannot expect the same high standard of fighting in the second and subsequent battles'.[96]

The psychological supremacy enjoyed by the Axis, due to the overwhelming effect of their firepower, could in some way explain the surrender statistics that drove Auchinleck and Ritchie to demand a reintroduction of the death penalty for a second time in July 1942. The desert environment meant that there was little scope for ambush and surprise, the natural ally of a poorly armed force.[97] It was often possible to weigh up the odds of success or defeat miles away by identifying

---

[92] AWM 54 883/2/97 MEFCWS, no. XXXII (17 to 23 June 1942), p. 1.
[93] AWM 54 883/2/97 MEFCWS, no. XXXIII (24 to 30 June 1942), p. 1.
[94] AWM 54 883/2/97 MEFCWS, no. XXXII (17 to 23 June 1942), p. 2.
[95] IWM 94/41/1, Sir Robin Dunn.
[96] NA WO 216/85 Some Notes on Operations, 26 May to 8 July. GHQ MEF for CGS, 12 July 1942, p. 12.
[97] John A. Nagl, *Learning to Eat Soup with a Knife: Counterinsurgency Lessons from Malaya and Vietnam* (Chicago, 2005; first published 2002), p. 16.

numbers and types of armoured vehicles and comparing them with one's own. Throughout the desert war, surrenders made up a large proportion of casualties on both sides, while it was comparatively rare for defenders to fight to the last man as they did on the eastern front and in the Pacific. Opposing forces would size each other up and decide on merit whether an engagement might produce a fruitful or futile outcome. In such circumstances, the attitude of each side to their own and the enemy's weapons was crucial. More often than not, the Germans were able to win this psychological battle during the summer months of 1942, due to Eighth Army's lack of confidence in its own equipment. Once a perfunctory effort to retaliate had been made, satisfying the defenders' own conscience, groups of men would surrender if they felt the fight could not be won.

Certainly, the disasters at Gazala and Tobruk, in May and June 1942, finally brought the technology/morale debate to the forefront in the minds of the high command, the press and the troops. Churchill wrote to Auchinleck, on 14 June, stating that a 'retreat would be fatal. This is a business not only of armour but of will-power.'[98] Chester Wilmot, an Australian correspondent in the desert, bemoaned the fact that 'for the past few years we've explained away our reverses by pleas of lack of equipment. There's been some justification for this but we've been so concerned about material factors that we've rather forgotten about morale ones.'[99] Cyril Falls had been expressing similar sentiments since March in the *Illustrated London News*. In his view, poor morale was the problem besetting the British forces from Singapore to the desert. The consequences were that 'people who considered not long ago that if we maintained our output of war material the war could not be lost, are now admitting that the war might be lost'.[100]

Following Gazala and the fall of Tobruk, the censorship summaries reported a widespread demand by the troops for a 'full and searching inquiry' into the debacle that had befallen Eighth Army.[101] Such an inquiry, by officers of Eighth Army and by officers flown out from the United Kingdom, was held in July 1942. It found that inadequate weapons had played a major role in deflating the morale of the troops. The inquiry reported that 'to put infantry in battle against tanks without adequate means of defending themselves is not only useless but unfair

[98] NA WO 236/1 *Egyptian Gazette*, Sunday, 29 October 1950. 'The Hinge of Fate', XV, The Battle for Tobruk.
[99] National Archives of Australia (NAA) SP300/4 Item 145, 'Discipline and Morale', 21 May 1942 (Chester Wilmot ABC radio talk script) Box 2.
[100] NA WO 259/64 *Illustrated London News*, 14 March 1942.
[101] AWM 54 883/2/97 MEFCWS, no. XXXIII (24 to 30 June 1942).

to the troops and exceedingly bad for their morale'.[102] Not only did the defenders of Tobruk have no adequate means of defending themselves from armour but they had endured the psychological blow of 'witness[ing] the decisive defeat of our armour', their only potential protectors in the open spaces of the Gazala line.[103]

It was also highlighted that the troops must be 'given sufficient opportunity to train in the technical and tactical use of th[eir] arms before going into action'. The report stated that 'it is wrong for troops to be sent into battle with only a training scale of equipment or for changes in their equipment to be made in the forward areas'. Significantly, the report recommended that the capabilities of forces arrayed against each other in the desert should no longer be calculated by numbers of tanks and guns alone. Instead, it advised that 'the fighting capacity of formations and units must be measured ... also by their morale and the state of their equipment'.[104]

The pervasive sense of shock that reverberated through Eighth Army after the fall of Tobruk was clearly reflected in the censorship summaries. The men of Eighth Army had been led to believe once again that they were now, finally, ready to match the Germans in methods and technology. The fact that they were not adequately prepared left many of the men bitter and frustrated. Out of this frustration did, however, come reflection and eventual understanding.

Middle East Command had begun, as early as the Battleaxe and Crusader offensives, to compile reports on the various methods employed by German armoured formations in both attack and defence. These reports identified the German practice of cooperation among all arms. The Germans did not see tanks as the primary weapon in destroying other tanks any more than they saw artillery as the primary weapon in destroying other artillery. Instead they preferred to use all their arms together as a collective fighting force. German tank-destroying tactics were particularly innovative. Their practice in this regard was to lay down a well-concealed line of anti-tank guns on encountering British armour and then attempt to draw the British tanks onto them through ruse and deception. The German force would then destroy the oncoming British armour with its

[102] SAMAD UWH, Published Books, Box 368, Court of Inquiry, Tobruk. Report of a Court of Inquiry Assembled by Order of the C-in-C, 8 July 1942, p. 4.
[103] SAMAD UWH, Draft Narratives, Box 364, Tobruk, Accounts from British Sources. Some personal opinions on the fall of Tobruk 1942, Brigadier L. F. Thompson, Comd. 88 Area Tobruk June 1942.
[104] SAMAD UWH, Published Books, Box 368, Court of Inquiry, Tobruk. Report of a Court of inquiry Assembled by Order of the C-in-C, 8 July 1942, p. 3.

anti-tank guns rather than with its armour, which would retreat safely behind the protection of the anti-tank screen.[105]

These tactics created considerable confusion among the units of the Royal Armoured Corps (RAC). More often than not, in the turmoil of battle, the British forces were left disorientated and failed to identify the German anti-tank guns. They wrongly assumed that they had been engaged and destroyed by the bigger guns of the German Mark III and IV tanks and not by the anti-tank guns which were well dug in at the rear and not easily observed. By March 1942, reports suggested that Eighth Army was beginning to learn from German tactics. One such report, on the 'Role of Armoured Formations' in battle, stated that 'it appears that the greatest losses we have inflicted on the enemy have been when he has attacked our guns in position. It should therefore be our aim, as it appears is the German practice, to draw the enemy tanks on to our guns. On almost every occasion that we have attacked his tanks with our own we have been drawn on to his guns, and this we must avoid.'[106]

Such notes and reports handed out to armoured formations on the tactical handling of their units in battle, struck many 'as being an exact reproduction of German armoured tactical doctrine'.[107] By mid-July 1942, the General Staff Committee on Weapons and Equipment was honest in its appraisal that the British lacked experience in the organisation of armoured units. While they lacked experience however, they admitted the Wehrmacht 'certainly did not'. The committee accepted that German methods, 'so far as armour is concerned, [are] based upon what has undoubtedly proved to be a fresh conception of war i.e. blitzkrieg'. If 'we are ever in serious doubt what to do', the Committee concluded, 'we might, with advantage, think of what they have done, follow it and, where possible, improve on it'.[108] Thus German armoured tactics became British armoured tactics.

However, these lessons did not appear to filter through to the troops on the ground. Time and again in May and June 1942 the British armour wasted its strength battering against lines of German anti-tank guns.

[105] NA WO 201/527 Armoured Formations: Tactical Handling of Armoured Forces, December 1941 to March 1942. Notes on employment of 'I' tanks based on conversation with Brig. Watkins 27 December 1941.

[106] Ibid., HQ Eighth Army MEF, Role of Armoured Formations.

[107] Ibid. Notes made by Paul Hobbes, who had commanded a troop of twenty-five-pounders and a troop of twenty-five-pounders and was Jock Campbell's adjutant in 4RHA, 10 March 1942.

[108] NA WO 163/183 Record of the first meeting of the General Staff Committee on Weapons and Equipment, held in the War Office 17 July 1942.

Furthermore, not only was the ordinary soldier unaware of German tactical methods but he was also ignorant of the German use of their 88 mm anti-aircraft gun as an anti-tank weapon.

The German 88 mm was regarded by many as the most effective weapon of the Second World War and certainly created a complex amongst soldiers that faced it. The gun earned the nickname of 'demoralizer' in the US Army during the Tunisian campaign of 1943.[109] Its shells could penetrate British armour at up to 2,000 yards range and travelled so fast that the 'crack' of firing them was often heard only after a tank was seen to be hit. 'Wherever it appeared, it dominated the battlefield.'[110]

The censorship summary for 24 to 30 June shows that British troops were completely surprised by the impact of the 88 mm during the Gazala and Tobruk battles. This was despite German use of the 88 mm as an anti-tank weapon from their first days in the desert. A report on the 'Lessons of the Second Libyan Campaign' in December 1941 had admitted that 'we were amazed to find that the enemy had such large numbers of these guns in every defensive position . . . it would appear that the tactics used by our tanks were not based on the knowledge that the enemy possessed a hard hitting A Tk gun'. The report noted that 'it would be interesting to know whether the characteristics of the 88 mm German A Tk gun had been circulated among our tanks units; and, if so, whether the tactics of attack had been modified accordingly . . . it is felt that the knowledge of it should have produced less expensive tactics'.[111]

By June 1942, the troops' attitude was that, 'our intelligence should have known about them' and that the Germans have once again 'pulled one out of the bag'.[112] Critics such as Chester Wilmot were vocal in their derision. 'It seems to me', he wrote, 'that the most disturbing thing about the fighting in the desert is that after two years of war we still haven't learnt enough to match the Germans in tactics or equipment. We are still being surprised.' Reports from the front 'suggest that we were surprised that Rommel . . . used his 88 mm. AA guns as an anti-tank weapon; surprised that our tanks were ambushed. If we were surprised, it is only because we are slow to learn.'[113]

It does seem remarkable that Eighth Army had failed to communicate German tactics and methods to its men. One explanation for this could be

[109] Atkinson, *An Army at Dawn*, p. 222.   [110] Bungay, *Alamein*, p. 29.
[111] AWM 54 519/7/26 'Lessons of the Second Libyan Campaign', Report of Lieut.-Col. S. H. Porter and Lieut.-Col. J. D. Rogers, 26 December 1941.
[112] AWM 54 883/2/97 MEFCWS, no. XXXIII. (24 to 30 June 1942), p. 2.
[113] NAA A5954/1 323/14 Criticism of Middle East Command by Wilmot. 'When Will We Learn Enough to Win?' Broadcast over national stations, Monday, June 29, 7.22 pm, by Chester Wilmot, pp. 2–3.

the rapid expansion of Eighth Army before and after Crusader. In the months between January and August 1942, 149,800 army reinforcements arrived in the Middle East from Britain. In addition, about 32,400 reinforcements came from India.[114] This expansion created a two-tier organisation, those who had experience of desert warfare and those who were newcomers. General Frank Messervy, who commanded 1st Armoured Division during its disastrous retreat, observed in February 1942 that it took new formations three months to learn the ropes of desert warfare.[115] The retreats of March 1941 and January/February 1942 were both largely caused by the disintegration of entirely new formations ignorant of German tactics. The British tendency to remove whole battalions or even divisions from the battlefield for rest and replace them with new units arriving from the United Kingdom appears to have been the problem. These new units did not have a cadre of experienced officers and men to pass on the lessons learned from previous battles. As Niall Barr has argued, the Eighth Army did not learn in a 'progressive way from previous experience'; instead 'most units had to relearn the same lessons' again and again.[116] Indeed Auchinleck, as far back as September 1941, recurrently asked Churchill for details and drafts to be sent to the Middle East to bring units already in the desert up to strength instead of sending new divisions and battalions.[117] Furthermore, as Barr has pointed out, it can be fairly assumed that officers had little time to read the plethora of pamphlets produced to educate them about German equipment and tactics.[118]

This pedagogic vacuum exacerbated the morale effects of German weapons such as the 88 mm anti-tank gun. The 1943 investigation into the morale effect of weapons (already alluded to) reported a 'fear of [the 88 mm] amongst all who . . . encountered it'. 'Apart from the very natural dislike of its qualities', the report argued that there were 'marked signs of an 88 mm neurosis' developing amongst the armoured corps, 'tank men tending to attribute all their troubles to it without always being justified.'[119]

Just as in the case of the Stuka dive-bomber, the 88 mm caused more damage psychologically than it did materially. A report by the Deputy Prime Minister, Clement Attlee, on the tank position in the Middle East in March 1942 showed that the 88 mm was not the universal killer it was

---

[114] Playfair, *The Mediterranean and Middle East*, vol. III, p. 372.
[115] Ibid., p. 153.   [116] Barr, *Pendulum of War*, p. 48.
[117] NA WO 259/38 Telegram from C-in-C ME to War Office despatched 21 September 1941. See also Telegram from PM to Gen. Auchinleck despatched 18 September 1941.
[118] Barr, *Pendulum of War*, p. 50.
[119] NA WO 222/124 The Moral Effect of Weapons, Investigation into Reactions of Group of 300 Wounded Men in North Africa, 1943, p. 6.

Table 3 *Reasons for disliking weapons*

Reason for disliking weapon	Percentage
Effectiveness (i.e. lethality and destructiveness)	19%
Accuracy	21%
Inability to retaliate	13%
Create a feeling of vulnerability	15%
Speed and surprise of attack	10%
Suspense	5%
Noise	5%
'Demoralizing effect' (admitted)	12%

Source: NA WO 222/124 The Moral Effect of Weapons, Investigation into Reactions of a Group of 300 Wounded Men in North Africa, 1943, p. 5.

assumed to be. Of forty-eight British tanks rendered unserviceable in action in operation Crusader and subsequently examined by GHQ Middle East Tank Directorate, only fourteen (29%) were damaged by the 88 mm anti-tank gun. Seven (15%) were damaged by the 50 mm gun (of either the German *Panzer* Mark III or the anti-tank gun), three (6%) by the 47 mm gun and twenty-four (50%) by lighter weapons, mines or mechanical breakdown.[120]

The *Panzerarmee* was aware of this British fear of the 88 mm and were known to play on it. By early July 1942, German units were found to create dummy 88s out of telegraph poles while mobile 88s would fire from nearby positions.[121] Such instances lend further credence to the contention that warfare in the desert was as much about bluff and psychological supremacy as anything else.

The study 'Moral Effect of Weapons' further illustrates this point (Table 3). The report pointed out that only the first two reasons for disliking weapons (effectiveness and accuracy), representing 40 per cent of the total explanations, were simple, rational physical reasons directly related to the real lethality of the weapon in question; 'and even they are frequently attributed to weapons which, on the facts, do not possess them'. The remaining 60 per cent were all dislikes of certain psychological sensations.[122] The report stated that all of the men questioned had had

---

[120] NA WO 259/61 Enquiry by the Rt. Hon. C. R. Attlee MP into Tank Position in the Middle East, March 1942.

[121] Latimer, *Alamein*, p. 155.

[122] NA WO 222/124 The Moral Effect of Weapons, Investigation into Reactions of Group of 300 Wounded Men in North Africa, 1943, p. 5.

experience of battle and had, in fact, been wounded. 'Yet in the majority of instances they would rather face weapons which they have logical reason to fear may kill them, than weapons which arouse instinctive fear.'[123]

Of crucial significance to the desert war, the report also pointed to a 'notable demoralising effect' arising from the disadvantageous comparison between British and German weapons. 'Those who particularly dislike the German mortars invariably compare their size and accuracy with our own mortars; and those who dislike the enemy machine-guns usually point out that their rate of fire is higher than ours. The feeling of inequality – almost of injustice – appears to be very important.'[124] Thus, the morale crisis that began to rear its head in the summer of 1942 can to some extent be attributed to the inadequate weapons provided for the troops of Eighth Army. Indeed Mark Johnston and Peter Stanley have blamed 'a loss of faith in equipment' as one of the key reasons for the crisis in the desert in 1942.[125]

By the beginning of July, a number of changes started to take place in the desert. The toll of a month's heavy fighting had begun to tell on the *Panzerarmee*. By 30 June the *Afrika Korps* could muster only 55 battleworthy tanks while the Italian XX Corps could manage a meagre 15.[126] In comparison, although an estimated 1,188 British tanks had been knocked out at Gazala, many of them in a matter of hours charging 'invisible' anti-tank screens, the British forces had 137 tanks at the front on 1 July. Auchinleck could also rely on another 42 tanks in transit from base workshops to the front.[127]

The Desert Air Force had also begun to wrest control of the skies from the Luftwaffe. The German war diaries show that this more than any other factor seemed to drain the offensive spirit and morale of the Axis forces.[128] The war diaries of the 90th Light Division commented that

The enemy throws all the Air Force at his disposal into the battle against the attacking Afrika Army. Every 20 or 30 minutes 15, 18, or sometimes even 20 bombers, with adequate fighter protection, launch their attacks. Although the visible success of these heavy and continuous bombing and low-flying attacks is negligible owing to the disposition of the fighting and supply units, the moral effect

---

[123] Ibid.   [124] Ibid.   [125] Johnston and Stanley, *Alamein*, p. 22,

[126] NA CAB 146/13 Enemy Documents Section, Appreciation No. 9, pp. 477–86.

[127] Barr, *Pendulum of War*, pp. 39–40. This was due to more efficient battlefield recovery techniques.

[128] SAMAD Div Docs, Box 54, Index to Advanced Air HQ Western Desert Intelligence Summary no. 167, 'Effects of Our Bombing'; SAMAD UWH, Narratives, Box 376, Crisis in the Desert, May to July 1942, El Alamein, p. 5.

on the troops is much more important. Everyone prays for German fighter protection ... Sometimes German fighters appear singly, greeted by the roaring applause of the troops, but naturally they are not in a position to attack such heavy bomber formations.[129]

Rommel had pushed his army so far and so fast that he had completely outrun the Luftwaffe's ability to provide air cover. General Enea Navarini, the commander of the Italian XXI Corps, considered the issue of such importance that, on 6 July, he issued an order of the day informing the troops that 'final victory is within your grasp. Do not let yourselves be overawed by some momentary predominance of enemy aviation.'[130] As Niall Barr has argued, 'the Axis air forces had put forth an enormous effort during the battle of Gazala and for the attack on Tobruk but could not sustain this level of activity indefinitely'.[131]

All through the month of July, the *Panzerarmee* had to labour under this constant bombardment, what the British soldiers began to refer to as the 'shuttle service'.[132] By 22 July, the German war diaries were still reporting that 'the enemy air force is numerically much superior to ours'. It has 'kept up continuous day and night attacks on our troops, it has caused us considerable losses, has brought the Italians' morale down to a very low ebb, [and] has hindered and partly curtailed supply'. Allied air superiority was so complete by late July 1942 that, in addition to the morale damage being done to the *Panzerarmee*, about thirty military transports were being lost a day to air raids.[133]

Matters had comparatively improved for Eighth Army. The censorship summary for 15 to 21 July reported that 'the outstanding feature of correspondence ... during the past week has been the magnificent work of the Allied Air Forces', which were 'responsible in a large measure for the high morale prevailing among all ranks'.[134] The report stated that 'there was hardly a letter which did not contain praise and admiration for the thorough and determined manner' in which the Air Force had 'carr[ied] out its blitzkrieg', and for the 'splendid protection' it had provided during the long withdrawal and in the new positions at El Alamein. 'Many writers considered th[e] withdrawal could not have

---

[129] AWM 54 526/6/19 The Crisis at El Alamein, 30 June to 4 July 1942, p. 58.

[130] SAMAD Div Docs, Box 54, Index to Advanced Air HQ Western Desert Intelligence Summary no. 167, 'Effects of Our Bombing'.

[131] Barr, *Pendulum of War*, pp. 35–6.

[132] IWM 93/19/1 W. R. Garrett, 'A Private Viewing', p. 9.

[133] AWM 54 492/4/76 War History Branch, Department of Internal Affairs Wellington New Zealand, 22 July 1942, and appendices to German War Narrative (African Campaign), June to July 1942.

[134] This short-lived morale revival is discussed in Chapter 1.

been successfully accomplished had it not been for the Air Force.'[135] This was in stark contrast to the numerous letters written earlier in the campaign that attributed the primary cause of the 'debacle' to the 'lack of air support'.[136]

As RAF effectiveness increased, soldiers became more and more confident in the capabilities of the RAF compared with those of the Luftwaffe. There was also evidence that 'morale' weapons such as the dive-bomber began to lose their effect on some of the more experienced veteran troops in the desert.[137] Private E. Kerans of the newly arrived 9th Durham Light Infantry described how 'the lads used to sit on the sides of their trenches [on the El Alamein line] and in comparative safety watch for hours one dog-fight after another'. The area he remembered 'was a graveyard of planes'.[138] Such dominance caused 'much satisfaction' among the troops, many of them having been frequently on the other end of aerial bombardment. There was also a regularly expressed conviction among the men, that 'eventually the morale of the enemy must break under the constant bombing and machine gunning' carried out by the Desert Air Force.[139]

The enormous increase in numbers and quality of weapons on the ground had a similarly positive effect on Eighth Army's morale. One private wrote how 'every day there is a continuous roar of trucks going up loaded with equipment and returning empty for more'.[140] An officer wrote, 'I thought I had seen a lot of supplies and stuff in the desert before, but it's colossal this time – tanks, guns, planes, trucks day and night passing here. Have seen scores of smashed tanks from Alamein dragged back but every one seems to be replaced by two more ... its great.'[141] The censorship summary for 22 to 28 July noted the effect of these changes on Australian morale. It remarked that morale was improving and that confidence in Australian ability to defeat the Hun was, 'if anything, strengthened'.[142] One of the main factors in sustaining this enhanced level of morale was 'the excellence of our equipment'.[143] As Johnston and Stanley have argued, the rearming and equipping of Eighth Army had 'a positive influence on ... morale'.[144]

---

[135] ANZ WAII/1/DA508/1 vol. 1, MEFCWS, no. XXXVI (15 to 21 July 1942), p. 1.
[136] AWM 54 883/2/97 MEFCWS, no. XXXIII. (24 to 30 June 1942), p. 1.
[137] AWM 54 883/2/97 MEFCWS, no. XXXII (17 to 23 June 1942), p. 3.
[138] IWM 86/61/1 E. Kerans, 'Proud to Be There', p. 9.
[139] ANZ WAII/1/DA508/1 vol. 1, MEFCWS, no. XXXVII (22 to 28 July 1942), p. 3.
[140] ANZ WAII/1/DA508/1 vol. 1, MEFCWS, no. XXXV (8 to 14 July 1942), p. 22.
[141] Ibid., p. 22.
[142] Australian morale appears to have been more resilient than other nationalities in Eighth Army, as is outlined in Chapter 1.
[143] ANZ WAII/1/DA508/1 vol. 1, MEFCWS, no. XXXVII (22 to 28 July 1942), p. 16.
[144] Johnston and Stanley, *Alamein*, p. 50.

Another major factor in affecting morale was the reorganisation of the Royal Artillery. Previously the artillery had been dispersed into Jock columns and brigade groups. Now, under Auchinleck's instruction, this practice was reversed and the artillery was concentrated once more to allow divisional shoots or 'stonks'. This change of plan was facilitated by the provision of more six-pounder anti-tank guns to the anti-tank battalions, which allowed these battalions to hand over some of their two pounder anti-tank guns to the infantry. This gave the infantry what they had asked for from the start, a means of protecting themselves against the German panzers. Freed from this role, the twenty-five-pounder regiments were able to return to providing concentrated and centrally controlled fire support for the infantry and armour.

The ability of Eighth Army to unleash concentrated firepower in the bottleneck of El Alamein had a devastating effect on the tired troops of the *Panzerarmee* as they tried to drive Eighth Army out of the El Alamein position. The war diary of 90th Light Division reported how 'a panic' broke out in the division when the *Afrika Korps* ran headlong into the newly concentrated fire of the South African artillery on 2 July. 'Supply columns and even parts of fighting units rush[ed] back under the ever increasing enemy artillery fire.' The energetic action of the divisional commander and chief of staff was all that prevented a 'rout', according to the diary.[145] Auchinleck wrote to the Chief of the Imperial General Staff, Alan Brooke, a couple of weeks later, saying,

The troops have recovered themselves wonderfully, I think, and have acquired a new tactical technique, based really on the proper use of artillery . . . They have still a great deal to learn of course, but the gunners have been very good indeed, and the Boshe does not like our shell fire at all, now that it is centrally controlled and directed.[146]

For perhaps the first time in the desert war, Eighth Army was able to boast superior firepower to the *Panzerarmee*. Nevertheless, in spite of the dominance of the Desert Air Force and the reconcentration of the artillery, a problem remained to hamper Eighth Army. The armour had lost confidence in its weapons and itself. That in turn had grievous consequences for the morale of the infantry, who relied heavily on armoured support during the July offensives.

Intimate cooperation was required between infantry and armour for the night attacks favoured by Auchinleck at El Alamein in July 1942 to

---

[145] SAMAD UWH, Narratives, Box 376, Crisis in the Desert, May to July 1942, part 3, El Alamein, p. 78.

[146] LHCMA Alanbrooke MSS 6/2/14 Auchinleck to Alanbrooke, 25 July 1942.

succeed. Once a position was taken by attacking infantry it was necessary to prepare the ground for an inevitable German counter-attack the next morning. These counterattacks were normally led by large numbers of panzers supported by infantry. The problem, according to Brigadier Les Inglis, the commander of 2nd New Zealand Division during the July battles, was that 'infantry could not protect itself against tank counter-attack for a period of 3 to 5 hours after daylight' the following day. Some reorganisation of the infantry was always necessary at first light. It then took an hour to reconnoitre the area in daylight and coordinate an anti-tank plan. It took a further hour for the infantry's anti-tank guns to be sighted. It then finally required a further one to three hours for everything to be dug in. Inglis argued that 'until all this is done the infantry is not in a position to meet any weighty A.F.V. [Armoured Fighting Vehicle] attack' and during the intervening period 'mobile A/Tk weapons, that is to say, tanks must be right up prepared to support immediately'.[147]

In spite of Inglis's concerns and forewarnings, the British armour repeatedly failed to support the infantry during the July battles on the El Alamein front. The New Zealanders suffered particularly, causing much bitterness among their battalions left to face German panzers without support. An officer wrote,

Our boys were supposed to have armoured support, as the Jerry always counter attack with tanks. Well our boys went through them like butter with the bayonet and gained the objective easily and started looking around for our tanks, not a tank of ours was to be seen, but they soon saw plenty of German tanks, they moved around and cut the whole lot of our boys off and shot them to pieces. As it turned out the Tommy tanks were sitting about two miles back waiting orders!!! The crews out frying sausages while our lads were being torn to pieces ... it was a disgraceful affair, it's terrible to see the best troops in the world slaughtered like sheep because of those Pommie bastards ... It was a stinking show ... The Germans regard the N.Z. as the best troops in the M.E. and they are correct, and consequently they have their best material facing us always. Our men do the job and then are let down by the armoured forces. Good as our blokes are they are not human tanks.[148]

The horrific casualties suffered by the New Zealanders during the July battles were roundly blamed on the incompetence of the higher command and the lack of tank support. These casualties destroyed the trust between the New Zealanders and the British and played a major role in the morale

---

[147] ANZ WAII/1/DA441.23/5 Brig. L. M. Inglis, Private Diary while GOC 2 NZEF, 25 July 1942.
[148] ANZ WAII/1/DA508/1 vol. 1, MEFCWS, no. XXXVIII (29 July to 4 August 1942), pp. 17–18.

crisis that developed in the New Zealand division during and following the battle. The censorship report for the week 29 July to 4 August reported how only about 1 per cent of New Zealand writers had a good word to say about 'Tommy'.[149]

By the end of July, Eighth Army was in an uncertain state. Although it found itself better equipped than ever before and there were signs that tactical lessons were being learned, victory had still not been achieved. Once again the promise of new and better equipment had given an initial boost to the confidence of the troops but failed to maintain morale for very long. Trust between the various nationalities was beginning to wane with both the British and South Africans (due to the surrender of Tobruk) seriously ridiculed for their performances during June and July. Following the horrific casualties at Gazala the armoured forces of Eighth Army had performed poorly on the El Alamein line, suggesting that they had lost their self-belief.

When Montgomery arrived, therefore, on 13 August, he had a massive task ahead of him. Montgomery, since the end of the Second World War, has gained the reputation of being a 'brute force' general of the First World War style. He has been criticised for being overcautious and for relying entirely on the firepower provided by superior amounts and quality of weapons to win his battles.[150] However, the two major engagements that he oversaw at the end of 1942 suggest that this judgement, at least in the context of North Africa, is potentially misplaced, and that his methodical and heavy-handed approach to battle was based more on the 'human factor' than on an over-reliance on technology. In fact, Montgomery's doctrine of command made it clear that he saw technology as an adjunct to morale rather than as the solution to success in battle.[151] He believed that battles were 'won primarily in the hearts of men'.[152] He dissented from interwar doctrine that focused almost entirely on technological solutions to overcome the problems of the modern battlefield. Whereas many of the generals before him in the desert had been obsessed with counting the number of tanks at their disposal, Montgomery saw his 'raw materials' as the 'men' under his command.[153] Whereas Auchinleck had delayed his offensives in order to obtain more armour, Montgomery delayed his offensive in order to train his men.

---

[149] Ibid., p. 16.   [150] Ellis, *Brute Force*, p. 535.
[151] IWM BLM 24/1 5 Corps Study Week for Commanders. 'Some Lessons Learnt during the First Year of War, September 1939 to September 1940'; BLM 28/3 'Lightfoot' General Plan of Eighth Army, 14 September 1942.
[152] Montgomery, *Memoirs*, p. 89.   [153] Ibid., p. 83.

At Alam Halfa in particular, Montgomery did not have an overwhelming superiority in weaponry. In fact, he fought the battle with much the same arsenal as Auchinleck had fought the July battles. The German war diaries show that Rommel expected to enjoy a material advantage when he attacked Eighth Army around the end of August.[154] They estimated that Eighth Army had only 400 tanks at the front and the Axis had a 50 per cent superiority in heavy artillery.[155] By 28 August, the strength of the *Panzerarmee* had been rebuilt and compared favourably with the forces that had begun the summer offensives on 26 May. The *Panzerarmee* now had 84,000 German and 44,000 Italian personnel,[156] with 250 German and between 200 and 250 Italian tanks.[157] Eighth Army had also rebuilt much of its strength, with 446 guns and 386 tanks arriving from Britain and America in August.[158] However, it was clear that it would take time for these forces to reach the front line. Rommel therefore had to attack in the brief window afforded him while the material situation was favourable.

The censorship summaries show that a nervous optimism pervaded Eighth Army on the eve of Alam Halfa. The confidence derived from the influx of new weapons was not as all-encompassing as on previous occasions in the desert war. The report for 3 to 9 September made 'many references to past mistakes and performances', and stressed the fact that the withdrawals of the summer 'still rankle in the minds of many' of the soldiers. These 'bitter blows of the recent past' rang, in the report's words, 'a warning note that we must be properly led and equipped before we tackle the job, that the many weary months spent in reforming and re-equipping must not be wasted'. It was important in the eyes of the troops that 'we must not make a present of large quantities of brand new equipment to the enemy – as we did last time'.[159]

Montgomery was aware of the frail confidence of Eighth Army, a fact he made abundantly clear in his diaries and memoirs. He therefore decided to fight Alam Halfa as a limited battle. The July battles had shown that Eighth Army's strength lay in its determined infantry, the artillery and the Desert Air Force. Its weaknesses were its armour and its inability to coordinate all arms in the attack. Alam Halfa was a battle entirely

[154] SAMAD UWH, Draft Narratives, Box 316, War Diary of Panzer Army Africa, 28 July to 23 October 1942, pp. 33–4.
[155] Kitchen, *Rommel's Desert War*, p. 295. Kitchen has estimated that Eighth Army had 700 tanks in the front line by the start of the battle; however, he does not provide a source for this figure.
[156] NA CAB 146/14 Enemy Documents Section, Appreciation no. 9, pp. 58–62.
[157] Kitchen, *Rommel's Desert War*, p. 295.
[158] Playfair, *The Mediterranean and Middle East*, vol. III, p. 371.
[159] ANZ WAII/1/DA508/1 vol. 3, MEMCWS, no. XLIII (3 to 9 September 1942), p. 1.

conceived and executed with these strengths and weaknesses in mind. Montgomery held his armour back and refused to allow it to become embroiled in a tank versus tank battle with the *Panzerarmee*. Instead he wanted to minimise casualties and concentrate on what Eighth Army could achieve, rather than, like previous commanders, relying on what it was hoped Eighth Army would achieve. He realised that his troops needed time to develop confidence in both themselves and in their weapons.[160] Montgomery therefore decided on an essentially defensive battle in which he would draw Rommel onto his own artillery and anti-tank screen. In many ways Alam Halfa was a British application of German tactics used on a grand scale with the significant help of the Desert Air Force.

Montgomery understood the intimate connection between firepower and morale. He wrote, as early as 1940, that 'the concentrated fire of artillery and mortars is a battle-winning factor of the first importance. By means of it the enemy troops can be shaken and their morale lowered.'[161] That is exactly the effect the combined and coordinated firepower of Eighth Army had on the advancing *Panzerarmee* at Alam Halfa. The *Panzerarmee's* daily report for 2 September acknowledged that the concentrated firepower of Eighth Army had 'caused serious losses to personnel and material' as well as affecting 'the morale of both the German and Italian troops'.[162]

A report by the 19th Flak Division for *Panzerarmee Afrika* HQ on the firepower unleashed by the Desert Air Force gave some idea of the morale damage it inflicted. The report stated that 15,600 bombs had been dropped on the *Panzerarmee* over the five days of the offensive. These had been distributed over a front averaging 12–15 km in length and 8–10 km in depth. That meant approximately 100 bombs were dropped per square kilometre during the offensive. The methods used by the Desert Air Force were specifically designed to undermine German and Italian morale. The report stated that 'bombs were not dropped simultaneously by all the aircraft in the formation; instead an extensive area was covered by bombs being dropped one after the other'. The effect of such action on the troops was that 'in addition to the extensive material damage caused, the effect on morale was … great. The spirit of the troops was considerably depressed owing to the totally inadequate German fighter cover. Incessant night attacks in particular served to reduce the degree of readiness for action of both officers and men.' This was due to the factors

---

[160] Montgomery, *Memoirs*, pp. 107–115.
[161] IWM BLM 24 Fifth Corps Study Week for Commanders. 'Some Lessons Learnt during the First Year of War, September 1939 to September 1940', p. 2.
[162] AWM 54 492/4/77 Panzerarmee Afrika Daily Report, 2 September 1942.

of 'no sleep, continual waiting for the next bombs, [and the] dispersal of units etc'.[163]

While the morale of the *Panzerarmee* was being worn away by the fire-power unleashed upon it, the morale of Eighth Army soared as the troops finally saw their equipment put to the kind of use they had long believed possible. The censorship summary for 10 to 16 September contained references to improved tactics, particularly in regard to the use of arm-oured formations. An officer wrote, 'we do not sacrifice the wretched tank crews as before, as this old fashioned idea of cavalry charges head on with tanks has been given up I'm glad to say'. Another stated, 'it does look as though the tanks are beginning to learn their lesson – and not charge straight at dug in 88 mm A/Tk guns two up with their flag flying'.[164] The same summary recorded that 'the predominant feature of correspondence from all ranks of British troops in the Western Desert' was the 'general appreciation of the massive support given to our land forces by the Allied Air Forces, which has affected morale to an incalculable degree'.[165] The summary for 17 to 23 September also emphasised the performance of the Allied Air Forces. A gunner wrote, 'air co-operation was perfect and we'd only to name a target to have the R.A.F. bombing it ten minutes later; artillery combined shoots ... worked perfectly. We drove their stuff ... into groups and then left them to the R.A.F.' Another soldier stated, 'we harried him a good deal on his way back but didn't get really heavily involved. Our artillery and the R.A.F. gave him absolute hell and I sat on one ridge all day about 5,000 yards from a *Panzer* Division which the R.A.F. bombed every 45 mins and which the big gunners put about 10,000 shells into in one day. It was the most incredible sight I have ever seen and gave our chaps considerable satisfaction. We took some of those particular Germans prisoner the following day and they said it was [by] far the worst day they had ever experienced.'[166]

Following Alam Halfa, new shipments of weapons and equipment con-tinued to arrive in the Middle East. The delivery of over 300 Sherman tanks from the United States midway through September was one of the most important additions to Eighth Army. The Sherman carried a 75 mm high velocity gun firing either armour piercing or high explosive shells. It

[163] SAMAD UWH, Draft Narratives, Box 316, War Diary of Panzer Army Africa 28 July to 23 October 1942, pp. 79–83. Reply to query about bombs dropped made on 6 September 1942 by 19th Flak Division, 8 September 1942.

[164] ANZ WAII/1/DA508/1 vol. 3, MEMCWS, no. XLIV (10 to 16 September 1942), p. 2.

[165] Ibid., p. 1.

[166] ANZ WAII/1/DA508/1 vol. 3, MEMCWS, no. XLV (17 to 23 September 1942), p. 1.

was very reliable and unlike the Grant carried its big gun on a revolving turret. Another addition was the British Crusader Mark III with a six-pounder gun. Seventy-eight of these new tanks were available by the beginning of El Alamein. However, they proved to be just as unreliable as previous Crusader versions. More importantly, by the middle of October, Eighth Army had at its disposal 849 six-pounder anti-tank guns. The arrival of these guns meant that every infantry battalion in Eighth Army received eight two-pounder anti-tank guns to add to its defences.[167] This was extremely important for morale, and gave the infantry confidence that it could deal with the German panzers without the aid of tanks.

Much has been made of the material advantage enjoyed by Eighth Army at El Alamein.[168] Walter Warlimont, who served as Hitler's Deputy Chief of the Operations Staff between September 1939 and September 1944, described El Alamein as 'a typical battle of material in which no military genius on the part of the commander, and no amount of courage on the part of the men, could make up for the catastrophic situation brought about by the failure of the [Axis] overseas supply lines'.[169] At El Alamein Eighth Army had twice as many troops (around 220,000 versus 108,000),[170] twice as many tanks (around 1,029 versus 548), a three to two advantage in artillery (around 892 versus 552) and anti-tank guns (1,451 versus 1,063) and nearly 200 more planes (around 530 versus 350).[171] Overall Eighth Army possessed a rough two to one advantage. However, Eighth Army had enjoyed quantitative advantages previously and still been defeated by the *Panzerarmee*.

The massive superiority Eighth Army had in tanks could only pay off if the armour was not only able to break free of the defensive minefields (consisting of some 400,000 mines) that accounted for a little over one-fifth of all British tank casualties in North Africa in 1942,[172] but also

---

[167] I. S. O. Playfair and C. J. C. Molony, *The Mediterranean and Middle East*, vol. IV, *The Destruction of the Axis Forces in Africa* (London, 1966), pp. 8–10. These were the guns freed up by the equipping of the anti-tank regiments with six-pounders.

[168] Kitchen, *Rommel's Desert War*, p. 341.

[169] Walter Warlimont, 'The Decision in the Mediterranean 1942', in Hans-Adolf Jacobsen and Jürgen Rohwer (eds.), *The Decisive Battles of World War II: The German View* (London, 1965), p. 203. In February 1943 Warlimont travelled to Tunis to confer with Rommel as to whether or not the Germans should abandon North Africa.

[170] NAA A5954/69 529/9 AIF Participation in 8th Army Offensive, October/November, 1942.

[171] Barr, *Pendulum of War*, p. 276.

[172] NA WO 222/65 Army Operational Research Group, Memorandum no. A16, 'The Comparative Performance of German Anti-Tank Weapons during World War II', prepared by H. G. Gee. Rommel called his minefield at El Alamein the 'devil's garden'.

overcome the Axis anti-tank screens.[173] Merely two-fifths of Eighth Army's tanks were Grants or Shermans, the only models that could realistically take on the German armour and anti-tank guns. The advantage Eighth Army had in anti-tank and artillery pieces was not decisive by any measure.[174]

It was clear to Montgomery that his supposed technological superiority did not guarantee him victory any more than it had his predecessor at Gazala or during the July battles. In a memorandum on his plans for operation Lightfoot, written on 6 October 1942, he stated that 'we have great superiority in tanks and in fire-power ... but it is a regrettable fact that our troops are not, in all cases, highly trained'. Montgomery realised that 'by doing foolish or stupid things' he 'could lose heavily in the first few days of the battle' as had happened at Crusader and Gazala 'and thus negative [his] superiority'. Montgomery was therefore determined to 'ensure that we fight the battle in our own way'.[175]

Niall Barr has pointed out that Eighth Army's numerical advantage was also negated by the fact that at the point of attack XXX Corps had well below the three-to-one ratio of forces that was generally considered necessary for a straightforward frontal assault to succeed.[176] In fact the plan was to attack on the basis of two to one, viz., where 1,000 men were thought to hold an enemy position 2,000 men were put in to attack it.[177] The advantage in manpower was also largely negated by a lack of flexibility due to the imperial make-up of Eighth Army. One could not simply disband an Australian unit and place the men in a British unit that needed reinforcements. Many of the infantry brigades were below strength and incapable of prolonged attritional activity. For these reasons, Montgomery concentrated on the morale issue. 'This battle', he warned, 'will involve hard and prolonged fighting. Our troops must not think that, because we have a good tank and very powerful artillery support, the enemy will all surrender. The enemy will NOT surrender and there will be bitter fighting. The infantry must be prepared to fight and kill, and to continue doing so over a prolonged period.'[178] The soldiers 'must be

[173] AWM 54 527/6/3 LHQ Tactical School, Lessons, Western Desert, in particular El Alamein Operations, 1942.
[174] Barr, *Pendulum of War*, p. 276.
[175] AWM 3DRL 2632 2/2 Lightfoot, Memorandum no. 2 by Army Commander, 6 October 1942.
[176] Barr, *Pendulum of War*, p. 277.
[177] ANZ WAII/2 Accession W3281, Box 1, 101d part 1, The New Zealand Division in Egypt and Libya, Operations 'Lightfoot' and 'Supercharge', part 1, Narrative and Lessons.
[178] Quoted in Keegan, *The Second World War*, p. 279.

worked up to that state which will make them want to go into battle and kill Germans'.[179]

Montgomery's doctrine of command was focused on the 'human factor'. He saw the raw material for success not as technology but the man and his psychology.

I have always held the view that an army is not merely a collection of individuals, with so many tanks, guns, machine-guns, etc. The real strength of an army is, and must be, far greater than the sum total of its parts; that extra strength is provided by morale, fighting spirit, mutual confidence between the leaders and the led and especially with the high command, the quality of comradeship, and many other intangible spiritual qualities ... The raw material with which the general has to deal is men ... and to handle an army well, it is essential to understand human nature ... The morale of the soldier is the single greatest factor in war.[180]

For Montgomery, arms and weapons were but a mechanical extension of the pride and aggressive attributes of the individual. Without pride and confidence in them the soldier was unlikely to have confidence in himself and his ability to fight.[181] He therefore saw the increasing material strength of Eighth Army not as a battle-winning element on its own, but as one of the key factors that would motivate his troops to withstand the 'hard and prolonged fighting' that he predicted at El Alamein.

Montgomery's words were not just rhetoric. He ensured that every soldier in Eighth Army was aware of the quantity and quality of material supporting him. This he hoped would improve morale. Sergeant L. Clothier, of 2/13 Battalion AIF, wrote the night before the battle: 'The hop over is a 4 divvy show with tanks and the barrage will be laid down by 820 25 pdrs, plus mediums and heavys. The 15th and 17th are cracking his first 2 lines and we're going thru [sic] them to attack his gun lines which consist of MG and A.Tk posts beside his infantry support guns. 8 mile away is the 15th Panzer div and they expect us to be counter attacked by them, but as we have 48 tanks in support plus 96 25 pdrs and 16 A/tk guns, we should be OK.' Of course Clothier realised that 'all this is on paper and theory. It is almost sure to be different with so much noise and confusion despite us having trained for it for 3 weeks.' Nevertheless he was aware that 'there is supposed to be 300 Shermans, 300 Grants, and 400 other types of tanks, plus 25 Pdrs on tank chassis (unknown number), 1,000 bombers and 700 fighters on our side'.[182]

[179] NA WO 201/444 'Lightfoot, Memorandum by Army commander', 28 September 1942.
[180] Montgomery, *Memoirs*, p. 83.
[181] A similar sentiment was expressed by Lieut.-Col. C. D. Daly, 'A Psychological Analysis of Military Morale', in *The Army Quarterly*, 32(1) (April 1936), p. 71.
[182] AWM PR 00588 Papers of Sgt. L. Clothier, 2/13 Battalion A.I.F. Diary, 22 October 1942.

The effect of improved weaponry on morale is perhaps best illustrated by the 2nd New Zealand Division. The vitriolic reaction of New Zealand forces to their British allies that threatened to lead to 'incidents' between New Zealand and British troops following the July battles was indicative of the morale problems of 2nd New Zealand Division in July and August 1942.[183] Combined with the general animosity directed towards the South Africans for surrendering Tobruk, the very fabric of Eighth Army was in danger of being torn apart. It was decided, therefore, following the July battles, to convert the New Zealand 4th Brigade to armour and to attach the British 9th Armoured Brigade to the 2nd New Zealand Division while the 4th Brigade was being retrained. This decision played a significant role in placating the concerns of Inglis and Freyberg and restoring damaged New Zealand morale.

Freyberg was convinced that the addition of 9th Armoured Brigade would prevent any repeat of the July debacle. He wrote to New Zealand detailing the forty-one Shermans, forty-eight Grants and over sixty Crusaders that 9th Armoured Brigade would bring to his command. These tanks, he said, would have 'turned the scales in any of our past battles'.[184] The reaction among the troops of the division was electric.[185] One soldier wrote, 'from the worst equipped div. in the army we will be the best equipped. In fact we are told the best equipped in the world. It is impossible to describe this wonderful change but there is no doubt about it, the boys will go to town in no uncertain manner with Rommel next time they go in.'[186]

The censorship summaries highlighted similar sentiments among many of the troops. By the end of September, the summaries were reporting that 'mail from 8th Army personnel made pleasant reading; the esprit de corps is amazingly high ... To get "on the job again" appears to be the earnest desire of all troops who are confident that we are stronger and better equipped than at any time, and that morale cannot be improved by too much waiting.'[187] By October, the summaries were reporting that

the offensive spirit continues to be dominant in correspondence from British troops in Egypt, and it is obvious that all ranks expect and are ready for a flare up on a grand scale at any moment. And what is more, they are absolutely

---

[183] ANZ WAII/8/26 Freyberg General Correspondence, February to October 1942. W. G. Stevens, Brigadier, Officer i/c Adm 2 NZEF to GOC 2 NZEF, 9 August 1942.
[184] ANZ WAII/8/26 Freyberg General Correspondence, February to October 1942. Letter 14 October 1942.
[185] ANZ WAII/1/DA508/1 vol. 4, MEMCFS, no. XLVIII (7 to 20 October 1942), p. 18.
[186] ANZ WAII/1/DA508/1 vol. 3, MEMCWS, no. XLVII (30 September to 6 October 1942), pp. 14–15.
[187] ANZ WAII/1/DA508/1 vol. 3, MEMCWS, no. XLVI (23 to 29 September 1942), p. 1.

convinced that this time there can be but one result to the impending campaign, since, as one man said, 'we've got the stuff and a General who knows how to use it.' ... There is no doubt [that] the most satisfactory feature of the mail was the confidence that [Eighth Army] can now face the Germans with parity in weapons.[188]

That is not to say that all soldiers were full of 'binge' and confidence. W. R. Garrett, a private with the Royal Sussex, who were newly arrived in the desert, recalled how he 'resented some of the desert veterans who predicted "just another complete cock-up"'.[189] Montgomery's message to the troops on the night of the battle was targeted at reassuring such worries. He stressed the sentiments that Eighth Army was 'ready' and well equipped and what mattered now was that the troops played their part in the bargain.

Eighth Army, Personal Message from the Army Commander.
1. When I assumed command of the Eighth Army I said that the mandate was to destroy ROMMEL and his Army, and that it would be done as soon as we were ready.
2. We are ready NOW.
3. We have first-class equipment; good tanks; good anti-tank guns; plenty of artillery and plenty of ammunition; and we are backed up by the finest air striking force in the world.
All that is necessary is that each one of us, every officer and man, should enter this battle with the determination to see it through – to fight and to kill – and finally, to win.
    If we all do this there can be only one result – together we will hit the enemy for 'six', right out of North Africa.

BL Montgomery, 23/10/42.[190]

The battle of El Alamein did indeed turn out to be a 'hard and bloody killing match'.[191] As Montgomery had predicted, the firepower of Eighth Army did not guarantee a swift and easy victory. It instead played a crucial role in reducing the Axis will to resist.[192] The lessons from operations derived from the battle of El Alamein acknowledged that 'several formations ... reported that considering the density of the artillery support during the various attacks, the number of enemy dead and wounded found by the leading troops was surprisingly light, and that enemy

---

[188] ANZ WAII/1/DA508/1 vol. 3, MEMCWS, no. XLVII (30 September to 6 October 1942), p. 1.
[189] IWM 93/19/1 Garrett, 'A Private Viewing', p. 18.
[190] IWM BLM 53 Eighth Army, Personal Message from the Army Commander, 23 October 1942.
[191] Montgomery, Memoirs, p. 138.
[192] IWM BLM 28/3 'Lightfoot' General Plan of Eighth Army, 14 September 1942.

automatic weapons quickly opened up when the barrage or concentration ... passed'. The report stressed that 'the killing power of artillery barrages or concentrations against well dug in infantry is often slight. The purpose of the artillery support in an attack is primarily to shake the enemy's morale, temporarily to stupefy him, (as was done on most occasions in the last break in battle) to enable the attacker to reach the objective with the minimum of casualties. The killing or capture of the enemy then follows.'[193] Reports and accounts written later and after the war tended to lend support to this conclusion.[194] One such report found that the morale effects of bombardments were anywhere between two to six times greater than the material effects.[195] It estimated that the suppressing result of Allied artillery on the German defenders on D-Day had reduced casualties to one-third of what they might have been in the assaulting British battalions.[196]

Eighth Army's superiority in tanks did not play a decisive role in success at El Alamein either. Montgomery found the lack of 'drive and pep' in X Corps extremely frustrating[197] and it was only in the very final phase of the battle that the armour ultimately managed to 'break out' and confirm the Axis defeat. By this stage of the desert war the ascendancy of the anti-tank gun over the tank was almost universally accepted and the *Panzerarmee* still had over 400 anti-tank guns of 50 mm and higher calibres.[198] Thus, in the end, El Alamein was an infantryman's battle. As 'Middle East Training Manual no. 7', which dealt with lessons from El Alamein stated, 'even with the introduction of new weapons, and new techniques,' the reality is that 'between two equally armed opponents the brunt of the fighting will still normally be borne by infantry formations, and, as was found at ALAMEIN, against a stubborn co-ordinated defence, there will seldom be enough infantry for all demands.'[199] At El Alamein Eighth Army suffered 13,560 casualties, about the same number it suffered during the July fighting. The German war diaries from the El Alamein battle were gracious in their praise of the British soldier who had 'once again demonstrated his tenacity and hardiness in fighting and in enduring losses'. In tacit recognition of British

---

[193] NA WO 201/2596 Lessons from Operations: Training. Preliminary Draft Lessons from Operations October and November 1942 (referring to the battle of El Alamein), p. 24.
[194] NA WO 291/904, Army Operational Research Group Memorandum no. 635. 'The Morale Effect of Bombardment'; Bidwell, *Modern Warfare* (London, 1973) pp. 156–7.
[195] NA WO 291/904, Army Operational Research Group Memorandum no. 635. 'The Morale Effect of Bombardment', p. 6.
[196] Ibid., p. 4.   [197] IWM BLM 28 Diary Notes, 23 October to 7 November 1942.
[198] Playfair and Molony, *The Mediterranean and Middle East*, vol. IV, p. 10.
[199] IWM 99/1/2, Maj.-Gen. Raymond Briggs. METM no. 7, Lessons from Operations, October and November 1942.

morale, the war diaries stated that, 'in spite of the very heavy losses which he is known to have sustained, he attacked repeatedly'.[200]

In comparison, on 2 November the German war diaries admitted that their troops were 'exhausted' and that, taking all things into consideration, 'it had to be admitted that after a desperate 10-day struggle against an enemy superior on land and in the air the Army was in no condition to prevent a further attempt at breaking through'.[201] The war diaries identified four reasons why further resistance would fail. The first was 'the enemy's great superiority in tanks and artillery'. However, X Corps had proved largely ineffectual at El Alamein and the artillery did more morale than material damage to the Axis forces. The second reason was 'the continual heavy day and night bombing attacks, against which there was no defence' and which 'only added to the feeling of inferiority' suffered by the troops of the *Panzerarmee*. However, air bombardment was notoriously inaccurate,[202] and, as has been already argued, it was seen by both sides as having primarily a morale, rather than material, effect on the enemy. The third reason was the 'almost complete failure of the Italian troops'. According to the report of the General Officer Commanding (GOC) *Afrika Korps*, the Axis problem lay once again with the morale of the Italian formations. In the words of the report, 'the Italian Littorio and Trieste Divisions co-operating with Afrika Korps had failed. Only the Italian artillery had fought well.' Due to the unreliability of the Italian formations, 'the defence [had to] be borne by the German formations alone'. Furthermore, the Italian command 'had only partial control over their troops'. According to another *Afrika Korps* report, the Italian 'Littorio Armoured Division was almost completely demoralised' and many Italian units with transport and tanks were known to be 'moving back' from the front line. Similar occurrences were apparently taking place among the infantry of the Trieste Division.[203] The fourth and final reason was the *Panzerarmee*'s 'own heavy losses in men and material on account of the enemy's vast superiority in the most modern weapons'. There can be no doubt that the weight of fire unleashed on the *Panzerarmee* caused many casualties. However, a large proportion of

---

[200] SAMAD UWH, Draft Narratives, Box 316, 15th Panzer Division Report on the Battle of Alamein and the Retreat to Marsa El Brega, 23 October to 20 November 1942.

[201] ANZ WAII/11/20 German–Italian Forces in Africa, 23 October 1942 to 23 February 1943. German War Narrative, 2 November 1942.

[202] Stephen Budiansky, *Air Power: The Men, Machines, and Ideas That Revolutionized War, from Kitty Hawk to Gulf War II* (London, 2004), p. 305; Richard P. Hallion, *Storm over Iraq: Air Power and the Gulf War* (London, 1992), p. 283.

[203] ANZ WAII/11/20 German–Italian Forces in Africa, 23 October 1942 to 23 February 1943. German War Narrative, 2 November 1942.

these casualties, as was the case with Eighth Army in the summer battles, can be attributed to morale as well as material causes. The statistics show that 40% of German and 63% of Italian casualties were missing or POWs; the rate for British and Commonwealth troops during the battle was 17%.[204] In addition, extremely high sickness rates, a sure sign of morale problems, removed large numbers of men from the front line.[205] Mark Harrison has estimated that nearly one in five Germans were listed as sick during the battle, with the elite 15th Panzer Division suffering a sickness rate as high as 38%.[206] Problems with desertion and surrender prompted Rommel to encourage use of the death penalty at courts marshal during July;[207] these problems persisted into October and November.[208] Finally, one of the more significant effects of heavy losses of any kind is the impact they have on primary group cohesion, which is generally recognised as a key factor in maintaining morale in the front line.[209]

The *Panzerarmee*, by any standard, did put up a determined defence at El Alamein and as Montgomery predicted the 'enemy did not all surrender' because Eighth Army had 'a good tank and very powerful artillery support'.[210] In the words of Niall Barr, by the end of the battle 'Eighth Army had virtually run out of formed infantry units that could still be used in the attack.'[211] Many of the front line battalions of Eighth Army suffered over 50 per cent casualties.[212] It is clear that Eighth Army won the 'killing match' that Montgomery predicted at El Alamein due to sheer determination and will power as much as any other factor. The arrival of large amounts of new and better weapons played a decisive role in developing this determination among the soldiers of Eighth Army while concurrently draining the *Panzerarmee* of its willingness to resist.

This chapter has shown that there was an evolution in the British understanding of the relationship between morale and technology during the desert war. It has suggested that British interwar doctrine was misplaced and that the British Army could not rely on technology to replace human beings, with all their physical and psychological vulnerabilities. Instead it became evident that a subtle balance was needed

---

[204] Derived from statistics quoted by Bungay, *Alamein*, pp. 196–7.
[205] Kitchen, *Rommel's Desert War*, pp. 312, 323, 346.
[206] Harrison, *Medicine and Victory*, pp. 88–9.
[207] Kitchen, *Rommel's Desert War*, pp. 264, 292.   [208] Ibid., pp. 323–4.
[209] See Chapter 8 for a discussion of primary group theory and the role played by the primary group in maintaining Eighth Army's morale in the desert.
[210] NA WO 201/444 'Lightfoot, Memorandum by Army Commander', 28 September 1942.
[211] Barr, *Pendulum of War*, p. 397.
[212] Eighth Army casualties are discussed in greater detail in Chapter 8.

Illustration 5 A Martin Baltimore of no. 55 Squadron RAF flies over the target area as salvoes of bombs explode on tanks and motor transport of the 15th Panzer Division during the battle of El Alamein, October 1942. The effective utilisation of air power played an important role both in building Eighth Army's morale and in eroding Axis morale during the critical battle of El Alamein.

between firepower and morale, and that victory did not depend on one without the other. Over the space of two years hard fighting in the desert the British forces gradually adapted their doctrine and methods and became far more aligned with the German viewpoint on firepower and morale. The British forces increasingly understood German warfare and how they used weapons to unnerve the front-line soldier as much as to kill him. This greater understanding led to the British designing a form of warfare under Montgomery that tried to maximise both the human and technological elements to overcome the problems of modern battle. This refinement in British doctrine led to a decisive victory in North Africa and saw Britain through the rest of the war.

The *Afrika Korps* war diaries claimed that the 'heroic troops' of the *Panzerarmee* 'were denied victory . . . due to enemy superiority in numbers and material, and not in leadership and morale'.[213] This viewpoint is however grossly misleading as to how the conflict in the desert was actually fought out. Both sides were keen to deflect criticism away from the conduct of their own troops. Similarly, both sides drastically exaggerated the significance of material shortcomings in defeat. The reality of war in the desert only proved Marshall's post-war contention correct. Morale endured only so long as soldiers' weapons were perceived to 'deal greater death or fear of death to the enemy' and, when that perception changed, 'morale dies and defeat occurs'.[214]

---

[213] SAMAD UWH, Draft Narratives, Box 316. 15th Panzer Division Report on the Battle of Alamein and the Retreat to Marsa El Brega, 23 October to 20 November, 1942.
[214] Marshall, *Men against Fire*, p. 67.

3 Quality of manpower and morale

Men and women remain the most important assets of an Army, even since the development of modern weapons. Economy of manpower means much more than operating with the smallest numbers possible; it is also essential to use every man and woman to the best advantage.

(General Ronald Adam)[1]

The object of training must be, firstly, to select those who possess within them the potentialities of leadership and, secondly, to develop these potentialities.

(Field Marshal B. L. Montgomery)[2]

We seem to have plenty of people who can read orders literally but precious few who can interpret them intelligently which is far from the same thing. According to the press I see every time British Forces take it in the teeth and get shoved back from or off of something, a howl goes up from the B[ritish].P[ublic]. to Govt. about supplies and quality or quantity of tanks, guns etc. Now however true that may have been I do not believe it to be the main fault now. In my considered opinion – here's high heresy – the fault in main lies from top to bottom with the personnel!

(An officer commenting on the summer 1942 crisis in the desert)[3]

In 1922, the Southborough Committee on Shell Shock unequivocally concluded that many of the manpower problems that had beset the British Army in the First World War could be overcome in a future war by better personnel selection and manpower policies.[4] The committee recommended that unsuitable men were 'unlikely to become efficient soldiers', and that their removal from the fighting services would be of 'prime importance in the successful conduct of the war' of the future.[5]

In spite of this recommendation no serious measures were taken in the interwar years to improve the quality of recruits available to the army.

---

[1] LHCMA Adam 3/13 Narrative Covering Aspects of Work as Adjutant-General, WWII, chap. 1, Manpower, p. 3.
[2] IWM Briggs Papers, 'Morale in Battle: Analysis', by B. L. Montgomery, 1946.
[3] ANZ WAII/1/DA508/1 vol. 3, MEMCWS, no. XLI (19 to 25 August 1942), p. 4.
[4] War Office, *Report of the War Office Committee of Enquiry into 'Shell-Shock'* (London, 1922).
[5] Ibid.

Instead, the army, as it struggled to attract adequate numbers to make up full establishments, was forced to admit into its ranks any man it could lay its hands on. The situation became so acute that Sir Cyril Deverell, the Chief of the Imperial General Staff between 1936 and 1937, had to admit that he had 'no objection to any man who is not an imbecile being enlisted'. In other words, he did 'not consider rejection on education grounds alone should be a sine qua non', although he did not want to proclaim such a policy 'loudly'. By the late 1930s, men who could scarcely read or write were being enlisted into the army in an attempt to maintain numbers.[6]

With the beginning of hostilities in September 1939, the army began to swell its numbers on a grand scale, expanding nearly two and a half times from 892,697 men in September 1939 to 2.2 million men by June 1941.[7] The Regular Army, the only fully trained element of the British Army, only made up 232,000 of the forces available in September 1939. By June 1941, therefore, this fully trained cadre made up at most just over 10 per cent of the heterogeneous force of Regulars, Territorials, conscripts and volunteers available to Britain.[8]

Ronald Adam, the Adjutant-General to the British Army from 1941 to 1946, recalled after the war that this accelerated expansion of the army was carried out largely without the input of the War Office. The Cabinet, hoping to frighten Hitler and Mussolini, rushed headlong into an expansion that the War Office was ill equipped to manage. Thus, the opportunity to plan a reorganisation of the army was missed.[9] Adam was further handicapped by the fact that the records that documented the creation of a volunteer and conscript army in the First World War had all been destroyed. Thus, Adam and the War Office were forced to relearn, by trial and error, the subtle policies necessary to select and motivate the citizen army thrust upon them.[10]

At the start of the desert campaign, there were 211,000 men in the British forces in the Middle East and East Africa. By June 1941, that number had risen to 370,000.[11] By the end of 1941, the number of men in the Middle East, including those on route from the United Kingdom, had

---

[6] French, *Raising Churchill's Army*, p. 49.
[7] NA WO 277/12 Piggott, *Manpower Problems*, p. 80.
[8] NA WO 163/50 Use of Manpower in the Army, part Two, app. A, Notes on the Growth of the Army, 21 November 1941. This does not take account of casualties among regular units between September 1939 and June 1941.
[9] LHCMA Adam 3/13 Narrative Covering Aspects of Work as Adjutant-General, WWII, chap. 1, Manpower, p. 3.
[10] Ibid., introduction.
[11] NA WO 163/50 War Office Progress Reports for December 1940 and June 1941.

swollen to almost 640,000.[12] During the first eight months of 1942, another 224,000 men were transported to the Middle East.[13] Between August and the outbreak of the battle of El Alamein a further 60,000 replacements arrived in the command to bring Eighth Army up to strength after the casualties of the summer battles.[14] Therefore, from the beginning of the desert campaign to the vital battle of El Alamein, the Middle Eastern Forces more than quadrupled the size of the forces at their disposal.[15]

The expansion of the armed forces and the replacements arising from wastage in battle created a problem for the army. There simply wasn't enough good human material to go around. The majority of the best intakes chose to join either the Royal Air Force or the Royal Navy (RN).[16] This left the army with what Brigadier John Rees, the Consultant Psychiatrist to the army, called 'the psychopathic tenth'[17] of the country's manpower, the least intelligent and often the least ambitious of the recruits. The army offered very little to prospective recruits. Few of the skills learnt by an infantryman were transferable to employment following service. On the other hand, both the RAF and RN provided training and skills useful to a vocation following the war.[18] The stigma of the Poor Bloody Infantry (PBI) was another stumbling block for the army. The memory of the 'holocaust' on the western front was still prevalent in the minds of the sons of the veterans who had fought in France and Belgium. Sixty per cent of men born between 1905 and 1927, and 70 per cent of those born between 1915 and 1927, served in the UK armed forces during the Second World War.[19] Many young men were not keen to relive their fathers' experiences of twentieth-century warfare.

In June 1941, Adam became Adjutant-General of the army, with responsibility for dealing with the problems of manpower, personnel

---

[12] NA WO 163/51 War Office Progress Report December 1941.

[13] Playfair, *The Mediterranean and the Middle East*, vol. III, p. 372. This includes RAF and RN personnel as well as 32,400 reinforcements from India.

[14] IWM BLM 62 Notes on the Maintenance of the Eighth Army and the Supporting Royal Air Force by Land, Sea and Air from El Alamein to Tunisia. Compiled by Q Staff, GHQ Cairo, 1942, p. 2.

[15] It must be noted that Middle East Command had responsibility at various times for areas as far ranging as Egypt, Sudan, Palestine, Iraq, Ethiopia, Eritrea, Libya and Greece.

[16] NA WO 163/123 Army No 72. Allocation of Man-Power in the Army: Statement of the WO Views on the 22nd Report of the Select Committee on National Expenditure (Session 1940–1941). Memorandum by the WO, 20 October 1941.

[17] LHCMA Adam 3/13 Narrative Covering Aspects of Work as Adjutant-General, WWII, chap. 2, Selection of Men and Leaders; Ahrenfeldt, *Psychiatry in the British Army in the Second World War*, p. 32.

[18] French, *Raising Churchill's Army*, p. 50.

[19] LHCMA Adam (Box 2), *White Paper on Strengths and Casualties 1939–1945*.

selection and morale. Like many of his peers, he had fought in France in 1940. He had commanded the final beachhead at Dunkirk and had witnessed in full the disintegration of the British Expeditionary Force at the hands of the Wehrmacht. Adam's experiences gave him a clear conviction that too many undertrained and poorly selected individuals had taken part in the debacle in France.

On returning to Britain in 1940, Adam was installed as GOC Northern Command in the United Kingdom. He immediately set about studying the problem of manpower in the army. With the cooperation of the Northern Command psychiatrist, Lieutenant-Colonel G. R. Hargreaves, he initiated a study to ascertain the intelligence of the men under his leadership and their suitability for the jobs to which they had been posted. He reported his findings to the War Office in January 1941.[20] Adam found a wide gap between the ideal of employing every man on the work most suited to him and the actual position as it pertained in the army. The figures he produced were quite staggering. He reported that 50% of every Royal Armoured Corps intake and 20% of every infantry intake did not have the intelligence for full efficiency in the corps to which they had been posted. Furthermore, 20% of every infantry intake and 50% of every Pioneer Corps intake in Northern Command were 'misplaced' and capable of more efficient service in a corps other than the one to which they had been posted. Overall, he found that 4% of intakes were totally useless for any training as a soldier at all.[21]

Another study, carried out in February 1941, concerned with Category 'C' men (those that were only fit for home service), produced similar findings. A total of 29,556 men were examined with a view to upgrading or, if they could not perform a useful day's work within the army, to discharge. The results were again quite astonishing; 12.8% of the men investigated were discharged and 17.7% upgraded.[22] In other words, on the basis of this study, nearly a third (30.5%) of Category 'C' men in the British Army were unsuited to the job in which they had been placed.

Adam believed that findings such as these presented a real problem to the army. In general, men of low intelligence were more likely to develop neurotic features, poor morale, low personal esteem and disciplinary

[20] Ahrenfeldt, *Psychiatry in the British Army in the Second World War*, p. 37–8.
[21] NA WO 163/50 The Army Council, Selection Tests for the Army (Report by the ECAC for Consideration by the Army Council on Tuesday 17 June 1941), Paper no. AC/P(41) 40, 13 June 1941.
[22] NA WO 163/50 Use of Manpower in the Army, part 2, app. B, Medical Categories, 21 November 1941.

problems and see themselves as useless in their jobs.[23] A study carried out in Western Command, in August 1941, found that, of 300 soldiers under sentence for going AWOL, 'one half had the intellectual capacity found in the least intelligent quarter of the population, i.e. this group of men contained twice the number of dullards and defectives usually found in homologous conscript groups'.[24] Another study, carried out in 1942, found that nine out of ten men who reached a minimum level in intelligence tests were successful in training. Below that minimum intelligence level, four out of five men either failed in training, or were reported as unsatisfactory by their field units.[25] Men of low intelligence were also more likely to break down if they were placed in the wrong post ('misfits') or put in a position of heavy stress.[26] 'Misfits', who also included intelligent men placed in jobs below their capabilities, tended to feel, and become, 'outsiders' in their unit.[27] Their loyalty to their unit was therefore always doubtful and they were liable, as a circular to all medical officers written later in the war entitled 'Morale Discipline and Mental Fitness' noted, on slight cause to become openly resentful of authority. Their 'poor individual morale' could, therefore, 'affect group morale'.[28]

The situation convinced Adam that proper selection procedures had to be introduced.[29] Since July 1940, recruits had undergone intelligence tests subsequent to joining a corps in the army.[30] Uncoordinated testing had also taken place in various commands under the supervision of Command psychiatrists. However, no central authority had been concerned with the allocation, transfer or discharge of personnel in the army. The system clearly required an immediate overhaul. Not only did the acute shortage of manpower[31] make it 'imperative that the Army should apply its resources to the best possible advantage', but the 'efficiency and contentment of the Army depended to a large extent upon putting the

[23] Ahrenfeldt, *Psychiatry in the British Army in the Second World War*, pp. 77–81.

[24] Ibid., p. 78.

[25] NA WO 32/11972 Notes on the Use Now Being Made of Psychologists in the Army, 1942.

[26] Ahrenfeldt, *Psychiatry in the British Army in the Second World War*, p. 78.

[27] NA WO 222/218 Circular to all Medical Officers, ND, 'Morale, Discipline and Mental Fitness'.

[28] NA CAB 21/914 'The Work of Army Psychiatrists in Relation to Morale', The War Office Directorate of Army Psychiatry, January 1944.

[29] LHCMA Adam 3/13 Narrative Covering Aspects of Work as Adjutant General, WWII, chap. 1, Manpower, p. 9. Adam became Adjutant-General about the same time as the Beveridge Committee was set up to look into manpower allocation in the Army.

[30] NA WO 32/11972 Memorandum on Army Psychiatry, 1942.

[31] Ahrenfeldt, *Psychiatry in the British Army in the Second World War*, p. 77; the extent of this problem is also highlighted in French, *Raising Churchill's Army*, pp. 243–4.

right man in the right place'.[32] Adam, therefore, brought the issue before the Executive Committee of the Army Council (ECAC) in June 1941. His view was that 'the Army was wasting its man-power in this war almost as badly as it did in the last'. He pointed out that men were being posted to a corps almost entirely on the demand of the moment and without any effort to determine their fitness for the corps in question. He argued that the American Army, which had carried out selection testing on every man in the Great War, was continuing the policy into the Second World War and that the German Army was employing as many as 1,000 psychologists on testing. He thought the Red Army was also conducting intelligence tests.[33]

As a result of Adam's proposal, the Directorate of Selection of Personnel (DSP) was set up, in June 1941, under Brigadier Alick Buchanan-Smith. The purpose of the directorate was to provide testing, at medical examination centres, for all new recruits, as well as for units in formations due for conversion to other corps, in particular for transfer to the RAC.[34] The directorate had two branches, one to deal with the allocation of personnel, and the other to maintain liaison with the appropriate directors in the War Office.

The extent of the challenge facing the new directorate was immense. By the second half of 1941, the army was discharging about 1,300 men every month because of diagnosable, and therefore avoidable, psycho-neurotic problems during training.[35] Furthermore, Major W. R. Bion (the inventor of the leaderless group test) wrote a report, in August 1941, on the many new units being converted into tank battalions. He pointed out that the intelligence of an appreciable number of soldiers in these newly formed units was too low to allow for efficient or reliable performance of their duties. Bion argued that, sooner or later, a decision would have to be made whether 'armoured divisions subjected to the stress of active warfare could afford the risk of retaining hard-working and pleasant dullards who were slower than the average man to learn what was required of them'. There was, in his opinion, an obvious advantage in employing men of superior intelligence, for 'backward' men 'encumbered, and perhaps endangered, military enterprise'.[36]

---

[32] NA WO 163/50 The Army Council, Selection Tests for the Army (Report by the ECAC for Consideration by the Army Council on Tuesday, 17 June 1941), Paper no. AC/P(41) 40, 13 June 1941.

[33] Ibid.

[34] NA WO 163/50 Army Council, WO Progress Report June 1941 Selective Testing of Personnel.

[35] NA WO 32/4726/MAC19 Detection of Psycho-neurosis by Medical Boards, January 1942.

[36] Ahrenfeldt, *Psychiatry in the British Army in the Second World War*, pp. 40–1.

The new directorate was advised by a committee of civilian psychologists, including the professors of psychology at Cambridge, Edinburgh and London Universities, as well as Dr. Charles Myers. Myers had experience of psychiatry in the First World War as Chief Specialist in Nervous Shock and as Consulting Psychiatrist to the British Army in France, and added considerable experience. The directorate's staff consisted of a nucleus of officers who were professional psychologists and approximately 150 NCOs. The officers devised suitable selection procedures and the NCOs carried out the tests.[37] Matrix tests (general intelligence tests similar to modern-day aptitude tests), seen as 'the best established and most reliable' form of evaluation at the time, were designed to assess recruits by testing their reasoning abilities and spatial awareness. The intelligence levels for various army jobs were established and it was then up to recruits to meet the standard required. Those scoring particularly low on the tests were referred to psychiatrists to ascertain the best use of their abilities.[38] Testing began in some commands in August 1941, and, by November 1941, two-thirds of intakes were being subjected to tests on enlistment.[39] By July 1942, some 23,000 men a month were being tested on entering the army.[40]

The manpower situation in the desert was also affected by the problems on the home front. As Brigadier G. W. B. James, Consultant in Psychological Medicine in the Middle East, wrote, in June 1942, 'fighting, especially in desert warfare, and in tank and mechanised infantry battles, requires high and varied mental qualities'. There was, in his opinion, no room in the desert 'for the dull and backward soldier'.[41]

A report, written in July 1942 by Major H. B. Craigie of the Department of Army Psychiatry in the Middle East, described how 'the poor material' being sent to the desert from the UK and the low standard of local recruits, particularly Palestinians and Cypriots, in the Command, were contributing to significant numbers of 'mental cases'. He pointed out that the number of psychological cases in the three services in the Middle East

---

[37] NA WO 32/11972 Notes on the Use Now Being Made of Psychologists in the Army, 1942; WO 163/50 The Army Council, Selection Tests for the Army (Report by the ECAC for Consideration by the Army Council on Tuesday 17 June 1941), Paper no. AC/P(41) 40, 13 June 1941.

[38] Ahrenfeldt, *Psychiatry in the British Army in the Second World War*, p. 39.

[39] NA WO 163/50 Army Council, WO Progress Reports for August and October 1941; Use of Manpower in the Army, part 2, app. G, Selective Testing.

[40] NA WO 163/51 Army Council, WO Progress Report July 1942.

[41] NA WO 32/11972 App. B to Report: Extracts from Report on Psychiatric Services, Middle East, 5 June 1942, by Brigadier G. W. B. James, Consultant in Psychological Medicine, Middle East.

in 1941 was 7,269 and it was estimated that the probable number in 1942 was going to be 11,000, a projected increase of 51 per cent in one year.[42]

Craigie's labelling of 'poor material' as the cause of mental cases in the Middle East reflected British understanding of the treatment of psychological casualties at that stage of the war. As front-line psychiatry developed, during and after the war, psychiatrists increasingly understood that neurosis and breakdown in battle was not caused solely by 'inadequate personalities' but also as a result of the collapse of unit morale and/or of individual morale in specific battle situations. Stable personalities were just as likely to break down under stress in battle as those with previous psychological problems.[43] Nevertheless, poor quality personnel did tend to suffer greater individual morale problems and were more likely to commit crime and question authority.[44] They could, therefore, undermine unit morale and thereby contribute to the number of battle exhaustion cases suffered by units.

To back up his arguments, Craigie provided statistics of a draft of eighty men to a searchlight regiment. He recounted that twenty-seven of these men, who arrived in the Middle East in November 1941, were examined before more thorough testing and that seven were diagnosed as 'feeble-minded mental defectives' and eleven as 'dull' and 'backward' men.[45] On testing with the matrix tests, fifty copies of which were sent to the MEF in August 1941,[46] twenty-four out of these twenty-seven men were shown to be intellectually defective or below average and only three were intellectually average.[47]

The censorship summaries show that medical officers in the desert were well aware of the problems that they faced in this regard. One wrote that

Some of the drafts we have been getting have been sheer sweepings. Obviously when told to provide a draft, the R.S.M. has been allowed to make a list of all the nit-wits and chronic sick paraders in the unit. We've had chronic bronchitis, dyspeptics, and gentlemen 'who have always suffered with me nerves doctor.'

---

[42] NA CAB 21/914 Expert Committee on the Work of Psychologists and Psychiatrists in the Services, Note by Major H. B. Craigie of the Department of Army Psychiatry in the Middle East to Sir Stafford Cripps (Lord Privy Seal) on Psychiatric Cases in the Middle East, 21 July 1942.

[43] Copp and McAndrew, *Battle Exhaustion*, pp. 5, 23, 46.

[44] NA CAB 21/914 'The Work of Army Psychiatrists in Relation to Morale', The War Office Directorate of Army Psychiatry, January 1944.

[45] Ibid.

[46] NA WO 165/101 War Diary of Directorate of Selection of Personnel, June 1941 to December 1942, 25 August 1941.

[47] NA CAB 21/914 Expert Committee on the Work of Psychologists and Psychiatrists in the Services, Note by Major H. B. Craigie of the Department of Army Psychiatry in the Middle East to Sir Stafford Cripps (Lord Privy Seal) on Psychiatric Cases in the Middle East, 21 July 1942.

Table 4 *Number of persons suffering from psycho-neurosis and other mental conditions evacuated to the UK from the Middle East, September 1941 to April 1942*

	Officers	Other ranks	Others
September, 1941	2	29	2
October, 1941	3	39	1
November, 1941	5	33	–
December, 1941	12	75	2
January, 1942	7	107	5
February, 1942	3	10	1
March, 1942	2	22	–
April, 1942	7	62	13
Total	41	377	24

Source: NA CAB 21/914 Major H. B. Craigie, Department of Army Psychiatry in the ME, to Sir Stafford Cripps on Psychiatric Cases in the Middle East, 21 July 1942.

James told me that one draft of 80 contained 27 people who were boardable as 'dull and backward.' . . . If they want results they must not only send us proper weapons but also decent human material.[48]

In addition to these cases, Brigadier Rees, the Consultant Psychiatrist to the army, estimated that around a further 1,000 men had been evacuated from the Middle East to the UK for diagnosable mental conditions by June/July 1942 (Table 4).[49]

The problem of 'low quality men' was not confined to the British elements of Eighth Army. Between October and December 1941, 607 men of the AIF were admitted to medical units in the Middle East for nervous and mental diseases, 135 of whom were evacuated back to Australia. These casualties cost the medical units of the AIF 17,236 days of treatment.[50] By 18 March 1942, 813 Australians had been returned home for reasons of nerves, anxiety state, and mental and nervous diseases. This was fully 16 per cent of all those, including battle casualties, returned to Australia during this period. In addition, another 156 men were returned for being over age.[51] A report by 6th Australian Division, written

[48] ANZ WAII/1/DA508/1 vol. 1, MEMCWS, no. XXXIX (5 to 11 August 1942), p. 3.
[49] NA CAB 21/914 Expert Committee on the Work of Psychologists and Psychiatrists in the Services, Note by Major H. B. Craigie of the Department of Army Psychiatry in the Middle East to Sir Stafford Cripps on Psychiatric Cases in the Middle East, 21 July 1942.
[50] AWM 54 267/4/5 Disease Groups, AIF Middle East. Statistical Breakdown of Diseases and Disabilities in their Categories (Numbers and Period of Treatment), October to December 1941, p. 6.
[51] AWM 54 903/2/3 Personnel Returned to Australia by Cause.

during the summer of 1941, pointed out that many of the other ranks (ORs) arriving as reinforcements in the desert were 'far too old', and it was considered that insufficient proof was required to be produced by applicants for enlistment in Australia. These men, the report contended, became 'a burden on the unit to which they are posted after arrival in [the] ME' and ultimately had a negative effect on the Australian war effort.[52]

The New Zealand Expeditionary Force (NZEF) suffered similar problems. In August 1942, in the midst of the morale crisis besetting 2nd New Zealand Division, Lieutenant-General Bernard Freyberg wrote to Major-General Edward Puttick, Chief of the General Staff in Wellington, requesting permission to send large numbers of low quality men back to New Zealand. Freyberg estimated that there were about 200 such men in the base camp area alone. Most of the cases Freyberg mentioned were Grade II (men fit for service in certain arms only or for employment in base or back areas) but some were Grade I (men fit for service in any arm or any part of a theatre of war) with no definite physical disability. Freyberg classified these low quality men in six different categories.

(1) Men of 45 years and above, some with last war service, now 'burnt out'.
(2) Men who in one way or another spent all their time off duty with varying minor complaints.
(3) Grade I men of subnormal mentality who required constant supervision.
(4) Men who had lost their nerve, including many escaped prisoners.
(5) Men of objectionable personal habits, e.g. methylated spirit or alcohol addicts.
(6) Bad conduct men who spent the majority of their time in detention and who in some cases were really criminals.[53]

In Freyberg's opinion, 'all these men' were 'useless for service in the field even in [an] emergency'. They were 'responsible for much crime and indiscipline' and had a 'demoralising influence on comrades'. Large numbers of fit men were also engaged in 'controlling them in one way or another'. Freyberg believed that the 'climate and surroundings' in Egypt and the Middle East generally tended 'to aggravate any tendency to ill health, low morale, or crime'. He was convinced that the presence of these men was 'definitely detrimental to our war effort'.[54]

---

[52] AWM 54 839/1/2 Liaison Officer Reports on Officer Reinforcements, Reinforcements Generally and Standards of Training of Other Ranks Arriving in the ME, July 1941. Notes for LO (Australia) – submitted by 6 Australian Division.

[53] ANZ WAII/8/26 Freyberg General Correspondence, February to October 1942. From Fernleaf Cairo to Defender Wellington, 13 August 1942.

[54] Ibid.

In September 1942, Brigadier W. G. Stevens, who was in charge of administration in the 2nd NZEF, wrote a memorandum proposing to extend Freyberg's 'purge' of misfits to six New Zealand divisional units and instigate a regular process of removing unsuitable men 'as the occasion warrants and as passages are available' back to New Zealand.[55] On 25 September, Stevens received permission from New Zealand to rid the NZEF of these men, who 'should never have been sent overseas', providing the 'selection of these people ... is carried out with the greatest care'.[56] The obvious worry was that such a policy would only serve to encourage malingering and 'bad conduct' in units. Therefore, selection of any personnel to go back to New Zealand was to be carefully based on a soldier's general record and medical grading, and a special board was to be set up to determine the degree of each soldier's employability.[57]

The situation among South African soldiers was no different. The field censorship summaries pointed out that many references were made to the fact that some of the men from the Union were not able to stand the pace and had been sent home. One soldier wrote home demonstrating his rather unsympathetic contempt for such men. 'A few men have gone back from here – some genuinely unfit – others just can't take it and some bomb-happy and can't take it. Yes, plain gutless moaners and squeakers ... we are glad to be rid of a few yellow gutless rats.'[58]

By the summer of 1942, news of the large numbers of men being returned to Britain and the Commonwealth homelands began to filter back to the War Office and Cabinet.[59] The Lord Privy Seal, Sir Stafford Cripps, heard that 'thousands' and 'shiploads' of men were being sent back from Libya because of their defective psychological outlook. He even heard rumours that such men had comprised 14 per cent of one particular convoy.[60] The War Cabinet discussed the issue on 4 August. The problem in their eyes was that some units had used drafts for the Middle East 'as a means of getting rid of their worst personnel, with most unfortunate

[55] ANZ WAII/8/26 'Return to New Zealand of Undesirable and Unemployable Soldiers'. HQ 2 NZEF to HG 6 NZ Div and PA to GOC, 19 September 1942.

[56] ANZ WAII/8/26 Freyberg General Correspondence, February to October 1942. HQ 2 NZ Div to HQ 2 NZEF, 25 September 1942.

[57] ANZ WAII/8/26 Freyberg General Correspondence, February to October 1942. From Fernleaf Cairo to Defender Wellington, 13 August 1942.

[58] AWM 54 883/2/97 British Troops in Egypt, no. 93 Field Censorship Report Week Ending 7 August 1941, p. 3.

[59] NA CAB 21/914 Letter to Lord Privy Seal (Sir Stafford Cripps) from Sir Edward Mellanby, Medical Research Council, 14 July 1942.

[60] NA CAB 21/914 Expert Committee on the Work of Psychologists and Psychiatrists in the Services, Note by Major H. B. Craigie of the Department of Army Psychiatry in the Middle East to Sir Stafford Cripps (Lord Privy Seal) on Psychiatric Cases in the Middle East, 21 July 1942. The actual figure had been 14 per cent of one shipload.

Table 5 *Intelligence levels of group of 2,000 RAC reinforcements sent to Middle East, 1942*

Selection groups	Ideal make up of draft based on job analysis	Actual RAC drafts to Middle East		
		From training regiments	From field units	Average
SG1, 2 and 3 plus	72.8%	73%	71%	72.4%
SG3 minus	17.1%	17%	14%	15.6%
SG4 and 5	10.1%	10%	15%	12%

and wasteful results',[61] a contention that was reaffirmed later in the war by Brigadier G. W. B. James.[62] The Secretary of State for War, P. J. Grigg, was asked to look into the matter,[63] and confirmed that there was indeed a problem, but that it was well on the way to being overcome by the DSP.

Grigg provided the Army Council and War Cabinet with a report by the DSP on a 'test audit' carried out on 2,000 drafts of the RAC due to leave for the Middle East that summer (Table 5). Grigg's sample was taken from both training regiments and field units and made up one-third of the total RAC drafts sent to the desert during the period. Recruits were banded into groups, based on their scores in the matrix test, to identify their suitability for active operations. Selection Group 1 (SG1) were the best material; SG2 were above average; SG3 were average; and SG4 and 5 were below average and useless.[64]

It is apparent from Table 5 that the type of men being sent to the desert matched the 'ideal make up of drafts based on job analysis'. In the words of the Deputy Adjutant-General, it provided strong proof that 'the increased use of selective testing is bearing fruit', and that the quality of drafts, from this point of view, should 'certainly show progressive improvement' into the future. In fact, it appeared that 'if the RAC figures are representative of the Army as a whole – and there is no reason to think that they are not', the army had 'already achieved a satisfactory standard of drafting insofar as selection groups are concerned'.[65]

[61] NA WO 32/11972 Extract from Conclusions of the 103rd (42) Meeting of the War Cabinet, Tuesday 4 August 1942.
[62] G. W. B. James, 'Psychiatric Lessons from Active Service', *The Lancet*, 1945, p. 801.
[63] NA WO 32/11972 Extract from Conclusions of the 103rd (42) Meeting of the War Cabinet, Tuesday 4 August 1942.
[64] NA WO 165/101 War Diary of Directorate of Selection of Personnel, June 1941 to December 1942, 25 August 1941.
[65] NA WO 32/11972 Correspondence between the Army Council Secretariat (ACS) and the Deputy Adjutant-General (DAG), Letter from DAG to ACS, 7 August 1942.

Illustration 6 A new recruit undertakes a general intelligence test, February 1942. Selection procedures such as this played an important role in ensuring that individuals were placed in the right jobs within the army – a crucial factor in building morale.

The quality of men by selection groups in RAC training regiments was high owing to the specialist nature of the corps. It is interesting to note that the intelligence composition of RAC field units in the UK, based on another sample of 10,000 RAC men taken in the summer of 1942, was 62% SG1, 2 and 3 plus, 20% SG3 minus and 18% SG4 and 5.[66] The intelligence composition of the first fourteen general service intakes as a whole was 59% SG1, 2 and 3 plus, 19.7% SG3 minus and 21.3% SG4 and 5 (Table 6).[67]

At the same time, field artillery regiments in Southern Command were complaining that they no longer had 'sufficient men of high enough intelligence for training as specialists', due to the fact that overseas drafts were

---

[66] NA WO 32/11972 Correspondence between the Army Council Secretariat and the DAG, Memorandum from the DAG, 1 August 1942; NA WO 201/2870 General Martel's Report on his Visit to the Middle East, 26 January 1942.
[67] NA WO 222/103 Consolidated Psychiatric Recommendations for the First Fourteen General Service Intakes.

Table 6 *Intelligence levels of sample of 10,000 RAC men, summer 1942*

Selection groups	Ideal make-up of draft based on job analysis	Sample of 10,000 men, summer 1942	First 14 general service intakes
SG1, 2 and 3 plus	72.8%	62%	59%
SG3 minus	17.1%	18%	19.7%
SG4 and 5	10.1%	20%	21.3%

taking their best men.[68] This shows that, by the summer of 1942, in the midst of the crisis in the desert, training and field units were sending their very best men to the Middle East to combat the *Panzerarmee*. These were the men who made up the replacements needed after the Gazala and Tobruk disasters and the July battles on the El Alamein line. These were the men who, alongside the desert veterans, fought Montgomery's El Alamein and the battles following it west into the desert and into Tunisia.

By September 1942, a Joint Memorandum by the Lord Privy Seal, the First Lord of the Admiralty, the Secretary of State for War and the Secretary of State for Air noted that many of the manpower problems besetting the British Army were solved. It stressed that men who were 'definitely sub-normal mentally' and who were effectively 'unemployable' in civilian life were by this time fitted into jobs within their capacity and in some cases were sent to the new unarmed units of the Pioneer Corps, where they were 'happy, efficient, clean, and useful members of the Army'. The report stated that the most important method of preventing habitual offending and mental illness in the army was putting men in jobs that were not beyond their mental capacity. The memorandum stressed that the reduction in the number of cases of absence without leave in the army since 1941 was traceable to better personnel selection and the role played by psychiatry in the process. Overall, the report concluded that there could 'be no doubt that morale has gained as a result of the intro-duction of psychiatry' in the army.[69]

Reports from the desert also suggested that the problem, as it was per-ceived, was all but resolved by the end of the summer of 1942. By this time, there were some thirty psychiatrists in the Middle East.[70] Brigadier Rees regarded these men as 'the cream of the psychiatrists available at the time

---

[68] NA WO 199/1656 Notes on C-in-C's Conference, 14 May 1942.
[69] NA CAB 21/914 Extract from a Joint Memorandum by the Lord Privy Seal, the First Lord of the Admiralty, the Secretary of State for War and the Secretary of State for Air, 17 September 1942.
[70] Ibid.

when they were sent out'. Brigadier James, for instance, had received a Military Cross and bar in the First World War and was, in Craigie's view, 'an excellent man'.[71] In July, Craigie reported that 'the position' in the Middle East was 'improving' and that the 'indiscriminate posting overseas of backward or unstable men' had become 'less likely'.[72] Adam, on a tour to the Middle East in August 1942, expressly to ascertain the state of the fighting troops' morale, noted that 'so far as the "fighting troops" are concerned ... the reinforcements appeared to be satisfactory'.[73] Later he stated that the application of selection procedures to the 363,000 men inducted into the army in 1942 had provided the army with an intake 'predominantly of an age, medical category and type suitable for the fighting arms'.[74]

By the end of 1942, it was clear that not only had better selection procedures improved the quality of intakes into the army as a whole, but the introduction of intelligence tests, for those who had already joined the army, meant that many misplaced individuals were freed up for better service. Large numbers of men were downgraded from posts that were beyond their capacity. In January 1942, just under 6,000 men were downgraded. By the later months of 1942, over 10,000 men were being downgraded per month. During the same period, approximately 99,000 soldiers classified in high intelligence categories, including 600 category 'A' men from the Pioneer Corps and 1,950 from the Royal Army Pay Corps, were released for more active employment.[75]

Even more important than the selection of ordinary recruits, in the eyes of Adam and the War Office, was the quality of officers inducted into the British Army.[76] In September 1939, there were 53,500 officers in the British Army. By October 1941, this number had more than doubled to 136,500 officers. However, the army list had only comprised 13,800 regular officers in September 1939; the rest had been made up of Territorials and reserves, who all required a significant amount of further training. By October 1941, therefore, at most 10 per cent of serving

---

[71] NA CAB 21/914 Expert Committee on the Work of Psychologists and Psychiatrists in the Services, Note by Major H. B. Craigie of the Department of Army Psychiatry in the Middle East to Sir Stafford Cripps (Lord Privy Seal) on Psychiatric Cases in the Middle East, 21 July 1942.

[72] Ibid.

[73] LHCMA Adam 3/6/1 Report by the Adjutant-General on his Tour to the Middle East, India and West Africa, August 1942.

[74] LHCMA Adam 3/3 Notes on the S-of-S Estimates Speech, February 1943, AG's Department. As Adam suggested, these men would have started reaching the Middle East around August 1942.

[75] Ibid.

[76] NA WO 163/51 Retention and Review of Suitability of Officers, January 1942.

officers had been Regulars at the outbreak of war. As David French has argued, 'the vast majority of regimental officers during the Second World War had ... been civilians in 1939 and the wartime officer corps was composed overwhelmingly of amateur soldiers'.[77] This massive increase in both manpower and training requirements for the officer corps put a great strain on the capacity of the army to deliver the appropriate level of quality manpower and leadership.

This problem was exacerbated by the fact that modern weapons and conditions of battle threw an 'increasing responsibility on junior commanders'. Success in battle, according to the 1935 Field Service Regulations (FSR), ultimately depended 'largely on their efficiency'. Experience during the Second World War tended to confirm that this viewpoint was well founded. The average platoon typically included 'three or four heroes, three or four irreconcilables' and a remainder of men who responded 'in direct relationship to the quality of their leaders'.[78]

Leadership, in the words of the FSR, 'depended on simple and straight-forward human qualities' and 'above all' on the ability of the leader to gain the confidence of his men. To do this, the potential leader had to earn his men's respect.[79] He achieved this, according to the FSR, by showing determination and a ready acceptance of responsibility; by the clearness and simplicity of his orders and the firm way that he carried them out; by his thorough knowledge of his profession and by his sense of justice and common sense; by his keenness, energy and habit of forethought; by his sense of humour and his indifference to personal danger; by his readiness to share in his men's hardships; by his cheerfulness in the face of difficulties; and by the pride he took in his command.[80]

As well as possessing these basic martial qualities, the officer was expected to maintain the morale, discipline and welfare of his men. To fulfil these roles, officers were required to act as stern but benevolent 'parental figures'. This, according to a circular, 'Morale, Discipline and Mental Fitness', was 'the essential basis' of an officer's 'position, authority and functions'. Good officers were thus like good parents; 'they exercise a controlling (paternal) function' and at the same time a welfare or 'maternal function'.[81] This dual role required the highest standard of individuals and put a huge strain on officers unused to such responsibility in civilian life. To exacerbate the problem, many of the best officer

[77] French, *Raising Churchill's Army*, p. 73.
[78] NA WO 231/14 Notes by Col. T. N. Grazebrook, Lately Comd. in N. Africa, Sicily and Italy, 3 January 1944.
[79] War Office, *Field Service Regulations*, vol. II (1935), p. 2.   [80] Ibid., pp. 2–3.
[81] NA WO 222/218 Circular to All Medical Officers, n.d. but Second World War, 'Morale Discipline and Mental Fitness'.

candidates, just like many of the best ordinary recruits, were drawn into the RAF and RN. The War Office, as Sparrow wrote after the war, 'had to work on the material that came to its hand'.[82]

In early 1942, reports reached the War Office that officers in field units were struggling to cope with the dual 'paternal' and 'maternal' functions of maintaining the troops' discipline and welfare.[83] The morale report for February to May 1942 made clear that a number of junior officers in home formations were 'lacking in interest in their men and [were] ignorant of man-management'. This was having a bad effect on the welfare of the troops as well as destroying respect and confidence between officers and men. The report stated that the two characteristics that the troops objected to most in officers were 'selfishness and lack of efficiency'.[84]

The situation in the desert was similar. K. J. Bowden, of the Tower Hamlets Rifles, described how, in early 1941,

One of the Tower Hamlets officers had a deep belief in the comforts of life. He had a bell-tent, a tin bath and a carpet which went with him everywhere in the desert, and fresh water being short, his batman would very often fetch sea-water for his ablutions. They usually managed an officers' mess somehow. The German officers ate with their men, and were ready at all times when required to move off in five minutes flat. Can you imagine packing tent, bath and carpet into the 15-cwt lorry in the middle of a flap?[85]

Much later, Auchinleck's morale report for the period December 1941 to March 1942 highlighted the extent of 'criticism of officers in the letters of other ranks'. He recounted that 'occasionally the criticism is regarding [officer's] technical or training abilities, but more frequently it is regarding their selfishness'. The Regular Army tradition of thought and care for subordinates before self appeared, in Auchinleck's view, 'to be lacking in some regimental officers who, with a background of business life, are convinced that the application of "business methods" is all that is required for success and Victory'.[86] The morale report for January 1942 detailed incidences where officers who had carried out censorship of their men's mail in the desert discussed and joked about items they had censored, resulting in 'acute resentment and lowering of morale'.[87] The field censorship summary for 5 to 11 March 1942 admitted that it could not 'be denied that criticism of the ability and enterprise of officers both in the field and

[82] NA 20 277/16, Sparrow, 'Morale', p. 21.
[83] NA WO 163/51 Retention and Review of Suitability of Officers, January 1942.
[84] NA WO 163/51 Report of Morale Committee on the Summary of Divisional and District Reports at Home and Censorship Reports. February to May 1942.
[85] IWM 91/26/1 K. J. Bowden, *Four Years behind Barbed Wire*, p. 41.
[86] NA WO 163/51 Morale Report, December 1941 to April 1942.
[87] NA WO 193/456 Morale Report, January 1942.

at the base is increasing'. Other ranks' complaints centred specifically on officers demonstrating 'too much self-indulgence rather than on specific incompetence'.[88] The censorship summary for 8 to 14 July pointed out that 'many officers fail to inspire confidence in their men, who feel more and more that they should share the hardships of the men'.[89]

Conditions in the Union Defence Force (UDF) were no better. Towards the end of 1941, ministerial pressure forced the South African Chief of the General Staff to write to the General Officer in charge of Administration in the UDF complaining about the issue. Field Marshal Jan Smuts himself drafted a special routine order drawing the attention of all officers in the desert 'to the fact that complaints have been received with regard to high-handed and inconsiderate treatment' of other ranks at the hands of their officers. Smuts felt that discipline would be better maintained if officers could win the 'respect and esteem of the soldiers under their command' as current practices caused much 'dissatisfaction' and threatened to 'seriously impede the war effort'.[90]

A 1st South African Division memorandum on the 'Morale of SA troops in the Middle East', written in August 1942, highlighted that the problem of inefficient officers was a 'theme of endless discussion' amongst the men. The memorandum stated that it was generally felt that officers 'of proved incompetence should be demoted and replaced much more often than actually happens'. The report stressed that many men in the UDF felt that the army was 'too soft' in its treatment of incompetence, and that there had to be a practice of demotion of officers, whatever their rank, who had failed. It was equally believed that successful officers should be promoted. A frequent statement among the troops was that the 'Russians would have shot an officer for this or that.'[91]

Similar problems were evident in the Australian Imperial Force in 1941. A report submitted by 6th Australian Division, in July, pointed out that there was 'a general criticism throughout th[e] division that reinforcement officers arriving in the ME' were 'very poorly trained'. The report highlighted that, in many cases, the replacements were 'not of suitable type and in all cases their standard of technical training is low'. In addition to these criticisms, it was argued that these men lacked

---

[88] AWM 54 883/2/97 MEFCWS, no. XVII (5 to 11 March 1942), p. 4.
[89] ANZ WAII/1/DA508/1 vol. 1 MEFCWS, no. XXXV (8 to 14 July 1942), p. 5.
[90] SAMAD CGS (War), Box 151, Ross, for the Lt.-Gen. CGS) to GOA, UDF, ME Cairo, 12 November 1941; Union Defence Force, Special Routine Order issued by the Rt. Hon. Field Marshal Jan Christian Smuts, C-in-C, Union Defence Forces. It is not clear whether he ever released this RO.
[91] SAMAD, Div Docs, GP 1, Box 1, Memorandum on Morale of SA Troops in ME, 8 August 1942, p 6.

'experience in handling men'. As there were neither facilities nor time to train such officers once they arrived in the Middle East, it was suggested that in future lower numbers of officers should be drafted to the Middle East from Australia. Instead, the AIF should find the greater proportion of vacancies for commissions from units in the field. That way, potential officers would only be chosen after 'careful selection of personnel who have been tried in battle'. The report suggested that the restrictions that prevented large numbers of men from being promoted from the ranks should be lifted, as they were 'not in the best interest of unit esprit de corps'.[92]

By March 1942, the situation was arousing enough attention that P. J. Grigg, the Secretary of State for War, stated at a press conference that 'the question of suiting people to the job, of doing their best to get the right leadership, and to promote the right officers, is one which is being taken seriously by the military'. Grigg stressed that it was his belief that the quality of officers was 'about the most important single consideration affecting the morale of the Army' and 'the most important thing to get done'.[93] Such concerns were not new. Adam, since taking over the role of Adjutant-General, had adopted a two-sided approach to the problem. First, he concentrated on better officer selection procedures and second, he focused on educating potential officers in the essentials of man-management.[94]

Traditionally, officers were selected in the British Army by a small Command Interview Board in a ten- or fifteen-minute interview designed to test the personality of the officer candidate. By the summer of 1941, however, it was evident that this system was not working. Selection boards were turning down approximately 30 per cent of commanding officers' nominations[95] and as many as 20 to 50 per cent of candidates sent to Officer Corps Training Units (OCTUs) were failing the course.[96] By mid-1941, the Secretary of State for War was receiving as many as thirty parliamentary questions each week that were critical of the officer selection system.[97] It was clear that many men felt they were poorly treated by the single command interview,[98] and that the lack of transparency in the

---

[92] AWM 54 839/1/2 Liaison Officer Reports on Officer Reinforcements, Reinforcements Generally and Standard of Training of Other Ranks Arriving in the Middle East, July 1941. Notes for LO (Australia) – submitted by 6 Aust Div.

[93] NA WO 259/64 War Office, Press Conference, Wednesday 18 March 1942.

[94] NA W0 277/16 Sparrow, 'Morale', p. 22.

[95] NA WO 216/61 Training of Officers, Report of a Meeting Called by the Secretary of State for War, 29 January 1941.

[96] NA WO 163/89 Adjutant-General, The Officer Situation, 28 September 1942; Ahrenfeldt, *Psychiatry in the British Army in the Second World War*, p. 54.

[97] French, *Raising Churchill's Army*, p. 74.

[98] NA WO 32/11972 Memorandum on Army Psychiatry, 1942.

system was dissuading many potential candidates from putting their names forward for commissions. As a result, during 1941, OCTUs were frequently running below capacity because enough willing recruits could not be found.

Adam was aware that the Germans had a far more scientific method of selecting their officers. Since 1926, they had subjected their potential candidates to two days of rigorous personality and psychological testing along with more traditional selection procedures. Adam put the possibility of instituting a similar type of test for OCTU candidates to the Army Council in June 1941.[99] In the same month, at the suggestion of Rees, the Consulting Psychiatrist to the army, the Command Psychiatrist Scottish Command began investigations designed to test the value of psychological methods in the assessment of officer candidates. An effort was made to reproduce and try out the German Army methods of officer selection and the results of the study proved encouraging. As a consequence of these preliminary investigations, a conference was held in Edinburgh, in late 1941, at which the tests used were demonstrated to Adam, the Director of Selection of Personnel, and the army commander in Scotland. By 20 October 1941, Adam had convinced the War Office that 'an intelligence test supplemented by a commanding officer's report and a really well planned interview might produce a good result'.[100]

The new officer selection procedure was introduced in January 1942 in Scottish Command and the first batch of officer candidates were examined there in February.[101] The tests became widespread throughout all commands by March 1942 and later with overseas OCTUs,[102] such as the one that was set up in Cairo at the end of 1940.[103] Overall, seventeen new War Office Selection Boards (WOSBs) were set up in 1942.[104] New Officer Selection Units (NOSUs) were also established, with the advice of psychiatrists, to assist the presidents of WOSBs in selecting potential officers. The selection procedure itself was lengthened from a single interview to three days of rigorous psychological and military situation tests. Cutting-edge selection techniques, such as leaderless group tests, were introduced to observe men's capacity for maintaining personal

---

[99] NA WO 163/50 Army Council, War Office Progress Report, June 1941; Ahrenfeldt, *Psychiatry in the British Army in the Second World War*, p. 53.

[100] NA WO 163/123 Army no. 72. Allocation of Man-Power in the Army: Statement of the WO Views on the 22nd Report of the Select Committee on National Expenditure (Session 1940–1941). Memorandum by the WO, 20 October 1941.

[101] Ahrenfeldt, *Psychiatry in the British Army in the Second World War*, p. 57.

[102] Ibid., p. 58.   [103] Quilter, *No Dishonourable Name*, p. 113.

[104] LHCMA Adam 3/3 Notes for the S-of-S Estimates Speech, February 1943. AG's Department.

relationships in situations of strain that tempted them to disregard the interest of their fellows for the sake of their own.[105] At the end of the course, individuals underwent an interview of the traditional type to ascertain whether candidates' personalities fitted the British view of an officer.[106]

The reaction to the new selection procedures was extremely positive. Candidates at several WOSBs, who were surveyed in the summer of 1942, expressed unanimous enthusiasm about the new process.[107] Psychiatrists involved in the project noticed that new candidates felt they were getting a square deal from a more 'fair' procedure.[108] The upshot was that the supply of candidates to OCTUs rose by 65 per cent over the summer of 1942.[109] *Picture Post* declared that the new system was one of the most progressive initiatives of the war and that it would put an end of all talk of 'class favouritism'.[110]

The old system of the command interview had rejected at least one out of three of the best candidates appearing before selection boards.[111] The new system also rejected about one in three candidates. However, the better candidates did not get rejected to the same extent in the revised selection procedures.[112] An investigation, carried out at the end of the war on men selected for OCTUs by the two methods, showed that the standard of men who passed out of OCTUs selected under the WOSBs was higher than those selected under the old command interview system.[113] Jeremy Crang, in *The British Army and the People's War*, has argued that the increased number of candidates willing to put themselves before selection boards, combined with the more efficient selection techniques introduced in 1942, resulted 'in nearly two-and-a-half times as many above average candidates being sent to OCTUs during the period than would have been sent under the old system'.[114]

The second initiative that the War Office focused on in order to improve the quality of officers was education in the essentials of man-management. In the British Army, the welfare of the soldier had always

---

[105] Ahrenfeldt, *Psychiatry in the British Army in the Second World War*, pp. 60–1.
[106] NA WO 32/11972 Memorandum on Army Psychiatry, 1942.
[107] Ahrenfeldt, *Psychiatry in the British Army in the Second World War*, p. 66.
[108] NA WO 32/11972 Memorandum on Army Psychiatry, 1942.
[109] Jeremy A. Crang, *The British Army and the People's War, 1939–1945* (Manchester, 2000), p. 34.
[110] Ibid., p. 33.
[111] Ahrenfeldt, *Psychiatry in the British Army in the Second World War*, p. 66.
[112] LHCMA Adam 3/3 Notes for the S-of-S Estimates Speech, February 1943. AG's Department.
[113] Parliamentary Debate, 5th Serv., Lords, 155: 1064–6; 26 May 1948.
[114] Crang, *The British Army and the People's War*, p. 34.

been regarded as the responsibility of the regimental officer. This princi-ple was fundamental to the tradition of British military leadership and was inextricably linked with the issue of man-management and morale. Major-General H. Willans, who was appointed Director-General at the Directorate of Welfare in December 1940,[115] realised that the weight of responsibility on newly commissioned officers was overwhelming for many of the new citizen army.[116] 'The present war' was, in his opinion 'far more complicated' than wars in the past, including the Great War. The duties of the officer were more numerous, more varied and more difficult to master. Moreover, the ordinary recruit also had 'many more problems', some of which were 'beyond the reasonable scope of the Regimental Officer's knowledge and experience' – problems raised by the bombing of the soldier's home, the evacuation of his relations and those connected with his business and property.[117]

Willans summarised the significance of these issues in a speech that he gave at the beginning of 1942.

You will agree with me, or, at any rate you will not quarrel with me, for saying that leadership is the most important of all the sinews of war, and it is not too much to say that one instant of toil denied at this moment by any leader, great or small, senior or junior, may well make the difference between victory or defeat ... And I say, without fear of contradiction that no part of the leader's duty is more insistent or more unforgiving than that part which charges him to cater for the spiritual, moral, physical and mental well-being of the men who are under his command; to cater for them in such a way that it will bring out their best qualities, courage, resolution, and stiffen their fibre and their morale and will make them in due course better soldiers; so much better soldiers that they may be described as the 'Crusaders', as we hope they will be, of 1942, or 1943, or of the following years.[118]

Willans believed that the responsibilities of leadership in such times were 'crushing', the opportunities 'endless'. The officers and men of the British Army would 'not fail us' as long as their welfare was properly considered. The problem, as he saw it, was that such a situation was far from reality at the beginning of 1941.[119]

Throughout 1941, therefore, Willans oversaw the publication of a series of pamphlets on the subject of welfare in the army in an attempt to educate

---

[115] LHCMA Adam 3/13 Narrative Covering Aspects of Work as Adjutant-General, WWII, chap. 6, Welfare, pp. 1–3.

[116] For this reason he helped to introduce a centralised welfare system in the British Army to help regimental officers bear the load. This is dealt with in further detail in Chapter 5.

[117] LHCMA Adam 3/13 Narrative Covering Aspects of Work as Adjutant-General, WWII, chap. 6, Welfare, pp. 4–5.

[118] NA WO 277/4 Brig. M. C. Morgan, *Army Welfare* (War Office, 1953), p. 28.

[119] Ibid., p. 15.

officers in man-management. 'The Officer and Fighting Efficiency', for instance, told officers that 'in order to care for their men properly, they must first know and understand them'.[120] Another pamphlet, 'The Soldier's Welfare, Notes for Officers', released by order of the Army Council, also in 1941, clearly listed the two main aims of welfare work in the army as,

(1) To make the men as happy and contented as possible, in the varying circumstances of war, so that they would be at all times fighting fit and fit to fight.

(2) To link officers and men together in a bond of mutual friendliness and respect, which would not only stand the hardest tests of war, but would be strengthened by them. [121]

The pamphlet went on to list a number of principles the officer should adhere to in order to realise these two aims. Among them were the following:

The care of his men is an officer's first concern, which he puts before his own comfort and convenience.

Discontent seldom arises from hardship, provided that the men feel the hardship is reasonable, i.e. that it is a necessary part of the business of winning the war. They are ready to endure cheerfully anything which they believe to be unavoidable, but they are easily disgruntled if they feel that the hardships are caused by red tape or inefficiency or by lack of understanding, rather than by military necessity.

Every man is entitled to be treated as a reasonable human being, unless he has shown himself unworthy of such treatment. Whenever possible, therefore, the reason for irksome orders or restrictions should be explained to him ... Such action strengthens discipline and is not a sign of weakness.

Men are more easily upset by treatment that they believe to be unfair and by supposed inequality of sacrifice than by any other cause.[122]

The pamphlet concluded that the reward for officers would be not only 'happy and efficient men, but a loyalty and devotion from them out of all proportion to the services rendered'.[123]

Lectures to regimental officers on man-management, welfare and morale were also given on a large scale by consultant and specialist psychiatrists, and were a standard part of staff courses, OCTUs and battle schools throughout 1941 and 1942. Lectures focused on topics such as measures to maintain the mental health of the soldier; how to weed out unsuitable men before battle; the handling of incipient breakdowns

---

[120] Ibid.; NA WO 163/123 Army Pamphlet 'Welfare and Education', produced by the Director-General of Army Welfare and Education, Maj.-Gen. H. Willans, in March 1941, used the same language, p. 3.

[121] NA WO 163/123 The Soldier's Welfare, Notes for Officers, 1941.

[122] Ibid.   [123] Ibid.

during a campaign; the principles of group feeling (esprit de corps); the place of discipline in mental health; the foundations of morale; the morale effects of various enemy weapons; the proper place and use of battle inoculation; factors militating against individual and group morale; methods of upholding mental health under difficulties; and the function of leadership in the field of morale.[124]

These pamphlets and lectures represented a concerted drive by Willans and the War Office to educate officers in the art of leadership and man-management. They also demonstrate that, although the War Office was determined to be accountable for the welfare of its soldiers, ultimately responsibility rested on the shoulders of the regimental officer, just as it had done in the First World War.

Indeed, by the summer of 1942, there was evidence to suggest that these initiatives were having a positive affect on officer–men relations. The morale report dealing with home forces from May to July 1942 announced that 'Commanders' reports state the relationship between officers, N.C.Os. and men is generally good, and that the standard of junior leadership and man-management, though it leaves much to be desired, is improving. Favourable references to their officers outnumber the unfavourable references in the men's letters.'[125] The report also stated that a decrease in minor cases of absence had occurred and that 'several Commanders suggest that it is due to an improvement in officers' care for their men and an increase in the attention paid to the men's domestic difficulties'.[126] Much credit for this could be given to the OCTUs and lectures given at battle schools throughout the UK. By May 1942, 'training in these establishments' was 'concentrated on Leadership and not, as [be]fore, on training the cadet to be the perfect private soldier'.[127]

In the desert, however, in the midst of the summer crisis of 1942, there was still much adverse comment from officers and men on the quality of officer reinforcements from the UK. Officers from the Middle East, who had received their commissions from the Middle East OCTU, were generally preferred to inexperienced officers from home.[128] The Commander-in-Chief Home Forces, when referring to the death penalty debate in August 1942, reiterated that the solution to the problem of

[124] NA CAB 21/914 The Work of Army Psychiatrists in Relation to Morale, The War Office Directorate of Army Psychiatry, January 1944; NA CAB 21/914 The Work of Army Psychiatrists in Relation to Morale, app. C, Battle Inoculation, January 1944.
[125] NA WO 193/453 Morale Committee Papers, Draft Morale Report, May to July 1942.
[126] Ibid.
[127] NA WO 199/1656 Extracts from Minutes of the Commander-in-Chief's Conference Held at GHQ, 14 May 1942.
[128] NA WO 193/453 Morale Committee Papers, Draft Morale Report, May to July 1942.

surrender in the desert lay principally 'in the training of a corps of officers, whose efficiency, example and instinctive interest in their work and the troops would compel the respect of the men'.[129] He acknowledged that OCTU training had greatly improved and that this would be an important factor in the future performance of Eighth Army.[130]

It can certainly be argued that the many manpower initiatives carried out during 1941 and 1942, relating to both men and officers, were not just a matter for the 'future' (which they clearly were), but also that they had a real impact even as early as El Alamein. The replacements that poured into the Middle East to make up war establishments after the heavy casualties of May, June and July 1942 would have benefited from such initiatives in both the UK and the Middle East.

From 1 August to 23 October 1942, Eighth Army received approximately 60,000 reinforcements, including units such as the 51st Highland Division.[131] The Highland Division, which was reformed after its destruction in France in 1940, benefited from better personnel selection and officer training in the United Kingdom. It spent six weeks attending battle schools at Aldershot in April and May 1942 where medical officers 'did their bit by purging units of the unfit', and officers attended classes on welfare and man-management.[132] Douglas Wimberley, the commander of 51st Highland Division, believed that its quality 'owed not a little to [the] Divisional Battle School'.[133] Certainly, the Highland Division outperformed other new divisions that had fought in the desert before it. Both the 2nd and 1st Armoured Divisions had been routed in their first contact with the enemy in the spring of 1941 and 1942, while the 50th Division had suffered heavy casualties for little gain in its engagements in the summer of 1942.

The weeding out of unsuitable material from units already in the Middle East also played a crucial role in removing 'misfits' and problem makers from Eighth Army. As Brigadier Rees said in 1943, such practices 'produced a revolutionary change in the Army's utilization of

---

[129] NA WO 32/15773 The Army Council, Minutes of the Fourteenth Meeting, 11 August 1942. Army Morale: The Death Penalty in Relation to Offences Committed on Active Service, p. 4.

[130] Ibid., p. 5.

[131] IWM BLM 62 Notes on the Maintenance of the Eighth Army and the Supporting Royal Air Force by Land, Sea and Air from El Alamein to Tunisia. Compiled by Q Staff, GHQ Cairo, 1942, p. 2.

[132] J. B. Salmond, *The History of the 51st Highland Division 1939–1945* (Durham, 1994), p. 25. First published in Edinburgh in 1953.

[133] IWM 430 PP/MCR/182 Maj.-Gen. D. Wimberley, 'Scottish Soldier: An Autobiography', vol. II, part 4, 'World War II', p. 26.

Illustration 7 Troops charging with fixed bayonets on an assault course at the 51st Highland Division battle school in the UK, May 1942. Battle schools such as these played an important role in training officers how to lead and manage their men in stressful battle scenarios.

manpower'.[134] Adam later wrote that 'if we had had selection procedures earlier, we would have prevented a number of men unsuitable for battle being sent to fighting units'. This would have, in his opinion, drastically reduced the number of desertions from the front line.[135] The introduction of selection testing also reassured the army and the public that something was being done to end the uneconomical use of manpower in the army. Selection testing, therefore, dissipated uneasiness and restored confidence in the running of the war.[136]

It is safe to say, based on the evidence already adduced in this chapter, that the quality of ordinary recruits improved between the battles of mid-1942

---

[134] Ahrenfeldt, *Psychiatry in the British Army in the Second World War*, p. 50.

[135] LHCMA Adam 3/13 Narrative Covering Aspects of Work as Adjutant-General WWII, chap. 5, Morale and Discipline.

[136] NA CAB 21/914 'The Work of Army Psychiatrists in Relation to Morale', The War Office Directorate of Army Psychiatry, January 1944.

and El Alamein. The situation regarding the quality of officers in the desert is not so clear-cut however. Improved officer selection techniques were not introduced throughout the UK until March 1942. It took, according to Sparrow, on average three months to train an officer and four months to train an infantry officer during the Second World War. If the time it took to ship officers out to the Middle East is taken account of, it is unlikely that the new selection and man-management measures could have made a significant difference by the time of El Alamein.

However, the censorship summary for 5 to 11 August 1942 indicated that the new initiatives had already begun to have a positive impact. It stated that officers who passed out of the Middle East OCTU were of a far higher quality than those who had gone before them. These officers, the summary reported, were granted their commissions on 'merit and experience after what must be one of the most exacting courses existing'.[137] At the same time, a sapper wrote,

We have new officers and we hardly know what has happened to us. We feel imbued with new courage because these new officers consider us as the old ones never did. We are not accustomed to officers having much interest taken in our welfare and it almost makes one feel as if you have just started so pleasant is the atmosphere. While the old officers always ignored us or tried to get rid of us with the least trouble, these new officers are doing all they can for us. They have to travel over more than a 100 miles of desert to bring our post to us, but they do it whereas the others would not have bothered about it. Yes, I thank God that the old crowd have gone, and I hope I never see them again. It was just the treatment meted out to us by our former officers that upset me, hard work and hardship never affected me or made me despondent.[138]

The censorship summary for 3 to 9 September reported that mail from 'training units and Base Depots' offered 'many interesting comments on Senior and Junior Officers. The majority of these were favourable and gave the impression that officers who inspire their men by their ability and courage by far outnumber those who do not. For some time past much adverse criticism was registered and it is therefore a pleasant feature to see this change of tone.'[139] The censorship summary a week later commented that 'one of the happiest features of the mail was the confidence expressed by other ranks in their officers [and] unit commanders'.[140] The summary for 23 to 29 September remarked that 'there is much pleasing evidence to show that officers, senior and junior, are putting their best into their work, a

[137] ANZ WAII/1/DA508/1 vol. 1, MEMCWS, no. XXXIX (5 to 11 August 1942), p. 7.
[138] Ibid., pp. 18–19.
[139] ANZ WAII/1/DA508/1 vol. 3, MEMCWS, no. XLIII (3 to 9 September 1942), p. 7.
[140] ANZ WAII/1/DA508/1 vol. 3, MEMCWS, no. XLIV (10 to 16 September 1942), p. 2.

fact which never fails to be appreciated by the men'. The censor believed that 'a good deal of [the] friendliness and understanding between officers and men is due to a keener appreciation [by officers] of the importance of man-management'.[141]

It is likely that this improvement was derived primarily from better officer selection and education in man-management in OCTUs in the Middle East. In addition, some units may have initiated the new selection and training procedures at an earlier date in the United Kingdom, as is instanced by the case of the 51st Highland Division. Some form of better officer selection and training, for example, had taken place in Scotland since June 1941.[142]

Furthermore, Montgomery's style of command played a role in high-lighting the importance of man-management. Montgomery understood the vital role that junior officers had to play in battle and how important they would be in rebuilding and maintaining the morale of Eighth Army. In his first training memorandum, issued on 30 August 1942, he highlighted their critical role in combat. 'Once battle is joined', he said, 'the issue passes to the junior commander and his sub-unit ... Success depends on a high standard of initiative and skill on the part of the[se] junior leaders, and on the tactical efficiency of units and sub-units.' It was essential, in his view, that 'the standard of junior leadership, sub-unit efficiency, and individual efficiency' be 'very high'. If it was not, then Eighth Army would 'fail', however good the higher leadership.[143] Montgomery set an uncompromising example by making a clean sweep of the commanders whom he considered unsuitable for the battle ahead. His purge applied to the highest echelons of Eighth Army (as high as corps commanders) as well as the lower levels of brigadiers and colonels.[144] All units engaged in training in the Middle East for the critical battle of El Alamein also attended battle schools, under Montgomery's instruction, where lectures on welfare and man-management were likely to have been given.

Montgomery issued another memorandum, in August 1942, on the subject of 'Commanders speaking to their men', with the aim of improving officer–man relations. He professed to being 'seriously alarmed at the idea', which seemed prevalent at the time in Eighth Army, 'that units or sub units in the Army area cannot be assembled in a compact body to be addressed

---

[141] ANZ WAII/1/DA508/1 vol. 3, MEMCWS, no. XLIII (23 to 29 September 1942), p. 2.

[142] NA WO 163/123 Army no. 72. Allocation of Man-Power in the Army: Statement of the WO Views on the 22nd Report of the Select Committee on National Expenditure (Session 1940–1941). Memorandum by the WO 20 October 1941.

[143] IWM 99/1/2 Briggs, Eighth Army Training Memorandum no. 1 by B. L. Montgomery, 30 August 1942.

[144] Barr, *Pendulum of War*, pp. 256–7.

by their own C.O. or by their Coy, Sqn, Bty etc Commander' (presumably due to the threat of enemy shelling or air attack). He stated that 'a unit has got to be welded into a fighting machine, with the highest possible morale. The men have got to be given inspiration, and be imbued with infectious optimism and offensive eagerness.' Montgomery believed that 'in a unit the men draw their inspiration from the officers' and therefore the unit 'must be assembled regularly and the men addressed personally by their officers'. The great danger, he believed, was that 'Officers should think they cannot ever assemble their men and speak to them personally; ... officers who have this mentality are a menace.' Montgomery wished to tackle the matter at once, noting that 'if there are any orders in existence which forbid the assembly of personnel in forward areas, they will be considered as cancelled'.[145] Officers, therefore, in the run-up to the battle of El Alamein, were clearly ordered to focus on man-management and morale.

Throughout the three years of war leading up to the summer of 1942, the British Army gradually rediscovered how to create a battle-worthy citizen army. It did this by learning from the Germans and using the 'new' sciences of psychiatry and psychology. Adam proved himself to be at the forefront of innovative methods of personnel selection and, following the war, he became the Chairman of the National Institute of Industrial Psychology.[146] His initiatives paved the way for the decidedly different style of warfare practised by the British Army in the second half of the war, a style that revolved around the 'human factor'. The gradual improvement in British weapons and material towards the second half of 1942 was combined with more enlightened and forward-thinking policies about the manpower available to the army. As Hew Strachan has argued, 'the origins' of the victory at El Alamein were found as much 'in the personnel policies of the Adjutant General, Sir Ronald Adam' as in any other factor.[147]

---

[145] NA WO 32/10810 Army Commander's Personal Memorandum, 20 August 1942.
[146] Ahrenfeldt, *Psychiatry in the British Army in the Second World War*, p. 66.
[147] Hew Strachan, *Military Lives: Intimate Biographies of the Famous by the Famous* (Oxford, 2002), p. vii.

4   Environment, provisions and morale

Where men are living and fighting in trying conditions, whether of terrain, climate or other circumstances, small grievances assume undue proportions, particularly when it may reasonably be thought that they could be removed. Even though a straw does not break a camel's back, it may profoundly irritate the animal, particularly if it thinks that its master cannot be bothered to remove it ... therefore ... action is called for on the lesser matters as urgently as it is on those of major importance.

(Inter-Service Committee Report on Morale, 1944–1945)[1]

As each type of terrain approaches its extreme it ... tends to emphasize the personal resources of the ranks, down to the private soldier.

(Carl von Clausewitz, *On War*)[2]

The Second World War 'was a truly global conflict'. Soldiers fought in climates and terrains as diverse and 'alien' as the jungles of Burma, the Russian steppe and the deserts of North Africa. One of the consequences of waging war in such inhospitable environments was that soldiers had to develop ways of living and fighting in the most trying of circumstances.[3]

Literature on the North African campaign has generally acknowledged the difficulties of waging war in a desert many thousands of miles from the British, Commonwealth and Dominion homelands.[4] The desert was a hostile environment that required armies to adapt to a tempo, style and character of warfare all of its own. Correlli Barnett referred to the desert war as 'unique in history'. Keith Douglas described it as an 'extraordinary war' that was fought in a territory 'neutral' to both sides, and 'being barren, a landscape almost neutral to man'.[5] The desert had virtually no roads, but, as the whole area was mostly 'good going', movement 'was almost as free as that of a fleet' on the high seas. There were, apart from a

[1] NA WO 32/11194 Morale: General (Code 105(A)): Inter-Service Committee Report on Morale, 1944 to 1945, p. 5.
[2] Clausewitz, *On War*, p. 418.   [3] Ellis, *The Sharp End*, p. 22.
[4] See, for example, Alan Moorehead, *The Desert War* (London, 1984), p. 10; Barnett, *The Desert Generals*, p. 23; Bungay, *Alamein*, p. 46; Latimer, *Alamein*, p. 6.
[5] Keith Douglas, *Alamein to Zem Zem* (London, 1992), p. xiii. Douglas fought with the Nottingham (Sherwood Rangers) Yeomanry.

few inhabited places along the coast, neither towns nor villages to provide shelter or obstacles to armies. There were hardly any civilians to get in the way of the battle. The desert campaign was therefore, in Barnett's words, 'war in its purest form'.[6]

Living and fighting in the desert pushed soldiers to the limits of human endurance. An Italian soldier wrote in 1940 that Italy had 'committed the wildest folly in coming into this appalling desert. The flies plague us in millions from the first hour of the morning. The sand seems always to be in our mouths, in our hair and our clothes, and it is impossible to get cool. Only troops of the highest morale and courage would endure privations like these.'[7] The experience of living and fighting in the desert also featured heavily in the letters and memoirs of the soldiers who fought with the Western Desert Force and Eighth Army. Many of the greatest hardships that the men recounted resulted not only from the actions of the German and Italian forces that they faced but also from the conditions imposed by living in a wilderness. Thus, the impact that the environment had on how the men perceived their struggle against the Axis forces played a part in determining their morale. The ability, or inability, of Eighth Army to mitigate these hardships and allay the men's concerns was of significance in both causing the morale crisis of the summer of 1942 and in fixing it, with all that this implied for the army's combat performance.

Surviving in a desert with little cover was an extraordinary challenge for men unused to such an environment.[8] During the summer months, which lasted roughly from May to October, daily temperatures ranged from 20 °C to 60 °C in the shade, the highest temperatures being reached in the late afternoon. As a result, very little action tended to take place between 12 and 4 p.m., as effort expended during these hottest hours caused men to sweat and consequently become dehydrated. Even during the winter months, daily temperatures reached over 20 °C with a rapid drop in temperature once the sun set.[9] Colder weather in November usually required men to don winter clothing. This caught out British divisions such as the 51st Highland Division which, in 1942, was forced to request an issue of woollen drawers as it had 'under-estimated the coldness of the North African climate'.[10]

[6] Barnett, *The Desert Generals*, p. 23.   [7] Moorehead, *African Trilogy*, p. 65.
[8] IWM 04/15/1 H. Lee, Diary entry 16 April 1942; IWM 96/50/1 R. L. Crimp, p. 121. Diary Entry for 19 April 1942; IWM DS/Misc/63 G. F. Morrison, Lieut., Letter to his Mother, 13 August 1942.
[9] Bungay, *Alamein*, pp. 69–70.
[10] NA WO 177/324 Monthly Report of Assistant Director of Hygiene, Eighth Army, November 1942. Compiled 26 December 1942.

The desert 'was not inviting'. It was 'a trackless waste, with rocky escarpments enclosing valleys part-filled with drift sand'.[11] It was like scrubland, all dried up, badly needing rain. Small stunted bushes and rocks and stones were scattered across its surface.[12] There were yellow rolling sand dunes, such as can be found in the Sahara, in areas like the Nile Valley, the coastal plain bordering the Mediterranean and the vast sand seas to the south. However, the greater part of the area of battle was a plateau standing on average some 500 feet above sea level, with a light covering of sand, and as barren as its name implied. For young and inexperienced men from England's 'green and pleasant land' it was frightening to contemplate.[13]

The desert war was, for the most part, a mechanised war. Even infantry units comprised 'armadas' of vehicles, and formations left without transport could be easy prey to mobile units in a theatre ideal for manoeuvre warfare. To take a British motorised infantry unit as an example, each section had its own truck, making four to a platoon, including one for platoon headquarters. There were three infantry platoons to a company, and one scout platoon, which normally comprised a dozen Bren-gun carriers. Allowing four vehicles to company HQ and half a dozen more to the echelon, there were more than thirty vehicles per company. So with four of these 'fighting' companies, plus a far more numerous HQ company as well, a whole battalion could have as many as 150 vehicles.[14]

While the going was 'generally good for both wheeled and tracked vehicles on the plateau, there were many traps for the inexperienced and unwary'. According to Barrie Pitt, in *The Crucible of War*, the burning sun overhead made it difficult to see sudden hollows down which vehicles could drop at the cost of broken springs. Sharp rocks could rip tyres and boulders could buckle a wheel or crack a sump. Tracked vehicles strained their springs and ruined their tracks on the rough terrain. Wheeled vehicles were prone to sinking in deep and soft sand in which the wheels quickly became embedded to the axles. This often necessitated hours of 'unsticking' with spades and sandmats, and unloading and reloading heavy stores.[15]

Navigation was made difficult by the lack of readily identifiable landmarks. The infinite vastness and emptiness of the landscape 'fostered a dangerous illusion of freedom' that could easily lead units to get 'lost for ever'.[16] Each unit, therefore, had its own 'expert navigator whose task it

[11] IWM 87/44/1 K. W. Morris, 'Another Man's Meat: An Affectionate Tribute to All Ranks of the HQ Squadron, 4th Armoured Brigade 1942–1946', p. 32.
[12] IWM 91/26/1 K. J. Bowden, 'Four Years behind Barbed Wire', p. 31.
[13] IWM 93/19/1 W. R. Garrett, 'A Private Viewing', p. 4.
[14] IWM 96/50/1 R. L. Crimp, Diary, 14 September 1941, p. 39–40.
[15] Pitt, *Wavell's Command*, p. 14.
[16] IWM 93/19/1 W. R. Garrett, 'A Private Viewing', p. 4.

was to ensure that he could give a map reference of his position whenever asked'. On any particular journey, a course was plotted by using a compass and the distance travelled was measured by keeping an eye on the speedometer and a clock. At the end of a fifty-mile trip it was not considered poor form if units finished two miles from their intended destination.[17]

A typical day for the soldier, when moving and fighting in the desert, began with stand to before dawn, at approximately 0500 hours.[18] Stand to was described as 'a definite low'. Soldiers 'stood about, rifles in hand ... mouths corroded with the fur of sleep and shivering, with that empty stomached feeling that can only be felt and not described'. When the all clear was sounded the men would stand down and head straight to breakfast and a brew up.[19]

Once officers had been issued with their orders, the signal was given and units prepared to move out. Vehicles whose engines failed to start would be left to the fitters to look after.[20] This could be extremely dangerous during a retreat. As the convoy pulled out it would move at little more than walking pace until the leaders were satisfied that all vehicles had taken up sufficiently well dispersed stations (in case of air attack) and that everyone was on the move. Then, as the speed increased, the vehicles would 'develop a great, grey plume of dust which could be seen for miles'. This cloud of dust made travelling in the back of trucks almost unbearable.

[The trucks] seemed to set up a vacuum as the vehicles went along and sucked in the choking dust. We were all covered in the stuff but the unfortunates in these vehicles were practically suffocated. We used the gas goggles out of our gas masks to protect our eyes but, as it grew hotter, sweat irritated where the sharp edged celluloid cut into our cheekbones. There was nothing anyone could do about it, just suffer.[21]

Units could travel a hundred miles in a day or alternatively be driven mad by constant delays.[22] Sometimes, travelling 30 or 40 miles across the desert in a day was good going and the equivalent physical effort of about 120 miles on better going.[23] The hard work and discomfort was compounded by the fact that the men would rarely eat at midday during

[17] George Forty (ed.), *Leakey's Luck: A Tank Commander with Nine Lives* (Stroud, 2002), p. 16.
[18] Hugh Lock, *War Was a Cross to Bear* (Self-published, 1998), p. 15.
[19] IWM 85/35/1 L. E. Tutt, 'Gentleman Soldier', pp. 171–2.
[20] NA WO 202/33 Spears Mission, Western Desert, Notes on Desert Warfare, December 1941 to March 1942.
[21] IWM 85/35/1 L. E. Tutt, 'Gentleman Soldier', p. 95.
[22] Ibid.   [23] Jack Swaab, *Field of Fire: Diary of a Gunner Officer* (Stroud, 2005), p. 20.

the summer (they would still stop for a brew-up) because flies and heat made any such attempt extremely unpleasant. This meant waiting until the end of the day for a decent meal. At day's end the men would halt and stretch while still dispersed and brew up and prepare a meal. When darkness came, the vehicles would come together to laager for the night, make repairs and refuel.[24]

Soft-skinned vehicles such as petrol and ammunition lorries were usually placed in the centre of the laager, surrounded by artillery, Bren-carriers, anti-tank guns and tanks on the outside – 'just like the old covered wagon days'. Units 'adopted this formation every night' and drivers 'used to be able to drive into it in pitch darkness and half asleep'.[25] If there were infantry units available, listening posts would be set up around the exterior for protection. Armoured personnel usually had to perform a couple of hours of maintenance and repairs on their vehicles before sleep. This could often reduce their rest to no more than three or four hours a night, with potentially catastrophic effects on morale and combat performance. During battle few of the men would get any sleep at all.[26]

The brief periods of static warfare in the desert, around Tobruk, Knightsbridge and El Alamein, involved more digging and boredom than life on the move.[27] These monotonous days could prove 'demoralising' as one soldier recounted.

Picks and shovels were our only tools and were soon blunted on the unyielding rock. We welcomed the nights and a respite from the torment and toil and sweat. We welcomed the sunrise for its relief from the night's chill.[28]

The empty days of static warfare could melt into one indefinable consciousness. Len Tutt, of the 104th Regiment (Essex Yeomanry) Royal Horse Artillery, recalled a conversation with his mate while holed up in Tobruk.

> 'Is it Monday or Tuesday today Dump?'
> 'I thought it was Thursday,' I answered, 'but I'll look in the log in the Command Post.'
> When I returned I said,
> 'We're well out. It's Saturday.'
> 'Yes. But Saturday of this week or last?'[29]

[24] IWM 85/35/1 L. E. Tutt, 'Gentleman Soldier', p. 95.
[25] Forty (ed.), *Tanks across the Desert*, p. 32.   [26] Ibid., p. 37.
[27] IWM 02/19/1 C. H. Butt, Letter to His Dad, 22 November 1942; IWM 84/13/1 J. E. Brooks, Letter to Bill (His Brother) Describing His Experiences in the War so Far, 12 February 1943, p. 19.
[28] IWM 93/19/1 W. R. Garrett, 'A Private Viewing', p. 7.
[29] IWM 85/35/1 L. E. Tutt, 'Gentleman Soldier', p. 168.

Living in the desert, like living in any theatre of war, required the soldier to survive in the open without permanent shelters for protection. This made men particularly vulnerable to the elements, especially sand, wind and sun.

The omnipresent sand spread lightly over the surface of the rocky plateau was a constant feature of life in the desert. 'Sand found its way into everything, medical instruments, bandages, food, clothing, vehicles, guns, eyes, ears, noses and behinds' when men were 'obliged to go to the latrines'.[30] Rifleman K. L. Philips, of the 1st Battalion the Rifle Brigade, commented in February 1942 that 'in spite of all the sand that we've swallowed in the last few months there still seems to be as much lying about as ever . . . we are in our usual state of eating, smoking and drinking sand – as well as being smothered in it from head to foot'.[31] All the guns and rifles had 'to be cleaned two or three times every day' or they wouldn't fire.[32]

In addition to these basic hardships, the discomfort of sand increased dramatically when combined with the presence of wind. A strong and persistent wind usually blew in the desert and local gossip often revolved around 'when this — wind will leave off'.[33] The wind tended to blow from the northwest or the southeast. The northerly wind was cold and the prevailing southerly one was hot 'like the draught from an oven',[34] or 'the hot blast on a Tube Station'.[35] This meant that in the morning the soldiers were 'slowly roasted' and in the evening, when the wind had died down, they often needed to wear 'pullovers and greatcoats'.[36]

Every day, when the sun had dried out the surface of the desert, a superfine dust was whipped up by the wind. 'Six days out of seven this was of no real moment, for the streams kept close to the ground and did not affect the senses.' However, when a really strong wind blew, signalling the arrival of a sandstorm, 'there was nothing else to do but don eye shields and get to earth'. This wind was usually the Khamseen, a hot wind that blew from the south at 60–80 mph at temperatures of up to 50 °C.[37]

A soldier recalled that

When it comes [the Khamseen] all work has to cease. Everything is suspended until it blows itself out. Friend and foe alike retire to any shelter they can find and bury their heads in anything likely to stop the dust. If you succeed too well you are

[30] IWM 87/12/1 J. H. Witte, *The One That Didn't Get Away*, p. 84.
[31] IWM (Not yet referenced in IWM) K. L. Philips, Letter to Parents, 2 February 1942.
[32] IWM DS/Misc/63 G. F. Morrison, Lieutenant, Letter to his Mother, 6 September 1942.
[33] IWM (not yet referenced in IWM) K. L. Philips, Letter to Parents, 11 January 1942.
[34] IWM 80/37/1 E. W. Cope, Letter to Dad, 19 April 1942.
[35] IWM (not yet referenced in IWM) K. L. Philips, Letter to Parents, 29 March 1942.
[36] IWM 80/37/1 E. W. Cope, Letter to Dad, 19 April 1942.
[37] IWM 98/35/1 A. S. Harris, Letter to David, 13 August 1942; IWM 87/44/1 K. W. Morris, 'Another Man's Meat', p. 48.

Illustration 8 A soldier watches an approaching sandstorm from beside his jeep, October 1942. The desert environment had a major impact on the morale of the troops of Eighth Army.

likely to die of suffocation, if you settle for more air you breathe in great lungfuls of the fine abrasive dust.[38]

Another soldier described how 'our hair turned yellowish-white, our eyes smarted, our throats were dry and tingling, our faces took on a queer bronzy hue; it coated clothes, kit, tables, papers'.[39] When the Khamseen blew, soldiers had to 'subsist on a few dry, gritty biscuits and gulps of tepid water from . . . water bottles', as there was no chance that the cooks could prepare food.[40] A bit of paper with writing on it would be covered in a 'brown coat with the writing completely obscured' within ten minutes.[41] As far as Len

---

[38] IWM 85/35/1 L. E. Tutt, 'Gentleman Soldier', pp. 73–4.
[39] IWM 02/19/1 H. W. F. Charles, Letter to Parents, 15 December 1941, p. 38.
[40] IWM 85/35/1 L. E. Tutt, 'Gentleman Soldier', pp. 73–4.
[41] IWM 02/19/1 H. W. F. Charles, Letter to Parents, 15 December 1941, p. 38; IWM (not yet referenced in IWM) K. L. Philips, Letter to Parents, 29 March 1942.

Tutt was concerned the Khamseen was the final arbiter in the war; 'plan as the Generals might, that awful wind brought everything to a halt'.[42]

There was much folklore surrounding the Khamseen among old desert hands. They were said to always blow for an odd number of days, one, three, five or seven, although they generally did not last longer than three days.[43] It was not uncommon to have a sandstorm once or twice in a week. At other times they might not blow for two weeks.[44] The Khamseen, when it eventually blew itself out, died in the late evening or during the night. For the men 'it was a relief to wake up to find clear, cool air'. The temperature always dropped for a short while when the Khamseen ended. Then there would be a great shaking out of kit and equipment to get rid of its coating of dust and sand.[45]

The desert supplied little but the arena of battle and presented both armies with the unalterable fact that just about everything needed for existence had to be carried with them to the front.[46] The most important of these supplies was water. In an effort to address the critical importance of water, General Wavell requested, in mid-1941, that a pipeline be built from Daba to Sidi Barrani to improve supply in the battle area. Later that year the Eighth Army Water Plan, of 29 October 1941, reminded formations that they should include water reconnaissance as one of the first duties of their Royal Engineers Detachments and that any substantial quantities of potable water located should 'at once be taken under control and reported to H.Q. Army'.[47] Indeed, great improvements in the supply of water were made prior to the Crusader offensive of November/December 1941. In fifty-six days, between September and December, 145 miles of mixed 8 in., 6 in. and 4 in. pipe, together with seven new pumping stations and ten large reservoirs, were laid down in the desert ready to deliver water to the front-line troops.[48] Previously, all water for troops on the escarpment had to be brought from Matruh by water lorry. On the last two days before Crusader, 600 tons of water from the pipeline were issued daily to units on the escarpment and it could be relied on for 400 tons on normal days.[49]

[42] Ibid.   [43] IWM 85/35/1 L. E. Tutt, 'Gentleman Soldier', pp. 73–4.
[44] IWM 04/15/1 H. Lee, Diary 1942; IWM 84/13/1 J. E. Brooks, Diary 1941.
[45] IWM 85/35/1 L. E. Tutt, 'Gentleman Soldier', pp. 73–4.
[46] Pitt, *Wavell's Command*, p. 14.
[47] NA WO 201/666 Water Supply Western Desert, October 1941 to April 1942.
[48] NA WO 227/22 Middle East Diary of Western Desert Pipe Line Work September to December 1941. Over 3,000 tons of water was needed to fill these new pipelines and reservoirs west of Matruh before delivery could begin. This large quantity was brought by water ship to Matruh and the actual filling of the line took more than four weeks of pumping.
[49] Ibid.

These great improvements, although an organisational and administrative triumph, did not radically affect the supplies available to the men on the front line. They still received about the same amount of water, only it took the supply echelons one convoy instead of six to meet their daily needs.[50] In any event, by the second half of 1942, Eighth Army had retreated well to the east of Daba and Sidi Barrani and the pipeline became irrelevant. When units of the 51st Highland Division arrived in the desert in August 1942, their water ration was two gallons a day, the same as for their predecessors in 1940 and 1941. Alastair Borthwick, in *Battalion*, reported troops of the 5th Seaforths as saying 'it was impossible to do anything with two gallons'. Nevertheless, the Seaforths, just like those who fought before them, in time became happy to survive on two pints a day when fighting in the open desert after El Alamein.[51]

The exigencies of manoeuvre warfare exacerbated the logistical difficulties of supplying water to formations in battle. The much-used hook south into the vast open spaces of the plateau meant units often left supply columns and the main coast road far behind. Borthwick wrote that the men 'learned to tolerate the heat, to save our shaving water for the washing of socks, and to drink in the morning and in the evening – the only times, we discovered, when the drink was not sweated out in minutes, leaving us thirstier than before'.[52]

Lieutenant-Colonel R. J. Awdry, commander of the 32nd Field Regiment, RA, described the kind of conundrum faced by the men daily; 'shall we put the showering water in the tea, or shave in the tea!!' Nevertheless, he assured his wife that a soldier could live on such meagre rations. The trick was to first fill your water bottle, then shave in an egg cup of water, and save the rest to cover a sponge to wash 'in three stages!!' Anyway, he finished wryly, 'the sand here is fairly clean'.[53] To save water, men would avoid washing bodies and clothes.[54] Shaving became a luxury and men might go weeks without putting a blade to their faces.[55] In the end, petrol, infinitely more abundant than water, was used extensively to wash clothes and equipment, and to carry out many of the menial chores for which water would normally be used.[56]

The fact of the matter was that for the most part the men were constantly thirsty. The censorship summary for 7 to 13 January 1942 made it clear that 'the shortage of water' was one of the two 'main complaints to

---

[50] Ibid.   [51] Alastair Borthwick, *Battalion* (London, 1994), p. 19.   [52] Ibid., p. 22.
[53] IWM Lieut.-Col. R. J. Awdry, Letter to His Wife, 22 July 1942.
[54] IWM 93/19/1 W. R. Garrett, 'A Private Viewing', p. 7.
[55] IWM 87/42/1 Len Waller, *When Bugles Call*, p. 36.
[56] IWM 96/50/1 R. L. Crimp, Diary, 9 November 1941, p. 54.

be found in letters' from the forward areas. The problem, it said, 'was mentioned in 80 per cent of the correspondence examined; the ration is considered inadequate and the taste unpleasant'.[57] In March the censors reported that 'the main complaint' from troops was in 'regard to the shortage of water and its salty taste'.[58]

Matters had not improved by the end of April. The censors pointed out that the 'shortage of water' was still a 'major problem and with the recent "khamseens" and sandstorms, creating as they do greater thirst, this question is ... a regular feature of letters'.[59] R. L. Crimp, a rifleman with the 2nd Battalion, the Rifle Brigade, noted, in his diary for 18 April 1942, what many men must have been thinking.

Very hot [today]. What makes it worse the water situation is bad, barely a gallon a day per man. So we're always thirsty. How marvellous it would be to drink glass after glass of clear, cold water, filling oneself right up – just as one used to take for granted at home![60]

By the start of June, as Rommel's summer offensive gathered momentum, the situation began to improve. The censors noted that 'only units exceptionally situated appeared to be suffering from an "acute" water shortage, as distinct from the "general" shortage which is causing discomfort rather than actual hardship'.[61] By July, with Eighth Army having retreated to the El Alamein line, there were 'no complaints regarding the water issue'.[62] Indeed, the New Zealand censors were able to report, by August 1942, that 'the increased water supply' was 'doing much to alleviate the discomfort' of the troops in the front line.[63] The summary for 5 to 11 August, just before Montgomery assumed command in the desert, pointed out that 'not a single complaint of lack of water was made'.[64] By the end of August, the censors were happily able to testify that 'in the front line a very considerable number of writers referred to ... water, and all agree that ... water [is] more plentiful than ever before'. This was due, in the censor's opinion, to the proximity of Alexandria and other centres of supply.[65] Nevertheless, it is important to note that supplies of water to front-line troops were always contingent on the local situation and the slightest change in supply could have a big effect on morale.

---

[57] AWM 54 883/2/97 MEFCWS, no. IX (7 to 13 January 1942), p. 1. The other main problem was that of mail.
[58] AWM 54 883/2/97 MEFCWS, no. XVI (26 February to 4 March 1942), p. 3.
[59] AWM 54 883/2/97 MEFCWS, no. XXIV (23 to 29 April 1942), p. 2.
[60] IWM 96/50/1 R. L. Crimp, Diary, 18 April 1942, p. 121.
[61] AWM 54 883/2/97 MEFCWS, no. XXIX (27 May to 2 June 1942), p. 1.
[62] ANZ WAII/1/DA/508/1 vol. 1, MEMCWS, no. XXXVII (22 to 28 July 1942), p. 19.
[63] ANZ WAII/1/DA/508/1 vol. 1, MEMCWS, no. XXXVIII (29 July to 4 August 1942), p. 18.
[64] ANZ WAII/1/DA/508/1 vol. 1, MEMCWS, no. XXXIX (5 to 11 August 1942), p. 15.
[65] ANZ WAII/1/DA/508/1 vol. 3, MEMCWS, no. XLI (17 to 25 August 1942), p. 15.

The little water that made its way to the front line was, in most men's opinion, 'foul stuff to drink in its natural form' and 'much more satisfying to have as a brew'.[66] The desert brew consequently became something of an institution, as most men hydrated through drinking tea rather than water. The men's diaries and letters make it clear that the brewing of tea played a hugely important part in developing bonds between the men and the process itself became 'almost a ritual' in the desert.[67]

It was not uncommon for a battalion to burn the best part of a hundred gallons of petrol daily just in the process of brewing up.[68] Nevertheless, such an expenditure might well have been worth it. Days of continuous discomfort, with tea without sugar or milk or either, in water that was salt or petrol tainted, could leave men with a sense of futility.[69] As long as there was no lack of 'char' everyone was happy. When there was a shortage 'morale slump[ed]'.[70] One soldier wrote that good morale was 'directly proportional' to the 'supply of brews'[71] as 'tea had become a drug to us'.[72]

'Without tea,' Ian Mackay, a regimental medical officer with the 64th Medium Regiment Royal Artillery, remembered, 'we would never have won.'[73] Recognising the importance of tea supplies, the British government bought the world's entire tea crop for 1942.[74] According to John Ellis, at any one time there were over 30 million tons of tea stored in England. One thousand tons of tea made about 500 million cups of desert char. It would appear that His Majesty's government was well aware of the importance of tea to the British people and their armed forces.[75]

For long periods of the desert war, soldiers ate much the same as their fathers had done on the western front of the First World War. The basic ration still consisted of bully beef, hard biscuits, tea, sugar, tinned milk, jam and margarine. David French has argued that adequate supplies of food and drink could be more important than many other factors in maintaining the morale of troops. 'They were essential not merely because they provided physical sustenance, but because their preparation and

---

[66] IWM 85/35/1 L. E. Tutt, 'Gentleman Soldier', p. 201; Ellis in *The Sharp End*, p. 285, has said that this was often caused by the petrol and oil cans that the water was transported in. 'Even in those cases where the water did not taste of petrol and chlorine, the internal coating of the cans – paraffin wax or bitumen and benzine – tended to flake off and add its own unmistakable taste.' The water in the desert was also heavily chlorinated.

[67] IWM 96/50/1 R. L. Crimp, Diary, 9 November 1941, p. 54.   [68] Ibid.

[69] IWM 96/50/1 Crimp, Diary, 1 April 1942, p. 118; IWM 80/37/1, E. W. Cope, Letter to Doreen, 1 May 1942.

[70] IWM 96/50/1 Crimp, Diary, 9 November 1941, p. 54.

[71] IWM 85/35/1 L. E. Tutt, 'Gentleman Soldier', p. 82.   [72] Ibid., p. 201.

[73] IWM 94/8/1 I. Mackay, 'Fighting Fit, The Story of a Regimental Medical Officer in World War II', p. 43.

[74] Latimer, *Alamein*, p. 21; Bungay, *Alamein*, p. 70.   [75] Ellis, *The Sharp End*, p. 287

Illustration 9 Grant tank crews sit down to a brew near their vehicles, Libya, June 1942. The desert brew became a ritual in the North African campaign and played an important role in hydrating men and developing group bonds. Note the use of the 'Benghazi cooker'.

consumption bonded men together.'[76] The shell-shock committee of 1922 had found that hot food and tea could reduce the incidence of psychological breakdown in combat by representing a slender thread linking men with normal life.[77] Richard Holmes has made a similar

[76] French, *Raising Churchill's Army*, p. 143. See also Irina Davidian, 'The Russian Soldier's Morale from the Evidence of Tsarist Military Censorship', in Hugh Cecil and Peter H. Liddle, *Facing Armageddon: The First World War Experienced* (London, 1996); Richard C. Hall, '"The Enemy Is Behind Us": The Morale Crisis in the Bulgarian Army during the Summer of 1918', *War in History* (April, 2004).

[77] David French, 'Discipline and the Death Penalty in the British Army in the War against Germany during the Second World War', *Journal of Contemporary History*, 33(4) (October, 1998), p. 533.

point, emphasising that food was particularly important in times of stress, for among the physiological effects of stress is a speeding-up of the metabolic rate, making men hungrier and thirstier than they normally are.[78]

The Middle East Field Service Ration was supposed to contain at least 3,700 calories and the battle ration 3,100. 'But the constituent parts of these ration scales were often not all available at any one time' and chronic deficiencies resulted in 'long periods of subsisting on the same few items'. Special issues of lime juice, tinned fruit, groundnuts, and vitamins compensated for dietary deficiencies in the basic ration.[79] Jack Swaab, a gunner with the 51st Highland Division, recalled members of his unit passing round vitamin C tablets to the cry of 'will you have an orange?'[80]

Many of the men, not used to cooking for themselves, had to learn the hard way, as even company cooking was difficult to organise in the middle of the desert. To cook and heat meals, units used what they called the 'Benghazi cooker', which they also used for heating water. The Benghazi was a simple device, and owed its practicality to the fact that petrol at that time was easier to come by than firewood. Each section carried a tin in which holes were stabbed with a bayonet. This was half filled with sand, and a pint or so of petrol was stirred into it to form a thick paste. A match thrown from a safe distance was all that was necessary after that. It would burn for half-an-hour with no more attention than an occasional stir with the point of a bayonet.[81]

This somewhat haphazard form of cooking could lead to burn injuries. The 'Monthly Report on the Health of Eighth Army' for April 1942 pointed out that accidents were the greatest single cause of hospital admissions, constituting approximately 20 per cent of the total.[82] Other reports showed that around 30 per cent of accidental injuries were caused by burns.[83] Burns could, therefore, cause as much as 6 per cent of hospital admissions in Eighth Army.

Throughout 1941, the censorship summaries consistently reported that one of 'the chief complaints voiced by men in forward areas' was 'the quality and quantity of food'.[84] However, they also indicated that food supplies were noticeably better during some of the key battles that the WDF and Eighth Army won in the desert. This was especially evident

---

[78] Richard Holmes, *Acts of War: The Behaviour of Men in Battle* (London, 2004), pp. 128–9.
[79] Ellis, *The Sharp End*, p. 275.   [80] Swaab, *Field of Fire*, p. 11.
[81] Borthwick, *Battalion*, p. 21.
[82] NA WO 177/324 Monthly Report on Health Eighth Army, April 1942.
[83] NA WO 177/324 Monthly Report on Health Eighth Army, September 1942.
[84] AWM 54 883/2/97 British Troops in Egypt. No. 89 Field Censorship Report Week Ending 3 July 1941, p. 3.

during the siege of Tobruk in 1941, when the Royal Navy's ability to supply the garrison was crucial to its successful defence.[85]

Nevertheless, those units involved in mobile warfare in the open desert had to face more considerable supply issues. The South African censor noted at the start of November that 'there have been more complaints this week about food', although these complaints represented 'not more than 10%' of South African correspondence. One man wrote 'the food we are getting here is mostly not to be eaten and if for once it can be eaten then it is just enough not to starve'.[86] The censors believed that the criticisms of 'the poor quality of the rations' did not show any 'lowering in the spirit of the writers'. Generally speaking, they said, 'it is evident the troops appreciate that what they are sacrificing is little in comparison with what they have to lose'.[87]

By the beginning of January 1942, complaints about the quantity of food in the desert began to diminish, but not die away altogether. The morale report for January summarised the situation by saying that 'general satisfaction is expressed regarding food and conditions, under the circumstances'.[88] But the real problem, according to Ellis, 'was the monotony of the diet which could easily cause men to lose all interest in food, with a consequent deleterious effect on efficiency and morale'.[89] This contention is supported in the censorship summaries.[90] One man wrote 'food out here is plain but plentiful. We have bully fried plain, bully fried in butter, bully stewed, curry and bully, and, of course bully. So you see we have got quite a variety of dishes – including bully.'[91]

The monotony of the daily menu could get men down. Breakfast almost always consisted of fried bully or porridge made from crushed biscuits. This was known, among other names, as 'Burgee porridge', 'Biscoo', 'Burgoo'[92] or 'Biscuit la-la'[93] and was designed to make use out of the large and otherwise inedible army biscuit. The biscuits were first put into a sandbag and then pounded into powder. The powder was mixed with a small quantity of boiling water, and sugar and tinned milk were added if available.[94]

---

[85] AWM 54 883/2/97 British Troops in Egypt. No. 107 Field Censorship Report Week Ending 11 November 1941, p. 2.
[86] AWM 54 883/2/97 British Troops in Egypt. No. 106 Field Censorship Report Week Ending 4 November 1941, p. 4.
[87] AWM 54 883/2/97 MEFCWS, no. I (12 to 18 November 1941), p. 2.
[88] NA WO 193/456 Sundry Morale Papers, Morale Report January 1942, M.E.F.
[89] Ellis, *The Sharp End*, p. 275.
[90] AWM 54 883/2/97 MEFCWS, no. X (14 to 20 January 1942), p. 1.
[91] AWM 54 883/2/97 MEFCWS, no. VIII (31 December 1941 to 6 January 1942), p. 1.
[92] Ellis, *The Sharp End*, p. 274.
[93] AWM 54 883/2/97 British Troops in Egypt. No. 104 Field Censorship Report Week Ending 21 October 1941, p. 2.
[94] Forty (ed.), *Leakey's Luck*, p. 62.

However, in a 'flap', or if the unit were on the move, breakfast would only consist of 'some army biscuits with a scrape of marge and jam'.[95] Lunch tended to consist of biscuits and cheese, and dinner of bully stew and rice pudding.

Some units fared worse than others. The censorship summary for the week of 28 January to 3 February 1942 reported that

The only complaint of any consequence in connection with rations came from the 3rd Coldstream Guards, several correspondents expressing strong dissatisfaction. The following were characteristic extracts: (a) "I'm still existing but not living on this so-called food, which is just about getting all the men fed up." (b) "Do you get any grub, we don't, well hardly any ... Bread is not rationed ... there has not been any during the last 60 days, just Army biscuits."[96]

Partly to deal with the problem of monotonous food, the battle ration was improved to include oatmeal, margarine and bacon in 1942.[97] Desert magazines, such as *Crusader*, made efforts to teach the soldiers recipes that they could use to spice up their diets and by the end of March many of these problems appear to have disappeared.[98]

Nevertheless, by late July, even though the withdrawal had shortened Eighth Army's lines of communication, there were still 'isolated complaints' about rations.[99] These did not persist however, and the censors were soon testifying that the typical comments from troops were extremely positive.[100] By the end of July, the New Zealand censors were able to report that 'rations have received head-line prominence. Practically without exception the old desert food problem has been praised. That the ration receives assistance from mobile canteens and other sources is admitted, but that the ration itself has been good is borne out by the lack of adverse comments.'[101] South African troops were especially pleased that 'fresh provisions and many commodities which were out of their reach for so protracted a period at Tobruk [during 1942] and beyond, are now available in abundance'. The censors noted that 'whoops of joy at this change' were 'clearly manifested in many letters'.[102]

The variety of food, therefore, had clearly improved before Montgomery arrived in the desert,[103] with the troops 'receiving hitherto unobtainable

[95] IWM 85/35/1 L. E. Tutt, 'Gentleman Soldier', pp. 90–4.
[96] AWM 54 883/2/97 MEFCWS, no. XII (28 January to 3 February 1942), p. 3.
[97] Ellis, *The Sharp End*, p. 275.
[98] AWM 54 883/2/97 MEFCWS, no. XX (25 to 31 March 1942), p. 2; AWM 54 883/2/97 MEFCWS, no. XXI (1 to 7 April 1942), p. 4.
[99] ANZ WAII/1/DA/508/1 vol. 1, MEMCWS, no. XXXVI (15 to 21 July 1942), p. 5.
[100] ANZ WAII/1/DA/508/1 vol. 1, MEMCWS, no. XXXVII (22 to 28 July 1942), p. 5.
[101] Ibid., p. 19.   [102] Ibid., p. 15.
[103] ANZ WAII/1/DA/508/1 vol. 1, MEMCWS, no. XXXIX (5 to 11 August 1942), p. 5.

"luxuries"'.[104] By the end of August, the South African censor was able to say that the situation had improved again, as it had 'never been as good as it is now',[105] while the Australian censor remarked less dramatically that 'no complaints were noted regarding rations'.[106] The summary for 3 to 9 September mentioned the 'high standard' of rations and the 'the good variety' which was 'considered even more vital'.[107] By the end of the month, the censors observed that 'the quality and variety of rations were repeatedly praised by forward and base troops alike; never has there been such unanimity and it is obvious that the men consider themselves far more fortunate in this respect than their rationed relatives at home'.[108]

By the beginning of October, the quality of rations had improved to an even greater extent.[109] The censorship summary for 21 October to 3 November, the period that covered the climactic battle of El Alamein, reported that 'most units in the Western Desert stated that rations were very good and superior to those obtained on previous desert campaigns'.[110] The morale report for August to October 1942 listed 'rations' as one of the three main topics of praise from Egypt and Libya.[111]

However, the biggest improvement was the introduction of the 'compo ration' in late 1942, in time for the invasion of Tunisia. 'Compo rations' were widely considered to be an improvement mainly because they contained a much greater variety of foods, exactly what the troops had called for.[112] However, the 'Compo ration' was not available before or during El Alamein and its introduction following the battle suggests that the provision of food was still not perfect.

There can be little doubt that the quality of rations improved throughout 1942 and particularly in the months leading up to the battle of El Alamein. Much of this improvement was due to the short lines of communication that allowed mobile canteens to reach the front line and supplement the standard rations of Eighth Army. The battles on the El Alamein line (July to November, 1942) were examples of static warfare that also facilitated the supply situation. They were an exception in the desert. For most of the

---

[104] Ibid., p. 15.
[105] ANZ WAII/1/DA/508/1 vol. 3, MEMCWS, no. XLI (17 to 25 August 1942), p. 15.
[106] ANZ WAII/1/DA/508/1 vol. 3, MEMCWS, no. XLII (25 August to 2 September 1942), p. 17.
[107] ANZ WAII/1/DA/508/1 vol. 3, MEMCWS, no. XLIII (3 to 9 September 1942), p. 4.
[108] ANZ WAII/1/DA/508/1 vol. 3, MEMCWS, no. XLV (17 to 23 September 1942), p. 6.
[109] ANZ WAII/1/DA/508/1 vol. 3, MEMCWS, no. XLVII (30 September to 6 October 1942), p. 5.
[110] ANZ WAII/1/DA/508/1 vol. 4, MEMCWS, no. XLIX (21 October to 3 November 1942), p. 24.
[111] NA WO 193/453 Morale Committee Papers, Morale Report, August to October 1942.
[112] IWM 82/37/1 E. P. Danger, 'Diary of a Guardsman', TS Memoirs, pp. 50–1.

time, units were far away from organised base depots and the reliability of food supplies was poor. Although inadequate supplies of food can hardly be blamed entirely for the morale crisis in the summer of 1942, as the quality and quantity of food gradually improved during this period, or for the deficient performance of British, Commonwealth and Dominion troops in manoeuvre warfare, it adds one more thread to the intricate web that explains the combat performance of the WDF and Eighth Army in the North African desert.

The supply of cigarettes was also an issue for the men of Eighth Army. Each man was entitled to fifty cigarettes every week, usually the much-maligned Indian 'V' cigarettes. The men could also supplement their supply by buying more 'decent ones' (two tins a man)[113] in a NAAFI (Navy, Army and Air Force Institutes) whenever one came up the line.[114] Many men who had not smoked before the war became addicts under the stressful circumstances of living and fighting in the desert, and took stupid chances just to get a drag of tobacco.[115] After tea, cigarettes were the second major comfort of those fighting in the desert.

Many of the soldiers' diaries and letters made comments on the vital importance of cigarettes to morale. The role of nicotine in calming soldiers' nerves before going into battle therefore cannot be overlooked. It was not uncommon for soldiers to chain smoke in the hours preceding an action in order to calm their fear.[116]

The supply of cigarettes was never consistent, so the arrival of a NAAFI issue or a parcel with a luxurious brand of cigarettes from home often engendered much comment and excitement.[117] Men had to ration themselves and conserve as best they could in case of shortages in the future.[118] On the other hand, 'the possession of many cigarettes' could 'drive up' the soldier's 'desire to consume them with the greatest possible speed, and thus run out as quickly as possible!' All the men asked for, as they said frequently in letters home, was 'a chance to smoke themselves to death'.[119]

For the soldiers of Eighth Army, it was not unusual to go days or even weeks without a 'fag' issue. In the midst of the Crusader offensive in December 1941, Crimp noted that some men were even 'reduced to

[113] AWM 54 883/2/97 British Troops in Egypt. No. 105 Field Censorship Report Week Ending 29 October 1941, p. 4.
[114] IWM 96/50/1 Crimp, p. 54.
[115] IWM 85/18/1 C. T. Framp, 'The Littlest Victory' (unpublished memoir), p. 54.
[116] IWM 87/35/1 Lieutenant Donald A. Main, p. 81.
[117] IWM 86/72/1 Captain E. N. Sheppard, Letter, 4 January 1941 and Letter to Tom, 31 October 1941.
[118] IWM 86/72/1 Captain E. N. Sheppard, Letter to Tom, 31 October 1941.
[119] Swaab, Field of Fire, p. 49.

drying tea-leaves and rolling them in newspaper'.[120] The censorship summaries corroborate such accounts. The summary for the week ending 10 July 1941 showed that the supply of cigarettes was far from desirable and many men felt compelled to write home to ask for some to be sent to them.[121] Even in Tobruk, where the supply of other commodities such as food and water were on the whole better in 1941, the censors commented that 'the scarcity of cigarettes' had 'been noted in letters'.[122] In February 1942, the censors reported that the situation in the desert had improved and that 'there were no more references to shortage of cigarettes'.[123] However, in July 'more than a few letters ... bemoaned the lack of cigarettes'.[124] Even as late as October 1942 'the quality of issue cigarettes' continued 'to draw unfavourable reactions'[125] and it is clear that the problem of supplying the men with adequate numbers and quality of cigarettes was never overcome.

The problem of the North African fly was another factor of great concern to the men in the desert. With plentiful amounts of food, faeces and bodies (both living and dead) to feed off due to the war, the fly was able to breed and multiply to biblical proportions. No personal account of the war in the desert fails to mention them.

Soon after sunrise, the flies would arrive in hordes. They would then plague the soldiers 'with malign persistence all throughout the day, swarming and buzzing round, trying desperately to land on faces, in eyes, ears and nostrils, on arms, hands, knees and necks'. According to Crimp, 'everything unwholesome, filthy and putrefied' was 'manna to them' and, accordingly, units had to completely seal off latrines and burn refuse dumps with petrol daily in order to prevent them feeding and breeding.[126]

The flies made eating and drinking a real trial. One man recalled that 'whenever I commenced to eat any food – it was covered with [flies]. Even my cup of tea, which I had kept covered with a handkerchief, revealed a few saturated flies at every sip.'[127] It was 'the devil's own job' to keep 'food from their clutches, and as soon as a meal's on the plate they always get the first nibble ... You can whack them a hundred times, and still they'll

[120] IWM 96/50/1 Crimp, Diary, 22 December 1941, p. 84.
[121] AWM 54 883/2/97 British Troops in Egypt. No. 90 Field Censorship Report Week Ending 10 July 1941, p. 3.
[122] AWM 54 883/2/97 British Troops in Egypt. No. 106 Field Censorship Report Week Ending 4 November 1941, p. 2.
[123] AWM 54 883/2/97 MEFCWS, no. XIII (4 to 10 February 1942), p. 2.
[124] ANZ WAII/1/DA/508/1 vol. 1, MEMCWS, no. XXXVI (15 to 21 July 1942), p. 17.
[125] ANZ WAII/1/DA/508/1 vol. 3, MEMCWS, no. XLVII (30 September to 6 October 1942), p. 5.
[126] IWM 96/50/1 Crimp, p. 45.
[127] IWM 01/32/1 H. Ashworth, 'Filling the Breach', p. 38.

Illustration 10 Two members of a Crusader tank's crew write home, August 1942. Note the mosquito nets round their faces to keep the flies away. Flies were one of the greatest torments of living and fighting in the desert.

come back.'[128] Len Tutt remembered watching some telephone engineers at work shortly after the war. 'They were having their break. One of them constantly waved his hand over the surface of his tea as he talked,' Tutt recalled. 'I knew immediately that he had served in the desert.'[129] It was a relief at sunset, when, 'as at some secret signal', all the flies simultaneously disappeared and the men could go about their business without their tormentors.[130]

The number of flies varied by the season. They were few in number in January, they increased appreciably in February, became a nuisance

[128] IWM 96/50/1 Crimp, p. 45.
[129] IWM 85/35/1 L. E. Tutt, 'Gentleman Soldier', pp. 95–6.
[130] IWM 96/50/1 Crimp, p. 45.

in March, and thereafter multiplied exceedingly to reach a peak in July, August and September. Subsequently they diminished slowly until they were few in number again by December.[131] Once the fly season began, there was little the men could do to avoid them.

By April 1942, 'the reappearance of the ubiquitous fly' was the 'subject of wide comment' in all correspondence.[132] In July, as the crisis in the desert was reaching its pinnacle, the censors noted that:

Overshadowing the loss of Tobruk, the German offensive in Russia, the possibility of a second front, unanimously condemned as the chief enemy and worse than Rommel were the millions of flies that are worrying the troops in the front line from dawn to dusk. As a Bdr remarked 'We can beat Rommel but not the flies.'[133]

The censorship summary for 5 to 11 August 1942, just before Montgomery assumed command in the desert, remarked that it was 'not too much to say that one out of two letters written by men out west of Alexandria, mentioned – usually with unstinted curses – the fly plague'. The plague was 'undoubtedly serious' and the flies were 'infuriating', driving the soldiers 'to distraction, and ruining all chances of rest during the daylight hours'. When Eighth Army had been fighting far out in the Western Desert, 'this scourge,' according to the censors, had been 'much less damaging'. With the withdrawal to native occupied areas, it had increased. The censors pointed out that 'now that there has been so much fighting within a limited area [El Alamein], and hundreds of dead bodies have been left to decompose on the battlefield, the plague of flies has multiplied beyond belief'.[134]

The authorities did make considerable efforts to address the fly problem. Eighth Army issued orders for each man to kill at least fifty flies per day.[135] The men took great pleasure in carrying out these orders.[136] Lieutenant G. F. Morrison noted that the flies loved to roost on the roofs of his unit's dugouts – 'so we all make paper spills, dip them in paraffin and burn the little dears to death – you can kill about 200 at one go in one dugout that way – marvellous!! Its lovely to hear them cracking and popping like chestnuts on a fire!!'[137] One unit bought a swatter per truck out of regimental funds, some invented ingenious traps, while others received an issue of liquid poison which caused, according to the censors, 'great havoc'.[138]

[131] AWM 54 883/2/97 MEFCWS, no. XXIX (27 May to 2 June 1942), p. 4.
[132] AWM 54 883/2/97 MEFCWS, no. XXIII (15 to 21 April 1942), p. 1.
[133] ANZ WAII/1/DA/508/1 vol. 1, MEMCWS, no. XXXVI (15 to 21 July 1942), p. 15.
[134] ANZ WAII/1/DA/508/1 vol. 1, MEMCWS, no. XXXIX (5 to 11 August 1942), p. 5.
[135] Latimer, *Alamein*, p. 143.
[136] IWM 02/19/1 H. W. F. Charles, Letter to Family, 19 December 1942, p. 38.
[137] IWM DS/Misc/63 G. F. Morrison, Lieut., Letter to his Mother, 3 October 1942.
[138] ANZ WAII/1/DA/508/1 vol. 3, MEMCWS, no. XLI (19 to 25 August 1942), p. 18.

Nevertheless, such practices were stopped after a time as the flies' burst bodies increased the risk of disease and infection.[139]

In addition to these initiatives, Auchinleck formed a Fly Control Unit in early August 1942, which, according to the censors, did 'good work'.[140] Fly nets 'which fitted over the helmet and covered face and neck' were also issued. They were 'grotesque looking affairs made of muslin or fine net with celluloid eye-pieces,' but they did 'keep the flies off the face'.[141] By the end of August, the New Zealand censors confirmed that the 'determined efforts' being made to combat the fly 'plague' were being gratefully received by the troops.[142]

In general, the number of cases of diarrhoea and dysentery in the desert reflected the extent to which Eighth Army had or had not achieved control of the fly problem.[143] In July, the 'Monthly Statistical Report on the Health of Eighth Army' noted a 'tremendous increase in fly-borne disease'.[144] By the end of August, it was apparent that dysentery had become 'prevalent' in Eighth Army,[145] making up 24.4 per cent of all hospital admissions.[146] A sister in 2 General Hospital stated that she had '142 patients stricken with this disease, and that with the crowded wards and people sleeping on the floor' it was like 'the Crimean war'. In 6 General Hospital, a medical officer stated that 'they were working the full 1600 beds' with 'eleven officers from one unit alone being under treatment'. Other hospitals, such as 27 and 42 General Hospitals, also mentioned being 'rushed off their feet' with dysentery cases, while there were between '200 and 240 in the dysentery block at 63 General Hospital'.[147]

By 9 September, the censors were referring to this outbreak as an 'epidemic'. A memo on hygiene and sanitation, issued by Eighth Army in August 1942, stated that two of the main causes of sick admissions were dysentery and diarrhoea/gastroenteritis, both caused by flies.[148] 'The prevalence of this epidemic', in the opinion of doctors, orderlies and nurses, was 'caused by carelessness on the part of new arrivals in the country who are said to be "not sufficiently fly-minded"'. One doctor

---

[139] Bungay, Alamein, p. 69.
[140] ANZ WAII/1/DA/508/1 vol. 3, MEMCWS, no. XLII (25 August to 2 September 1942), p. 6.
[141] ANZ WAII/1/DA/508/1 vol. 3, MEMCWS, no. XLI (19 to 25 August 1942), p. 19.
[142] Ibid., p. 18.
[143] AWM 54 883/2/97 MEFCWS, no. XXIX (27 May to 2 June 1942), p. 4.
[144] NA WO 177/324 Monthly Statistical Report on Health of Eighth Army, July 1942.
[145] ANZ WAII/1/DA/508/1 vol. 3, MEMCWS, no. XLI (19 to 25 August), p. 15.
[146] NA WO 177/324 Monthly Statistical Report on Health of Eighth Army, October 1942.
[147] ANZ WAII/1/DA/508/1 vol. 3, MEMCWS, no. XLII (25 August to 2 September 1942), p. 6.
[148] NA 177/324 Memo on Hygiene and Sanitation, Compiled 3 August 1942.

Table 7 *First attendees at regimental aid posts, November 1942*

	No. first attendances	% of all first attendances caused by desert sores
50 (N) Div	680	21%
51 (H) Div	1186	40%
1 Arm Div	528	28%
2 NZ Div	1774	35%

Source: AWM 519/3/7 The Last Campaign in North Africa 1942–1943. Operations as Affecting the Medical Services 1941–1942.

wrote that 'we have 450 extra beds put up to cope with the dysentery epidemic, the first we have had really – and that was avoidable'.[149] By the end of September, the problem began to diminish as new units in Eighth Army became more 'fly-minded' and as the flies began to disappear with the approach of cooler weather. Whereas dysentery and diarrhoea had made up 24.4% of hospital admissions in August, they made up 16.9% in September and 12.6% in October.[150]

Another medical concern caused by flies was the desert sore. While working and fighting in the desert soldiers constantly suffered abrasions to their skin, mainly on the knuckles and the back of the hands (about 90% of cases).[151] These cuts and abrasions 'were constantly covered with flies and sand and developed into "desert sores" that festered and refused to heal'.[152] The censors noted that the problem of desert sores became prominent in July 1941, during what was, for most of the men, their first summer in the desert.[153] Thereafter, they developed into a constant nuisance and became part of everyday life for the soldier. A study carried out by the 11th Hussars in the summer of 1942 showed that 25% of the regiment suffered from these sores, while 4% of the regiment had six or more sores. Desert sores accounted for fully 14% of those evacuated from the 11th Hussars, for all causes, including battle casualties, during this period.[154] Even as late as November 1942, desert sores remained a nuisance for the troops (Table 7).

The significance of flies to morale is illustrated by the fact that some elements of Eighth Army used them as a tool to attack German and Italian

---

[149] ANZ WAII/1/DA/508/1 vol. 3, MEMCWS, no. XLIII (3 to 9 September 1942), p. 6.
[150] NA WO 177/324 Monthly Report on Health of Eighth Army, October 1942.
[151] NA WO 177/324 Desert Sores, RMO XI Hussars, September 1942.
[152] IWM 93/19/1 W. R. Garrett, 'A Private Viewing', p. 7.
[153] AWM 54 883/2/97 British Troops in Egypt. No. 89 Field Censorship Report Week Ending 3 July 1941, p. 3.
[154] NA WO 177/324 Desert Sores, RMO XI Hussars, September 1942.

health and morale. The Australians, for example, used to take 'all their rubbish out on patrol with them and dump it' near the German and Italian lines.

The [Australians] are on the seawards side of the Jerries so that the wind takes the flies inland to the Jerries and what with the usual filth of the Italians their lines must be unbearable. We think they are suffering from dysentery or some similar thing for on our patrols we find they have walked out of some spots leaving blankets, tin hats, clothes and rifles just where they were in their defensive positions.[155]

Indeed, the censors made it clear that the universal belief held by Eighth Army was that 'the chief cause of the [fly] pest' was the Italians 'for not burying [their] dead properly' and that they deserved what they got in this regard.[156]

As early as July 1941, it was clear to the Allied troops in the desert that the German intervention in North Africa would prolong the desert war for many months or even years to come. As this realisation dawned on the men, the censors began to note many incidences of 'complaints about conditions', such as those already described, in the soldiers' mail. Many units had already spent months 'up the blue'[157] and the effects of little rest, harsh terrain and monotony were beginning to tell in a way detrimental to morale. The men could handle many of the hardships that they faced in the desert. However, it was the combination of all these hardships experienced together over a considerable period of time, without break or rest, that played a role in causing the morale crisis of the summer of 1942.

On 10 July 1941, the censors noted that

Some men ... suggest that they have almost reached the limit of physical and mental endurance. The fear of 'desert lunacy', as one man puts it is becoming more prominent among those who have served long unbroken periods in the desert; and it would seem that an important factor has been the withdrawal into the arid wastes of the desert after having seen the comparatively fertile regions of Cyrenaica.[158]

The censorship summary for 17 July 1941 noted that monotony appeared to be the 'greatest curse of life' in the desert and its effect varied 'according

---

[155] ANZ WAII/1/DA/508/1 vol. 3, MEMCWS, no. XLIII (3 to 9 September 1942), pp. 14–15.

[156] ANZ WAII/1/DA/508/1 vol. 3, MEMCWS, no. XLI (19 to 25 August 1942), p. 18.

[157] The desert was often referred to as 'the blue' by the men, in reference to the vastness of the desert and to the sky that composed nine-tenths of its landscape.

[158] AWM 54 883/2/97 British Troops in Egypt. No. 90 Field Censorship Report Week Ending 10 July 1941, p. 2.

to individual temperament'.[159] One soldier noted in his journal a month before the Crusader battle that

There's a sort of psychological complaint some chaps get after long exposure on the Blue called 'desert weariness', though I can hardly claim to have reached that yet, but for months now we've been cut off from nearly every aspect of civilised life, and every day has been cast in the same monotonous mould. The desert, omnipresent, so saturates consciousness that it makes the mind as sterile as itself. Its only now you realise how much you normally live through the senses. Here there's nothing for them. Nothing in the landscape to rest or distract the eye; nothing to hear, but roaring truck-engines; and nothing to smell but carbon exhaust-fumes and the reek of petrol. Even food tastes insipid, because of the heat, which stultifies appetite. The sexual urge, with nothing to stir it, is completely dormant.[160]

Australian and South African units, who felt that they had been longer in the desert than most, were especially vocal.[161]

By February 1942, many units were clammering for some rest and leave. This was all the more evident following the Axis counteroffensive in January and February 1942. The censorship summaries stated that 'most of the men had placed such high hopes on the rapid outcome of this campaign that their dismay over recent developments is all the greater. A large number state that they are "fed up" and "browned off" and many appear to dread having to spend the summer "out in the blue" again.'[162] J. E. Brooks, of the 64th Medium Regiment RA, summed up the situation rather well in February 1942, when he said that 'I'm sick and tired of this bloody desert and the sooner I get out of it the better I shall like it. I think I've done more than my share in this war, and it's about time somebody took my place.'[163]

The summary for 15 to 21 April 1942 stated that 'the scorching sun and absence of shade have evoked a marked increase in "grousing"'.[164] The same summary noted that New Zealand units in the Western Desert did not show 'high spirits'. Much has been written, it said, 'on the very trying weather conditions and the unwelcome prospect of spending another summer in the "Blue"'. One NCO wrote that 'most of us are getting very browned off with this life of ours out here now; it is really sickening; here we are, 18 months in the desert and no signs of a move'. Another

[159] AWM 54 883/2/97 British Troops in Egypt. No. 91 Field Censorship Report Week Ending 17 July 1941, p. 3.
[160] IWM 96/50/1 R. L. Crimp, pp. 44–5.
[161] AWM 54 883/2/97 British Troops in Egypt. No. 92 Field Censorship Report Week Ending 24 July 1941, p. 3.
[162] AWM 54 883/2/97 MEFCWS, no. XIV (11 to 17 February 1942), p. 1.
[163] IWM 84/13/1 J. E. Brooks, Letter 12 February 1943 to Bill (His Brother), Describing His Experiences in the War so Far, pp. 19–20.
[164] AWM 54 883/2/97 MEFCWS, no. XXIII (15 to 21 April 1942), p. 1.

NCO complained that 'after such a long time in the desert with only two leaves in 19 months and one is supposed to get leave one week every three months you can understand why one gets as the saying is "browned off".[165]

A South African NCO wrote in March 1942 that 'the boys definitely need a break – just a few days in Cairo would put them right. We have been 8 months in the desert – honestly solitary confinement couldn't possibly be worse than this.'[166] Not much had changed a couple of weeks later when a warrant officer wrote,

The 1st Div have not had any [home] leave for 22 months and were told the other day that they need not give it a thought so you can imagine what chance we have. It is even a job to get six days Cairo leave from here. The present plan is that one man goes at a time with a period of 14 days in between and we have 50 odd men in the troop it will take more than two years before we all have a chance to get to Cairo for a break. The way things are being done up here just gives me and others a pain in the neck.[167]

The South African censor summed the situation up well when he wrote at the end of April 1942 that

Several interesting letters have been read which cast a strong light on the struggle which men in the front lines, surrounded by the vast grey monotony of the desert, tortured by dirt, dust, heat, thirst, cold, vermin and insects and bereft of all the freedom, individuality, amenities, associates and privileges of their normal lives have to wage against forces which would destroy all morale and courage, balance and sanity if not actively and constantly resisted.[168]

It must be noted that a number of the units that performed most poorly in the critical fighting around Gazala and Tobruk later in 1942 had been in the desert for well over six months without a break.[169] The 1st South African Division, which surrendered at Tobruk, and had seen fighting in East Africa, and then in the desert, was particularly in need of a respite from the harsh morale sapping desert environment.

By 29 April, the censors were reporting that it was not only the desert environment but also 'the vagaries of the weather' that 'were the main features of the correspondence from British troops in the Libyan battle areas ... frequent and detailed descriptions of violent sandstorms,

[165] Ibid., p. 15.   [166] AWM 54 883/2/97 MEFCWS, no. XX (25 to 31 March 1942), p. 12.
[167] AWM 54 883/2/97 MEFCWS, no. XXII (8 to 14 April 1942), p. 11.
[168] AWM 54 883/2/97 MEFCWS, no. XXIV (23 to 29 April 1942), p. 11.
[169] NA WO 177/324 Memo 'Sickness, Army Troops', by DDMS Eighth Army, 26 July 1942; Report on Tour of Eighth Army, 18 to 24 July 1942 by Consultant in Psychological Medicine (Brig. G. W. B. James), 28 July 1942.

extreme heat one day with cold winds sweeping unhampered across the desert the next,' were noted. 'These conditions were responsible for the tone of the mail being lower than usual, and while some men regard them as "another hurdle to be jumped", the majority are heartily sick of the desert and are only spurred on by the thought that the sooner the enemy is pushed out of Libya the quicker they will get home.'[170]

By July, there was little change in the tone of the mail. The censorship summary for 15 to 21 July stressed that the fighting was taking place 'under gruelling desert conditions' with 'dust and terrific heat, 110 degrees and more in the shade' to contend with.[171] The summary for 22 to 28 July noted 'frequent references to ... excessive heat and desert weariness' in mail from British troops in the forward areas.[172] The South African censor remarked that 'correspondence from Union Defence Force personnel indicated that the forward units' were 'undoubtedly feeling the strain of eight months continuous desert service, but are carrying on through sheer determination and hoping to obtain a rest as soon as the improvement in the situation allows'.[173] By the start of August, during the height of the morale crisis affecting Eighth Army, the censors noted that 'there were many indications that many men are suffering from desert weariness and the desire for a much needed rest was frequently expressed'.[174] The difficult weather conditions and the stalemate in the operations were responsible for a 'spate of grouses and an increase in the number of writers who stated they were "browned off"'.[175]

It is clear that the morale of the soldiers who fought in the desert was affected by the difficult conditions they experienced. Some of these conditions arose from the 'normal' exigencies of industrial level war (such as supplying food and water to large numbers of troops) and some were attributable to the particular difficulties that were special to North Africa (sun, sand, flies, etc.). It must be noted that Eighth Army performed better in the cooler winter months than during the hotter summer months of the North African desert. The censorship summary for the week 19 to 25 November 1941, right in the middle of the Crusader battle, noted that 'the coming of cooler weather ... seems to have brightened the men's outlook considerably'.[176] Eighth Army's two great victories over the

---

[170] AWM 54 883/2/97 MEFCWS, no. XXIV (23 to 29 April 1942), p. 11.
[171] ANZ WAII/1/DA/508/1 vol. 1 MEMCWS, no. XXXVI (15 to 21 July 1942), p. 20.
[172] ANZ WAII/1/DA/508/1 vol. 1 MEMCWS, no. XXXVII (22 to 28 July 1942), p. 1.
[173] Ibid., p. 13.
[174] ANZ WAII/1/DA/508/1 vol. 1, MEMCWS, no. XXXVIII (29 July to 4 August 1942), p. 12.
[175] ANZ WAII/1/DA/508/1 vol. 1, MEMCWS, no. XXXIX (5 to 11 August 1942), p. 1.
[176] AWM 54 883/2/97 MEFCWS, no. II (19 to 25 November 1941), p. 1.

combined German and Italian *Panzerarmee*, Crusader and El Alamein, were both achieved in the more manageable heat of October, November and December, when the mean maximum and minimum temperatures were about 25 °C and 14 °C.[177] When considering the performance of Eighth Army, it must be remembered and accepted that, whether in advance or in retreat, not only did the men go through an awful ordeal of conflict under arms, but, in addition, the flies were intolerable, the sand was unbearable and hunger and thirst were inevitable.

[177] NA WO 177/324 Monthly Report of ADH Eighth Army for October 1942.

5   Welfare, education and morale

I have always regarded as the primary object of both branches of my directorate the maintenance of the morale of all ranks.

(General H. Willans, the Director-General of Welfare and Education, 1941)[1]

There is nothing more soulless than ... a patriotism which does not concern itself with the welfare and dignity of the individual.

(S. L. A. Marshall)[2]

Hew Strachan has stated that one of the main reasons why the British Army suffered a crisis in its morale in 1941–2 was that the army's institutions were 'ill-adapted to the needs of a citizen army in a world war'.[3] The expansion of the pre-war professional army into a citizen army of millions put tremendous stress on those normally assigned the duty of maintaining morale.[4] Even before the war, Ronald Adam, while Deputy Chief of the Imperial General Staff (DCIGS), suggested that 'outside help' was needed for regimental officers to deal with matters affecting morale, such as welfare, in a newly expanded wartime army.[5] On the outbreak of hostilities, it was soon apparent that he was right. Not only were officers fully occupied with the basic organisation of the many new recruits, and were thus less able to devote time to the question of welfare, but some of the problems that they had to deal with were outside the experience of the average junior officer.[6] The War Office looked into the matter and, in the autumn of 1939, appointed Lieutenant-General John Brown to the post of War Office Adviser on Welfare. Brown immediately invited the territorial associations, in conjunction with the GOCs of the various commands, to

---

[1] NA WO 32/9735 Memorandum by the Director-General of Welfare and Education for Consideration by the ECAC on Monday, 9 June 1941.

[2] Marshall, *Men against Fire*, pp. 161–2.

[3] Hew Strachan, 'Training, Morale and Modern War', *Journal of Contemporary History*, 41(2) (2006), p. 224.

[4] Conscription was introduced in April 1939.

[5] LHCMA Adam 3/13 Narrative Covering Aspects of Work as Adjutant General, WWII, chap. 6, Welfare, pp. 1–3.

[6] NA WO 277/4 Brig. M. C. Morgan, *Army Welfare* (War Office, 1953), p. 178.

set up a welfare organisation for the army at home. Local Army Welfare Officers (LAWOs) were appointed throughout the country to coordinate welfare on a local level and, by 1940, 700 of these officers were in place.[7]

As the 'phoney war' dragged on, the War Office became increasingly concerned about welfare, and its possible impact on morale. In January 1940, it set up a small committee under the Vice Chief of the Imperial General Staff (VCIGS), Lieutenant-General Robert Haining, to consider educational, welfare and recreational needs in the army.[8] Haining recommended that a director-general of welfare should be appointed and that a Treasury grant should be made to fund the new directorate. Accordingly, the Directorate of Welfare, with welfare officers in commands and localities throughout the United Kingdom, was established, in the autumn of 1940, again under John Brown. In December 1940, with vast numbers of troops having returned from France after Dunkirk, Major-General H. Willans, who was then commanding a territorial division, was appointed Director-General for Welfare, in place of Brown, at an expanded Directorate of Welfare at the War Office.[9]

The introduction of a central welfare organisation marked a break from previous tradition in the British Army, as no comparable organisation had existed in the First World War.[10] Willans saw the primary aim of this new directorate as 'the maintenance of morale'.[11] In a speech he gave on 7 March 1941 to the Royal Society of Arts, later released as a pamphlet for officers entitled 'Welfare and Education', he announced that in order to achieve this object it was necessary 'to cater for the whole needs of the man – the needs of his mind, his body and his spirit . . . to aim at a high standard of physical, mental and moral well-being which together will result in a contented soldier and so in a contented Army'. Army welfare, in Willans's view, aimed at 'linking officers and men together in a bond' that would 'stand the test of adversity'. It was 'not merely something to relieve boredom'; it had to be proactively 'planned as part of the soldier's life'.[12]

By early 1941, the War Office had begun issuing a monthly welfare memorandum, containing directives, information and advice, to welfare

[7] Crang, *The British Army and the People's War*, p. 91.
[8] WO 163/48 Notes of the Proceedings of a Meeting of the Army Council, 12 February 1940: NA WO 199/1644 Minutes of the GOC-in-C's Conference, Southern Command, 20 January 1940.
[9] LHCMA Adam 3/13 Narrative Covering Aspects of Work as Adjutant-General, WWII, chap. 6, Welfare, pp. 1–3.
[10] NA WO 277/4 Morgan, *Army Welfare*, p. 1.
[11] Ibid., pp. 27–8.
[12] NA WO 163/123 Army pamphlet, 'Welfare and Education', by Maj.-Gen. H. Willans. Reprint of address given on Friday 7 March 1941 before the Royal Society of Arts, p. 3.

officers throughout the country.[13] Pamphlets on 'The Soldier's Welfare' were also released, with the aim of explaining the details of the new welfare organisation and facilitating a coordinated approach across the country and overseas.[14] These initiatives were also introduced in the Middle East, and, by the first months of 1942, all units in Eighth Army of a strength equal to or over that of a battalion were ordered to assign a unit welfare officer as part of their strength.[15]

There were three main issues of significance for army welfare in the desert. The first was maintaining a constructive connection between the soldier and his homeland, with all that this entailed regarding the quality of radio broadcasts and reading materials available, the promptness of mail, and problems with loved ones back home. The second concerned issues arising directly from the soldiers' service in the desert, such as the provision of appropriate supports and entertainments. The third related to educating the soldier for his role in the great aims of the war.

The men in the desert remained tied to home and hearth just as their fathers had done in the First World War. The front was not an island but a living, breathing extension of the homeland.[16] Montgomery commented, following the war, that 'the home front and the battle front are now-a-days, as never before, very closely linked. If the soldier thinks that things are not well at home, he gets worried and his morale drops.'[17] The main sources of information about home and the progress of the war, such as the radio and whatever reading material the soldiers could get their hands on, therefore, played a crucial role in maintaining the morale of the troops. They represented the most tangible links between home and front and their management became of paramount importance. Lack of news was depressing, particularly when under fire. Morale, as a collection of the Australian 2/23 Battalion's wartime newsletters noted, could 'sink very low in these circumstances'.[18] Until the summer of 1942, however, the media in the Middle East often played a more destructive than constructive role in regard to

[13] NA WO 277/4 Morgan, *Army Welfare*, pp. 25–6, 39–40.
[14] Crang, *The British Army and the People's War*, p. 93.
[15] SAMAD Div Docs, Gp 1, Box 1, Army Routine Orders by Lieut.-Gen. N. M. Ritchie, General Officer Commanding-in-Chief, Eighth Army, 6 May 1942; AWM 54 883/2/97 MEFCWS, no. XII (28 January to 3 February 1942), p. 3.
[16] Stephane Audoin-Rouzeau, 'The French Soldier in the Trenches', in Cecil and Liddle, *Facing Armageddon*, pp. 223–6.
[17] IWM 99/1/2 Papers of Maj.-Gen. Raymond Briggs, Lecture on Military Leadership given at the University of St. Andrews by Field Marshal Sir Bernard Montgomery on 15 November 1945, p. 22.
[18] Dick Fanke (ed.), *Mud and Blood in the Field* (Hughesdale, 1984), p. vii.

morale. The BBC especially seemed inexplicably incapable of judging the sensitivities of the soldiers. One characteristic of the BBC's coverage that really vexed the troops was its 'over-exultant presentation of the news'. For example, during the Crusader offensive at the end of 1941, the BBC virtually proclaimed victory a week after the beginning of hostilities. Such coverage unsettled troops in the midst of the fighting, who knew that success on the ground was anything but assured and who worried how families back home would perceive a defeat after claiming victory.[19]

By February 1942, as a result of the overweening attitude of the BBC, many soldiers appeared no longer willing to accept the 'stock phrases' of the corporation. One British soldier wrote, 'will you tell the BBC from all the MEF in the name of God to call a withdrawal a withdrawal when they're describing it',[20] while the New Zealand censor noted a 'certain amount of sarcasm' being levelled at the reports that 'we retreated "according to plan"'.[21]

A report to the South African Director of Military Training on the morale of Union troops in the desert, written in March 1942 by the South African Director of Military Intelligence, Lieutenant-Colonel E. G. Malherbe, stated that BBC broadcasts were having a 'rather disturbing effect' on South African troops. Malherbe recounted how one of the BBC 'News from South Africa' talks, broadcast on 13 February 1942 by Penn Smith, started off with the remark 'total war has now come to South Africa' and ran through 'a horrifying list of shootings, crimes, sabotage and the evacuation of Durban (!)'. According to Malherbe, this caused 'considerable alarm amongst troops' in the forward areas. He reported that he had other evidence to show that irresponsible broadcasts from the BBC were 'causing a good deal of trouble also in a military way to our forces in the field' and he suggested that the matter was so grave that it should be taken up by the Chief of the General Staff (CGS) with the BBC.[22] The censorship summary for 8 to 14 July described how the 'BBC and particularly its observer in Cairo [Richard Dimbleby] is under fire from all sides.' Dimbleby was the subject of particularly vicious ridicule and savage sarcasm, and many of the troops believed that his reports did 'an awful lot of harm'. Furthermore, he was reputed to have undermined Eighth Army operations by giving unwanted publicity to certain units, who

[19] AWM 54 883/2/97 MEFCWS, no. IV (3 to 9 December 1941), p. 2.
[20] AWM 54 883/2/97 MEFCWS, no. XIII (4 to 10 February 1942), p. 37.   [21] Ibid., p. 7.
[22] SAMAD CGS (War), Box 155, Lt.-Col. E. G. Malherbe to Director of Military Training (DMT), 'Morale of Troops', 28 March 1942.

had to abandon their 'prize shows' because his programmes alerted the Germans to their plans.[23]

Another memorandum, written in August 1942 on the state of South African morale in the desert, highlighted how a war commentary, just before the attack on Tobruk, had 'expressed the opinion that the defence of Tobruk w[as] not essential to the defence of Egypt. This [wa]s said to have had a depressing effect on the morale of the defenders.' There was, according to the memorandum, 'a tendency [among soldiers] to regard news commentaries as an expression of the highest official opinion; there is very little realisation that the speakers have no official status'.[24] It was, therefore, all the more important that the BBC took great care in what it broadcast.

The BBC's regular praise of Dominion and Commonwealth forces, at the expense of the far more numerous British contingents in the desert, exacerbated many of these problems for the men from the UK. The British soldiers of Eighth Army wanted their loved ones to know that they too were fully contributing to the endeavour that caused their separation. It was demoralising to hear only praise for the Australians and hear nothing of their own efforts. Programmes such as 'Tribute to Tobruk', broadcast in October 1941, made some progress in dissipating such feelings, and the men were 'pleased to hear that prominence has at last been given to the fact that soldiers from the Home country are fighting here'.[25]

A memorandum, written in January 1942 by Major W. Stan Scrivenor, Australian Area Commandant ME Base Area, highlighted the problems that Australian troops experienced with Middle East news broadcasts. He wrote that 'the sessions at present, and for some time past, have been too short, and badly presented. The announcer from Australia quite frequently appears to be very tired, and puts the news over in such a way that it seems to be a trouble to do so. The impression here is that it is "just another job". This, I consider, is an insult to the troops.' It appeared to Scrivenor that many of the news items were badly chosen.

After many discussions with members of the AIF in many units, and of many grades, from privates to generals, news of a domestic character is required, such as floods in Gippsland, buses in Bourke Street, a fire at Hordens and even robberies and accidents. These are talking points among the troops, who pass such news on.

---

[23] ANZ WAII/1/DA508/1 vol.1, MEFCWS, no. XXXV (8 to 14 July 1942), pp. 6–7.
[24] SAMAD Div Docs, Gp 1, Box 1, Memorandum on Morale of SA Troops in ME, 8 August 1942, p. 8.
[25] AWM 54 883/2/97 British Troops in Egypt no. 105 Field Censorship Report Week Ending 29 October 1941, p. 4.

Anything pertaining to the welfare of dependents at home is readily acceptable, and indeed, looked for. Items on schemes for repatriation and the betterment of returned soldiers are listened to eagerly.

The only 'political items required' were 'responsible statements by Mr. Curtin or other ministers, and THEY MUST BE SHORT. Once a month there should be a resume of the activities in all sporting spheres, such as the positions on the list of the various football or cricket teams, and if possible, the Saturday broadcast should give the first, second and third of the main races.'[26] As another memo written on the subject announced, 'the news we want is the very big, and the very human and personal. The "middles" are of no interest to our men, who have outgrown them.' Broadcasters, it said, should consider the 'collective mind' of the AIF and address information 'to men who are all somewhat home-sick'.[27]

The BBC, as the troops consistently pointed out, was clearly out of touch with their needs. The censorship summaries noted many requests for improved or alternate programming and, in particular, for more 'easy listening'. The summary for 22 to 29 October 1941 stressed that 'music instead of talk is the cry as far as the entertainment side of the BBC programmes are concerned and many troops appear to listen to the German radio for musical programmes' instead of the BBC.[28] The popularity of the German song 'Lili Marleen' illustrates the extent of this practice. Written by Norbert Schultze and Hans Leip, and originally recorded by Lale Andersen in 1939, 'Lili Marleen' became a huge hit with both armies after its first broadcast on Radio Belgrade on 18 August 1941.[29]

In the spring of 1942, Willans set about dealing with the problem of broadcasts in the desert. He complained to the BBC that the *Forces Programme* was of an unacceptable quality. Standards, he argued, needed to be raised and the forces given a say in the direction of a 'real forces programme'.[30] In May, the BBC issued a questionnaire through *Parade* magazine to ascertain the types of programmes and items desired by military listeners.[31] With the backing of Adam, and with the objective of studying and developing the use of broadcasting by the army, a broadcasting section was set up in the Directorate of Welfare in July 1942. At the same time, an Army Broadcasting Committee was inaugurated, under the chairmanship of Willans, to frame an official army policy with regard to

[26] AWM 54 805/7/5 AIF News Service, 3 January 1942.
[27] AWM 54 805/7/5 Broadcasts to AIF, 6 January 1942.
[28] AWM 54 883/2/97 MEFCWS, no. XIII (4 to 10 February 1942), p. 7.
[29] Latimer, *Alamein*, p. 42.   [30] Crang, *The British Army and the People's War*, p. 96.
[31] AWM 54 883/2/97 MEFCWS, no. XXVIII (20 to 26 May 1942), p. 2.

broadcasting, and a joint planning committee was established with the BBC to work out programmes.[32]

In July 1942, a new daily programme for the MEF was begun and it gradually changed the MEF's opinions about the Corporation. By August, the BBC had toned down its propagandistic tendencies and reacted to the troops' desires regarding music and news.[33] A memorandum on the state of South African morale, written on 8 August, stated that 'on the whole the news bulletins are accepted as reliable, and there is little tendency to doubt facts given'.[34] Following El Alamein, during the advance westwards, Lieutenant-Colonel A.K. Main, an army psychiatrist, joined Eighth Army to ascertain what the men wanted in the way of programmes. When he returned to the UK, Adam arranged for him to discuss his findings with the staff responsible for the *Forces Programme*, and, as a result, the programme was considerably amended and 'we had no more trouble'.[35] Dimbleby was also removed, in September 1942, a measure which pleased almost all of the troops.[36]

There is little doubt that the quality of radio broadcasts to the Middle East improved in the run up to El Alamein. However, the troops' reliance on the radio for news was hampered by the fact that there were a limited number of radios available to units. 'Generally', according to the Australian 2/23 Battalion newsletter, 'there was only one "wireless set" to a Battalion, and this was heard by only a few' of the men.[37] The consequent transmission, and inevitable filtering, of news from man to man meant that rumours played a significant role in shaping the soldiers' experience and expectations in the desert.[38] As one South African soldier wrote, after Crusader, 'the men in the Desert scarcely know the situation ... as there is a grave lack of information once we get in the Desert. The result is that when we score a comparatively small victory as we did quite lately everyone thinks it's final and that they can go home.

---

[32] LHCMA Adam 3/3 Notes for the S-of-S Estimates Speech, February 1943. AG.'s Department.

[33] ANZ WAII/1/DA508 vol. 1, MEFCWS, no. XXXVII (22 to 28 July 1942), p. 6.

[34] SAMAD Div Docs, Gp 1, Box 1, Memorandum on Morale of SA Troops in ME, 8 August 1942, p. 8.

[35] LHCMA Adam 3/13 Narrative Covering Aspects of Work as Adjutant-General WWII, chap. 6, Welfare, p. 7.

[36] NA WO 193/453 Morale Report, August to October 1942.

[37] Fanke (ed.), *Mud and Blood in the Field*, p. vii.

[38] ANZ WAII/1/DA21.1/9/G4/12 part 2, 2 NZ Div Field Censor Reports; WAII/1/DA21.1/9/G4/12 Part 1, HQ 2 NZ Div (G Branch) Security and Intelligence Reports (16 June 1941 to 31 January 1942).

Now had they been better informed, they would not feel so blue as they do now when we suffer from reverses.'[39]

The 1st South African Division Security Report for the week ending 28 December 1941, illustrates this problem. It called for 'an increased scale' of 'lectures to other ranks . . . as despicable attempts are . . . being made to undermine the morale of troops by spreading of false rumours . . . All ranks should be requested to report immediately to FSS [Field Security Sections] any rumour coming to their notice, also to hand in any letters received in this connection, so that the necessary investigation can be made without delay.'[40] The virulence of such rumours was so extreme, and their relevance to the everyday experience of fighting in the desert was so important, that the New Zealand Security Report for 7 September to 19 October 1941 suggested that 'at suitable times judicious use be made of "rumours" of a heartening nature'. The contents of these 'rumours' could be decided on by general staff officers and spread discreetly by New Zealand FSS.[41]

A 9th Australian Division training instruction, released in late December 1941, pointed out that 'during battle, the enemy's attack on morale is often aided by . . . rumours of the most amazing character. Some are from their nature, depressing; others are so optimistic, that when time proves them untrue, their non fulfilment leads to depression.' Alarmist reports of heavy casualties and the early reports of losses in battle always tended to exaggerate problems. The report pointed out that in order to ensure that 'the soldier has a firm background as to the real situation against which he can assess rumours at their true value, it is essential, especially in difficult situations, that the troops are kept fully informed as to the true position. This can be done by the issue of news sheets and by explanation of the situation to the troops by their officers.'[42] By August 1942, the censorship summaries were still reporting that 'rumours and propaganda over here are rife and it is best to turn a deaf ear to all the wild furphies one hears every day'. Men were 'heavily fined' for passing on such tales[43] and in order to undermine them some units began issuing

[39] AWM 54 883/2/97 MEFCWS, no. XIV (11 to 17 February 1942), p. 10.
[40] SAMAD Div Docs, Gp 1, Box 49, 1st SA Division Security Report for week ending 28 December 1941.
[41] WAII/1/DA21.1/9/G4/12 part 1, HQ 2 NZ Div (G Branch) Security Report 7 September to 19 October 1941.
[42] AWM 54 519/7/26 9 Australian Division Training Instructions no. 5, Training Points with examples from ME campaign. HQ 9 Australian Div, 23 December 1941 (written by Lt.-Col. H. Wells, GS 9 Australian Division).
[43] ANZ WAII/1/DA508/1 vol. 1, MEFCWS, no. XXXIX (5 to 11 August 1942), p. 21.

news sheets to their troops derived from information from the battalion radio.

The printing and issuing of items such as news-sheets, however, was the exception rather than the norm in the fluid battles of the desert. Reference to the shortage of reading material was mentioned in almost every censorship summary, until the run-up to El Alamein. The general opinion among troops was that 'anything would be welcome'.[44] British troops in particular fared very badly in this regard. Most of the reading material they obtained towards the end of 1941 was passed on to them by the Australians, 'who seem[ed] to fare better in the way of comforts'.[45] One man, from the 2nd Battalion York and Lancaster Regiment, wrote, 'I was very impressed with the Australians' rations, comforts and papers, etc., sent from Australia, so much so that as often as not they had too much. Now, as you know, our fellows get next to nothing.'[46] Australians received 170 issues of the *AIF News* per infantry battalion and this number increased to 285 per battalion in May 1942. This was an increase from one copy per five men to one copy per three men.[47] The *AIF News* was the military newspaper with the highest circulation in the Middle East and the army postal authorities estimated that 90 per cent of the papers issued were posted on by the soldiers to their homes in Australia.[48]

By October 1941, in response to constant demand for more newspapers and periodicals,[49] South African authorities began printing their own newspaper, *The Springbok*, in place of the 'rancid sheets' that South African troops received at the time.[50] The *NZEF Times* was started around the same time and distributed on the basis of one copy per three men in field units and one copy per five men in base units.[51] *Eighth Army News* began production in September 1941 and the desert weekly, *Crusader*, began distribution in April 1942. These publications gained dedicated and enthusiastic readerships due to their ability to portray themselves as being 'by and for the ordinary soldier'. Articles focused on news and issues

---

[44] AWM 3DRL 2632 2/3 Morshead, Tobruk Fortress Censorship Report, ND but 1941.
[45] AWM 54 883/2/97 British Troops in Egypt no. 105 Field Censorship Report Week Ending 29 October 1941, p. 3.
[46] Ibid.
[47] AWM 54 805/7/5 Distribution of *AIF News*, 18 May 1942.
[48] AWM 54 805/7/2 *AIF News*, Copy of Final Report and Supporting Details, February 1943.
[49] AWM 54 883/2/97 British Troops in Egypt no. 102 Field Censorship Report Week Ending 7 October 1941, p. 4.
[50] AWM 54 883/2/97 British Troops in Egypt no. 104 Field Censorship Report Week Ending 21 October 1941, p. 4.
[51] William George Stevens, *Problems of 2 NZEF, Official History of New Zealand in the Second World War 1939–45* (Wellington, 1958), pp. 126, 249.

that the troops were interested in, and 'perhaps most important of all – letters from soldiers disgruntled over pay and conditions'. As the editor of *Crusader*, Warwick Charlton, wrote, in May 1942, 'this is a desert paper. It originates in the desert and is for the desert rats. Our chief interest is what you want and not what other people think you should have.'[52]

By May 1942, other publications such as the *World Press Review* and *Parade* magazine were available throughout the Middle East. The *World Press Review* provided a weekly selection of articles of interest that had appeared in the international press. It was produced by GHQ, MEF, and the material was drawn from what was considered the best and most informative matter relating to current affairs. Individuals or units could subscribe at discount rates.[53] *Parade*, with its feature 'Home Town News', took the laurels for the most popular publication in the desert, and many troops were known to send copies home.[54]

In spite of these initiatives, in August 1942 the morale reports and censorship summaries were still highlighting a continued and 'most disturbing' need for information in the desert. This was required, among other reasons, to counter Axis propaganda that was affecting not only Eighth Army's morale but also its combat performance. In particular, the censorship summaries reported the serious development that 'a positively friendly feeling towards the Afrika Korps' had arisen amongst the men of Eighth Army that was having the effect of making 'men become readier to surrender'. It was suggested that it was high time a fresh endeavour was made to encourage men to realise what defeat would mean.[55] German propaganda had 'all the more effect', according to the summary for 12 to 18 August, the height of the morale crisis, 'as it comes on top of recent reverses, and there is a complete lack of any adequate counter-measures on our part. A growing number of men feel they have been deceived about the enemy and in their present temper are prepared to jump to conclusions and assume they are being misled in regard to other factors too.' The censor clearly thought the problem was that 'many of the troops still want to know what we are fighting for'.[56]

[52] S. P. MacKenzie, 'Vox Populi: British Army Newspapers in the Second World War', *Journal of Contemporary History*, 24(4) (October, 1989), p. 666.
[53] SAMAD Div Docs, Gp 1, Box 1, Army Routine Orders by Lieut.-Gen. N. M. Ritchie, General Officer Commanding-in-Chief, Eighth Army, 23 May 1942, p. 7.
[54] AWM 54 883/2/97 MEFCWS, no. XXX (3 to 9 June 1942), p. 5.
[55] ANZ WAII/1/DA508 vol. 1, MEMCWS, no. XXXVIII (29 July to 4 August 1942), p. 2; ANZ WAII/1/DA508 vol. 1, MEMCWS, no. XL (12 to 18 August 1942), p. 2.
[56] NA WO 193/453 Draft Morale Report, May to July 1942; ANZ WAII/1/DA508 vol. 3, MEMCWS, no. XL (12 to 18 August 1942), pp. 2–3.

To counter German propaganda, a number of articles were released in *Crusader* magazine and a reproduction of a *New York Times* story addressing the issue was published in the *World Press Review*. The censorship summary for 3 to 9 September noted that 'comment on the virtues and humane qualities of the German troops was definitely on the decrease,' and it gave 'not a little' credit for this turnaround and the 'spiking of the enemy's invisible weapons' to both publications.[57] The morale report for August to October 1942 recounted the positive news that 'perhaps the most important change of feeling [among the troops in the desert] is the disappearance of the friendliness towards the Afrika Korps (largely the result of German propaganda), which was assuming such dangerous proportions during the preceding quarter'.[58]

The same report noted that 'morale has been greatly strengthened' by the publication of unit and service magazines. The improved amount of reading matter that was available to the troops in the desert, in the lead up to El Alamein, was attributed by many to the intervention of Churchill following his visit to the desert in August 1942.[59] By El Alamein, newspapers were being carried forward to troops to provide a distribution of 4,500 copies per corps with the aim that units could receive the previous day's paper with their rations.[60]

The need for information was not confined to news about operations and general current affairs. Information that might have relevance to loved ones and friends back home was considered of equal if not greater importance by the men in the desert. A great worry for British soldiers in 1941 was the Blitz in England.[61] Willans made the issue one of his priorities. In his address to the Royal Society of Arts, in March 1941, he stated that he planned for the anxious soldier serving overseas 'to be able to receive rapid and accurate information as to the welfare of his close relatives and his home, whenever he has reason to fear that they have been the subject of attention by the enemy'. At the time, the soldier serving overseas was informed by the War Office when anyone carrying his name and address with their identity card was admitted to hospital as a casualty or a fatality. In Willans's opinion, this information was 'inadequate' because the soldier was 'left wondering about developments for what can be a very long period of time'. He made it clear

---

[57] ANZ WAII/1/DA508 vol. 1, MEMCWS, no. XLIII (3 to 9 September 1942), p. 7.
[58] NA WO 193/453 Morale Report, August to October 1942.
[59] Ibid.
[60] IWM 99/1/2 Papers of Maj.-Gen. Raymond Briggs, METM no. 7, Lessons from Operations, October and November 1942, p. 62.
[61] NA CAB 21/914 'The Work of Army Psychiatrists in Relation to Morale', January 1944.

that it was his goal to arrange that the soldier received follow-up cables to inform him of progress when his property was damaged, and, in all cases, the definite assurance that his interests were being properly looked after.[62]

The War Office, therefore, requested the Soldiers', Sailors' and Airmen's Families Association (SSAFA) to open an overseas branch at their head office in London.[63] This was done in May 1941, and the SSAFA was entrusted, having received representations from the Consulting Psychiatrist Middle East Forces,[64] with dealing with all enquiries from British soldiers serving overseas relating to air raids, family and personal problems. In June 1941, a leaflet produced by command of the Army Council, 'Injury or Damage from Enemy Action. Important Information for All Soldiers Serving at Home or Overseas', informed soldiers that a special welfare organisation had also been set up by the Commander-in-Chief in the Middle East.[65]

By September 1941, the War Office was able to claim in a memorandum that a scheme had been put in place, (a) to prevent the soldier overseas from worrying unnecessarily and to reassure him so far as possible in the event of bomb damage; (b) to relieve him as quickly as possible of his anxiety about what had happened to his wife and family; (c) to help him and his family get assistance as quickly as possible if they had suffered from enemy action; and (d) to afford help on the spot, as necessary, by extension of leave and pay.[66]

Nevertheless, as the situation appeared to improve for British contingents of Eighth Army, it deteriorated for the Commonwealth and Dominion elements. The Japanese advances in the Far East, in early 1942, caused considerable concerns for many of the men.[67] The censorship summary for 18 to 25 February 1942 stated that the weakness of the Allied position in the Far East had 'led to an obvious drop in the tone of correspondence from the NZEF' and that a 'large majority of the troops expressed the desire to be fighting in the defence of their own country'. One soldier wrote, 'this business with Japan is taking more out of us in

---

[62] NA WO 163/123 Army Pamphlet, 'Welfare and Education', by Maj.-Gen. H. Willans, reprint of address given on Friday 7 March 1941 before the Royal Society of Arts, pp. 6–7.

[63] NA WO 163/123 Injury or Damage from Enemy Action. Important Information for All Soldiers Serving at Home or Overseas, 7 June 1941.

[64] NA CAB 21/914 'The Work of Army Psychiatrists in Relation to Morale', January 1944.

[65] NA WO 163/123 Injury or Damage from Enemy Action. Important Information for All Soldiers Serving at Home or Overseas, 7 June 1941.

[66] NA WO 163/123 Army Welfare and Education, Memorandum by the War Office, 12 September 1941.

[67] AWM 54 883/2/97 British Troops in Egypt, no. 93 Field Censorship Report Week Ending 7 August 1941, p. 1.

worry than the actual fighting . . . I guess there isn't one of us over here who wouldn't change places with someone at home.'[68] Another New Zealand soldier wrote, 'we should all be home now, darling, to look after our own people. I hate to contemplate the thought of those Japs ever attacking our country . . . I don't know what I should do, and if such a calamity did happen, I would feel that I had let my people and my country down by coming away instead of staying to fight for them and my own country.'[69] A spate of white feathers, sent to the 9th Australian Division from home, accusing them of abandoning their country in its hour of need, only exacerbated Australian soldiers' anxieties.[70]

Freyberg, Commander of 2nd New Zealand Division, was so concerned about the situation that he wrote to Major-General Puttick, Chief of the General Staff in Wellington, in March 1942, detailing the measures he had undertaken to allay the soldiers' fears. 'The matter has been receiving constant attention here', he wrote, 'and Brigadiers have been kept in touch through Middle East censorship with the tone of correspondence. We have also been dealing with various questions affecting morale through "NZEF Times".' Freyberg was able to report that lecturettes, based on a 'proper appreciation of the position', which had been sent by Puttick from New Zealand and delivered to the troops, had helped to allay the anxiety of men 'who [were] naturally worried at the speed and success . . . of Japanese attacks'.[71]

In addition to news bulletins, news-sheets and official communications, the other key source of information on matters at home was personal mail. The arrival or non-arrival of mail played a crucial role in determining the soldiers' morale. One soldier wrote, 'you should have witnessed the crowding around the mail bag in our canteen tonight . . . I got 5 letters. Mail does so much to keep one cheerful and in good spirits, for quite often this existence in the desert, day after day gets one down in the dumps.' Another soldier, who received eight letters, airgraphs and Christmas cards, in January 1942, wrote that 'this is one of the happiest days in my life'.[72]

Soldiers were able to send mail home as often as they liked, but it was usually censored by the officers in their unit and often took weeks, if not months, to reach its destination, as it had to travel by boat all the way around the Cape of Good Hope. Every week soldiers were also permitted

[68] AWM 54 883/2/97 MEFCWS, no. XV (18 to 25 February 1942), p. 9.
[69] AWM 54 883/2/97 MEFCWS, no. XII (28 Jan to 3 February 1942), p. 8.
[70] AWM 54 883/2/97 MEFCWS, no. XXX (3 to 9 June 1942), p. 16.
[71] WAII/8/26 Freyberg to Maj.-Gen. Puttick (Chief of the General Staff, Army HQ, Wellington), 20 March 1942.
[72] AWM 54 883/2/97 MEFCWS, no. XII (28 January to 3 February 1942), p. 2.

to send home one 'green envelope', which was censored centrally, allowing the soldier some freedom to write what he wanted to say without his commanding officer reading his correspondence.[73] Men were also allowed to send home one 'air letter' or 'airgraph' every month. This was extremely popular with the troops as their correspondence reached home relatively quickly. The volume of mail that was sent to and from the Middle East was staggering. To give an example, 2nd New Zealand Division alone sent approximately 150,000 letters home a month during the summer of 1942.[74]

Throughout 1941, the speed and reliability of mail services in the desert was a persistent problem. The question of mail became so important to morale that the matter provoked debate in the House of Commons.[75] The government reacted by instigating the airgraph service, between Britain and the Middle East, in August 1941. The airgraph was invented in the 1930s by the Eastman Kodak Company in conjunction with Imperial Airways (now British Airways) and Pan American World Airways, as a means of reducing the weight and bulk of mail carried by air. The airgraph forms, upon which the letter was written, were photographed and then sent as negatives on rolls of microfilm. Around 1,600 letters on film weighed just 5 oz, while 1,600 ordinary letters weighed 50 lbs. At their destination, the negatives were printed on photographic paper and delivered as airgraph letters through the normal postal systems. Around 70,000 airgraphs were sent in the first batch from the UK to the desert in 1941[76] and it was hoped by the censors that more and more people would make use of this facility 'to convey welcome news to the troops in the desert'.[77]

In spite of this innovation, the problem of mail was never adequately solved in the Middle East. The censorship summary for 24 to 30 December 1941 noted that the only item criticised by fighting units was the mail.[78] Almost a year later, the censorship summary for 3 to 9 September 1942 reported that 'dissatisfaction with the postal services, which had practically disappeared in the course of the past six months, is on the increase again, notably in regard to incoming mail'.[79] Australians and New Zealanders were especially unfortunate, again due to the Japanese invasion of Southeast Asia, which, in the first half of 1942,

---

[73] ANZ WAII/1/DA21.1/9/G4/11 part 1, Notes on Green Envelope, HQ NZ Div, 7 November 1940.
[74] WAII/1/DA302/15/1–31, History 1 and 2 NZ Fd Censor Sections, p. 35.
[75] AWM 54 883/2/97 British Troops in Egypt No. 95 Field Censorship Report Week Ending 21 August 1941, p. 5.
[76] www.remuseum.org.uk/specialism/rem_spec_pcsww2.htm
[77] AWM 54 883/2/97 British Troops in Egypt no. 100 Field Censorship Report Week Ending 23 September 1941, p. 4.
[78] AWM 54 883/2/97 MEFCWS, no. VII (24 to 30 December 1941), p. 4.
[79] ANZ WAII/1/DA508/1 vol. 3, MEFCWS, no. XLIII (3 to 9 September 1942), p. 4.

slowed down mail to the antipodeans' homelands. The New Zealand forces were told to expect delays to parcel services, while airmail services would still work as efficiently as possible, although, in March 1942, even airmail services were suspended. At the same time, the authorities also asked New Zealand soldiers to reduce letter writing to a minimum and restrict letters to approximately two pages.[80] The irregularity of mail meant that the impact of news from the BBC and newspapers and journals was all the more powerful. It also meant that it was almost impossible for men to develop coherent streams of contact with their loved ones.

It was not just the arrival of the mail that was important but also the contents of the written correspondence, with all that this entailed in regard to relationships and family affairs. As it was pithily put by one officer, 'the two main factors affecting morale of the soldier overseas are the mail and the female'.[81] The men, separated from their wives, fiancées and sweethearts, worried especially about the fidelity and loyalty of their loved ones back home. The exigencies of the Second World War meant that many Allied soldiers, especially Canadians and Americans, spent time in Britain, Australia, New Zealand and South Africa. Unsurprisingly, many of these men met and had relations with women in the countries where they were posted. The censorship summaries make it clear that this issue was almost more important to the troops than any other during the desert war.

By September 1941, Canadian troops in England had already developed a bad reputation. An officer wrote,

The boys are getting very scared of the Canadians upsetting their domestic life at home. We have three instances of it in this unit during the last month. It started when I got a letter addressed to the O.C. Would I be good enough to inform Pte. X that his wife was an expectant mother and had gone to live with another man . . . Poor chap . . . He couldn't speak for three days. Since then two more have had letters breaking off engagements. What with that and the delay in the mail, the whole crowd are worried to death.

Such grim stories, in the censor's opinion, 'in virtue of their appeal, are subject to wide and quick circulation' and did 'in consequence cause considerable uneasiness'.[82] By January 1942, the summaries pointed to an almost hysterical pandemic of worry and jealousy among the troops in the desert.

The censorship summary for 4 to 10 February 1942 pointed out that comments about Canadian troops on home soil were enough to 'fill a

[80] AWM 54 883/2/97 MEFCWS, no. XII (28 January to 3 February 1942), p. 8.
[81] NA WO 193/453 Draft Morale Report: Overseas Commands: November 1943 to January 1944.
[82] AWM 54 883/2/97 British Troops in Egypt no. 100 Field Censorship Report Week Ending 23 September 1941, p. 4.

Illustration 11 A soldier of 50th Battalion, Royal Tank Regiment, shaving beside his Valentine tank, October 1942. A photograph of his wife and new baby is propped up alongside his mirror. The soldiers' relationship with home played a crucial role in maintaining morale. The high incidence of relationship breakdown contributed to the morale crisis that beset Eighth Army in the summer of 1942.

book'. The censor reported that 'very few letters did not mention this subject'.[83] The Australians, New Zealanders and South Africans were not immune to such worries either. The arrival of US troops on Australian and New Zealand soil, in the first half of 1942, was of concern to many of the men. Their misgivings appeared to be all the greater when Australians recollected their own activities abroad.[84] One writer stated, 'our biggest worry at present is the rumour that there are a lot of Yanks in Brisbane,

[83] AWM 54 883/2/97 MEFCWS, no. XIII (4 to 10 February 1942), p. 4.
[84] By February 1943 there were 116,420 US soldiers and airmen in Australia. See NA WO 162/318 Indian and Dominion Forces, Strengths and Casualties as Reported to Central Stats Office.

and remembering the good time we had in South Africa and the British Isles we want to get home in a hell of a hurry to see how our girls are behaving themselves. Believe me this is a big worry.'[85] The censorship summary for New Zealand troops for 5 to 11 March reported that the most discussed topic of mail was the arrival of US Forces at home. One man wrote, 'I suppose they are having a good time. I only hope they don't get the same name that the Canadians have in England, it's pretty rotten.'[86] The censorship summary for 23 to 29 April recounted how the 'Springboks advise their womenfolk not to be led astray by R.A.F. personnel training in South Africa. Concern over the activities of the "blue plague" as the R.A.F. trainees are being increasingly called, has been growing in recent weeks.'[87]

The extraordinary prevalence of 'women problems' among the men of Eighth Army and their effect on morale almost defies belief. The censorship summary for 27 May to 2 June, right at the start of the Axis summer offensive, commented that 'there appears to be no slackening of mail from home relating to domestic tragedies and this type of news seems to have an increasingly adverse effect on the morale of the troops. The hatred the troops show for overseas troops in Britain is very real and finds a great deal of expression throughout the mail.'[88] In July 1942, one man wrote to his wife, 'I tell you what our tent is called now, love, it is called the "Jilted Lovers Tent," because there are four chaps in this tent who were engaged, but now their girls have broken it off and in three cases the girls have married Canadians.' Another stated, 'unfortunately the women of England are not playing the game, we have just had another chap whose wife has been put in the family way by another man – that makes 15 out of 160 of us [c. 9 per cent], good going eh?'[89]

The censor described these examples as 'by no means being isolated case[s]'.

The ... men believe that they have been away so long that it is becoming increasingly difficult for their girls to remain loyal to their engagements and friendships. Younger married men are worried about their wives as they feel they are still attractive and may be in danger from unwelcome attention while older married men are worried that their wives will be too old to rear children by the time they return. This subject, apart from the ebb and flow of the battle itself, has a greater effect on the men's morale than any other single factor.[90]

---

[85] AWM 54 883/2/97 MEFCWS, no. XIII (4 to 10 February 1942), p. 9.
[86] AWM 54 883/2/97 MEFCWS, no. XVII (5 to 11 March 1942), p. 11.
[87] AWM 54 883/2/97 MEFCWS, no. XXIV (23 to 29 April 1942), p. 12.
[88] AWM 54 883/2/97 MEFCWS, no. XXIX (27 May to 2 June 1942), p. 2.
[89] ANZ WAII/1/DA508/1 vol. 1, MEFCWS, no. XXXIV (1 to 7 July 1942), pp. 7–8.
[90] Ibid.

A chaplain, writing in July 1942 to the wife of a soldier who had caused him to seek a divorce, did not mince his words: 'The most efficient fifth column work done out here is carried out by the women in England, who seem to be incapable of faithfulness or courage when they're separated from their husbands.'[91] By August 1942, newspapers were reporting that Free French, Czech and Polish troops in the UK were marrying on average 600 English girls a month. The censor stated that these reports were 'doing more harm among our men than anything Dr. Goebbels can produce'.[92]

One particular story took hold of the troops' imagination. In January 1942, the English and US press published a photograph depicting Italian prisoners of war 'making merry' with land girls on a farm in England. A week later, the *Egyptian Mail* published a paragraph on the photo entitled 'Storm in a Teacup', drawing attention to the matter in not unfavourable terms. The troops reacted with outrage. The censorship summary for the week 21 to 27 January 1942 reported that one field censor had found as many as 50 per cent of the letters examined contained some reference to the subject.[93]

The publication of the article in Britain also created a furore, causing the Minister for Information, Brendan Bracken, to answer questions on the topic in the House of Commons.[94] What was clear was that the British press had no concept of the great danger inherent in such articles. 'This is just a sample of what upsets us out here', one man wrote, 'it makes us feel as if England isn't worth fighting for ... You see what I mean, don't you, things like that in the newspapers are so distressing, the lads think their girls may be doing the same thing.'[95] The censorship summary for the week 28 January to 3 February remarked, 'the men are all the more incensed by this unfortunate affair [because] it is generally agreed that the Italians have behaved very badly towards our own prisoners'.[96] Five months later, the effect of the story had still not diminished. The censorship summary for 22 to 28 July discussed a rumour that a member of the women's Land Army was expecting a child by an Italian prisoner of war. The report stated that 'to determine the truth of these statements is very

[91] AWM 54 883/2/97 MEFCWS, no. XXXVII (22 to 28 July 1942), p. 3; NA WO 193/453 Draft Morale Report, May to July 1942. Although there are some references to the consoling effects of chaplains and of religious services in the censorship summaries, these are not sufficiently consistent or recurring to warrant particular attention here.
[92] ANZ WAII/1/DA508/1 vol. 1, MEFCWS, no. XXXVIII (29 July to 4 August 1942), p. 3.
[93] AWM 54 883/2/97 MEFCWS, no. XI (21 to 27 January 1942), pp. 1–2.
[94] Ibid., p. 2.   [95] Ibid., p. 3.
[96] AWM 54 883/2/97 MEFCWS, no. XII (28 January to 3 February 1942), p. 3.

difficult, but they are discussed at great length ... and morale is certainly very adversely affected by [them]'.[97] Similar stories in the Australian press had just as negative an effect on AIF morale. One Australian Army chaplain wrote that 'the "Roger the Lodger" and "Hank the Yank" stuff that some papers publish is ... bad psychology – good fifth column. It is bad enough for the lads to face the interminable waiting out here with a mail that seldom arrives, and the Jap in the north, without this type of stuff being added. In peace it might slip in, but in war, when men are living in abnormal conditions under abnormal strain, it is at best stupid and at worst damnable.'[98]

At the start of 1942, the BBC produced a radio play, 'Front Line Family', that had a similar effect on the troops. The play was about a family whose son met the fiancée of a soldier who was stationed in the Middle East. The soldier's fiancée fell in love with the other boy and then broke off the engagement.[99] One man in the desert wrote despairingly about the BBC's choice of programmes for the troops. 'You know the BBC really are the most incredibly short sighted lot. The other day they put out to the MEF a story of some woman playing fast and loose ... in England while her husband was in Libya. Can you beat it? It is just what is causing some of our men the worst awful mental anguish as they hear the most colourful stories of life in complacent England. I must admit that such thoughts have crossed my mind on more than one occasion, and it needs quite strong willpower to put it out of one's mind.'[100]

The significance of women troubles was highlighted at a conference of medical specialists held at GHQ Middle East in April 1942. The medical officers (MOs) present agreed that experience in the Middle East had proved the 'immense importance of minor psychological upsets in the causation of disease'. Among such psychological upsets, the MOs included 'marital infidelity' and 'broken homes', and emphasised that, in units with 'a few men so circumstanced, morale may become generally undermined'. From the military medical standpoint, the MOs concluded that 'psychological upset through worry' caused the 'deterioration' of a man's 'psychological condition', with a consequent impairment in his 'fighting quality'.[101]

The implications of 'women troubles' for morale and fighting effectiveness was also noted by officers in the field. One officer reported how a lack

[97] AWM 54 883/2/97 MEFCWS, no. XXXVII (22 to 28 July 1942), p. 3.
[98] ANZ WAII/1/DA508/1 vol. 1 MEMCWS, no. XXXVIII (29 July to 4 August 1942), p. 16.
[99] AWM 54 883/2/97 MEFCWS, no. XVII (5 to 11 March 1942), p. 4.
[100] AWM 54 883/2/97 MEFCWS, no. XVI (26 February to 4 March 1942), p. 5.
[101] AWM 54 883/2/97 MEFCWS, no. XXXVII (22 to 28 July 1942), p. 4.

of concrete emotional connections with loved ones at home could leave soldiers detached and ultimately lead to surrender.

Many of these troops of ours have been out here upwards of two years ... It is difficult at this time and distance for them to feel that they have their backs to the wall of their own homes. Many are obsessed with the fear or knowledge of the infidelity of their womenfolk and desire for 'revenge'. All in all, it is possible that if suddenly confronted with the choice between the likelihood of death in the desert and twelve to eighteen months in a prison camp, the latter alternative might prevail. This is of course, far from universal, but at the same time I suspect it is not exceptional, and it is not the way to set out to win battles.[102]

During 1941, 16,000 men applied for compassionate leave from Home Command for causes of urgent domestic hardship. That number jumped to 100,000 in 1942 for both Home Command and overseas troops,[103] while the number of men who applied for release or posting nearer home, on the grounds of domestic hardship, during 1942, was 39,000.[104] The censorship summary for 29 July to 4 August reported that in some units in the desert with poor morale, such as the 1st Buffs, an inordinately high percentage of NCOs and men began to attempt 'to get home on compassionate grounds'.[105] Needless to say, there was not much chance of such men being successful. For example, up until 18 March 1942, only 177 members of the AIF were returned home for compassionate reasons.[106]

To deal with such numbers of domestic worries, the War Office relied heavily on the SSAFA, who processed enquiries into the problems presented by applications from soldiers overseas. By April 1942, the Welfare Directorate had taken the step of initiating a reconciliation scheme, where representatives of the SSAFA would visit soldiers' wives and try to patch up relations between soldiers and loved ones before family allowances were withdrawn or any legal action was taken. By October 1942, there were 6,000 cases of this sort on the lists of the SSAFA bureau in London and it was receiving over 1,000 additional enquiries by letter each week.[107]

---

[102] ANZ WAII/1/DA508/1 vol. 1, MEFCWS, no. XXXIV (1 to 7 July 1942), p. 7.

[103] NA WO 277/4 Morgan, *Army Welfare*, p. 32.

[104] LHCMA Adam 3/3 Notes for the S-of-S Estimates Speech, February 1943. AG's Department.

[105] ANZ WAII/1/DA508/1 vol. 1, MEMCWS, no. XXXVIII (29 July to 4 August 1942), p. 3.

[106] AWM 54 903/2/3 Personnel Returned to Australia by Cause.

[107] NA WO 277/4 Morgan, *Army Welfare*, p. 116; Crang, *The British Army and the People's War*, p. 101; LHCMA Adam 3/3 Notes for the S-of-S Estimates Speech, February 1943. AG's Department, p. 23.

The SSAFA also set up an office in the Middle East[108] to give free legal advice to men wishing to petition for divorce. By the autumn of 1942, some 2,000 cases were awaiting attention and new cases were being received at a rate of about 12 a day.[109] The War Office was so concerned that a representative of the Directorate of Welfare visited Eighth Army to investigate the matter in the autumn of 1942. At XIII Corps headquarters, he found 'many cases of domestic problems'; at 7th Armoured Division headquarters, the 'need' for 'legal advice' for domestic issues was stressed 'from the point of view of morale'; at 1st Battalion Rifle Brigade head-quarters, the men were 'concerned about some of their domestic problems at home'; while at 22nd Armoured Brigade headquarters, the main difficulties found 'were delays in mail and home problems'.[110]

At the end of the desert campaign, the figures for infidelity by wives and loved ones were still extremely high. According to the Commander-in-Chief Middle East, an average of just under a hundred 'anxiety' cases were dealt with by the SSAFA daily. Of these, one-third were proven infidelity of wives, one-third were suspected infidelity (in most cases the suspicion proving to have been well founded), and the remaining one-third were comprised of other forms of domestic trouble. In addition there was an average of thirty applications per day made to the legal advice section for divorce. This made a total of 'over 60 definite and 30 suspected cases of infidelity per day'.[111] By the end of the war, the free legal advice initiatives set up by the War Office had dealt with 175,000 cases of all types, of which 140,000 were concerned with matrimonial affairs. Of these cases, 94,000 divorce applications were made, of which 50,000 were carried through to a conclusion. The fact that 44,000 applications for divorce lapsed (c. 47 per cent), suggests, as the War Office claimed after the war, that the reconciliation scheme achieved a measure of success.[112]

While 'women troubles' never diminished as a problem for the men of Eighth Army, the efforts of the Directorate of Welfare, such as utilising the SSAFA and introducing free legal aid, were key in shaping morale in the desert. As long as the soldier felt his best interests were being looked

[108] SAMAD Div Docs, Gp 1, Box 1, Army Routine Orders by Lieut.-Gen. N. M. Ritchie, General Officer Commanding-in-Chief, Eighth Army, 6 May 1942. The SSAFA was changing offices in Cairo in May 1942 so it almost certainly had been present in the Middle East for some time before then.
[109] NA WO 193/453 Morale Report, August to October 1942.
[110] NA WO 277/4 Morgan, *Army Welfare*, p. 116.
[111] NA WO 193/453 Morale Committee Papers, 25 February 1942 to 25 October 1945, Morale Report, May to July 1943.
[112] NA WO 277/4 Morgan, *Army Welfare*, p. 37–8.

after, he could shoulder much difficulty and heartache. The War Office initiative, in which welfare officers and the SSAFA played a role in effecting reconciliation between soldiers and their wives, proved, in Adam's opinion, to be very successful.[113] Indeed, all officers were encouraged to show interest in the domestic affairs of their men and to treat the soldier's family as if it were actually a part of the army.[114] Freyberg, for instance, organised short talks for the New Zealand Division to counteract enemy propaganda on the subject of American soldiers stationed on 'home soil'. By the end of March 1942, he had ordered all companies to issue lecturettes to all ranks on the subject.[115] In this way, it was hoped that the effect of bad news, or no news, from home could be minimised.

The men of Eighth Army were concerned about their loved ones in other senses as well. In particular, they worried about the extent to which army pay could cover the living costs of families left behind. The draft morale report for May to July 1942 stated that it was 'generally accepted as axiomatic that a private soldier's wife with children in an urban area who had no resources other than his pay and allowances simply could not manage'.[116] Many of the men in the desert were forced to send items such as food and cigarettes home[117] or to encourage wives to work in the war economy to support themselves. This upset men who felt that their sacrifice of fighting in the desert was enough for their whole family. One man in the 1st Army Tank Brigade wrote to his wife, 'I do hope you like being back at work again but when I think that such a step was made necessary because the miserable pittance allowed by the Army is not sufficient to keep you and John going, I feel like getting up and hitting somebody's head off. It's b ... y disgusting and the more I think about it the worse I feel. To say the least it can hardly be said to encourage any feeling of patriotism.'[118] The increase in family allowances paid to soldiers' families from March 1942[119] and the increase in soldiers' basic pay that accompanied it in the autumn[120] all played a role in placating such worries. Nevertheless, British soldiers were well aware that their

---

[113] LHCMA Adam 3/3 Notes for the S-of-S Estimates Speech, February 1943. AG's Department, p. 23.

[114] WO 222/218 Circular to all medical officers, n.d. but Second World War, Morale Discipline and Mental Fitness.

[115] ANZ WAII/8/26 Fernleaf Cairo to Defender Wellington, 15 March 1942.

[116] NA WO 193/453 Draft Morale Report, May to July 1942.

[117] AWM 54 883/2/97 MEFCWS, no. XXIV (23 to 29 April 1942), p. 3.

[118] AWM 54 883/2/97 British Troops in Egypt no. 102 Field Censorship Report Week Ending 7 October 1941, p. 2.

[119] SAMAD Div Docs, Gp 1, Box 1, Army Routine Orders by Lieut.-Gen. N. M. Ritchie, General Officer Commanding-in-Chief, Eighth Army, 23 May 1942.

[120] NA WO 193/453 Morale Report, August to October 1942.

Commonwealth and Dominion Allies were better paid than themselves and this did not necessarily promote good relations between the different nationalities of Eighth Army.[121]

As well as these welfare schemes, which were targeted specifically at ameliorating the morale problems arising from the soldiers' separation from home and loved ones, there were other welfare initiatives, focused more directly on the soldiers' immediate needs in the desert.

Direct welfare provisions, such as comforts parcels, sports gear and entertainments, were important in maintaining morale. Among the articles despatched overseas from the Army Comforts Depot in England, during August 1941, were 133,272 woollen articles, 782 articles of sports gear, 20 wireless sets, 43,200 cigarettes and 1,600 ounces of tobacco.[122] The field censorship report for September 1941 made reference to 'very favourable comments on organised recreation, mental and physical' that provided relief from boredom and helped the soldiers' morale.[123]

The exigencies of mobile warfare in the first half of 1942 effectively negated the possibilities of front-line welfare. However, in the run-up to El Alamein, in the more static positions that prevailed from July 1942, it became more accessible. Montgomery focused on bringing welfare amenities right up to the front line to improve morale.[124] This was something his predecessor had never really been in a position to do. ENSA (Entertainments National Service Association) concerts and mobile cinemas were possibly the most popular form of welfare in the forward areas and Montgomery made special efforts to ensure that the troops were able to enjoy such entertainments.[125] The censorship summary for 17 to 23 September reported that these performances, when they 'made their appearance in the front lines [were] mentioned with great appreciation'. Many front-line troops, the report continued, 'have not seen any sort of show for nine months and the effect of these recent entertainments have been so excellent that every effort should be made to provide more'.[126] One officer wrote, 'they have laid on a mobile Cinema Unit, and we are

[121] Ibid.

[122] NA WO 163/50 War Office Progress Report, August 1941.

[123] AWM 54 883/2/97 British Troops in Egypt no. 100 Field Censorship Report Week Ending 23 September 1941, p. 4.

[124] ANZ WAII/1/DA508/1 vol. 3, MEMCWS, no. XLIII (3 to 9 September 1942), p. 16.

[125] IWM 99/1/2 Briggs, METM no. 7, Lessons from Operations, October and November 1942, p. 62.

[126] SAMAD CGS (War), Box 248, Summary of 'I' Summaries for CGS. MEMCWS (17 to 23 September 1942).

having shows up here right in the front line. Fortunately there is a disused underground well, that we are using for a Hall ... we can seat 100 at a time. We send 5 from each company for each performance.'[127] A warrant officer made similar comments: 'This afternoon the E.N.S.A. Concert Party were right out here in Alamein and put on an excellent show. There were two girls (one a Yank) and 3 fellows and they were very good. The fellows appreciated it terrifically and it is pushing their morale up to overflowing ... these shows help one to stand it a little better.'[128]

The fact that the El Alamein line was so close to Cairo, Alexandria and the Delta made it far easier for entertainments to be brought up to the men. It was also noticeable that the cooler weather of the winter months encouraged soldiers to play football and other sports. There were no grass pitches, so they would rig up posts in the desert and start a game. Rugby was not played much owing to the danger of desert sores.[129]

The government provided a general grant of 3s per man and 1s 3d extra for men serving overseas for welfare amenities. In addition, grants for objects such as wirelesses and cinemas were commonplace. Total welfare spending worked out at about £1,500,000 a year.[130] Lord Nuffield also spent about £750,000 during the war on army welfare. Cinema proprietors often gave the proceeds of the first night of new films to welfare funds. On the whole, it is extremely difficult to calculate exactly how much money was collected locally and nationally and spent for the benefit of the services overseas on welfare,[131] but efforts were always appreciated and they played a key role in maintaining morale.

Army education was an integral part of welfare in the desert. The 1934 Training Regulations explained that 'the conditions of modern warfare necessitate considerable decentralisation of responsibility to junior leaders and individuals'. The soldier therefore had to 'be intelligent, adaptable, and capable of acting on his own initiative'. These qualities, according to the training regulations, were 'developed by educational training, which though it includes instruction and study not purely military in character, is an integral part of military training'.[132] The conditions

---

[127] ANZ WAII/1/DA508/1 vol. 3, MEMCWS, no. XLV (17 to 23 September 1942), p. 17.
[128] Ibid., p. 18.
[129] AWM 54 883/2/97 British Troops in Egypt no. 104 Field Censorship Report Week Ending 21 October 1941, pp. 2–4.
[130] NA WO 32/10462 Army Education: Memorandum by AG for Consideration by the ECAC, 10 September 1943.
[131] LHCMA Adam 3/13 Narrative Covering Aspects of Work as Adjutant-General WWII, chap. 6, Welfare, p. 17.
[132] War Office, *Training Regulations 1934*, p. 4.

of fighting in the desert made such qualities even more important. 'Middle East Training Pamphlet no. 10', which dealt with the lessons from the December 1940 to February 1941 campaign against the Italians, stated clearly that

The maintenance of discipline on active service was difficult enough when troops fought and moved in close order. In modern war under Eastern conditions, wide frontages and great dispersion prevent close control of individuals by their superiors. Instead, the individual must discipline himself and this is only possible where the individual has learnt to understand and respect the cause for which he fights and to take pride in his Army, his unit and himself. Where these incentives are lacking, lamentable things happen which bring disgrace on our cause and may expose the Army to a dangerous reverse.[133]

In a citizen army, it did matter enormously that men should, as Cromwell said, 'know what they fight for and love what they know'.[134] In 1941, the British soldier in the desert appeared either too ignorant or too apathetic to care what he was fighting for. This kind of attitude was, in Willans's opinion, 'liable in times of pressure to transform a retreat into a rout or a setback into a disaster'.[135] The Western Desert Force, by July 1941, had been 'routed' from Cyrenaica by the Germans and had suffered two defeats in its attempts to recapture the territory lost. It seemed to the War Office that British morale was not resolute enough to stand up to the trials of modern warfare against a politically indoctrinated foe. The censorship summaries, in the summer of 1941, suggested that the desert army was 'browned off', bored and lacking in personal commitment to the war. P. J. Grigg, the future Secretary of State for War, noted in the spring of 1941 that the majority of soldiers were 'listless and lazy', doing 'what was absolutely required of them but nothing more ... civilians in khaki' in the worst sense of the term.[136] Adam and Willans believed that the general decline in morale was linked to a lack of understanding among the troops about why they were fighting and about current affairs. Adam himself had overseen an experiment in army education, over a period of six months while GOC Northern Command, which had convinced him of its benefits. As part of the experiment, platoon and equivalent commanders had addressed their men at least once a week on campaigns and other educational subjects of

---

[133] NA WO 201/2586 'Middle East Training Pamphlet no. 10'. Lessons of Cyrenaica Campaign: Training Pamphlet, December 1940 to February 1941, p. 60.
[134] S. P. MacKenzie, *Politics and Military Morale: Current Affairs and Citizenship Education in the British Army, 1914–1950* (Oxford, 1992), p. 75.
[135] NA WO 32/9735 ABCA, Current Affairs in the Army: The Outline of a New Plan, 21 July 1941, p. 2.
[136] MacKenzie, *Politics and Military Morale*, p. 86.

general interest. The experiment proved a success. The troops had eagerly absorbed the information, which was all the more welcome because, like the men in the desert, they were stationed in places where it was difficult to obtain newspapers.[137]

On the outbreak of war, official education in the army had virtually ceased.[138] However, by 1940, with concern about morale increasing during the 'phoney war', the Army Council assigned the Haining Committee the task of drawing up a plan for adult education in the army. The Haining scheme was announced in September 1940 and introduced voluntary education for those that were interested when off-duty. An education officer was appointed in each unit and the Army Education Corps (AEC), which had almost died away during the interwar years, was expanded and returned to work. The Directorate of Education, which was formed in the autumn of 1940, was intended to cooperate with its welfare counterpart, set up at the same time, and this arrangement was formalised at the end of 1940 when General Willans was appointed Director-General of Welfare, with the Directorate of Education within his remit.[139]

By the spring of 1941, it was estimated that only 20 per cent of troops in the UK were receiving educational provisions.[140] At the same time, news of defeats in the Middle East and the prospect of a continued sedentary existence for the troops at home raised fresh concerns over morale.[141] Willans was convinced that education and welfare had to go hand in hand. 'Welfare was concerned with the morale of the army' and, in his mind, 'so too was education.'[142] In June 1941, he proposed to the Army Council a new project designed, above all, 'to maintain the morale of the troops'. It would also have the added effect of forcing junior officers to get to know their men better and prepare the men for the requirements of the post-war world.[143]

The proposal, encapsulated in a paper, 'Current Affairs in the Army: The Outline of a New Plan', made a number of far-reaching recommendations

[137] NA WO 32/9735 Extract from the Minutes of the Eighth Meeting of the Army Council held on Tuesday, 17 June 1941.
[138] Crang, *The British Army and the People's War*, p. 115.
[139] Ibid., p. 116.
[140] LHCMA Adam 3/13 Various Administrative Aspects of the Second World War, chap. 6, Welfare, p. 3.
[141] Crang, *The British Army and the People's War*, p. 116.
[142] NA WO 163/123 Pamphlet: 'Army Welfare and Education', by Maj.-Gen. H. Willans, Director General of Army Welfare and Education. Reprint of an address given on 7 March 1941 to the Royal Society of the Arts, p. 14.
[143] NA WO 32/9735 Extract from the Minutes of the Eighth Meeting of the Army Council held on Tuesday 17 June 1941.

that linked education and morale in an intimate relationship that was designed to drive towards success in battle. It stated that the soldier who neither knew nor cared why he was under arms was a danger to national safety. Morale was 'fundamentally a matter of discipline' and true discipline was 'a matter of understanding'.[144]

In brief, the argument amounted to this:

(a) The soldier who understood the cause for which he was fighting was likely to be a more reliable soldier than the one who did not.

(b) Many soldiers in the British Army had no such understanding, and many others were losing touch with the sources of knowledge and information they used to possess.

(c) It was the business of the army to make good this deficiency of knowledge and therefore to devise what means were possible to keep the men abreast of current affairs.[145]

To oversee this radical new plan, a new directorate, the Army Bureau of Current Affairs (ABCA), was formed. It was headed by W. E. Williams, who was, at the time, secretary of the British Institute of Adult Education[146] and was viewed by Willans as a 'pioneer' of his profession.[147]

The new plan for current affairs instruction was to be introduced as a part of the soldiers' general training. The regimental officer would take his men aside once a week and lead a discussion on current events.[148] In order to help the already overloaded regimental officer carry out these new duties, ABCA issued two fortnightly, alternating bulletins. The first was 'War', the second 'Current Affairs'. 'War' provided military intelligence in the widest sense. It printed vivid narratives of what was happening in the various theatres of war and illustrated these records with accounts of outstanding achievements by the British Army, Royal Navy and RAF. It was designed to educate the troops about the march of events.[149] 'Current Affairs', on the other hand, aimed to provide a background of knowledge against which events could be assessed and understood.[150] It was expected that these publications would contain sufficient material to enable officers of average

---

[144] NA WO 32/9735 ABCA, Current Affairs in the Army, The Outline of a New Plan, 21 July 1941, p. 1.

[145] Ibid., p. 4.

[146] LHCMA Adam 3/13 Narrative Covering Aspects of Work as Adjutant-General WWII, chap. 6, Welfare, p. 4.

[147] NA WO 32/9735 ABCA, Current Affairs in the Army, The Outline of a New Plan, 21 July 1941, p. 6.

[148] Ibid., p. 2.

[149] NA WO 163/123 Army no. 71, Army Welfare and Education, Memorandum by the War Office, 12 September 1941.

[150] Ibid.

ability to talk usefully to their men on a particular topic for at least half an hour every week.[151]

In August 1941, Williams officially became director of ABCA and, in the same month, 'Current Affairs in the Army: The Outline of a New Plan' was released in pamphlet form to all commanding officers in the army.[152] This initiative, in conjunction with other educational schemes, represented a major attempt by the War Office to combat the 'crusading zeal' of the German Army with its own intellectual and emotional appeal to British troops. Adam and Willans knew that junior officers in the Wehrmacht were required to spend time with their men discussing the causes and political aims of the war. These activities involved:

(a) Discussion of daily political events. For an hour every day, officers gathered their men for an explanation of the political acts of the Nazi leadership so as 'to give every soldier an immediate participation in the decisive events of the function of state and race'.

(b) Patriotic education. This concentrated on the presentation of historic military examples to develop the soldier's sense of duty and desire for emulation.

(c) Social evenings of comradeship.

(d) Weekly hour of the company. Cultivation of music and community singing, particularly German classics and folk songs. Political, scientific and cultural lectures.

(e) Festive Hours. Commemorating historic events to give soldiers direct contact with German history.

(f) '10 Minutes Front-Spirit'. Ten minutes were set aside every day to whip up militant spirit in the conscripts. Officers who participated in the last war talked about their own experiences in combat.

(g) Planned recreation.[153]

ABCA was intended, unlike comparable German initiatives, to be apolitical and it was certainly not supposed to be propagandistic. Nevertheless, it contained many elements that could be viewed as propaganda. It therefore represented the strongest effort deemed possible by the War Office to inculcate morale amongst the troops by keeping them informed about the war and confirming that they had a cause worth fighting for.

In November 1940, it was decided that education would be extended overseas and, as a result, a war establishment for the AEC was approved

---

[151] NA WO 32/9735 ABCA, Current Affairs in the Army, The Outline of a New Plan, 21 July 1941, p. 4.
[152] MacKenzie, *Politics and Military Morale*, p. 94.
[153] NA WO 193/456 and NA CAB 21/914 'German Psychological Warfare', p. 24.

for the Middle East. By November 1941, army education along the same lines as in Britain was up and running in the Middle East.[154] By December, the AEC establishment in the theatre had twenty-four officers and fifty other ranks. Soon after December 1941, three more divisions joined the command, bringing with them their own AEC officers (one officer and seven other ranks to each division). The total establishment then worked out at approximately one AEC officer to every ten thousand troops and one other rank instructor to every five thousand troops.[155]

Classes were initiated in a wide range of vocational and cultural subjects.[156] In a similar fashion to the wartime education schemes in the UK, classes involved correspondence courses and lectures in general educational subjects.[157] These were held at or organised by establishments such as the British Institute of Engineering Technology at Cairo and Jerusalem, the British Council at Cairo, Alexandria, Port Said, Tanta, Mehalla, Mansura, Zagazig, Minia, Assiut and Jerusalem, the Anglo-Egyptian Union and the Fouad I University. Although courses were initially only available to officers, by May 1942 they were made accessible to all British officers and other ranks.[158] By the end of 1943, more than two thousand courses covering 150 different subjects were in progress.[159] A South African memorandum claimed that the staffs of the British Council and British Institutes were 'amongst the best informed men on current affairs and social conditions anywhere' and that they were able to give officers 'a great deal of useful information'.[160] Officers were then able to pass on such information to the troops, thus keeping them informed of current affairs.

In May 1942, General Ritchie, Commander Eighth Army, announced, in a general routine order, that all units of a strength equal to or over that of a battalion were to have both a unit welfare and a unit education officer. In small units and detachments it was accepted that 'Welfare, Education and A.B.C.A.' could be organised by one officer.[161] In June 1942, a Middle East School of Education was formed to train unit education officers on the same

[154] NA WO 32/10462, app. A to ECAC/P(43)98, 'Brief Notes on the Development of Army Education from 1939 to 1943'.
[155] Major T. H. Hawkins and L. J. F. Brimble, *Adult Education: The Record of the British Army* (London, 1947), pp. 238–9.
[156] Ibid., p. 239.
[157] NA WO 165/85 War Diary of the Directorate of Army Education.
[158] SAMAD Div Docs, Gp 1, Box 1, Army Routine Orders by Lieut.-Gen. N. M. Ritchie, General Officer Commanding-in-Chief, Eighth Army, 6 May 1942; Div Docs, Gp 1, Box 49, British Council Lecture Scheme, UDF Admin, HQ, MEF, 4 April 1942.
[159] Hawkins and Brimble, *Adult Education*, pp. 239–40.
[160] SAMAD Div Docs, Gp 1, Box 49, British Council Lecture Scheme, UDF Admin, HQ, MEF, 4 April 1942.
[161] SAMAD Div Docs, Gp 1, Box 1, Army Routine Orders by Lieut.-Gen. N. M. Ritchie, General Officer C-in-C, Eighth Army, 6 May 1942.

Illustration 12 An Army Bureau of Current Affairs course at the American University in Beirut for officers stationed in the Middle East, April 1943. A medical officer is shown giving a lecture on plans for a post-war health service. Army education initiatives such as this played an important role in building morale in the run-up to the battle of El Alamein.

lines as the syllabus pursued in Britain. The unit education officers were given an outline of the army education scheme, background information about current affairs, and direction on the general principles of instruction. According to the commandant of the school, 'the personnel attending were for the most part keen and appreciative, and the results achieved proved … that much good had been derived from the School's peregrinations'.[162]

Besides these courses, the staff of the school gave numerous evening lectures to any units that were stationed near them and who cared to invite them. Interspersed with the courses, the school carried out two lecture tours, of which the second was with the Eighth Army on the eve of the El Alamein offensive. This was received, in the words of Major

[162] Hawkins and Brimble, *Adult Education*, p. 244.

T. H. Hawkins and L. J. F. Brimble, in *Adult Education: The Record of the British Army*, 'with unparalleled enthusiasm by the seventy audiences who listened to the talks of which they themselves had chosen the subject'. At the end of the first tour, the school embarked on the much more ambitious programme of making units 'ABCA conscious'. This was achieved by holding courses of two and a half days' duration for junior officers at any location where enough units were stationed.[163]

ABCA pamphlets, similar to those in use in Britain, were reproduced locally in the Middle East and circulated to units.[164] At the same time, touring teams of AEC personnel held short courses to give demonstrations of the main principles of ABCA instruction. An interesting feature of ABCA in the Middle East, according to Hawkins and Brimble, was that it was well received by field force units but with little enthusiasm by the base units. Nevertheless, it could still have a positive effect on those units who were initially unenthusiastic about implementing it.

Two big base units in Egypt, for example, were working at high pressure in the days before El Alamein. Their commanding officers cordially 'admitted' to the visiting Army Education Corps officer that their job was production and that they had no time for superfluities. In spite of their wishes, these commanding officers were persuaded to allow the men in their workshops to discuss current events for half an hour a week in working hours. This was agreed to as an experiment; but when the commanding officers found that, not only did their production not decrease but that it slightly increased, the experiment remained as a permanent feature.[165]

The school possessed a considerable amount of apparatus and paraphernalia. This was made up of various visual aids and consisted of a series of charts, maps, posters and diagrams. The school's equipment, in the commandant's words, consisted of

Outline maps in two colours with no complicated physical features or elaborate details to mislead the readers; simple block and circle methods of illustrating proportions to 'put over' the ever increasing mass of modern statistics; charts on plain paper to simplify the concept of government; wall quizzes composed of photographs; cut outs of periodicals, aeroplane silhouettes from cheap pamphlets, or snippets of old atlases; the day's news taped to an outline map of the battle-front with coloured ribbons; the headline news of the day pasted to a board with a coloured flash for the particular front to which the item referred.[166]

In the first year of the school's existence, its staff, which was never larger than four and was usually only three and sometimes two in number, conducted thirty-four courses, made two lecture tours and delivered

---

[163] Ibid., pp. 244–5.   [164] 'British Way and Purpose' booklets were also produced locally.
[165] Hawkins and Brimble, *Adult Education*, pp. 240–1.   [166] Ibid., p. 245.

more than a hundred and fifty lectures to units. During that period, more than six hundred and fifty students passed through the school, representative of all branches of the army, and including small numbers of RAF and Royal Navy officers, as well as members of the Free French Forces.[167]

Education was not only introduced to the British elements of Eighth Army. Towards the end of 1940, E. G. M. Malherbe, at that time South African Director of Census and Statistics, reacted to spontaneous educational initiatives instigated among troops both in the desert and in South Africa by setting up education provisions for Union soldiers. He wrote a memorandum entitled 'Educating the Troops in the Political, Social and Economic Reasons for Our Being at War' to the South African Prime Minister, Field Marshal Smuts, the Minister for Education, Jan Hofmeyr, and the Director-General of Training and Operations, Major-General George Brink. In the memorandum, Malherbe asserted that the major purpose of the education scheme he proposed was to 'improve the fighting force against Nazism'.[168]

In February 1941, the Chief of the General Staff, Sir Pierre van Ryneveld, approved the Army Education Scheme (AES) with two major aims, to enable soldiers to 'defend democracy', and to 'equip citizen-soldiers to build a better democracy once the threat of Fascism has been removed'. The AES, just like ABCA, relied on officers to instruct their men in current affairs. The first month-long course for education officers (later known as information officers, or IOs) began in March 1941. Candidates were selected with particular attention to their level of English/Afrikaans bilingualism and sent to units in South Africa and the Middle East.[169]

By June 1941, Malherbe believed that 'the idea of the Army Education Scheme' had been 'effectively "sold" to all ranks'. Troops were expected to attend one AES lecture a week, and by many accounts, large numbers of white troops did indeed participate enthusiastically in discussions organised under the auspices of the AES.[170] Malherbe was determined that the AES reach as many troops as possible and the evidence from the desert was that IOs played a major role in keeping troops up to date with current affairs and news from South Africa and around the world.[171]

---

[167] Ibid.
[168] www.queensu.ca/sarc/Conference/1940s/Roos.htm. Neil Roos, 'The Second World War, the Army Education Scheme and the "Discipline" of the White Poor in South Africa', Workshop on South Africa in the 1940s, Southern African Research Centre, Kingston, September, 2003.
[169] Ibid.   [170] Ibid.
[171] SAMAD Div Docs, Gp 1, Box 49, 1st SA Division Security Report for week ending 28 December 1941; SAMAD CGS (War), Box 155 Morale of Troops in the Field.

IOs, by 'mixing with ... the rank and file', were in an 'ideal position to experience and analyse the causes of any weakening of morale, and to suggest practical remedies'.[172] They censored letters and generally 'kept their fingers on [the] pulse' of the troops.[173] They were required to write regular reports, which were sent to Malherbe (who became Director of Military Intelligence) in South Africa, ensuring cooperation and understanding on issues of morale. At the same time, Malherbe supplied IOs with information he deemed important to the troops' morale.[174] They were also encouraged to attend British Council and Institute lectures and a major drive was begun, in April 1942, to encourage IOs to do so while on leave out of the desert. In addition, 1st SA Division, 2nd SA Division and SA non-divisional units took it in turn to send an IO on special leave to attend courses every month. IOs and ordinary officers were also allowed to apply for extensions of leave to attend special educational lectures in the rear areas.[175]

The establishment of an equivalent education scheme in the Australian Army was approved by the Australian War Cabinet in March 1941. The Australian plan was modelled largely on the British initiative and became fully operational in June 1941. The role of education, according to the 'War History of the Australian Army Education Service', 'involved finding solutions for a number of allied problems, all of which had to be solved if the welfare and morale of troops was to be maintained at the highest possible level'.[176] The service was designed explicitly to meet the 'demands of total war' and combat the 'fanatical faith' of the German enemy. 'This was done by breeding confidence in the soldier that the ideals for which he fought are worth far more than the sacrifices required to preserve them.' The Australian soldier joined to the military skills he was taught 'a full mental and emotional acceptance of his part of the struggle'. His acceptance of this role was obtained 'only by a process which was in the fullest sense of the word educational'. Thus it was 'evident that the great task of Army Education was to assist in the building and sustaining of morale'. Education toughened the soldier's spirit 'so

[172] SAMAD CGS 2, Box 585, Training Memorandum, February 1942.
[173] CGS (War), Box 155, Memorandum, DMT, 7 March 1942.
[174] CGS (War), Box 155, Memorandum, 'Morale of UDF Troops up North', E. G. Malherbe, 20 April 1942.
[175] SAMAD Div Docs, Gp 1, Box 49, British Council Lecture Scheme, UDF Admin, HQ, MEF, 4 April 1942; SAMAD Div Docs, Gp 1, Box 49, Minute from GOA on British Council Lecture Scheme, 1 SA Div HQ, 9 April 1942.
[176] AWM 54, 492/4/34 War History of the Australian Army Education Service 1939–1945, pp. 1–6.

that he resolutely faced privation and loss and ever strove toward the goal'.[177]

A New Zealand scheme for education was not introduced until the middle of 1944, three years too late, as the official history remarked. Nevertheless, many of the functions of education and information officers were carried out by field security NCOs in the NZEF. Each brigade had two security NCOs who issued fortnightly reports to GHQ ME on matters relating to morale, rumours and security.[178] These NCOs performed 'useful work' in 'forward areas by disseminating accurate and recent news bulletins' to the troops.[179] They played an especially important role, throughout the whole campaign, in counteracting the rumours that were a remarkable feature of life in the desert, by coordinating with HQ NZ Division and the *NZEF Times*.[180] From 1940 to 1942, the University of New Zealand also arranged that reputable bodies in Cairo (e.g. the British Council) could conduct examinations on its behalf for such men as could sit them. This procedure ceased, partly because men could not keep up their studies, and partly because the only ones who ever could sit them were those who happened to be serving at Maadi or in other sedentary employment.[181]

By May 1942, the censorship summaries show that a number of the men in the back areas of Eighth Army were 'availing themselves of [the] educational facilities placed at their disposal'. Lectures were 'proving undoubtedly beneficial' and army education generally was 'becoming increasingly popular'.[182] Throughout August, the censors reported that many men referred to 'attending lectures on "war aims", "our plans after the war" and even "Prussianism"'.[183] Indeed, the War Office historical monograph on the 'History of Army Education' stated that, by August 1942, education had begun 'to take definite root in the Eighth Army'.[184] In addition, a Command education officer arrived in the desert in September 1942. His main focus was education of 'a field

---

[177] Ibid., p. 7.
[178] ANZ WAII/1/DA21.1/9/G4/12 part 1, Note from Brig.-Gen. Staff 10 Corps to 2 SA Div and NZ Div, 27 August 1941; Duties of a Unit Security Officer, n.d. but likely to be 1941.
[179] ANZ WAII/1/DA21.1/9/G4/12 part 2, Weekly Extracts of 2 NZ Div FS Section, 27 November 1942.
[180] ANZ WAII/1/DA21.1/9/G4/12 part 1, HQ 2 NZ Div (G Branch) Security and Intelligence Reports (16 June 1941 to 31 January 1942).
[181] Stevens, *Problems of 2 NZEF*, pp. 254–5.
[182] AWM 54 883/2/97 MEFCWS no. XXV (29 April to 5 May 1942), p. 4.
[183] ANZ WAII/1/DA508 vol. 1, MEMCWS, no. XL (12 to 18 August 1942), p. 3.
[184] NA WO 277/35 War Office, Historical Monographs: 'History of Army Education'.

nature' due to the upcoming battle at El Alamein.[185] From his initial visits to the front, he became convinced that education could be of real service to army operations, not only providing relief from monotony and boredom, but also helping to keep alive interest in home and outside affairs generally.[186] S. P. MacKenzie has since written that Montgomery 'pragmatically incorporated the various education schemes into his plan to build up the efficiency and esprit de corps of the units under his command' in Eighth Army and that it 'proved a great success in every sense'.[187]

The war diaries of the AEC reported that 'excellent work' was indeed carried out 'in the front line' with 'Eighth Army in its advance westwards across Africa'. For example, the Command education officer prepared a series of lecture summaries, which were distributed to those interested. He chose subjects of both a general educational interest, such as 'The British Empire: what it is and how it works', and also those of a purely local interest, like 'The history of Egypt, Libya and Barbary'. These summaries proved most popular and, at the end of the journey westwards, the main ones were produced in booklet form and issued on request. In addition, he provided material for the lighter and more informal activities needed to amuse an army. These included lists of words for spelling competitions and questions for quizzes for those who asked for them. During the advance, publicity for the various phases of the educational scheme was obtained by printed articles in the Eighth Army's weekly newspaper, *Crusader*. In this way, such matters as the availability of correspondence courses, provision of textbooks and facilities for taking examinations like the London Matriculation were advertised throughout the army, and according to Hawkins and Brimble, a surprisingly large number of queries from individuals and units was received. Through the medium of *Crusader*, a poetry competition was organised, and, in two months, 403 poems were received from 276 competitors. An essay competition was similarly organised, though not with quite the same success.[188]

AEC instructors also organised educational activities in the back areas during the advance. The first opportunity came with the opening of a leave and rest camp at Derna. At this centre it was possible not only to provide recreational education by means of quizzes, brains trusts and music recitals, but also to interest men straight from battle in talks and discussions based on the news of the moment. News had been scarce in the desert, and every opportunity was taken, when the men were withdrawn

---

[185] Ibid.   [186] Hawkins and Brimble, *Adult Education*, pp. 245–6.
[187] MacKenzie, *Politics and Military Morale*, pp. 157–8.
[188] Hawkins and Brimble, *Adult Education*, pp. 246–8.

from the fighting, to satisfy their insatiable thirst for knowing what was going on.[189]

Adam himself remarked that education and its partner, ABCA, 'played an important part' in Eighth Army's advance from 'Alamein to Tunisia'.[190] In 'no formation' he said, 'had appreciation been more evident' for education 'than in the Eighth Army'. He pointed out that 'the growing appetite for education was not solely stimulated by his department. It sprang also from Army Commanders at home and abroad who regarded it as an indispensable contribution to the sustenance of morale.'[191] Army authorities reported that, by 1943, 30 per cent of units in North Africa were running ABCA discussions satisfactorily.[192] In September 1943, the South African Chief of the General Staff commented that IOs had 'done a magnificent job' in the army.[193] Adam stated that the 'morale value' of education in the army had 'been so great' that he most strongly deprecated any reduction in the increasing volume of its activities or any attempt to narrow its scope.[194] The education initiatives proved so successful that it was possible to hold the London Matriculation and City and Guilds examinations in Tripoli in June 1943.[195]

It is evident that, by the second half of 1942, education officers and information officers were integral parts of units. Both personal diaries and mail show that the men were interested in current affairs and concerned about their future following the war.[196] Education, as well as having an immediate relevance to the 'job at hand', was also able to provide the soldier with a link to home and the future that he was fighting for. In addition, by September 1942, 6,000 troops were attending other classes of various kinds in the Middle East.[197] By May 1943, more than 150 education centres had been set up in the theatre, including several in Cyrenaica and Tripolitania.[198] Army education cost the exchequer just over £500,000 a year, representing a cost of less than 5s per soldier. The

---

[189] Ibid.
[190] NA WO 32/10462 Army Education: Memorandum by AG for Consideration by the ECAC, 10 September 1943.
[191] NA WO 32/10462 Extract from the Minutes of the 127th Meeting of the ECAC held on Friday 10 September 1943.
[192] Crang, *The British Army and the People's War*, p. 128.
[193] SAMAD CGS (War), Box 155, Apathy towards War, Morale/Training, September 1943.
[194] NA WO 32/10462 Army Education: Memorandum by AG for Consideration by the ECAC, 10 September 1943.
[195] NA WO 165/85 War Diary AEC, 1 November 1943 to 30 November 1943, AEC Quarterly Bulletin no. 2, November 1943, p. 5.
[196] NA WO 193/453 Draft Morale Report, May to July 1942; AWM 54 883/2/97 British Troops in Egypt No. 92 Field Censorship Report Week Ending 31 July 1941, p. 4.
[197] Hawkins and Brimble, *Adult Education*, p. 239.   [198] Ibid., p. 241.

total amount spent on education for the whole army in one year was roughly the equivalent of the cost of thirty-five tanks or twenty bombers, i.e. the number of bombers that might be lost in one night's action.[199] The importance of education to the troops was therefore out of all proportion to the financial expenditure required to make it function. The work of education in the desert meant that another element in the intricate web of human needs and motivation was put in place. No better praise of the success of army education, in the months up to and following El Alamein, can be garnered than the fact that the services of 'education' were especially requested for the invasion of Sicily in 1943 and beyond. It seems reasonable to conclude, therefore, that army education 'had contributed something of real worth' to Eighth Army 'on active service'.[200]

Willans remarked, in March 1941, that 'the soldier takes the ups and downs of war as they come, he does not brood upon hardships; he goes where he is sent and suffers and endures and lives and works and plays, and takes it all as part of the game. But he does worry about his family and his home, and he does worry about the future.' These things, he said, are 'being thought about, and I hope that the thought will in due course produce results'.[201]

The manner in which Willans and the War Office went about allaying these worries was through army welfare and education. The success of these initiatives was attributable not least to those who took on such roles as welfare officer, education officer and information officer.[202] Here again the building and maintenance of troops' morale was linked with better officer selection and training in man-management.

Nothing that was in the power of the authorities could remove the soldier from the horrors of war or from the tedium and discomfort of life in the desert. There was little that they could do to change the situation at home. But they could keep the soldier informed and they could provide the supports that strengthened the soldier's belief that he was part of a great national effort. They could also make it clear that those who commanded in the desert and on the home front appreciated the difficult trials that the soldier had to endure. These initiatives strengthened the soldier's morale and increased his will to fight.

---

[199] NA WO 32/10462 Army Education: Memorandum by AG for consideration by the ECAC, 10 September 1943.
[200] Hawkins and Brimble, *Adult Education*, pp. 246–8.
[201] NA WO 163/123 Pamphlet Army Welfare and Education by Maj.-Gen. H. Willans, Director-General of Army Welfare and Education. Reprint of address given on Friday 7 March 1941 before the Royal Society of Arts.
[202] NA WO 163/123 Army no. 71, Army Welfare and Education: Memorandum by the War Office, 12 September 1941.

6   Leadership, command and morale

> The most important thing about a commander is his effect on morale.
> (Field Marshal William Slim)[1]

> My theory is that an army commander does what is necessary to accomplish his mission and that nearly 80 percent of his mission is to arouse morale in his men.
> (General George Patton)[2]

> The art of leading, in operations large or small, is the art of dealing with humanity.
> (S. L. A. Marshall)[3]

Since the publication of Correlli Barnett's *The Desert Generals*, a debate has raged on who should take the credit for Eighth Army's victories at Alam Halfa and El Alamein. This debate has highlighted both the excesses of Bernard Montgomery's character and the important contribution of Claude Auchinleck to victory in the desert. It has also played a vital role in bringing balance to the historiography of the desert war.[4] However, the dialectical Montgomery versus Auchinleck approach that has developed has distracted historians from some of the key factors that led to victory in North Africa. In particular, it has pushed the issue of morale to the sidelines of the search for explanations of victory and defeat in the desert.[5]

The reality of a morale crisis in the summer of 1942 clearly brings into question the contribution and performance of Auchinleck as Commander-in-Chief MEF. It is hardly surprising, therefore, that supporters of Auchinleck, such as Barnett, have queried the existence of

---

[1] Field Marshal Viscount Slim, *Defeat into Victory* (London, 1999), pp. 36–7. First published in 1956.
[2] Atkinson, *An Army at Dawn*, p. 138.   [3] Marshall, *Men against Fire*, p. 160.
[4] See for example, Barnett, *The Desert Generals*; Carver, *Dilemmas of the Desert War*; Connell, *Auchinleck*; Hamilton, *The Full Monty*; Pitt, *Wavell's Command*; Pitt, *Auchinleck's Command*; Pitt, *Montgomery and Alamein*.
[5] Montgomery's biographer, Nigel Hamilton, is an exception.

such a crisis and argued that 'it would be wrong to place too much emphasis on the moral effects produced by [Montgomery]: for in the words of the Official History, Auchinleck "had retained to a remarkable degree [his army's] admiration and confidence"'.[6] More recently, Jon Latimer, in *Alamein*, has described it as a 'legend' that 'Eighth Army ... had completely lost faith in its commanders'. The army was not 'beaten or dispirited,' he said, 'it just wanted to be led to victory'.[7] Latimer argued that 'Montgomery did not transform a beaten army, but rather took a blunt but fundamentally sound blade and sharpened it before wielding it with maximum force.'[8] Martin Kitchen has similarly claimed that Churchill's rationale for replacing Auchinleck with Montgomery, to 'restore confidence in the Command, which I regret does not exist at the present time', was 'both blatantly untrue and exceptionally mean spirited'.[9]

The evidence already adduced in this book, however, confirms the reality of a morale crisis in the summer of 1942. What is more, the sources suggest that leadership and command played a significant role in causing the crisis. Command can be defined as the purposeful exercise of authority, by virtue of rank or appointment, 'over structures, resources, people and activities'.[10] It involves setting forth or asserting 'a vision that has an impact upon and defines the mission, culture, and values o[f] an organization', and encompasses the defining of directions, time perspectives and organisational structures for the achievement of goals and objectives.[11] Leadership is a distinctly different concept; it can be defined as 'the art of influencing and persuading those assigned to particular goals to work willingly, energetically and in unison towards the attainment of those goals'.[12] It has been impossible to adhere to any strict definitions of command or leadership in the course of writing this chapter due to the inconsistent use of these terms in the sources. Nevertheless, it should be noted that the quality of both leadership and command played a significant role in affecting the morale of the men in the desert.

For example, the censorship summary for the end of June 1942, as Eighth Army retreated to the El Alamein line, stated categorically that the

[6] Barnett, *The Desert Generals*, p. 258.   [7] Latimer, *Alamein*, pp. 97–8.   [8] Ibid., p. 4.
[9] Kitchen, *Rommel's Desert War*, p. 286.
[10] Canadian Defence Academy, Canadian Forces Leadership Institute, *Leadership in the Canadian Forces: Doctrine* (Kingston, ON, 2005), pp. 3–7; Glyn Harper and Joel Hayward (eds.), *Born to Lead?: Portraits of New Zealand Commanders* (Titirangi, 2003), p. 25.
[11] Allister McIntyre and Karen D. Davis (eds.), *Dimensions of Military Leadership* (Kingston, ON, 2006), p. 101.
[12] Harper and Hayward (eds.), *Born to Lead?*, p. 25.

summary 'would not give a fair cross-section of the criticisms levelled if it did not emphasise that many letters suggested that Rommel is a better general than our own, and more than one correspondent has stated that the "8th Army have more respect for Rommel than for our own high command"'.[13] The summary for 1 to 7 July stated that 'the Eighth Army is without doubt a very angry army ... Our reverse in Libya is attributed by a number of writers from Field Rank to Trooper to the fact that "Rommel seems to be a better General."' It was commonly believed that under the right leadership, 'we would prove more than a match for the Axis forces'.[14] The summary for 8 to 14 July concluded that

The outstanding criticism was undoubtedly that of leadership; the opinion that we have been out-generalled is unfortunately widely held. Epithets ranged in the men's letters from 'miserably inept', 'pathetic', 'gross ignorance' and 'appalling optimism' to more restrained but not less forceful expressions in some of the officers' mail, one of whom pithily stated what many had in mind, 'the fundamental trouble is Rommel'. Another remarked, 'if we had him on our side I don't think any force in the world could stop us'.[15]

A memorandum written, in August 1942, on the state of South African morale, expressed similar sentiments. The UDF 'assume in general that German leadership and staff work are and will be superior to ours. They have rather little faith in their higher commanders, or in the general direction of the war.'[16]

The soldiers' own diaries and memoirs tell a similar story. Jake Wardrop, of the 5th RTR, remarked, 'it seemed to me that there was just about enough stuff on the blue to lick them, but I don't know, we never seemed to get going. Of course, a poor General makes a lot of difference.'[17] Len Clothier, of the 2/13 Battalion AIF, noted in his diary that 'there's everything here to do with plenty of tanks, A.Tk. guns, arty and fresh infantry. I think we're sadly lacking good leaders.'[18] Robin Dunn, of the 2nd Armoured Brigade, commented that 'British soldiers will fight today as well as they fought at Agincourt or Blenheim or Waterloo or Ypres, provided they are well led. But without inspired leadership, personal leadership on the field of battle, they are useless.

---

[13] AWM 54 883/2/97 MEFCWS, no. XXXIII (24 to 30 June 1942).
[14] ANZ WAII/1/DA/508/1 vol. 1, MEFCWS, no. XXXIV (1 to 7 July 1942), p. 3–5.
[15] ANZ WAII 1/DA/508/1 vol. 1, MEMCWS, no. XXXV (8 to 14 July 1942), p. 5.
[16] SAMAD Div Docs, Gp 1, Box 1, Memorandum on Morale of SA Troops in ME, 8 August 1942, p. 1.
[17] Forty, *Tanks across the Desert*, p. 45.
[18] AWM PR 00588 Papers of Sgt. L. Clothier, 2/13 Battalion, Diary, 27 July 1942.

That inspired leadership was sadly lacking in the 8th Army in June 1942.'[19]

The men's criticisms were clearly targeted at Auchinleck, C-in-C MEF, and Neil Ritchie, his Commander Eighth Army (until Auchinleck sacked Ritchie and took overall control of the MEF and Eighth Army on 25 June 1942). Divisional commanders were equally caustic about the state of affairs. Freyberg commented, in a letter written to the New Zealand Prime Minister in October 1942, that, on arrival at Mersa Matruh on 25 June, he had received three separate sets of orders: (1) to go to the frontier, (2) to take up a defensive position west of Mersa Matruh, (3) to occupy the defences of Mersa Matruh. He informed the Prime Minister that 'this continual vacillation shook me'.[20] Les Inglis, commander of the 2nd New Zealand Division during the July battles, wrote that 'the strategic direction of the show as a whole beats me ... I feel very much that we need a commander who will make a firm plan, leave his staff to implement it, crash through with it; and once the conception is under way, hove about the battlefield himself and galvanize the troops who are looking over their shoulders.'[21] He commented, after the war, that 'it was apparent that the 8th Army was not going to deliver any decisively successful attack until it recuperated in strength and morale and got some new blood and new ideas at the top'.[22] Lieutenant-General 'Strafer' Gott, commander of XIII Corps, noted, in a report in July 1942, that 'the success of the enemy has been primarily accomplished ... under the direction of one man. There was the one magnetic personality giving orders, which resulted in a unity of effort and a clear picture in the mind of the Commander ... no such circumstances existed on our side.' He concluded that 'to defeat the enemy, the first requisite is a Commander of the right calibre. A quick brain and a flair for moving warfare are essential qualities.'[23]

Auchinleck himself was aware of his subordinates' attitudes. He emphasised, in a memorandum on 'discipline' released to officers on 25 July 1942, that he was 'greatly concerned about the growing habit of criticism' in the army by individual officers. 'These criticisms have been overheard in public places. They are obviously most dangerous, quite apart from the fact that an individual officer is seldom in a position to criticise operations over a wide area with justification. Such criticism will

[19] IWM 94/41/1 Sir Robin Dunn papers.
[20] ANZ WAII/8/26 Freyberg to Fraser (NZ PM), 14 October 1942.
[21] ANZ WAII/8/24 Inglis to Freyberg, 11 July 1942.
[22] ANZ WAII/1/DA21.1/10/9 L. M. Inglis. Ruweisat Ridge, comments on narrative by J. L. Scoullar, 18 October 1952, pp. 19–20.
[23] NA WO 216/85 Some Notes on Operations, 26 May to 8 July, GHQ MEF for CGS, 12 July 1942.

not be tolerated, and officers who are heard indulging in them will be Court Martialled.'[24]

The press was also vociferous in its criticism of British leadership and command, an issue that the War Office took extremely seriously. In March 1942, the Secretary of State for War, P.J. Grigg, fearing that negative press coverage was having an adverse effect on morale, asked the press to reduce its criticism of generals.[25]

It cannot be too strongly stressed [noted Grigg] that the effect of such campaigns is to undermine the confidence of the Army in its leaders ... the morale of the Army is to a very great extent dependent upon the Press ... The undermining of the confidence of the Army in their leaders by ill-advised articles – which are widely read by soldiers and civilians alike – will mean that when the soldier finally gets into a tight corner he won't fight: and if the Army won't fight we shall lose the war. We have not such a margin of safety in this war that we can afford to run any risks with our morale – war in the end is a war of morale.[26]

By July 1942, it was evident that the press had not changed their tack. The Army Council, as it debated the reintroduction of the death penalty, concluded that one of the reasons for the possible deterioration in morale in the desert was 'adverse criticism and ridicule by the Press of military leaders and of everything military; in fact, the "Brass-hat" complex'. The Army Council concluded that 'this cannot fail to shake the confidence of the troops and to undermine discipline and lower morale'.[27]

It was Auchinleck's attempts to reinstate the death penalty that perhaps said most about his leadership and its effect on morale in the summer of 1942. As Gary Sheffield has argued, 'the ideal leader is one who relies mainly on personal and expert power. A poor leader is one who relies mainly on institutional and coercive power.'[28] The Field Service Regulations of 1929 stated that

A commander maintains the moral of his force and exerts his authority, as much by the confidence and loyalty which he inspires as by discipline. Strong personality, knowledge of human nature, a well-balanced sense of proportion and a mutual understanding with subordinates are vital moral factors in producing military

---

[24] SAMAD Div Docs, Box 119, Memorandum on Discipline by A.A.G. Eighth Army, 25 July 1942.

[25] NA WO 259/64 War Office, Press Conference, 18 March 1942.

[26] NA WO 259/64 Notes for Secretary of State for interview with Editors, n.d., but almost certainly March or April 1942.

[27] NA WO 163/51 The Army Council, Death Penalty in Relation to Offences Committed on Active Service (Note by the Joint Secretaries), 31 July 1942, p. 3.

[28] Gary Sheffield, *Leadership in the Trenches: Officer–Man Relations, Morale and Discipline in the British Army in the Era of the First World War* (London, 2000), p. 42.

efficiency; impersonal, passive, weak command inevitably results in loss of moral, in want of resolution and ultimately in failure.[29]

Auchinleck had clearly failed to maintain morale by power of his leadership and command style. Instead, he was forced to turn to policies of coercion to maintain his troops' willingness and discipline to fight, even to the extent of advising his officers, in May 1942, that 'if necessary in order to stop panic, there must be no hesitation in resorting to extreme measures, such as shooting an individual who cannot otherwise be stopped'.[30]

By 23 June Auchinleck's relationship with his troops had deteriorated to such an extent that he felt that he had no choice but to tender his resignation. He wrote to Alan Brooke in London, accepting full responsibility for all that had occurred in the desert. He offered to vacate the post of Commander-in-Chief, admitting to a 'loss of influence' with the troops 'due to lack of success, absence of luck and all other things which affect the morale of an army'.[31]

Auchinleck was fully aware of the importance of his role as Commander-in-Chief in the maintenance of morale. He wrote to Grigg, in March 1942, describing how one of his 'main tasks here, if not *the* main one, is to study the psychology of this very mixed array we call an Army, and I spend most of my time doing this in the hope that it will not disintegrate altogether!'[32] He had set an example by sleeping outdoors on the hard desert floor like his men. Many of his decisions were based on questions of morale. He explained the appointment of Ritchie in Cunningham's place, in the middle of the Crusader battle in November 1941, with the rationale that the army was 'morally shaken and ... needed a strong, unflustered, self-confident commander'.[33] He had tried to inspire his men with a stirring message as Eighth Army retreated to the El Alamein line on 30 June 1942. Rommel, he wrote, 'thinks we are a broken army' and 'hopes to take Egypt by bluff ... Show him where he gets off.'[34] At the beginning of August 1942, he wrote a précis of the situation, insisting that 'our policy should be to harass the enemy by all possible means, morale as well as physical'.[35] Even his demands, in April and July 1942, for the death penalty to be reintroduced were driven by his concerns about morale.[36]

---

[29] Daly, 'A Psychological Analysis of Military Morale', p. 65.
[30] NA WO 201/538 Corbett to 8, 9 and 10 Armies, 24 May 1942.
[31] Barnett, *The Desert Generals*, pp. 180–1.   [32] Connell, *Auchinleck*, p. 460.
[33] Barnett, *The Desert Generals*, pp. 123–4.   [34] Scoullar, *The Battle for Egypt*, p. 148.
[35] AWM 54 519/6/15 Précis of an Appreciation by the C-in-C Middle East at Eighth Army, 0800 hrs 1 August 1942.
[36] NA WO 32/15773 Death Penalty for Desertion in the Field: Reintroduction, 1942.

It is evident from the morale reports that Auchinleck's efforts did pay some dividends and it would be unfair to simply label him as a failure in this regard. The report for May to July 1942 stressed that Auchinleck's decision to take over command of Eighth Army on 25 June 1942 had proved a fine boost to morale. 'After the initial disappointment the troops recovered their spirits remarkably; ... The personality of General Auchinleck seems to have had much to do with this: Letters from all ranks were enthusiastic in his praise.'[37] The censorship summaries similarly reported support for Auchinleck's assumption of command. The summary for 8 to 14 July recorded that 'during the regrouping period at El Alamein it apparently became generally known that the C-in-C had himself assumed command of the operations and this undoubtedly gave a great fillip to the troops' morale ... not a single adverse comment on General Auchinleck was noted.'[38] A field officer wrote that 'there is definitely a feeling of quiet confidence here now. Auchinleck is a great man and leader and there is no doubt that from now onwards the Bosch is in for a pretty rough time.'[39] The censorship summary for the week 22 to 28 July acknowledged that 'faith in General Auchinleck's ability and judgement continues to be recorded in all quarters'.[40] The South African censor noted that

great confidence was again expressed in General Auchinleck, and his natural, unassuming manner is making a happy impression. The nickname of 'The Auck' is gaining prominence, surely a sure barometer of esteem in the case of fighting men. A typical remark was 'the boys are full of beans and have the utmost confidence in their leader Gen. Auchinleck, in whom Rommel has met his boss.' No other British General in the course of the North African campaign has received such praise from or inspired such trust in the U.D.F. as has the C-in-C.[41]

Unquestionably, Auchinleck grasped the attention of many of his troops on taking over combined command of the MEF and Eighth Army in late June 1942. However, there was a larger problem at issue. The troops were still caustically critical of the high command, even if they did profess confidence in their Commander-in-Chief General Auchinleck. This seems somewhat anomalous as it was ultimately the Commander-in-Chief who took responsibility for the conduct of all operations in the Middle East. A memorandum written on the state of South

---

[37] NA WO 163/51 War Office Committee on Morale in the Army. Second Quarterly Report, May to July 1942, p. 5. The report is referring to the brief recovery in morale that took place in the second and third weeks of July 1942.
[38] ANZ WAII/1/DA508/1 vol. 1, MEMCWS, no. XXXV (8 to 14 July 1942), p. 1.
[39] Ibid., p. 2.
[40] ANZ WAII/1/DA508/1 vol. 1, MEMCWS, no. XXXVII (22 to 28 July 1942), p. 2.
[41] Ibid., p. 13.

African morale in August 1942 clarified the problem. It stated that the distrust of the high command was 'not focused on particular persons'; corps and army organisations remained 'nebulous' to the men, as did the 'personalities of the commanders'.[42] The key problem, as a study of the censorship summaries demonstrates, was that Auchinleck only became well known to Eighth Army in July 1942. That was exactly a year after he had taken command in the Middle East, when the censorship summaries had reported that 'allusions to the exchange of places of General Wavell and General Auchinleck have been very rare'. In fact, the summaries noted only two references to the change of command at all, one of which stated that 'I am very sorry Wavell is going ... his successor, I believe, is very good, but he will have to make his name for himself out here because to the troops he is very little known.'[43] There was a gap between Auchinleck and the troops that he never fully succeeded in bridging. In fact, the censorship summaries and the security reports make it very clear, not only that Rommel played a far more prominent role in the men's consciousness, but also that the troops had a fascination with Rommel that bordered on the extreme. In essence, Auchinleck's rise to prominence came too late for Eighth Army. The damage had been done; Rommel was already a hero and the influence of the British high command on morale was undermined and outdone. Auchinleck's efforts in July 1942 certainly caught the troops' attention but it was too little too late.

There are other issues that must be taken into consideration when assessing Auchinleck's impact on morale in the desert. It can be argued that Auchinleck was somewhat unfortunate[44] in that he presided over Eighth Army during a period when it was inferior to its enemy in many ways. Of particular importance was the perceived difference in weapons between the two armies, a crucial element in maintaining morale. A report written in 1943, on the 'Moral Effect of Weapons', showed that there was a notable 'demoralising effect' when 'our own' weapons were compared disadvantageously with the Germans. The sense of being 'vulnerable' or unable to hit back or 'retaliate' at the enemy left the soldier feeling a great sense of 'unfairness' and 'inequality', almost of 'injustice'. These feelings, since they were concerned with 'having a fair chance' and the whole sense of 'justice', had a 'particularly strong bearing on the attitude of the troops towards their own leaders'. The feeling of injustice did not 'turn on the

---

[42] SAMAD Div Docs, Gp 1, Box 1, Memorandum on Morale of SA Troops in ME, 8 August 1942, p. 1.
[43] AWM 54 883/2/97 British Troops in Egypt. No. 90 Field Censorship Report Week Ending 10 July 1941, p. 2.
[44] Bungay, *Alamein*, pp. 222–3.

enemy', but on those whom the troops felt to be responsible for 'giving them a chance'.[45]

It has also been suggested that Auchinleck was unlucky in that he had spent most of his professional career in the Indian Army, where he had not had the chance to acquaint himself with many of the men he worked with in the desert. Some authors have therefore exonerated Auchinleck on the grounds that he was not in a position to know the best men to pick and that it was his subordinates that let him down.[46] Auchinleck's biographer, John Connell, has certainly propounded such views, blaming Ritchie in the main for not obeying the instructions he received from his Commander-in-Chief in the summer of 1942.[47] Others, such as Lieutenant-General George Erskine, HQ British Troops in Egypt, Middle East Land Forces, emphasised, following the war, that these appointments were ultimately Auchinleck's responsibility.

He had a completely free hand in selecting his Army Commander and his own staff. If these people served him ill or he handled them wrongly it was his fault and nobody else's ... if this was not the team Auchinleck could drive, he should not have put them into harness.[48]

It is interesting to note that Auchinleck himself had a very poor view of the quality of some of his subordinates, especially his brigade and divisional commanders. He wrote to the War Office, in March 1942, summarising his views.

Result my experience so far this war and especially of last three months have reached conclusion that standard of leadership in all our brigade and divisional leaders not nearly high enough. This due almost complete absence systematic and continuous instruction in simple principles in peace time. Staff college training did not fill and is not filling this gap. Am convinced that we must act at once ... to have chance of meeting enemy equal terms.[49]

Whatever the possible excuses or reasons for the failures that transpired under Auchinleck's command, the facts as they are must be addressed. Auchinleck's army experienced a disastrous retreat in May and June 1942. The rate of surrender and desertion among his front line troops was so high that he had asked for the reintroduction of the death penalty. The

---

[45] NA WO 222/124 The Moral Effect of Weapons, Investigation into the Reactions of a Group of 300 Wounded Men in North Africa, 1943.

[46] Bungay, *Alamein*, pp. 222–3.

[47] Ibid., p. 222. Connell, *Auchinleck*, pp. 506–7.

[48] NA WO 236/1 Lieut.-Gen. Sir George Erskine, HQ British Troops in Egypt, Middle East Land Forces, 5 September 1950 to J. A. J. Agar-Hamilton, Union War History Section of the Prime Minister's Office, 724, Government Avenue, Pretoria.

[49] NA CAB 121/320 Telegram from C-in-C Middle East to the War Office, 7 March 1942.

number of cases of battle exhaustion was alarming[50] and, as Inglis, acting commander of the 2nd New Zealand Division, put it, the army was 'looking over [its] shoulders' for rear lines to which to withdraw.[51] Erskine concluded that 'I do not see why history should make excuses for Auchinleck when he gathered exactly what he had sown.'[52]

For instance, Auchinleck's contention that there was a dearth of quality commanders at brigade and divisional levels was only accurate to a degree. For sure, some of the generals who fought in the desert were not of the highest calibre. Others, however, were. Not all of these, unfortunately, survived until the critical battles of May and June 1942. Major-General Jock Campbell of the 7th Armoured Division, for example, was a daring and dramatic leader, much like Rommel. He had won a Victoria Cross during the Crusader campaign and his reputation among his men bordered on hero worship.[53] Campbell was given command of 7th Armoured Division in February 1942 but was tragically killed in a car crash a couple of weeks later. The censorship summary for 5 to 11 March commented that his 'reputation and popularity were such among all ranks that his death has come as a terrible blow'.[54] One man wrote,

There is no doubt that [his death] is more than tragic and he is an irreplaceable loss, for apart from his phenomenal courage and his magnificent leadership, I know no one who has ever heard of anyone who has such an effect on everyone in the field as he had … if when perhaps men were obviously tired, you could tell them that Jock Campbell was somewhere within 20 miles, it had a better effect on them than a good meal and good whisky would ever have had.

The writer, like many of the men, considered Campbell's demise of such significance that he equated it 'almost with the loss of Singapore'.[55] Another man wrote that 'if we had three more generals like that bloody Jock … the whole bloody Jerry Army would be screaming bloody murder by June at the latest'.[56]

Campbell unquestionably had a hold on his men like few other British generals during the desert war.

Ask any ordinary Gunner here his opinion, – they would not find the words they wished to use to express themselves, but to them 'if Jock said so' – NO power, no man, and no enemy would alter it, such was his simple faith and so he lived or died.

---

[50] See Chapter 1.   [51] ANZ WAII/8/24 Inglis to Freyberg, 11 July 1942.
[52] NA WO 236/1 Lieut.-Gen. Sir George Erskine, HQ British Troops in Egypt, Middle East Land Forces, 5 September 1950 to J. A. J. Agar-Hamilton, Union War History Section of the Prime Minister's Office, 724, Government Avenue, Pretoria.
[53] AWM 54 883/2/97 MEFCWS, no. XVI (26 Feb to 4 March 1942), p. 2.
[54] AWM 54 883/2/97 MEFCWS, no. XVII (5 to 11 March 1942), p. 1.
[55] AWM 54 883/2/97 MEFCWS, no. XVIII (12 to 18 March 1942), p. 3.
[56] AWM 54 883/2/97 MEFCWS, no. XX (25 to 31 March 1942), p. 3.

Illustration 13 General Claude Auchinleck, Commander-in-Chief, Middle East (right) and Major-General Jock Campbell VC (left), in the Western Desert, February 1942. Auchinleck was in command in the Middle East during the morale crisis of the summer of 1942.

For myself, for the first time I have met 'greatness' and seen all that people have ever tried to mean and express in 'leadership'. I can understand how legendary figures have risen in the past, for I have lived, worked, and fought with one. But more, I have known that men, – real, hard, 'Tough', men, have 'loved' another man with a love I've never felt or seen before but one that anyone of them would die to save. A 'love' of such a character that no one would ever even think of hesitating to die, whatever the circumstances, if to die was to obey. This was never just school-girl 'hero-worship' – that suggestion is sacrilege! – but I suppose, almost akin to the true 'Christian love' in character. We might have all been under a 'spell' so profound was it – but I wish we could be put under it again.[57]

The loss of Campbell clearly denied Auchinleck and Eighth Army the influence of a leader who might have challenged Rommel in the minds of the men. Other effective and charismatic commanders, however, did survive to fight the crucial battles of May, June and July 1942. 'Straffer'

---

[57] AWM 54 883/2/97 MEFCWS, no. XXIX (20 to 26 May 1942), p. 1.

Illustration 14 General Neil Ritchie, Commander-in-Chief Eighth Army (centre), with his Corps Commanders, Generals Charles Norrie (second from left) and 'Strafer' Gott (second from right), during the battle of Gazala, May 1942. Ritchie's handling of the battles on the Gazala line and around Tobruk contributed to the morale crisis of the summer of 1942 and ultimately led to his dismissal.

Gott, for instance, fought on until he died in unfortunate circumstances, in a plane crash, on 7 August, ironically while preparing to take over command of Eighth Army from Auchinleck.[58] His men recounted that he was 'as brave as a lion'.[59] An officer in 2nd Scots Guards regarded Gott's death as a 'great loss to the country – in my estimation almost as great as that of a battleship'. Another officer wrote, 'we all mourn the death of General Gott who was an inspiration to all troops in the MEF and a great leader of men. His loss is on the same parallel as that of Major-General Campbell.'[60]

It is, however, fair to say that no man, until Montgomery arrived in the desert, commanded as much respect from his men, or as much comment

---

[58] ANZ WAII/1/DA508/1 vol. 1, MEMCWS, no. XL (12 to 18 August 1942), p. 16; ANZ WAII/1/DA508/1 vol. 1, MEMCWS, no. XLI (19 to 25 August 1942), p. 7.
[59] ANZ WAII/1/DA508/1 vol. 1, MEMCWS no. XL (12 to 18 Aug 1942), p. 16.
[60] ANZ WAII/1/DA508/1 vol. 1, MEMCWS no. XLI (19 to 25 Aug 1942), p. 7.

from the censors, as Major-General Dan Pienaar of the UDF.[61] Following the Crusader offensive, the censors noted that many correspondents showed 'great admiration for Brigadier Pienaar'.[62] These sentiments were just as strong in May 1942:

> Every week yields fresh tributes to the outstanding qualities of Maj. Gen. Dan Pienaar. This commander has the distinction which has fallen to very few in this war, namely, that the passing of time and campaigns have consistently added to his reputation with all ranks. In U.D.F. correspondence he stands alone. Confidence in him with the ranks is absolute and admiration for prowess and ability unequalled.[63]

Even by late July, after two months of hard fighting, the censors continued to report that

> The effect of Gen. Pienaar on the men of the UDF is tremendous and his influence with them is a factor of the utmost practical importance. The manner in which Gen. Pienaar keeps personal contact with his soldiers, his simple man to man approach, coupled with his proven ability has won for him unbounded loyalty and admiration.[64]

There were clearly, therefore, some capable commanders in Eighth Army, at least in the eyes of the troops.[65] Nevertheless, whether and to what extent Auchinleck made the best use of the leadership material he had at his disposal, even if he did view it as second rate,[66] remains open to debate.

For instance, the German high command assumed that generals, in addition to their basic training, would learn from experience and from their mistakes. British generals were, however, rarely given the same opportunity. While Rommel made himself a folk hero for both sides in the desert, he was opposed by no less than six different British commanders in the same period.[67] Auchinleck twice sacked his Commander Eighth Army in the midst of active operations. Montgomery wrote, before the war, that 'we must remember that if we do not trust our subordinates we will never train them. But if they know they are trusted and that they will be judged on results, the effect will be electrical. The fussy commander, who is for ever interfering in the province of his subordinates, will never train others in the art of command.'[68] Auchinleck had the choice, in the summer of 1942, of trusting Ritchie to do his job as Commander Eighth Army or of taking full control in the field like

[61] AWM 54 883/2/97 British Troops in Egypt. No. 96 Field Censorship Report Week Ending 28 August 1941, p. 4.
[62] AWM 54 883/2/97 MEFCWS, no. X (14 to 20 January 1942), p. 7.
[63] AWM 54 883/2/97 MEFCWS, no. XXV (29 April to 5 May 1942), p. 10.
[64] ANZ WAII/1/DA508/1 vol. 1, MEMCWS, no. XXXVII (22 to 28 July 1942), p. 13.
[65] Barr, *Pendulum of War*, p. 118.
[66] NA CAB 121/320 Telegram from C-in-C Middle East to the War Office, 7 March 1942.
[67] Neame, Beresford Pierce, Goodwin Austin, Cunningham, Ritchie, Auchinleck.
[68] IWM BLM 11/3 9th Infantry Brigade Individual Training, 1937/1938, Memorandum No. 2.

Rommel. Instead 'Auchinleck took neither of these courses' and choose to hamper and interfere with Ritchie's running of Eighth Army. Vital decisions were therefore delayed because 'two hands were on the helm'.[69]

Erskine recalled how, on 25 June,

> Ritchie's policy of making a stand at MERSA MATRUH was thrown overboard. The C-in-C changed the policy, which of course he was perfectly entitled to do, but he immediately introduced a feeling of uncertainty. Where the hell do we stand? He did not even say he would stand at EL ALAMEIN. He announced a vague policy of defeating the enemy in the open with Battle Groups. Only three days before X Corps had been told they were to hang on to MERSA MATRUH at all costs.[70]

These orders and counter orders created a great sense of bewilderment throughout Eighth Army and certainly did not encourage divisional and corps commanders to trust their Commander-in-Chief.

Such confusion necessarily filtered down to the men on the front line. This was especially evident during the fighting around Tobruk, at the end of June 1942, when faulty and inconsistent communication between the high command and the troops played a significant role in deflating morale. Lieutenant-Colonel P. T. Tower, commander 31/58 Field Battery RA, wrote following the war that the 'material and moral defences of Tobruk in June 1942 were in a very poor state'.[71] The root cause was the decision made by Auchinleck, in his operational instruction no. 110 on 19 January,[72] and again announced at the beginning of the summer campaign on 27 May, that Tobruk would not again be held.[73] This decision was well known to all ranks of Eighth Army and a scheme for the evacuation of Tobruk had been practised several times by way of signal exercises.[74] Tower argued that

---

[69] NA WO 236/1 Lieut.-Gen. Sir George Erskine, HQ British Troops in Egypt, Middle East Land Forces, 5 September 1950 to J. A. J. Agar-Hamilton, Union War History Section of the Prime Minister's Office, 724, Government Avenue, Pretoria.

[70] Ibid.

[71] SAMAD UWH Draft Narratives, Box 364, Tobruk, Accounts from British Sources. A Provisional Narrative of the Fall of Tobruk, 1942 by Agar-Hamilton: General Notes and Criticisms by Lt.-Col. P. T. Tower, then Commander 31/58 Fd Bty RA.

[72] Connell, *Auchinleck*, p. 430.

[73] NA WO 216/85 Some Notes on Operations, 26 May to 8 July, GHQ MEF for CGS, 12 July 1942, p. 13; SAMAD UWH Draft Narratives, Box 364, Tobruk, Accounts from British Sources. Some Personal Opinions on the fall of Tobruk 1942, Brigadier L. F. Thompson, Comd. 88 Area Tobruk, June 1942.

[74] SAMAD UWH Draft Narratives, Box 364, Tobruk, Accounts from British Sources. A Provisional Narrative of the Fall of Tobruk, 1942 by Agar-Hamilton: General Notes and Criticisms by Lt.-Col. P. T. Tower, then Commander 31/58 Fd Bty RA; SAMAD UWH Draft Narratives, Box 364, Tobruk, Accounts from British Sources. Some Personal Opinions on the fall of Tobruk 1942, Brigadier L. F. Thompson, Comd. 88 Area Tobruk, June 1942.

When the original decision was reversed, the new 'defenders' of Tobruk were caught with their 'pants down.' They had very little time to put their defences in first class shape, they had few documents, such as mine charts, to show them how their predecessors had done it, and, above all, their morale sagged considerably.

'Theirs', Tower continued, 'was almost a feeling of being sacrificed, and little was done to explain the reason for the new decision (even if there were a good one).'[75]

The situation that greeted Montgomery on his arrival in the desert in August 1942 was certainly serious. Montgomery noted in his diary that Eighth Army was 'in a bad state; the troops had their tails right down and there was no confidence in the higher command. It was clear that ROMMEL was preparing further attacks and the troops were looking over their shoulders for rear lines to which to withdraw.' The whole atmosphere, he wrote, 'was wrong ... The troops knew that they were worthy of far better things than had ever come to them; they also knew that the higher command was to blame for the reverses that had been suffered.'[76] He wrote to Major-General F. E. W. Simpson, on 12 October 1942, stating that the 'situation here when I arrived was really unbelievable; I would never have thought it could have been so bad'.[77]

The first and fundamental tenet of Montgomery's style of command was that morale should be at the centre of everything. As early as 1940, he had stated that 'all commanders from Generals down to junior leaders, and troops, must possess calm determination, "binge", enthusiasm and stout hearts. In the end it is the initiative and fighting spirit of the junior leader, and the soldier in the ranks, that wins the battle; if these cannot stand up to the conditions of modern battle then we must fail, however good the higher leading.'[78]

Montgomery, therefore, focused on four critical elements of leadership and command that directly impinged on morale in the desert in 1942: clarity of direction, communication with the troops, commanders' image and the handling of formations.

[75] SAMAD UWH Draft Narratives, Box 364, Tobruk, Accounts from British Sources. A Provisional Narrative of the Fall of Tobruk, 1942 by Agar-Hamilton: General Notes and Criticisms by Lt.-Col. P. T. Tower, then Commander 31/58 Fd Bty RA.

[76] IWM BLM 27/1 Situation in August 1942.

[77] IWM BLM 50 Montgomery to Simpson, 12 October 1942.

[78] IWM BLM 24/1 5 Corps Study Week for Commanders. Some Lessons Learnt During the First Year of War, September 1939 to September 1940; IWM BLM 24/4 Address, Minley Manor, 25 October 1940; he made similar comments in 1942; see IWM BLM 52 Eighth Army, Some Brief Notes for Senior Officers on the Conduct of Battle, December 1942.

During the summer of 1942, an atmosphere of uncertainty surrounded Eighth Army's plan of operations. The main issue was whether Eighth Army was to stand and fight at El Alamein or retreat to a defensive line under preparation in the Delta. At the end of June, as Eighth Army streamed back to El Alamein, Auchinleck had asked his Chief of Staff, Major-General Eric Dorman-Smith, to write an 'appreciation of the situation'. The appreciation envisaged, in a worst case scenario, that Eighth Army would retreat to the Delta if heavily attacked on the El Alamein line. Dorman-Smith passed the document on to Tom Corbett, Auchinleck's chief staff officer at GHQ in Cairo, who informed XXX and XIII Corps HQs of this provisional plan on 28 June 1942.[79] On 1 July, XXX Corps issued an operation order explaining how the retreat from El Alamein would be carried out, 'if considered essential to withdraw from the El Alamein position'.[80] The effect of Corbett's order on Gott, the commander of XIII Corps, and on Inglis, the acting commander of 2nd New Zealand Division, to whom Gott on 29 June unwisely repeated it, was confusion. Gott believed the appreciation created a 'psychological conception amongst some Commanders that the line in rear must be better than the one occupied!'[81] Inglis wrote to Freyberg, on 11 July, that Eighth Army was 'eastward leaning all the time', had 'been retreating too long', and seemed 'to be backing towards Alexandria'.[82] Hugh Mainwaring, Auchinleck's GSO 1 Operations, remembered that, around the end of July, he was ordered to reconnoitre the position at Mena for the defence of Cairo, and to practise evacuating HQ Eighth Army in case a retreat was necessary.[83] The situation was so uncertain that Auchinleck admitted, in a letter to Brooke on 25 July, that perhaps he had 'asked too much of [the troops]' and that 'we may yet have to face a withdrawal'.[84] With Auchinleck acting as Commander-in-Chief MEF and Commander Eighth Army, the staff at HQ Eighth Army necessarily became embroiled in GHQ staff work. In this way, strategic issues, such as the possibility of retreat from El Alamein, became 'popular knowledge'.[85]

It has been argued by some authors that Auchinleck did not intend to retreat to the Delta and that he was only being thorough in examining all

[79] NA WO 216/85 Some Notes on Operations, 26 May to 8 July, GHQ MEF for CGS, 12 July 1942, p. 14.
[80] AWM 54 526/6/19 The Crisis at El Alamein, 30 June to 4 July 1942, p. 12.
[81] NA WO 216/85 Some Notes on Operations, 26 May to 8 July, GHQ MEF for CGS, 12 July 1942, p. 14.
[82] ANZ WAII/8/24 Letter to Gen. Freyberg from Maj.-Gen. Inglis, 11 July 1942.
[83] Hugh Mainwaring, *Three Score Years and Ten with Never a Dull Moment* (printed privately, 1976), pp. 64–7.
[84] LHCMA Alanbrooke Papers, Auchinleck to Brooke, 25 July 1942.
[85] Mainwaring, *Three Score Years and Ten*, pp. 64–7.

Illustration 15 Field Marshal Erwin Rommel with his aides during the North African campaign, 1942. Rommel was regarded as a better general than Eighth Army's own commanders by many of the troops in the desert. This had a major impact on the troops' morale.

eventualities as his army fell back to El Alamein.[86] These authors have castigated Montgomery for claiming that Auchinleck planned to retreat in August 1942 when clearly the danger to the Delta had already passed. This argument, although it is essentially valid, misses the point. The significance of Auchinleck's plan was not whether he was seriously considering another retreat, but rather the effect this plan had on the morale of Eighth Army.[87] As one official historian put it, 'the High Command must have been aware that an order of this character, issued on the eve of a serious battle, was not calculated to improve morale'.[88]

After the El Alamein battles, an Australian memorandum, dealing with morale, discipline and training, explained the effect that such confusion could have on troops.

[86] Barnett, *The Desert Generals*, pp. 303–4; Barr, *Pendulum of War*, p. 188.
[87] Scoullar, *The Battle for Egypt*, pp. 142–5.
[88] AWM 54 526/6/19 The Crisis at El Alamein, 30 June to 4 July 1942, p. 12.

Troops must not be led into battle in the belief that the 'prepared positions' to their rear exist primarily to offer them refuge in face of a determined enemy. Over-reliance on static defensive measures and concrete fortifications will kill the fighting spirit of any army, and any officer who examines a prepared position with the unspoken thought, 'This is where I fall back to,' fails in the first essential of leadership – a resolve to win the day.[89]

Montgomery, on taking command of Eighth Army, immediately issued an order that there would be no more retreat. On 13 August 1942, he gathered his subordinates around him and put the matter to rest.

The defence of Egypt lies here at Alamein and on the Ruweisat Ridge. What is the use of digging trenches in the Delta? It is quite useless; if we lose this position we lose Egypt; all the fighting troops now in the Delta must come out here at once, and will. Here we will stand and fight; there will be no further withdrawal; I have ordered that all plans and instructions dealing with further withdrawal are to be burnt, and at once. We will stand and fight here. If we can't stay here alive, then let us stay here dead.[90]

This order, as Correlli Barnett has argued quite correctly, was strategically meaningless. But Barnett overlooks the key point. He belittles the 'moral impact of Montgomery's vaunted "No retreat" order',[91] showing a lack of understanding of the significance of the morale crisis affecting Eighth Army in August 1942. Eighth Army was confused and bewildered. It did not know whether it was to stand and fight or whether it was to retreat to the Delta. The effect of Montgomery's order, which completely clarified the situation, was, therefore, electric. Mainwaring believed it was 'the turning point of the war'.[92] A 9th Australian Division report on the battle of El Alamein stated that 'the effect of the new policy' had been 'quickly apparent ... General relief and satisfaction were felt when it became known that the enemy was to be met and fought in the prepared positions then held. Confidence and morale increased rapidly.'[93]

At a conference held at the 2nd New Zealand Division Headquarters on 16 August, Freyberg addressed his commanding officers on the new policy.

I want you to make the Army Commander's views clear to every body. This looking over your shoulder and cranking up to get back to the position in the rear is to cease. Here we are going to stay and here we are going to fight. There is no

---

[89] AWM 54 265/2/4 Esprit de Corps and Discipline. The Officer's Task. Army Discipline, Dress, Saluting, Drill and Physical Fitness, n.d., p. 4.
[90] NA CAB 106/703 Address to Officers of HQ Eighth Army by General Montgomery on Taking Over Command of the Army, 13 August 1942.
[91] Barnett, *The Desert Generals*, p. 304.   [92] Mainwaring, *Three Score Years and Ten*, p. 67.
[93] AWM 54 527/6/1 Part 1, 9th Australian Division Report on Operations. El Alamein, 23 October to 5 November 1942, p. 2.

question of going to any back position from here. We are to make this position as complete as we can.[94]

Howard Kippenberger, the commander of 5th New Zealand Brigade, later recalled that

The new Army Commander made himself felt at once. He talked sharply and curtly, without any soft words, asked some searching questions, met the battalion commanders, and left me feeling much stimulated. For a long time we had heard little from Army ... Now we were told that we were going to fight, there was no question of retirement to any reserve positions or anywhere else, and to get ahead with our preparations. To make the intention clear our troop-carrying transport was sent a long way back so that we could not run away if we wanted to! There was no more talk of the alternative positions in the rear. We were delighted and the morale of the whole Army went up incredibly.[95]

As a result of his meeting with Montgomery, Kippenberger sent this circular to his brigade before Alam Halfa.

We are now facing a very severe test. For the next few weeks we will be on the defensive and it is open to the enemy to make an attack which will test us to the limit. If he does not make it or if he makes it and fails, then the tide will quickly turn strongly against him, but these few weeks are critical. We hold an exposed and vital position of the line. Like the Australians, the South Africans, the Indians and British we are burning our boats by sending our transport many miles away and it is our duty to stand and fight where we are, to the last man, and the last round. It is probable, almost certain that we will be subjected to extremely severe attacks by dive bombers, arty, tanks and infantry and in fact it is probable that the supreme test of the New Zealand Division is close ahead of us.[96]

The censorship summaries and troops' diaries and memoirs show that Montgomery's 'no retreat' order reached the troops and did play a role in reinvigorating morale.[97] One South African officer wrote, 'there are three big factors in our favour, which were missing before – the Grant tank, the 6 pdr A/Tk gun and an Order of the Day that there will be no withdrawal, no retreat, but to fight to the last man, the last round. That is the kind of talk we can understand, and we have some equipment to back it up.'[98] A British field officer wrote that 'General Montgomery has issued some stirring orders and one feels his personality everywhere.' A private wrote,

---

[94] ANZ WAII/8/24 Conference Headquarters NZ Division Sunday 16 August 1942, Note of GOC's Address to COs.
[95] Howard Kippenberger, *Infantry Brigadier* (London, 1949), p. 196.
[96] ANZ WAII/1/DA508/1 vol. 3 MEMCWS no. XLII (26 August to 2 September 1942), p. 18.
[97] AWM 3DRL J. M. Butler, 2/23 Battalion AIF, Diary 3 September 1942.
[98] ANZ WAII/1/DA508/1 vol. 3, MEMCWS, no. XLIII (3 to 9 September 1942), p. 14; SAMAD CGS (War), Box 248, Summary of 'I' Summaries for CGS.

'our General out here said we have to fight to our last breath in our bodies, and we will'.[99] The censorship summary for 10 to 16 September revealed that 'the Order of the Day enjoining the troops to stand fast and fight on without withdrawal and surrender, definitely caught the imagination of all ranks and this change in policy, and the fact that in the recent trial of strength "Mr Rommel got a bloody nose" have encouraged the belief that the next desert battle will be the last'. A field officer wrote, 'our tails are up, anyhow, and we are all pleased with our new Generals – and faith in the Commander is half the battle – especially when his order is a simple one "Stand and Fight"'.[100]

Whereas Auchinleck's stirring message of 30 June 1942 to the effect that Rommel 'thinks we are a broken army' and 'hopes to take Egypt by bluff ... Show him where he gets off' made no impact on the censorship summaries or the troops' diaries and memoirs,[101] Montgomery's directive spread like wildfire throughout Eighth Army. Indeed, both Brian Horrocks, Montgomery's new commander of XIII Corps, and Francis de Guingand, his new chief of staff, described the effect of the order as 'magical'.[102]

Allied to Montgomery's 'no retreat' order was his determination to put an end to the extraordinarily high surrender rates affecting Eighth Army. Auchinleck had provided figures to the Army Council, in July 1942, establishing that prisoners of war were comprising up to 88 per cent of Eighth Army's casualties.[103] Such high surrender rates were quite contrary to the traditions of the British Army. The 1929 FSR made it clear that 'there is only one degree of resistance for troops actually allotted to the defence of any locality, that is to the last round and the last man, unless definite orders to the contrary are received by the commander of those troops'.[104] Montgomery, therefore, in his second memorandum on the upcoming battle of El Alamein, on 6 October 1942, issued clear instructions to his men to clarify what was expected of them.

It is essential to impress on all officers that determined leadership will be very vital in this battle, as in any battle. There have been far too many unwounded prisoners taken in this war. We must impress on our Officers, N.C.O's and men that when they are cut off or surrounded, and there appears to be no hope of survival, they

---

[99] ANZ WAII/1/DA508/1 vol. 3, MEMCWS, no. XLIII (3 to 9 September 1942), p. 2.
[100] ANZ WAII/1/DA508/1 vol. 3, MEMCWS, no. XLIV (10 to 16 September, 1942), p. 2.
[101] Scoullar, *The Battle for Egypt*, p. 148.
[102] Horrocks, *A Full Life*, p. 114; IWM BLM 56 Francis de Guingand to the Editor of the *Sunday Times*, 15 December 1958.
[103] NA WO 163/89 ECAC, The Death Penalty for Offences Committed on Active Service, 21 July 1942.
[104] *FSR* chap. 7 Sec. 77 (1929).

must organise themselves into a defensive locality and hold out where they are. By so doing they will add enormously to the enemy's difficulties; they will greatly assist the development of our own operations; and they will save themselves from spending the rest of the war in a prison camp. Nothing is ever hopeless so long as troops have stout hearts, and have weapons and ammunition.

He finished by saying that 'these points must be got across <u>now</u> at once to all officers and men, as being applicable to any fighting'.[105]

Leslie Morshead, the commander of 9th Australian Division, proffered a very similar message to the men under his command, repeating some of Montgomery's phrases verbatim. He began by saying that 'there must be no wavering. If you have anyone you are not sure of, then don't take the risk of taking him in. Give him some other job other than fighting.'

I cannot stress too greatly the value and necessity for <u>determined</u> leading, and it will apply in this battle as never before. Whatever the shelling or dive bombing, or the mortaring, we must stand firm, and not give way or run away. In the war there have been far too many unwounded prisoners taken. The modern term 'in the bag' is too excusable, it is not harsh enough, and it seems to mitigate having failed to make a proper stand and even to having just merely surrendered. We must make it unfashionable. I have closely questioned escaped prisoners and I know what actually happened in some instances, I am sure that those who did not put up a fight must often ruminate over it in their prison camps especially in the winter months.

You must impress on your officers, NCOs and men that when they are cut off or surrounded and there appears no hope of survival they must organise themselves into a defensive locality and hold out. They must be a good staunch Australian and not emulate the Italians. By so doing they will add enormously to the enemy's difficulties and will assist materially the development of our own operations. And they will live to have pride and satisfaction in themselves instead of spending the rest of the war and a long time afterwards in prison camps. Nothing is ever hopeless so long as troops have stout hearts, and have weapons and ammunition. In this too is the test of real leadership and manhood.[106]

To reinforce the point, Montgomery's personal message from the Army Commander to his troops on the eve of the battle of El Alamein had one section standing out in bold and in capitals so that it could not be missed. It read, 'LET NO MAN SURRENDER SO LONG AS HE IS UNWOUNDED AND CAN FIGHT.'[107]

It is impossible to establish the precise effect that Montgomery's communication may have had on the troops, but the outcome is indubitable.

---

[105] AWM 3DRL 2632 2/2 Lightfoot. Memorandum no. 2 by Army Commander, 6 October 1942.
[106] AWM 3 DRL 2632 Morshead Papers, El Alamein, 10 October 1942.
[107] IWM, BLM 53 Eighth Army, Personal Message from the Army Commander, 23 October 1942.

Only 17 per cent of casualties from the battle were POWs.[108] Taking into account the fact that Eighth Army was on the offensive, a situation where soldiers were less likely to be taken POW, this is still a remarkably low figure. The comparable statistic for the Crusader offensive at the end of 1941 was 42 per cent.[109] Montgomery, nevertheless, saw the issue of surrender as so important and the problem as so deep-rooted in Eighth Army, that, even after the victory at El Alamein, he continued to urge his troops not to surrender in the face of the enemy.[110]

The second leadership and command issue that affected morale was communication with the troops. The importance of information, of controlling the perceptions of soldiers with little to dwell on other than how unfortunate they were to be holed up in the Western Desert, was a key element in determining morale.[111] In the WDF's initial advance against the Italians in 1940 Wavell had taken a calculated risk when he informed his troops of the operations they were about to embark on. A 4th Indian Division report on the lessons learned from the operation noted that this communication had had a positive effect on morale. 'During the day', the report stated, 'the Divisional Commander visited all the troops, addressed officers and read out messages from General WAVELL and the Commander, Western Desert [Lieutenant-General Richard O'Connor]. The latter also visited the Division and addressed as many officers as possible in each Group. The morale of all ranks was high and all were filled with quiet confidence.'[112] The 9th Australian Division training instructions derived from the Crusader campaign made it clear that it was important 'to ensure that the soldier has a firm background as to the real situation against which he can assess rumours at their true value'. This was 'essential, especially in difficult situations'.[113]

Len Challoner, of the 2nd Regiment Royal Horse Artillery, advanced a similar argument a number of months later as Eighth Army retreated to the El Alamein line.

Mr Stephenson, previously of P Troop came to us here and made it his habit to come round daily with the fighting map and explain to us the position. What a

---

[108] Derived from statistics in Bungay, *Alamein*, pp. 196–7.
[109] Derived from statistics quoted by Playfair, *The Mediterranean and Middle East*, vol. III, p. 97.
[110] IWM BLM 52 Eighth Army, Some Brief Notes for Senior Officers on the Conduct of Battle, December 1942, p. 1.
[111] AWM 54 883/2/97 MEFCWS, no. XIV (11 to 17 February 1942), p. 10.
[112] NA WO 201/352 Report on Lessons of the Operations in the Western Desert, December 1940.
[113] AWM 54 519/7/26 Lessons of Second Libyan Campaign, 9th Division Training Instruction, Report of Lieut.-Col. S. H. Porter and Lieut.-Col. J. D. Rogers, 26 December 1941.

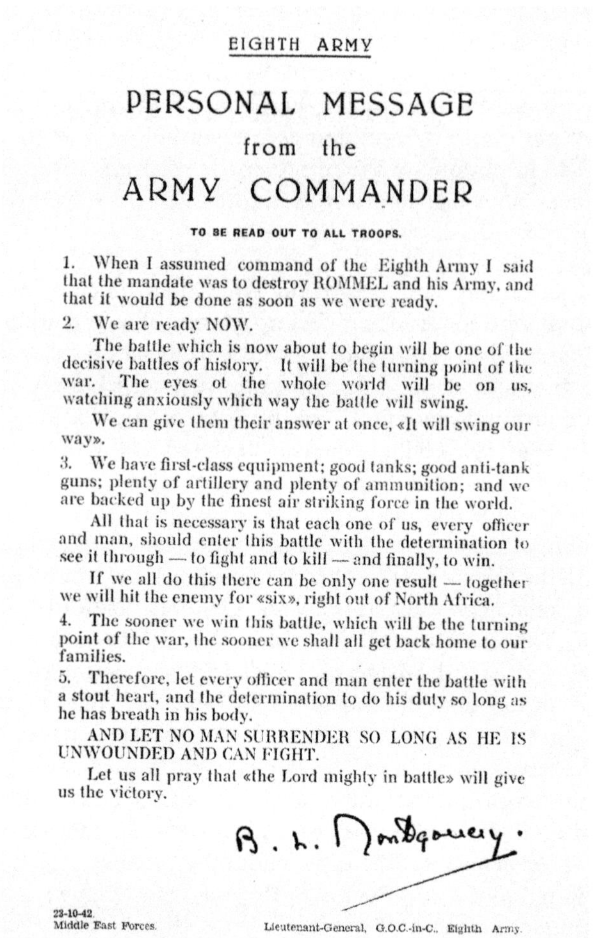

EIGHTH ARMY

PERSONAL MESSAGE

from the

ARMY COMMANDER

TO BE READ OUT TO ALL TROOPS.

1. When I assumed command of the Eighth Army I said that the mandate was to destroy ROMMEL and his Army, and that it would be done as soon as we were ready.

2. We are ready NOW.

The battle which is now about to begin will be one of the decisive battles of history. It will be the turning point of the war. The eyes of the whole world will be on us, watching anxiously which way the battle will swing.

We can give them their answer at once, «It will swing our way».

3. We have first-class equipment; good tanks; good anti-tank guns; plenty of artillery and plenty of ammunition; and we are backed up by the finest air striking force in the world.

All that is necessary is that each one of us, every officer and man, should enter this battle with the determination to see it through — to fight and to kill — and finally, to win.

If we all do this there can be only one result — together we will hit the enemy for «six», right out of North Africa.

4. The sooner we win this battle, which will be the turning point of the war, the sooner we shall all get back home to our families.

5. Therefore, let every officer and man enter the battle with a stout heart, and the determination to do his duty so long as he has breath in his body.

AND LET NO MAN SURRENDER SO LONG AS HE IS UNWOUNDED AND CAN FIGHT.

Let us all pray that «the Lord mighty in battle» will give us the victory.

B. L. Montgomery.

23-10-42.
Middle East Forces.   Lieutenant-General, G.O.C.-in-C., Eighth Army.

Illustration 16 General Bernard Montgomery's message to the Eighth Army before the battle of El Alamein, October 1942. A significant factor in Montgomery's leadership was his ability to communicate with and inspire his troops.

difference this makes to their morale only a gunner can tell; yet it should be obvious to the meanest intelligence that when men are ordered to fire, to retreat, to advance, to switch right and left without any explanation at all they very soon lose all interest and begin to think that the war is just a game that higher-ups play, in which they have no intelligent part.[114]

---

[114] IWM 10851 P479 L. Challoner, Diary, pp. 119–20.

A 50th Division report, on the 'Main Lessons Learned' in the months of May, June and July 1942, pointed out that the troops were 'often completely in the dark as to what is happening'. The report viewed it as 'important that [troops] should be given as much accurate information as possible, in order to heighten morale and to discourage wild rumours'. The 'only solution' was 'for officers, with due regard to secrecy, to give their men a picture of the general situation as they know it, at regular intervals'.[115]

Montgomery made a firm policy to keep the troops in the know at all times. In his inaugural address to the officers of HQ Eighth Army on 13 August 1942 he stressed the 'atmosphere' in which he wanted Eighth Army to work and fight. 'You must see that that atmosphere permeates right down through the Eighth Army to the most junior private soldier,' he demanded. 'All the soldiers must know what is wanted; when they see it coming to pass there will be a surge of confidence throughout the Army.'[116] This policy immediately endeared Montgomery to the troops and differentiated him from previous commanders. Indeed, it was key to the extraordinary surge in morale that preceded the battle.

In his first memorandum on the coming battle, issued on 28 September 1942, Montgomery insisted that 'Wed 21 October, and Thurs 22 October will be devoted to the most intensive propaganda as regards educating the attacking troops about the battle, and to getting them enthusiastic. All ranks must be told that this battle is probably the decisive battle of the war; if we win this battle and destroy the Panzer Army it will be the turning point of the war.'[117] Indeed, Douglas Wimberley recalled how, on 21 October, he was allowed to let his 51st Highland Division know 'what they were in for, and their part in the battle explained to them'.[118] The 9th Australian Division report on the operation stated that, during the two days preceding the offensive, an intensive drive was made to ensure that every man knew the object of the battle, the part his formation and unit had to play and the part that he himself had to play.[119]

The morale report for August to October 1942 stated that

Morale reached its peak as a result of the Army Commander's message to his troops on the eve of the offensive, and of the fact (commented on widely in the mail) that all ranks, down the whole chain of command, were taken into

[115] NA WO 201/538 app. to 50 Div Main Lessons Learned since 27 May 1942, 20 July 1942.
[116] NA CAB 106/703 Address to Officers of HQ Eighth Army by General Montgomery on taking over command of the Army, 13 August 1942.
[117] IWM BLM 28/4 Lightfoot, Memorandum no. 1 by Army Commander, 28 September 1942.
[118] IWM 430 PP/MCR/182 Wimberley, 'Scottish Soldier', p. 40.
[119] AWM 527/6/1 Part 1, 9th Australian Division Report on Operation. El Alamein, 23 October to 5 November 1942, p. 4.

confidence about the plan of attack. In the words of the censor 'the fact that the G.O.C.-in-C., 8th Army, took the whole army into his confidence right down to the last man and stated exactly what he hoped to do and how he was going to do it, the belief that the plan was good, and the knowledge that the tools at their disposal were more numerous and effective than they have ever been, brought the spirit of the troops to a new high level and intensified their assurance and grim determination which was to be fully tested and proved to the hilt in the twelve historic days that followed. On the evidence of this mail no army ever went to battle with higher morale.[120]

The morale report for November 1942 to January 1943 stated that 'all ranks were in the picture from the outset; this evidently made all the difference'.[121]

The third key leadership and command factor was the issue of commanders' image. Eighth Army's lack of confidence in its own commanders was reflected in Rommel's standing as a folk hero amongst the troops. Rommel was 'believed to possess more drive and enterprise than our own leaders'. One officer wrote, 'there is no news of interest here at the moment except that I have often heard fellows say "I wish we had Rommel on our side"'. An OR wrote, 'I can only say if General Rommel had been an Englishman we would have pushed the Jerries out of Libya months ago.'[122] A memorandum on the 'Morale of South African Troops' in the desert, written in August 1942, made a similar point. 'It is interesting to compare the attitude towards General Rommel, who has been built up by propaganda into an imposing figure, and the attitude to General Auchinleck, where little has been done to make his personality familiar or impressive to the men.'[123] Even Churchill held Rommel in high esteem. During a debate in the House of Commons, on 27 January 1942, he remarked, 'we have a very daring and skilful opponent against us, and, may I say across the havoc of war, a great general'.[124]

The authorities in the Middle East made a considerable effort to counter Axis propaganda and undermine the Rommel legend. The 'MEF Weekly Military Newsletter no. 74', dated 26 February 1942, argued that 'Axis propaganda had gone to considerable pains to build up the legend of Rommel, one of the aims being to give us a feeling of inferiority in face of this photogenic General who is supposed to be master of the Libyan

[120] NA WO 193/453 Morale Report, August to October 1942.
[121] NA WO 193/453 Morale Report, November 1942 to January 1943.
[122] AWM 54 883/2/97 MEFCWS, no. XVI (26 February to 4 March 1942), pp. 3–4.
[123] SAMAD Div Docs, Gp 1, Box 1, Memorandum on Morale of SA Troops in ME, 8 August 1942, p. 1.
[124] Raymond Callahan, *Churchill and His Generals* (Lawrence, KS, 2007), p. 97.

Illustration 17 General Bernard Montgomery issuing instructions, August 1942. Montgomery focused on clarity of direction, one of the critical elements of leadership and command that directly impinged on morale in the desert in 1942.

desert.' The publication insisted that 'we should combat this insidious campaign, otherwise, we run the risk of being "gerommelt"'.[125] Another article in the *NZEF Times* at the end of March noted that 'it is foolish to deny that General Rommel is a doughty opponent but it is open to dispute that he is a brilliant general ... Axis propaganda has undoubtedly been successful in its application to the German soldier who has been persuaded that Rommel is infallible but it should not succeed with those who have fought and beaten the German soldier, for, to them, General Rommel is still the man who failed to take Tobruk and who had the initiative wrested from him in the last Libyan offensive.'[126]

Auchinleck's reaction to the problem was to send a letter to all Eighth Army commanders on the subject of 'our friend Rommel' forbidding them to mention Rommel by name. 'I wish to dispel by all possible

[125] AWM 54 883/2/97 MEFCWS, no. XVI (26 February to 4 March 1942), p. 3.
[126] ANZ WAII/1/DA457 Box 15, *NZEF Times* 1(40) (Monday 30 March 1942), Free to NZEF.

means [the idea] that Rommel represents something more than an ordinary German general ... The important thing now is that we do not always talk of Rommel when we mean the enemy in Libya. We must refer to "the Germans", or the "Axis powers", or "the enemy" and not always keep harping on Rommel ... PS. I am not jealous of Rommel.'[127]

Auchinleck's reserved and somewhat aloof character in some ways allowed the flamboyant Rommel to dominate the war of personalities in the desert. Montgomery, on the contrary, actively pursued publicity and the press limelight and purposefully took on the Rommel legend. He recounted in his memoirs after the war that

> The Eighth Army consisted in the main of civilians in uniform, not of professional soldiers. And they were, of course, to a man, civilians who read newspapers. It seemed to me that to command such men demanded not only a guiding mind but also a point of focus: or to put it another way, not only a master but a mascot. And I deliberately set about fulfilling this second requirement. It helped, I felt sure, for them to recognise as a person – as an individual – the man who was putting them into battle. To obey an impersonal figure was not enough. They must know who I was.[128]

Mainwaring remembered how Montgomery, on taking command of Eighth Army, ordered him to ensure that every man knew 'the name Montgomery by tonight'.[129] Montgomery's showmanship gave Eighth Army a figure they could look up to, a man who could combat Rommel's image of the 'Desert Fox'. It also helped ease tensions between the various nationalities and arms of Eighth Army. By wearing his Australian and tank corps hats he appealed to Australian and RAC sentiments. The same could be said for his practice of wearing various unit badges on his headgear.[130] The *Crusader* magazine for 5 October 1942 boasted a picture of Montgomery with the heading 'Commander's Badges'.[131] Such affectations worked and in a remarkably short time Montgomery impressed his personality on the troops in the desert and gave them their own hero to look up to.

The fourth leadership and command issue that impacted on morale in the desert was the practice of mixing and matching units in battle. It was common practice for Eighth Army to move units from one formation to the next as needs arose during operations. While this allowed a certain

[127] Bungay, *Alamein*, p. 40; Hamilton, *The Full Monty*, p. 544.
[128] Montgomery, *Memoirs*, p. 111. The extent to which improved provisions of reading material played an important role in developing morale is dealt with in Chapter 5.
[129] Mainwaring, *Three Score Years and Ten*, p. 66.   [130] Hamilton, *The Full Monty*, p. 538.
[131] LHCMA Crick Papers, *Crusader, Eighth Army Weekly*, 2(23) (5 October 1942).

amount of operational flexibility, it could at the same time affect morale by preventing commanders and men from creating meaningful and effective organisational relationships. For example, the 1st South African Infantry Brigade underwent ten changes of higher command during the Crusader operations at the end of 1941. At various times they were under 1st South African Division, 2nd New Zealand Division, 4th Indian Division, XXX Corps, XIII Corps and Eighth Army.[132]

Following Crusader, a 1st South African Division report criticised the way battalions, brigades and even divisions were being treated.

> It is a well established fact that troops ... are happier when serving under their own Commanders. It is disastrous to hand units and formations over from one formation to another during the progress of operations. Formation commanders know their subordinate commanders and understand the characteristics ... of their troops. They know, or should know ... how to get the best out of those troops. The handing over of units and formations from one formation Commander to another during the recent operations has led to a great deal of unhappiness and recrimination, which it is imperative should, in the interests of unity and co-operation of our forces, be avoided at all costs. Formations should, therefore, be of a composition and strength which will enable them to operate continuously over a reasonable period of the operations, even if heavy casualties have been incurred.[133]

Despite the warning, the same mistakes were made six months later during the critical battles of the summer of 1942. The 7th Medium Regiment RA were attached to Indians, Kiwis, Poles, Free French, South Africans and Australians in turn over the space of a few months. Furthermore, battalions in the Durhams and the Guards were combined into composite battalions following the fall of Tobruk.[134] The effect of this policy was so destructive to morale that the field censorship summary for 5 to 11 August described the morale of the Scots and Coldstream Guards as being the 'lowest' in the desert.[135] One officer of the Coldstream Guards recounted his 'horror' as 'we got sent off into the blue as a composite Bn'.[136] As casualties built up, the running of the battalion became an absolute shambles. He recalled,

> Finally we got a suicidal order and one of the S[cots] G[uards] Companies suffered heavily trying to carry it out ... Next time a similar party was suggested,

[132] SAMAD Div Docs, Gp 1, Box 5, 1 SA Infantry Brigade, Report on Operations in Cyrenaica, November to December 1941.
[133] SAMAD Div Docs, Box 62, 1 SA Div Operations Report Cyrenaica, 18 November to 2 December 1941, p. 17.
[134] See Chapter 1 for more details on the composite Guards Battalion.
[135] ANZ WAII/1/DA508/1 vol.1, MEMCWS, no. XXXIX (5 to 11 August 1942), p. 4.
[136] Ibid.

X who was commanding the composite bn. refused to comply; and refused again and got asked for reasons in writing. Meanwhile the div Comdr who couldn't have been bloodier about the whole thing, had already sent Y and Z back, for being decided and outspoken in their conviction that we weren't fit for enterprising harassing warfare.[137]

Another officer described the situation as 'chaos'. 'We didn't know their form and they didn't know ours … How I wish you could mobilise and come out complete with esprit de corps and officers and men knowing each other, the answer would be so much better and quicker than this patchwork of odds and sods to which everyone out here comes sooner or later.'[138]

The initial court of enquiry following Tobruk stressed the same points that had been made following Crusader. 'Esprit de Corps is as important today as ever it was and this applies as much to formations as to units. Formations which have been trained together must operate together. To change the composition of Brigades or to detach them without good reason from one Division to another destroys all team work, dislocates communications, upsets administration and has a bad effect on the morale of officers and men.'[139]

'Strafer' Gott, the commander of XIII Corps, expressed a similar opinion in a report he wrote in July 1942. 'We have got ourselves into a proper muddle with Regiments, Squadrons and Brigades all mixed up. Perhaps unavoidable in the middle of a battle, but to retain our efficiency, we must get sorted out now. Chopping, switching and changing of units from Brigade to Brigade, and Division to Division can only result in chaos.'[140]

John Connell, Auchinleck's biographer, has tried to shift the blame for these policies onto Neil Ritchie, Auchinleck's Commander Eighth Army. He points out that Auchinleck wrote to Ritchie on 20 May 1942 advising that 'I consider it to be of the highest importance that you should not break up the organization of … divisions. They have been trained to fight as divisions, I hope, and fight as divisions they should.'[141] He blamed Ritchie for not having heeded his Commander-in-Chief's advice. Nevertheless, Auchinleck's advice to Ritchie was just that, advice; it certainly was not an order. Such a late and tentative change of policy does not excuse Auchinleck from the defeats that ensued on the Gazala line and at Tobruk.

Montgomery, as soon as he took over command, put an end to the practice of mixing and matching units. 'Divisions would fight as

---

[137] Ibid.   [138] Ibid., p. 3.
[139] SAMAD UWH, Published Books, Box 368, Court of Inquiry, Tobruk. Report of a Court of Inquiry Assembled by Order of the C-in-C, 8 July 1942, p. 3.
[140] NA WO 216/85 Some Notes on Operations, 26 May to 8 July, GHQ MEF for CGS, 12 July 1942, p. 3.
[141] Connell, *Auchinleck*, pp. 506–7.

Divisions', he said 'and they were not to be split up into bits and pieces all over the desert.'[142] Following this change, Freyberg wrote home to New Zealand, in October 1942, emphasising that 'the changes here for the most part have been for the best, and I feel that from the point of view of military organisation we shall be on much better lines'.[143] Douglas Wimberley, the commander of the 51st Highland Division, wrote to Montgomery in 1953 recalling,

> I do not think I could have stood for long and seen the breaking up of formations, (indeed already threatened the week I arrived), and the lack of understanding of those little psychological matters, which, nevertheless, with soldiers ... make all the difference between their fighting really hard and their fighting more half heartedly, except of course in the imagination of the writers of the sit[uation] rep[ort]s, the intelligence summaries and the War Diaries where these things get covered up![144]

Montgomery has been described by his critics as a plodding and pedantic general.[145] Nevertheless, his practice of 'stage managing' his battles and ensuring that his army remained 'balanced' must be recognised, at least in the context of North Africa, as policies designed specifically to prevent the breaking up of units in battle and thereby protect morale. The lessons from the Crusader and summer offensives could not have been clearer. Troops who had been trained together needed to fight together under the command of leaders with whom they were used to fighting. Montgomery therefore ensured the disposition of his units was carefully prepared before any battle to avoid the necessity of 'dancing to Rommel's tune' and breaking up units to deal with threats as they arose. He could, therefore, ignore Rommel's counter-thrusts while continuing with his own 'master plan'. This approach was diametrically different from the *Auftragstaktik* (mission command) used by the Wehrmacht.[146] Although less flexible and dynamic than German methods of command and control, Montgomery fought in a manner that made victory possible with the material he had at hand. This astute understanding of what affected his troops' morale enabled him to fight a considered and realistic battle that he could win.

Underlying the many difficulties that affected the morale of Eighth Army in June, July and August 1942 was a nagging uncertainty about the quality of

---

[142] IWM BLM 27 Situation in August 1942, p. 3.

[143] ANZ WAII/8/26 Freyberg to NZ Minister of Defence, 14 October 1942.

[144] IWM BLM 57 Wimberley to Montgomery, 9 June 1953. As mentioned in Chapter 1, neither the history of the Scots Guards or that of the Coldstreams mentions the crisis that took place in the summer of 1942.

[145] Alistair Horne, 'In Defence of Montgomery', in Robert Cowley (ed.), *No End Save Victory* (London, 2002), p. 477.

[146] Bungay, *Alamein*, pp. 32–3.

its leadership and command. This lack of confidence in its own high command was exacerbated by the overblown reputation of Rommel among the troops. When Montgomery took over command on 13 August 1942, he set out quite deliberately to replace uncertainty with confidence, to communicate clearly to all levels where previously the army had been beset by confusion, to propagate his image where up to that time Rommel's had been paramount and to organise his formations in a manner that best suited their traditions and state of readiness. His thoughtful, thorough approach resulted in a level of morale in Eighth Army that allowed the troops to withstand a most terrible battle and emerge victorious.

The court of inquiry, set up following the fall of Tobruk in June 1942, recommended, among other things, that leaders 'must keep themselves informed of the state of efficiency, equipment and morale of the forward troops' under their command at all times. The report clearly stated that 'the fighting capacity of formations and units must be measured not only by their numbers but also by their morale'.[147] Montgomery did just that. He placed morale at the centre of everything he did as a leader. No more than a month after he had taken charge, Leslie Morshead, although aware that he was being overlooked for a corps command in favour of Oliver Leese, spontaneously averred in a letter to Sir Thomas Blamey, Commander-in-Chief Australian Military Forces, that Montgomery had 'revitalized' the Eighth Army.[148] The censorship summary for 23 to 29 September reported that 'the stimulating effect of the change in command followed by an almost immediate victory was everywhere apparent'.[149]

The role that leadership and command played in victory in the desert, therefore, cannot be disregarded. Since the publication of Correlli Barnett's *The Desert Generals* historians have tended to side with either the Auchinleck or Montgomery camps. This dialectical approach has been at the expense of a proper thematic debate on the relationship between leadership, command and morale in the desert in 1942. The approach followed in this chapter has shown that many of the decisions and policies pursued by both commanders affected morale and consequently combat performance. It is suggested, therefore, that the relative qualities of the two commanders might best be judged in this light.

---

[147] SAMAD UWH, Published Books, Box 368, Court of Inquiry, Tobruk. Report of a Court of Inquiry Assembled by Order of the C-in-C, 8 July 1942, p. 3.

[148] NAA A5954, 649/9 Report of General Morshead's discussions with Generals Alexander and Montgomery. Also in AWM 72 Item no. 22 Barton Maughan, 'Tobruk and El Alamein': chap. 15, 'The Dog Fight', October to December 1942 (typed and hand-written notes).

[149] ANZ WAII/1/DA508/1 vol. 3, MEMCWS, no. XLVI (23 to 29 September 1942), p. 1.

7 Training and morale

The philosophy of discipline has adjusted to changing conditions. As more and more impact has gone into the hitting power of weapons, necessitating ever widening deployments in the forces of battle, the quality of the initiative in the individual has become the most praised of the military virtues. It has been readily seen that the prevailing tactical conditions increased the problem of unit coherence in combat. The only offset for this difficulty was to train for a higher degree of individual courage, comprehension of situation, and self-starting character in the soldier.

(S. L. A. Marshall)[1]

Training, according to William L. Hauser, 'is habituation'. The soldier, in peacetime and in wartime, is required to 'practice his individual duties over and over and over again, until he has learned them so well that he can perform by rote under the most distracting of circumstances'. Threat of death or maiming, according to Hauser, was 'surely the ultimate distraction'. Unless the soldier had been drilled in his tasks to the point of boredom, he could not 'be expected to keep fighting ... under the stresses of shot and shell, confusion, uncertainty, and the infectious fear of his comrades.[2]

Hew Strachan has postulated that training has five fundamental functions over and above that of imparting the basic grammar of military service. Like Hauser, he has argued that training creates an 'instinctive' reaction to certain tactical circumstances and that it enables soldiers 'to come to grips with innovative technologies and to master them'. He has, however, also highlighted the role of training in countering boredom, generating professional pride and creating unit cohesion. Training is, in Strachan's opinion, more than simple habituation. It is 'in large part psychological; it is an enabling process, a form of empowerment, which

---

[1] Marshall, *Men against Fire*, p. 22.
[2] William L. Hauser, 'The Will to Fight' in Sarkesian (ed.), *Combat Effectiveness*, p. 189.

creates self-confidence'.[3] Training is, in other words, a fundamentally important determinant of morale.

For most of 1941 and 1942 the troops who fought in the desert were handicapped by a training regime that was doctrinally and operationally unprepared for war. Timothy Harrison Place has written that 'not only should it not be surprising but it should also be forgivable if troops sent into the North African fray in 1941 and 1942 lacked the full range of professional tactical skills one should expect in fully trained career soldiers'.[4] As has been outlined in Chapter 3, the British Army increased its numbers on an enormous scale following the declaration of war in September 1939.[5] By June 1941, its fully trained cadre of regular soldiers made up at most just over 10 per cent of the forces available.[6] The situation in North Africa was similar. From the beginning of the desert campaign to the vital battle of El Alamein, the MEF more than quadrupled in size.[7] The desert army was, with the exception of the Western Desert Force that fought against the Italians in 1940/1, a citizen army.

It was close to impossible to turn these newly raised forces into highly trained armies over night. David French has described how the War Office faced chronic shortages in 'equipment, accommodation, ammunition, and land for training' due to the understandable fact that 'priority was given to field force units rather than to the training organization'. It was not until March 1942, 'with the opening of a battle-training area on the South Downs, that Home Forces had sufficient land for a whole brigade to exercise with live ammunition and air support'.[8] He has also pointed to problems with a paucity of skilled instructors, the dispersal of billets, 'which made collective training difficult to organize', the wholesale conversion of units from one arm of service to another, 'which meant that troops who had just mastered one set of skills had to begin to acquire another set from scratch', and the requirements of home defence, which 'consumed time that might have been spent in field training'.[9]

The War Office was forced to admit that the best it could do under such circumstances was to try to ensure that formations were 'supplied with

---

[3] Strachan, 'Training, Morale and Modern War', *Journal of Contemporary History*, 41(2) (2006), p. 216. Hauser does also point out that training can play a role in 'unit cohesiveness'; see Hauser, 'The Will to Fight' in Sarkesian (ed.), *Combat Effectiveness*, p. 206.

[4] Timothy Harrison Place, *Military Training in the British Army, 1940–1944* (London, 2000), p. 3.

[5] NA WO 277/12 Piggott, 'Manpower Problems', p. 80.

[6] NA WO 163/50 Use of Manpower in the Army, part 2, app. A, Notes on the Growth of the Army, 21 November 1941.

[7] It must be noted that Middle East Command had responsibility at various times for areas as far ranging as Egypt, Sudan, Palestine, Iraq, Ethiopia, Eritrea, Libya and Greece.

[8] French, *Raising Churchill's Army*, p. 199.   [9] Ibid., pp. 199–200.

the latest tactical lessons and general information' from the theatres of war to which they might be posted. This would 'enable them to make a special study of the fighting in such areas'.[10] This solution, however, was limited by the exigencies of security and the quality of the information provided. In general, units were rarely given much warning whether they were being sent to Egypt, Iraq, India or Burma. This made a realistic training programme, specific to a particular theatre, all the harder to implement.[11] An officer wrote, in 1942, that 'although we saw regular pamphlets about the German Army', his brigade's knowledge of fighting in the desert was extremely poor as these pamphlets 'gave little idea of the actuality' of combat in North Africa.[12]

The long sea voyage to North Africa did not offer much opportunity for training either. There were some practical activities officers and men could carry out while aboard. Lieutenant Morrison of the 7th Black Watch noted, in a letter in July 1942, that all the officers in the battalion had risen at 6 a.m. one morning for a three-mile run round the boat deck.[13] By 10 August, Morrison reported to his mother that 'P.T. every day has been of immense value to us.'[14] Nevertheless, running around a boat deck was hardly sufficient preparation for the rigours of modern warfare in the hostile environment that awaited them.

On arrival in the Middle East, troops were immediately subjected to a more targeted and rigorous training regime that focused on hardening the men and on acquiring the basic skills required to survive in desert conditions. Private C. G. Beech, of the Queen's Own Cameron Highlanders, recalled two sandhills at the base in Geneifa that training officers employed to toughen up the new recruits. Men were ordered to run up and down these hills often sinking to their knees in sand.

The Major would suddenly bear down upon you for a one-sided exchange of confidences, which would start something like this, 'You lad! What's your name . . . where are you from' . . . You had to be very careful about the nature of your reply or even the way you said it, for God help you if he thought you were taking the mickey, as you could be up and down the hill at the drop of a hat.[15]

Private E. Kerans, of the 9th Durham Light Infantry, described his training on arrival as a replacement near Alexandria in 1942. His account highlights how rudimentary his military knowledge was at that stage.

[10] NA WO 260/16 DSD to C-in-C Home Forces, 9 March 1942.
[11] Barr, *Pendulum of War*, p. 157.   [12] Ibid., p. 159.
[13] IWM DS/Misc/63 G. F. Morrison, Lieutenant, letter to his mother, 15 July 1942.
[14] Ibid., letter to his mother, 10 August 1942.
[15] IWM 90/18/1 C. G. Beech, 'Bury me in a shallow grave – Dig me up Later', pp. 38–9.

Illustration 18 A detachment of troops newly arrived in Egypt leaving their camp for a route march, October 1940. Reinforcements had to be toughened up through rigorous training so that they developed confidence that they could live and fight in the unforgiving desert environment.

There were tips from the veterans . . . To lie with arms round the head, this not only protects the eyes but gets your body as close to Mother Earth as possible, explosions go up not down. Not to clench the teeth or tighten the muscles, to let the jaw sag. With tight muscles and concussion the least that will happen is that you will have to wash your under-pants. [We were] taught that lying at the bottom of a two or three foot slit-trench it would need a direct hit to kill you but if you are crouching it might take your head off.

Kerans recounted that 'many things were just common sense . . . Empty one's bowels before going on patrol. Even at night to watch, as far as possible, where one put one's feet. To pick them up, not shuffle them. If the enemy is listening make sure he does not hear you.'[16]

However effective this training was in acclimatising men to the desert, it certainly did not equip them with the tactical and operational skills they would need to face the German and Italian *Panzerarmee*. For instance,

---

[16] IWM 86/61/1 E. Kerans, From Its Start in the Middle East in 1941 to the End of the Job and the Battalion in the Capital of Berlin. As Compiled by a Private Who for Most of That Time was PROUD TO BE THERE, pp. 5–6.

tank troops, fresh from England, were often sent into battle without knowledge of how to find a hull-down position in the small folds of ground in the desert, or without training in how to cope with dust clouds or how to navigate properly in the prevailing conditions.[17]

Niall Barr has pointed out that there was a general perception within Middle East Command that the level of training received by units from the United Kingdom was insufficient and inappropriate for desert conditions.[18] Although many of these shortcomings were understandable, the costs to Eighth Army were substantial; the 'full drawbacks' of this deficient training system were fully manifested on the battlefields of North Africa in 1941 and 1942.[19]

In addition to the training provided for formations in the UK and on reaching the Middle East, units of the WDF and Eighth Army were subjected to further training in preparation for the major campaigns of the desert war. The quality of this training played a decisive role in preparing them, both physically and mentally, for battle. Those commanders who properly implemented rigorous training before operations, therefore, contributed significantly to the morale of their troops and their combat performance.

O'Connor had been a firm believer in the importance of training. In preparation for Operation Compass, in December 1940, he had ordered an exercise with troops 'firing live shell and machine gun ammunition' that resembled the requirements of the forthcoming campaign.[20] The exercise involved 'a long approach march, a night move, a dawn attack . . . followed by subsequent attacks supported by Artillery and "I" Tanks'. From this exercise, lessons were deduced 'and the tactical ideas and necessary tactical and administrative arrangements for the battle were studied, discussed, and prearranged' after 'considerable thought and discussion'.[21] Following Compass, a report on 'Lessons of the Operation' stated that 'all' were 'agreed that [the] preliminary rehearsal . . . was invaluable because it brought to light a great number of faults which it then became possible to rectify before the actual operation took place'.[22] The report made it very clear that 'the value of the training' many of the divisions received prior to hostilities with the Italians was 'abundantly demonstrated throughout the

---

[17] Barr, *Pendulum of War*, pp. 158–9.   [18] Ibid., p. 157.
[19] French, *Raising Churchill's Army*, p. 211.
[20] NA WO 201/3526 O'Connor to 4th Indian and 7th Armoured Divisions, 29 November 1940.
[21] NA WO 201/352 Report on Lessons of the Operations in the Western Desert, December 1940.
[22] Ibid.

operations'. It stated categorically that no inexperienced or untrained divisions 'could have done what [they] did during the recent operation'.[23]

The quality of training afforded the regular troops of the WDF without doubt played a decisive role in the success of Operation Compass. However, as the crisis in Greece and the Balkans developed, these regular soldiers were gradually replaced with citizen soldiers from the British, Commonwealth and Dominion homelands. These replacements were not adequately trained or prepared for the German advance that followed in March and April 1941 with a consequent devastating effect on morale.[24]

A report, written on the action of the 2nd Armoured Division during the withdrawal, stressed this very point. It concluded that the 'Division had not, in fact, had opportunity for adequate training as a team. It was a collection of Units, three of which had only joined shortly before the action, rather than a trained formation.'[25] A similar situation pertained in Brevity and Battleaxe in May and June 1941. Wavell himself admitted that the refitted 7th Armoured Division was not prepared for the actions he subjected it to in these operations. Hastily reformed, with a combination of cruisers and 'I' tanks, the division was not, in his view, a 'homogeneous formation' and 'had not had time to settle down'. The Western Desert Force was not 'organised or trained [to combat] the type of close support the enemy employs'.[26]

A 6th Australian Division report, written in July 1941, pointed out that 'generally the standard of training falls far short of what we are looking for'. Many recruits had 'fired as few as 5–10 rounds' in training in Australia. The report stressed that

We cannot rely on these personnel receiving this essential training here before we commit them to battle. Our campaigns in LIBYA, GREECE, and CRETE have established the fact that our units are not as weapons conscious as they must be for battle. Certain incidents of withdrawal have been traced to this fact that personnel just had not fired their rifles sufficiently to realise what that rifle could do. Similar remarks apply to Brens, Mortars, A Tk rifles and, to a lesser degree, the weapons of Arty.[27]

Men like this were, therefore, 'at first a liability rather than an asset, to the unit they reinforce'.[28]

---

[23] Ibid.   [24] Barnett, *The Desert Generals*, p. 149.
[25] NA CAB 66/17 Report on the Action of the 2nd Armoured Division during the Withdrawal from Cyrenaica, March to April 1941, p. 4.
[26] NA CAB 66/17/6 War Cabinet Memoranda: Morale of the Australian and New Zealand Forces in the Middle East and the Royal Air Force in Egypt. Annex II, C-in-C, ME, to CIGS, 18 June 1941.
[27] AWM 54 839/1/2 Notes for Liaison Officers (Australia), Submitted by 6 Australian Division, July 1941.
[28] AWM 54 839/1/2 2nd AIF, Visit of Liaison Officer to AHQ Melbourne, 19 July 1941.

On taking over command of the MEF in July 1941, Auchinleck immediately grasped the need for training in his army. He deliberately postponed
his next offensive because, as he informed Churchill, 'Battleaxe showed
that [the] present standard of training is not (repeat not) enough, and we
must secure that team spirit which is essential for efficiency.'[29] Some units
made ample use of this extra time. Freyberg, conscious that his 2nd New
Zealand Division had experienced reverses in Greece and Crete, set out
early in September 1941 to train for the upcoming Crusader offensive. By
13 September, the New Zealand Division, fully equipped and completely
mobile, started a six-week programme to train for the specialised type of
fighting that had developed in the desert. They prepared for the most
difficult operations they could imagine, an attack on a heavily defended
fortress protected by wire and mines. Two dummy fortresses based on air
photos of Axis defences, 'Sidi Clif' and 'Bir Stella', were prepared, wired
and covered by live minefields. A series of exercises was then carried out
to capture them. Each infantry brigade took part, supported by full divisional artillery and a 'mock up' battalion of 'I' tanks.[30] The New Zealand
Division's lessons from the campaign concluded that this extra training
had made all the difference. 'Training now is more necessary than ever.
Success depends on the will to win of a fully-trained force at the highest
pitch of physical fitness.'[31]

Nevertheless, a 1st South African Division report, written following
Crusader, highlighted the fact that all units and formations had still not
been 'afforded ample opportunity and scope for carrying out training in
order to prepare for the type of operations in which they [were] about to
engage'.[32] Many of the new tanks and guns that arrived in the Middle East
in time for Crusader had been rushed up to the front line and delivered to
the men on the eve of battle. This meant men had to fight with weapons
they were not trained to use, negating any advantage they might have
gained from proper use of the firepower available to them. The same
report stressed that 'there can be only one time for the issue of essential
kit and equipment for a formation entering battle. That time is before it
leaves its assembly area.'[33]

Crusader indicated that Eighth Army had not absorbed all the lessons
from Compass, Brevity and Battleaxe. In early January 1942, therefore,

---

[29] LHCMA Alanbrooke MSS 6/2/11, Auchinleck to Churchill, 15 July 1941.
[30] ANZ WAII/2 Accession W3281, Box 1, 101b part 1, The New Zealand Division in
Cyrenaica and Lessons of the Campaign, part 1, Narrative and Lessons, p. 2.
[31] Ibid., p. 30.
[32] SAMAD Div Docs, Box 62, 1 SA Div Operations Report, Cyrenaica, 18 November to
2 December 1941, p. 13.
[33] Ibid., p. 10.

Illustration 19 Infantry negotiating barbed wire during an exercise in
the Western Desert, November 1941. Realistic training of this kind was
often overlooked by the commanders of Eighth Army. This had a
significant effect on morale and combat performance.

the Brigadier General Staff Eighth Army issued orders that 'every opportunity will be taken to carry out training . . . so as to develop an established
technique for this type of operation' in the future.[34] Nevertheless, when
Rommel launched his counteroffensive, at the end of January 1942, the
parallels with what had happened in March 1941 were striking. The

---

[34] NA WO 201/527 Harding to 1st Armoured and 4th Indian Divisions, 4 January 1942.

Illustration 20 Grant tanks training in the Western Desert, August 1942. The troops of Eighth Army were often put into battle without proper training in the weapons they were expected to use, with a consequent effect on morale and combat performance.

freshly arrived, undertrained and inexperienced 1st Armoured Division proved completely incapable of dealing with the *Panzergruppe's* rapid offensive and retreated in disarray.[35]

The censorship summaries pointed out that, in many cases, the troops blamed this set back on the 'inadequate training' of some of the units engaged in the operation.[36] The summary for 26 February to 4 March noted 'a certain amount of criticism of the new armoured division, which is very generally blamed for the retreat, the men holding the view that they were unused to desert conditions, had in some cases had very little

[35] AWM 54 883/2/97 MEFCWS, no. XIII (4 to 10 February 1942), p. 1.
[36] AWM 54 883/2/97 MEFCWS, no. XVII (5 to 11 March 1942), p. 1.

training of any sort, and showed poor morale'.[37] One man wrote home complaining, 'if you could only see some of these "trained" men, who have just come out from Blighty, you wouldn't wonder at retreats ... When we see any newspaper article or anything like that, about the continuous hard training which the armies in Britain receive, we can't help smiling ironically, no comment indeed.' Another wrote how a 'supposed crack div. took over' their positions. 'They had all been home-trained and they seemed to think that desert warfare was the same as Salisbury Plain, the result being that they were cut up and those behind also.'[38]

In early 1942, Auchinleck's Director of Military Training, Major-General John Harding, in an effort to address the training deficit, began making plans to coordinate all training efforts in Eighth Army. It was hoped that the introduction of monthly meetings to coordinate training would help standardise practices across Eighth Army. He also suggested the establishment of schools and a higher commanders' course for selected senior officers. By allocating collective training areas, each large enough to exercise a complete division, it was hoped that commanders, staff and men would develop the skills that seemed to be lacking in the desert.[39]

In spite of these efforts, Harding and Auchinleck were hampered by the situation on the ground. Between January and August 1942, 149,800 reinforcements arrived in the Middle East from the UK. These included the 8th Armoured Division and the 44th and 51st Infantry Divisions. In addition, about 32,400 reinforcements came from India.[40] During the same period, 2,012 tanks and 2,580 guns arrived in the Middle East.[41] This massive influx of men and new equipment put an enormous strain on the training organisation that Harding and Auchinleck were trying to build in the desert.

The influx of weapons from Britain and the United States meant little if the troops were not trained to use them. Nevertheless, Lieutenant-General Charles Norrie, commander of XXX Corps, remarked, after the battle of Gazala, that the troops were once again, in spite of the lessons learned during the Crusader offensive, 'handicapped by the issue of 6-pdrs just before battle, when they had not been properly trained'.[42]

---

[37] AWM 54 883/2/97 MEFCWS, no. XVI (26 February to 4 March 1942), p. 2.   [38] Ibid.
[39] NA WO 201/2591 Notes on the Training Conference Held at GHQ ME, 10 May 1942; French, *Raising Churchill's Army*, p. 233.
[40] Playfair, *The Mediterranean and the Middle East*, vol. III, p. 372. These figures do not include RAF and Royal Navy personnel.
[41] Ibid., p. 371.
[42] SAMAD UWH, Published Books, Box 368, Court of Inquiry, Tobruk. Statement by Lieut.-Gen. Norrie, 1st Day, 7 August 1942, p. 13.

The court of inquiry set up by Auchinleck, following the Tobruk disaster, ruled that 'not only must troops be adequately armed but also they must be given sufficient opportunity to train in the technical and tactical use of those arms before going into action. It is wrong for troops to be sent into battle with only a training scale of equipment or for changes in their equipment to be made in the forward areas.'[43]

Gott pointed out on 12 July that it was 'no use having good material and untrained troops. Training demands time, and that time has seldom been forthcoming in the Middle East. This is a point well known out here, but forgotten at home. I consider neither 1st nor 2nd SA Divisions properly trained or fitted for mobile operations. They have never had the chance or the transport.'[44] Gott strongly believed that, 'unseasoned, inexperienced and poorly trained troops' had 'no place on any battlefield, but there were some who came under this category in the recent fighting [around Tobruk]'.[45]

The exigencies of war in the desert did not lend themselves to a sophisticated training system. Niall Barr has pointed out that units were so often 'busy moving, fighting and recovering from operations that there was little time available for training'. Once a unit had been acclimatised in a training camp in Egypt, it might receive little or no further training after it arrived at Eighth Army. The problem was exacerbated, according to Barr, 'by the distances involved in the campaign. Units fighting around Tobruk or the Egyptian frontier were more than 350 miles away from the training camps in Cairo and Alexandria.' Very little training, therefore, actually took place in the desert and most troops learned from their experiences in battle. 'This led to an informal approach to training and a lack of common understanding throughout the army.'[46]

Auchinleck believed that this lack of training, in addition to casualties and the frequent changes of COs, contributed to a 'deterioration' in the army's 'standard of discipline',[47] represented by the high number of desertions and surrenders in the army, and the poor dress and saluting of the men. The reasons for this 'deterioration', in Auchinleck's view, were 'apparent and must be overcome'.[48] An Australian memorandum, written on 'Esprit de Corps and Discipline,' noted, in a comment that does not easily resonate with Auchinleck's efforts to reinstate the death

---

[43] SAMAD UWH, Published Books, Box 368, Court of Inquiry, Tobruk. Report of a Court of Inquiry Assembled by Order of the C-in-C, 8 July 1942, p. 4.

[44] NA WO 216/85 GHQ MEF for CGS, 12 July 1942, p. 3.   [45] Ibid., p. 4.

[46] Barr, *Pendulum of War*, p. 50.

[47] SAMAD Div Docs, Box 119, Memorandum on Discipline by C-in-C Eighth Army, 15 July 1942, p. 3.

[48] Ibid.

penalty, that 'Army discipline should not be a cowed state of submission based on a system of punishments.' It should instead 'be based on mental, moral, and physical training designed to ensure that all respond to the will of the commander, even if he is not himself present'.[49] Chester Wilmot, an Australian correspondent in the desert, felt that the morale problem that beset Eighth Army in the summer of 1942 was best explained by the lack of training. It is 'important', he said, 'that there should be the discipline that comes from good leadership and the confidence in themselves of troops who are well-trained and fit . . . The basis of good morale is confidence to meet the situation. They can only have this confidence if they are trained hard.'[50]

The blame for allowing untrained units into combat in the desert in May, June and July 1942 does not rest entirely at the door of Auchinleck, as Commander-in-Chief MEF. Churchill put an enormous amount of pressure on him to begin operations before he felt he was entirely ready.[51] Nevertheless, Auchinleck admitted, in a letter to Brooke on 25 July, that perhaps he had 'asked too much of [the troops]'.[52] By the end of July, Auchinleck was well aware that his army needed significant training. He wrote, on 27 July, in an appreciation of the situation in the Western Desert, that 'none of the formations in Eighth Army is now sufficiently trained for offensive operations. The Army badly needs either a reinforcement of well trained formations or a quiet period in which to train.'[53]

This was the situation that faced Montgomery on taking over command on 13 August. Acknowledging the training deficit, just as Auchinleck did before him, Montgomery launched an unprecedented training regime for Eighth Army. Indeed, the one element of Montgomery's reputation that has remained untarnished is his ability as a trainer of men. In addition, Montgomery immediately began devising strategies that catered for the actual situation on the ground, i.e. an undertrained citizen army, rather than the ideal situation of a well-trained professional army. He believed that a commander had 'to relate what is strategically desirable with that which is tactically possible with the forces at his disposal'. If this was not done, he said, the commander was 'unlikely to win'.[54] His plan and conduct of the Alam Halfa battle, in September 1942, was an excellent

---

[49] AWM 54 265/2/4 Esprit de Corps and Discipline. The Officer's Task. Army Discipline, Dress, Saluting, Drill and Physical Fitness, n.d.
[50] NAA SP300/4 – Item 145, 'Discipline and Morale', 21 May 1942 (Chester Wilmot ABC Radio Talk Script), Box 2.
[51] Bungay, *Alamein*, p. 223.
[52] LHCMA Alanbrooke Papers, Auchinleck to Brooke, 25 July 1942.
[53] Connell, *Auchinleck*, p. 938.   [54] Montgomery, *Memoirs*, p. 87.

example of this shift in approach. Montgomery fought a deliberately limited battle at Alam Halfa because of 'the low state of training of [his] army'. He ensured that 'formations and units were not given tasks which were likely to end in failure' because of this 'low standard of training'.[55] This was one of Montgomery's enduring contributions; he based his plans on what the soldiers could achieve rather than what he hoped they might be able to achieve. In that way, he avoided 'asking too much' of his men, as Auchinleck had done in July.[56]

Following Alam Halfa, Montgomery made it clear to his commanders, and through them to the men, that Eighth Army would not attack at El Alamein until it was ready.[57] The censorship summaries showed that the long period of unbroken service in the desert had left many units in Eighth Army feeling very stale.[58] Experience had shown that when training was carried out in full, as was the case with Australian troops stationed in Syria before the summer battles, morale tended to improve.[59] A key reason, therefore, for what might be referred to as Montgomery's 'cautious' approach to the battle of El Alamein, was the need for proper training throughout the army to develop confidence and maintain morale. It was clear to Montgomery that he 'would have to be very careful' at El Alamein, as he feared that by doing 'foolish or stupid things' he could 'lose heavily in the first few days of the battle' and 'negative [his] superiority'. He therefore ensured that 'formations and units were not given tasks which were likely to end in failure'. Eighth Army had suffered around eighty thousand casualties over the summer months, and the 're-born Eighth Army was full of untrained units . . . It was clear that I must so stage-manage the battle that my troops would be able to do what was demanded of them, and I must not be too ambitious in my demands.'[60]

Any units that were deemed incapable, or undertrained, were left out of the hardest fighting. For instance, on 21 September, Major-General J. S. Nichols, commander of 50th Division, wrote to Eighth Army drawing attention to the low state of training of a large number of the men recently drafted to him as reinforcements. From a total of about 860 men posted to his division, several had never fixed a rifle and well over a hundred had never thrown a grenade (Table 8). In addition, very few men had fired the

---

[55] IWM BLM 27 Review of the Situation in Eighth Army from 12 August 1942 to 23 October 1942 by Lieut.-Gen. B. L. Montgomery, GOC-in-C Eighth Army, pp. 7–8.
[56] LHCMA Alanbrooke Papers, Auchinleck to Brooke, 25 July 1942.
[57] NA CAB 106/703 Speech to HQ Eighth Army, 13 August 1942.
[58] ANZ WAII/1/DA/508/1 vol. 3, MEMCWS, no. XLIV (10 to 16 September 1942), p. 13.
[59] AWM 54 883/2/97 MEFCWS, no. XXIV (23 to 29 April 1942), p. 13.
[60] IWM BLM 27 Diary Notes, 12 August to 23 October 1942. pp. 7–8; AWM 3DRL 2632 2/2 Lightfoot, Memorandum no. 2 by Army Commander, 6 October 1942.

Table 8 *State of training of reinforcements to 50th Division, September 1942*

Total no. of reinforcements	860
Men who had never fired the rifle	7
Men who had fired the rifle once only	1
Men who had fired the rifle twice only	8
Men who had never fired the Bren	9
Men who had fired the Bren once only	75
Men who had never fired the Thompson submachine gun	138
Men who had never thrown a live grenade	131

Source: NA WO 201/2590 State of Training of Reinforcements, Maj.-Gen. J. S. Nichols to B.T.E., Eighth Army, 21 September 1942.

anti-tank rifle or 2 in. mortar, while only about 25 per cent had ever done any field firing.[61] The 50th Division was not used for serious offensive purposes during the battle of El Alamein for these reasons.

Montgomery removed five divisions from the line for intensive training in the period running up to the battle. These were the 1st, 10th and 8th Armoured Divisions from X Corps, and the 2nd New Zealand Division and the 51st Highland Division from XXX Corps. These formations were well chosen. The armoured divisions of X Corps were required to break through the holes in the Axis defences once the four attacking infantry divisions had 'broken in'. The New Zealand Division needed rest and training after its heavy casualties during the July fighting. The newly constituted 51st Highland Division had not been tested in battle and, therefore, needed extra training as it was going to take part in the initial assault on 23 October. The remaining formations in Eighth Army were required to hold the line and train a brigade at a time, as each brigade was relieved to take on the role of reserve.[62]

On 6 October, Montgomery issued a memorandum on his intentions for the upcoming battle. Ordinarily, Eighth Army's plan for operations in the desert had been first to eliminate the enemy's armour and then to destroy the remaining unarmoured portion of their army. Montgomery decided he would reverse the process 'because of the low state of the training of my Army'. The modified plan was to contain the German panzer units, while Eighth Army carried out a methodical destruction of the unarmoured troops on the Axis side. He referred to this tactic as a

---

[61] NA WO 201/2590 State of Training of Reinforcements, Maj.-Gen. J.S. Nichols to B.T.E., Eighth Army, 21 September 1942.

[62] AWM 54 527/6/1 Part 1, 9th Australian Division Report on Operations. El Alamein, 23 October to 5 November 1942, p. 12.

'crumbling' process. Once completed, the panzer divisions would be dealt with at leisure.[63] In essence, as the 9th Australian Division report on the battle of El Alamein confirms, Montgomery accepted that his armoured forces were incapable of beating the *Afrika Korps* in a straight fight.[64] He therefore concentrated his best troops, the Australian, New Zealand, South African and Scottish infantry, against the infantry of the Germans and Italians. This forced the Axis armour to react and counterattack the anti-tank guns and armour of X and XXX Corps. Montgomery judged that it was far easier to train units for a frontal assault and then to fight behind anti-tank guns than to train them in the intricate combined arms operations that the Germans were so efficient at in the open spaces of the desert.

Montgomery, with this plan in mind, developed his training along three clear lines.

(a) further toughening and hardening of the troops;
(b) developing battle drills and battle inoculation;
(c) making training exercises so similar to the initial attack that every man and officer would become familiar with the part he was to play.[65]

First of all, Montgomery focused on physical fitness. In a release on 'Lessons Learnt during the First Year of War', written in 1940, he had said that 'physical fitness, and powers of endurance, are essential in modern war . . . Officers and other ranks have got to be imbued with that infectious optimism which comes from physical well being; they must be brought to that state of physical and mental fitness which will enable them to take on the Germans (or anyone else) with absolute and complete confidence.'[66] This was not an uncommon viewpoint in the desert. The 'Notes From Theatres of War no. 10: Cyrenaica and Western Desert, January to June 1942' stated that it was the side that 'sticks it out longest' who 'wins in the end'. The notes stressed that recent operations had shown that the officers and men of the *Deutsche Afrika Korps* were 'extremely tough, and that they retain their mental and physical alertness even after long periods of strain and hardship'. It was the report's conclusion that 'every officer and soldier who, through idleness, indifference, or self indulgence, fails to keep himself constantly up to the highest attainable standard of physical fitness is deliberately assisting the enemy'.[67]

[63] IWM BLM 27 Diary Notes, 12 August to 23 October 1942, pp. 7–8.
[64] AWM 54 527/6/1 Part 1, 9th Australian Division Report on Operations. El Alamein, 23 October to 5 November 1942, p. 12.
[65] Ibid., p. 4.
[66] IWM BLM 24/1 5 Corps Study Week for Commanders. Some Lessons Learnt during the First Year of War, September 1939 to September 1940.
[67] NA WO 106/2223 Notes from Theatres of War no. 10: Cyrenaica and Western Desert, January to June 1942, pp. 1–2.

In the run-up to the battle of El Alamein, Montgomery ordered all commanders to pay particular attention to physical fitness. Even head-quarters staff were not exempt from the new regime. 'It is essential to remember', he said, 'that it is the primary duty of all soldiers to fight. This is often forgotten ... Discipline, Esprit de Corps, and confidence in their weapons is just as necessary for all ranks in Headquarters as it is for the fighting troops themselves.' Montgomery ordered 'all young officers and men in Headquarters [to] carry out frequent parades, including drill, physical training, and weapon training'. 'In these days of M[ilitary]. T[ransport]. and in particular during the present lull in operations', he said 'there are seldom opportunities for troops to march long distances. It is essential for all troops to be physically fit for great exertions when the battle flares up again. All Commanders will, therefore, ensure that all ranks in their units are given opportunities to bring themselves to a high standard of physical efficiency.'[68]

The contents of these orders were brought to the attention of all officers and men in XXX Corps,[69] as well as X and XIII Corps. This initiative demonstrated considerable insight from Montgomery, who understood that a strong feeling had developed among the troops during the summer months that there was one rule for officers and another for the men; 'the Shepheard's Hotel complex' as it came to be known. Montgomery, by means of this policy, created a greater sense of equality, which in turn improved esprit de corps in Eighth Army.

Second, Montgomery preached the utility of battle drill and battle inoculation. Montgomery was fortunate that he inherited Eighth Army at a time when these techniques were beginning to become commonplace in the British Army.[70] He was further aided by the fact that Alexander, the new Commander-in-Chief MEF, was one of the original instigators of battle drill at the end of the First World War, and the initial driving force in reinitiating it in the Second World War.[71]

Battle drill provided the ordinary section or platoon with standard sol-utions to common tactical problems. It was intended that these drills would inculcate uniformity of practice throughout the army, making it easier to absorb new replacements in units, as well as facilitating the development of confidence through knowledge and understanding of how to deal with stressful and difficult tactical situations. Battle drill was taught at battle schools set up throughout the UK and Middle East during 1942.

---

[68] SAMAD Div Docs, Box 119, 'Discipline', Letter to all units in 30 Corps by DA and QMG, 26 September 1942.
[69] Ibid.   [70] Harrison Place, *Military Training in the British Army*, chap. 4.
[71] Ibid., p. 49.

These schools also included battle inoculation techniques in their training regimes.[72] The purpose of battle inoculation was to provide the soldier with experiences that would 'help him to face unmoved, the attack on his morale involved in battle'.[73] Battle inoculation was supposed to undermine the 'pacifist propaganda' which had, in the words of a report written in 1942, 'exaggerated the horror and danger of war, until the individual has a false inner mental picture of it as an overwhelmingly terrifying thing to which the only logical attitude is escape or extreme passivity'. This attitude of defence and retreat could 'only be resolved by letting each man learn for himself that his inner image is over-drawn' and that the 'real truth' was 'not so terrifying'. Battle inoculation was the slow application of battle effects, for example noise and gunfire, graduated in severity up to battle conditions which were as near reality as possible. By steady inoculation, applied with patience and understanding, the average man could be made tolerant of the worst noises and sights of war and the 'unreal fears from his imagination' could be dissolved.[74] Battle inoculation was of particular value to leaders and potential leaders on active service, as they needed to learn how to make decisions under the stress and noise of battle.[75]

Montgomery strenuously supported the use of battle drill and battle inoculation before El Alamein. In his first training memorandum, written on 30 August 1942, he stressed that 'battle drill must be highly developed. By means of this battle drill we ensure a common line of approach to the sub-unit battle problem, and a common procedure within the sub-unit. The fact that every Officer, N.C.O. and man is taught this common procedure ensures full co-operation in the battle area, even when casualties necessitate changes in junior commanders and reinforcements to replace wastage.'[76]

The evidence from El Alamein shows that battle drill played a crucial role in maintaining morale and cohesion throughout the thirteen-day battle. A report by the 26th Australian Infantry Brigade considered 'a sound and practised battle drill capable of carrying troops through heavy continuous fighting' as the most important lesson of the operation.[77] Following the battle, a number of troops in 1st South African Division were questioned about their experiences of battle drill. The men were

[72] NA CAB 21/914 The Work of Army Psychiatrists in Relation to Morale, January 1944, p. 2.
[73] NA WO 199/799 Note on Object of Battle Inoculation, n.d. but 1942.   [74] Ibid.
[75] NA WO 199/799 'Training Noise Effects'. To Under Sec of State, the War Office, 12 August 1942 from Lieut.-Gen. C-in-C, Eastern Command. Copy to GHQ Home Forces.
[76] IWM 99/1/2 Briggs, Eighth Army Training Memorandum no. 1 by B. L. Montgomery, 30 August 1942.
[77] AWM 54 527/6/9 26 Australian Infantry Brigade, Report on Operation 'Lightfoot', 23 October to 5 November 1942.

Illustration 21 A mortar section under simulated artillery fire at the 51st Highland Division's battle school in the UK, May 1942. Realistic training of this kind played an important role in preparing men for the morale-sapping reality of battle.

asked whether they considered that 'battle drill, as taught during training and as rehearsed during ... exercises ... produced as smooth a working machine as possible?' All respondents agreed that battle drill had been 'most beneficial' throughout. The troops were also asked whether they considered their 'basic infantry tactics stood the test in the "Lightfoot" operation?' Once again, all agreed that Eighth Army's basic tactics had stood the test excellently.[78]

Battle inoculation also played a vital role in preparing the men for El Alamein. By giving the individual soldier confidence that he could withstand the noise and horrors of war, battle inoculation allowed Montgomery a certain tactical flexibility that his predecessor, arguably, was denied. The mixing and matching of units, in Jock columns and brigade groups, during 1941 and 1942, had, in many ways, been conceived as a solution to the vulnerability of infantry to armour in desert warfare. Montgomery was determined that the infantry would develop its own capabilities and confidence to combat armour, thus leaving the RAC to fight properly concentrated against the German panzers. A training memorandum, released by the Brigadier-General Staff to Eighth Army in September 1942, stated that 'the moral effect of an attack on infantry positions by tanks has in the past often been out of all proportion to the danger to which the troops were in fact exposed. It has been proved that infantry in slit trenches are practically immune to the fire of tank weapons provided they keep down in their trenches. In fact properly equipped with A.Tk Grenades, Molotof [sic] Cocktails, etc., they are a very serious menace to the tanks themselves.' The memo insisted that all infantry should undergo battle inoculation.

(a) Infantry should take up their position in slit trenches and be instructed to remain down in the trenches whilst tanks are driven over them.

(b) Some personnel of each platoon should ride in the tanks whilst this is being done in order to see, and pass on, how impossible it would be to bring the tank weapons to bear on the men in the trenches.

(c) Subsequently, when men have gained confidence they should be taught to take offensive action immediately the tanks have passed over them. Dummy sticky Bombs, Molotof [sic] Cocktails, etc., should be used for this purpose.[79]

A psychiatrist, who had worked on battle inoculation with units in the UK before El Alamein, was able to obtain a check on the success of such methods in the Middle East in November and December 1942. He reported that 'the opinion was strongly held among fighting men and officers that battle inoculation was a most important part of the training of battle reinforcement and should be given to all troops before their first action'. The troops, he found, 'were emphatic that their first experience of

[78] SAMAD CGS, Gp 2, Box 654, Summary of Replies to a Questionnaire Submitted to Battalions in the 1st SA Division Based on their Experiences in the 'Lightfoot' Operation in the Western Desert, October to November 1942, 22 March 1943.

[79] NA WO 201/2590 Training Memorandum to 1, 8, 10 Armoured Divisions, 2 NZ Division and copy to Main Eighth Army from Brig.-Gen. Staff, September 1942.

a set battle at Alamein had been well prepared for' and that they had been 'the steadier for it'.[80] A few months later, another report concluded that 'without a preliminary battle inoculation on active service, even the best troops will suffer unnecessary casualties and fail to make the best of an unexpected situation'.[81]

Third, Montgomery ensured that the training regime for every unit of Eighth Army was focused as much as possible on the expected requirements of the upcoming battle. For example, the newly arrived 51st Highland Division, in the two months leading up to El Alamein, laid out exact replicas of the parts of the enemy's defences that they were supposed to attack. Douglas Wimberley, the commander of the division, recalled that

> I took my troops, a Brigade at a time, and practised every Battalion in the exact job I had decided it was to do in the initial attack ... The dummy trenches were made the exact distance from the mock start line as were the real entrenchments ... held by the enemy, on the frontage on which I had been told to attack. Then, I used our Divisional artillery to fire the exact barrage they would have to fire in the battle, at the same rate and with the same pauses for leap frogging. Meanwhile Div Signals carried out the same outline plan, reporting the capture of objectives; and the Sappers did their clearing of mines through dummy minefields, of what we believed were the same breadth as the ones we had actually to gap in the battle.[82]

J. B. Salmond, who wrote the history of the 51st Highland Division, recalled that the whole operation had been 'rehearsed to such an extent [in total there were four divisional scale exercises][83] that every man, before the actual operation began, knew absolutely in detail what he was expected to do, with the result that morale was so high that the personnel of the division were not even conscious of what morale meant'.[84]

In addition, the 'Jocks' were given the opportunity to send troops to learn from both the veteran Australian and New Zealand divisions. Wimberley remembered that 'this went on throughout most of September. Our officers in the line were attached to Australian officers, our sergeants to their sergeants. If the Australians sent out patrols they were composed of a mixture of Aussies, and Jocks under instruction.'[85]

Training along these lines had an equally beneficial effect on the 2nd New Zealand Division. Freyberg wrote home to New Zealand, in

[80] NA CAB 21/914 The Work of Army Psychiatrists in Relation to Morale, app. C, Battle Inoculation, January 1944.
[81] NA WO 231/10 Lessons from Tunisian Campaign, 1942–1943.
[82] IWM 430 PP/MCR/182 Wimberley, 'Scottish Soldier', pp. 36–7.
[83] Barr, *Pendulum of War*, p. 264.
[84] Salmond, *The History of the 51st Highland Division 1939–1945*, p. 22.
[85] IWM 430 PP/MCR/182 Wimberley, 'Scottish Soldier', p. 35.

September 1942, detailing the importance of the training his men were undergoing. 'The Division has been hard at training since we came out of the line on the 10th September. The period of training was very necessary because we now have almost a complete change in infantry battalion commanders. As a result of our training I can report to you that I believe that as a fighting force although reduced in numbers we shall be fit to take our part in every way.'[86]

The censorship summary for 30 September to 6 October noted the correspondence of men who pointed out that the new commanders had certainly got into training 'with a will'. The position, according to one man, was that 'training and fitness are of the utmost importance and we are continually exercising etc. It is all very tiring and annoying at times but if the lack of it in the past has caused the present position it is only right that it should be rectified.'[87]

Such coordinated and thorough training had not been undertaken in the desert since before O'Connor's and Wavell's first successful offensive against the Italians in late 1940; the results were unsurprisingly similar.[88] Following the battle, 'Middle East Training Memorandum no. 7', which dealt with the lessons from the operation, highlighted the fact that 'all formations from Headquarters to sub-units trained systematically for this operation, and to this must be attributed a large measure of the success obtained'.[89] The morale report for November 1942 to January 1943 showed a general 'appreciation of the careful and exact rehearsal of the El Alamein battle in preliminary divisional schemes'.[90] The 9th Australian Division Report on the battle stated that 'the operations proved the general soundness of our principles of training for war, some of which had been neglected during previous fighting in the desert'. The same report stressed that 'the value of experienced or well trained staff and regimental officers was shown by the success of operations which had been adequately prepared and the execution of which was within the scope of trained officers'. The report recognised that 'the state of training between formations and units differed' and that 'when orders [were]

---

[86] ANZ WAII/8/26 Freyberg to NZ Minister of Defence, 14 October 1942.
[87] ANZ WAII/1/DA/508/1 vol. 3 MEMCWS, no. XLVII (30 September to 6 October 1942), p. 3.
[88] NA WO 201/352 Report on Lessons of the Operations in the Western Desert, December 1940.
[89] IWM 99/1/2 Briggs, METM no. 7, Lessons from Operations, October and November 1942; NA WO 201/2596 Preliminary Draft Lessons from Operations, October and November 1942.
[90] NA WO 193/453 Morale Report, November 1942 to January 1943.

given for a task to be undertaken regard must be paid by commanders to the ability of the unit selected to understand and carry out its role'.[91] For the first time since Operation Compass, a British commander had obeyed this fundamental rule of warfare and only asked of the troops what they were capable of and trained to do. The effect on the morale of the troops was considerable, with a consequent improvement in their combat performance.

[91] AWM 54 527/6/1 Part 1, app. A to 9 Australian Division Report on Operations, El Alamein, 23 October to 5 November 1942, Extracts from Draft Report by 30 Corps, 21 November 1942, p. 1.

8   In search of a theory to explain combat morale in the desert

Since 1945, the dominant explanation of what maintains morale in modern war has been primary group theory.[1] Primary group theory stresses that 'men fight not for a higher cause but for their "mates" and "buddies", bound by war in a relationship which ... can achieve great intensity'.[2] John Ellis has argued that

For the average soldier, once he was in combat, his view became microcosmic, and he lived only from day to day, barely daring to think about the end of the war, increasingly unconscious that life had any meaning beyond the unremitting ghastliness of endless combat. The soldier became increasingly bound up with his tiny fraternity of comrades who shared his suffering and they alone came to represent the real world. In the last analysis, the soldier fought for them and them alone, because they were his friends and because he defined himself only in the light of their respect and needs.[3]

Two men in particular pioneered work on the primary group, S. L. A. Marshall and Samuel A. Stouffer.[4] Although Marshall's work has been subsequently criticised,[5] Marshall's and Stouffer's studies are still recognised as the first two comprehensive scientific investigations of combat morale and motivation among front line units. Their basic conclusions and findings, while based on American soldiers' experiences in the Second World War, have, in general, been accepted as relevant to all the armies that fought during that war, although they have been applied, perhaps, at times, without due consideration of the behaviours and cultural characteristics of the other combatants.[6]

---

[1] Hew Strachan, 'The Soldier's Experience in Two World Wars: Some Historiographical Comparisons', in Addison, and Calder (eds.), *Time to Kill*, p. 371.
[2] Hew Strachan, 'The Morale of the German Army 1917–18', in Cecil and Liddle, *Facing Armageddon*, p. 388.
[3] Ellis, *The Sharp End*, p. 315.
[4] Marshall, *Men against Fire*; Samuel A. Stouffer *et al.*, *The American Soldier: Combat and Its Aftermath*, vol. II (Princeton, 1949).
[5] Roger J. Spiller, 'S. L. A. Marshall and the Ratio of Fire', *RUSI Journal*, 133 (Winter 1988), pp. 63–71.
[6] Strachan, 'Training, Morale and Modern War', *Journal of Contemporary History*, pp. 211–12.

Marshall interviewed men from 400 infantry companies in the central Pacific and European theatres of war.[7] From these interviews, he constructed a theory of battlefield effectiveness focused on firepower and the vagaries of human nature. His research uncovered a remarkable fact; he found that only 25 per cent of troops fired their weapons in combat.[8] The majority of these active firers were 'heavy weapons men',[9] the 'big men', as John Keegan might refer to them.[10] To operate weapons such as machine guns, flame-throwers, or bazookas, a small group working together was required.[11] According to Marshall, 'men working in groups or in teams d[id] not have the same tendency to default of fire as d[id] single riflemen'.[12] This led Marshall to investigate the value of the other 75 per cent of men in battle. It was in the context of this dilemma that Marshall propounded the primacy of the primary group.

I hold it to be one of the simplest truths in war that the thing which enables an infantry soldier to keep going with his weapons is the near presence or the presumed presence of a comrade. The warmth which derives from human companionship is as essential to his employment of the arms with which he fights as is the finger with which he pulls a trigger or the eye with which he aligns his sights. The other man may be almost beyond hailing or seeing distance, but he must be there somewhere within a man's consciousness or the onset of demoralisation is almost immediate and very quickly the mind begins to despair or turns to thoughts of escape. In this condition he is no longer a fighting individual, and though he holds to his weapon, it is little better than a club.[13]

Counterintuitively, it did not greatly matter that the majority of soldiers were 'non-firers'. The important fact was that the non-firers were there to give moral support to the minority of men who were doing the fighting. The fighting man was therefore, in Marshall's opinion, 'sustained by his fellows primarily and by his weapons secondarily'.[14]

Samuel A. Stouffer carried out a similar study in both the Pacific and European theatres of war.[15] With the help of his aides, he surveyed more than 12,000 American soldiers, and, just like Marshall, his work pointed to the importance of the small group in maintaining morale and motivation for the fight. He found that the combat soldier, 'isolated as he was from contact with the rest of the world, . . . was thrown back on his outfit to meet the various affectional needs for response, recognition, approval,

---

[7] Joanna Bourke, *An Intimate History of Killing* (London, 2000), p. 112.
[8] Ibid., p. 54.   [9] Ibid., pp. 75–6.
[10] John Keegan, 'Towards a Theory of Combat Motivation', in Addison and Calder (eds.), *Time to Kill*, pp. 8–9.
[11] Bourke, *An Intimate History of Killing*, p. 56.
[12] Marshall, *Men against Fire*, pp. 75–6.   [13] Ibid., p. 42.
[14] Ibid., p. 43.   [15] Bourke, *An Intimate History of Killing*, p. 112.

and in general for appreciation as a significant person rather than a means ... Most aspects of combat as a stress situation served only to make these needs the more urgent. The group was thus in a favored position to enforce its standards on the individual.'[16] The connection of the group in battle was so strong, according to Stouffer, that soldiers out of action, exhausted or wounded, would often report feelings of extreme guilt for being away from their comrades.[17]

Stouffer's surveys provided quantifiable evidence of the link between the primary group and good combat motivation. In one survey, Stouffer found that men who reported 'pride in outfit' or a 'strong identification with the unit' were 'more likely to hold together when orders called for combat action'.[18] In another survey, Stouffer established that the most commonly reported mistake in combat, made by both veteran and fresh troops, was the practice of 'bunching up'. This was the tendency of men to huddle together in groups when under fire. Such evidence, according to Stouffer, signified 'the strength of the need of combat men for mutual support'.[19]

Marshall's and Stouffer's theories on the primary group were supported by another, less scientific, study on morale carried out during the Second World War.[20] Edward Shils and Morris Janowitz, who both worked for the intelligence section of the psychological warfare division of the Supreme Headquarters Allied Expeditionary Force, based their work mainly on the evidence of interrogated German POWs.

Shils and Janowitz argued that the decisive factor in motivating the ordinary German soldier was that 'he was a member of a squad or section which maintained its structural integrity and which coincided roughly with the social unit which satisfied some of his major primary needs'. They found that the German soldier 'was likely to go on fighting ... as long as the group possessed leadership with which he could identify himself, and as long as he gave affection to and received affection from the other members of his squad and platoon'. In other words, 'as long as he felt himself to be a member of his primary group and therefore bound by the expectations and demands of its other members, his soldierly achievement was likely to be good'.[21]

---

[16] Stouffer, *The American Soldier*, p. 98.
[17] Ibid., pp. 136, 143.   [18] Ibid., pp. 141–2.
[19] Ibid., p. 284; for a similar perspective on British troops in North Africa see Alastair Borthwick, *Battalion: A British Infantry Unit's Actions from El Alamein to the Elbe, 1942–1945* (London, 1994), p. 65.
[20] Edward A. Shils and Morris Janowitz, 'Cohesion and Disintegration in the Wehrmacht in World War II', *Public Opinion Quarterly*, 12 (Summer 1948), p. 314.
[21] Ibid., p. 284.

Although these studies of combat morale and motivation in the Second World War point to the primary group as the core explanation for what maintains morale in battle, primary group theory has been queried, more recently, by historians keen to comprehend, in particular, the 'apocalyptic' struggles on the eastern front and in the Pacific theatre of the war.[22] Marshall's and Stouffer's own studies also point to a number of factors that can hinder the functioning of the primary group as a motivating force in combat.

It would seem reasonable that the relevance of primary group theory, as it is generally understood, should be limited by the extent to which there are factors militating against the primary group operating as a positive motivating force in a given conflict situation. A number of such factors may be identified.

One is the effect of either high casualties or replacements on group morale. According to primary group theory the success of the primary group is derived from unity more than anything else.[23] In Marshall's view, 'the tactical unity of men working together in combat is in the ratio of their knowledge and sympathetic understanding of each other'.[24] However, he also acknowledged that 'when a soldier is unknown to the men who are around him he has relatively little reason to fear losing the one thing that he is likely to value more highly than life – his reputation as a man among other men'.[25]

Stouffer noted that in the American Army 'high casualty rates among combat personnel, together with an established system of replacing individuals rather than units, led to a constantly changing membership of the front-line combat unit'. Stouffer's studies showed that many veteran outfits that had seen much fighting contained a relatively small proportion of men who had come overseas as original members. In a survey of four infantry divisions in Italy in April 1945, Stouffer and his aids found that only 34 per cent of infantrymen in line companies had come overseas with their outfits. The remainder had joined their divisions as replacements.[26] Of these replacements, half said they went into combat less than three days after they joined their unit.[27] Ground combat was, therefore, not to be thought of as involving teams of men who had all trained together from enlistment.[28] Instead, it often involved groups of individuals fighting together who hardly knew each other's names.

---

[22] See especially Bartov, *The Eastern Front* and Dower, *War without Mercy*.

[23] Marshall, *Men against Fire*, p. 138, Stouffer, *The American Soldier*, p. 242, Shils and Janowitz, 'Cohesion and Disintegration in the Wehrmacht in World War II', p. 281.

[24] Marshall, *Men against Fire*, p. 150.   [25] Ibid., p. 153.

[26] Stouffer, *The American Soldier*, p. 242.   [27] Ibid., p. 277.   [28] Ibid., p. 242.

Shils and Janowitz also argued that high casualties, especially the loss of officers, impaired the cohesion and morale of the group. By January 1945, the ratio of officers to enlisted men in the Wehrmacht had fallen to about 50 per cent of what it had been at the start of the war.[29] They pointed out that 'once disruption of primary group life resulted through separation, breaks in communications, loss of leadership, depletion of personnel, or major and prolonged breaks in the supply of food and medical care, such an ascendancy of preoccupation with physical survival developed that there was very little "last ditch" resistance'.[30]

Omar Bartov has described the crippling losses sustained by the German Army on the eastern front after the launch of Barbarossa in June 1941. His research showed that some German combat divisions lost as many as 300 per cent of their men during the four years of fighting in Russia. He argued that the primary group could simply not survive under such conditions.[31] Niall Ferguson has made similar points relating to the First World War. 'The fact that units often went into action shortly after being formed, or that friendships were so often terminated by death' meant that individuals had to find other ways of coping.[32]

David French and Terry Copp have also questioned the extent to which the primary group could act as a motivational factor during some of the more attritional campaigns of the Second World War.[33] For instance, the battle of Normandy cost the Allies more than 200,000 casualties or 2,354 a day. This was comparable to the 105 days of the third battle of Ypres in the First World War, which included the struggle for Passchendaele, where British and Canadian forces suffered 244,000 casualties, or 2,121 a day.[34]

Nevertheless, the evidence suggests that from the start of the war the British Army saw the primary group as the mainstay of morale in combat. The Army Training Memorandum of July 1940, entitled 'Morale and Fighting Efficiency', stated that

Mere individual determination to refuse to succumb to 'frightfulness' is not enough; a corporate sense of discipline will alone maintain the fighting value of a unit or sub-unit under the strain of the technique of demoralization as now practised by the German Army and Air Force. Discipline in this context is not merely a question of blind and unquestioning obedience to orders, but a rhythmic

---

[29] Shils and Janowitz, 'Cohesion and Disintegration in the Wehrmacht in World War II', p. 295.

[30] Ibid., p. 281.   [31] Bartov, *The Eastern Front* and *Hitler's Army*.

[32] Niall Ferguson, *The Pity of War* (London, 1998), p. 354–5.

[33] French, *Raising Churchill's Army*, p. 147.

[34] Copp, 'If this war isn't over, And pretty damn soon', in Addison and Calder (eds.), *Time to Kill*, pp. 148–9.

and automatic surging of the cohesive spirit of a body of men in times of crisis, so that all can draw on the common fund of courage and endurance.[35]

Montgomery unquestionably saw the primary group as the mainstay of morale and combat motivation for British soldiers in the Second World War.[36] He wrote following the war that 'the method by which the conquest of fear is achieved is the unifying of men into a group or unit under obedience to orders. Men require to be united if they are to give of their best ... Men learn to gain confidence and encouragement from doing the same thing as their fellows; they derive strength and satisfaction from their company; their own identities become merged into the larger and stronger identity of their unit.'[37]

For Eighth Army, 'the effectiveness of primary group loyalty in persuading men to remain in the front line' depended just as much on 'the human stability of each primary group and the fact that leaders and men knew each other intimately', as it did for units on the eastern front, in the Pacific or in Normandy. Heavy casualties sustained over a brief period made it difficult to sustain such relationships.[38] The cohesion of the primary group was not only affected by the loss of those killed in action, however. Studies in the Middle East showed that just 25 per cent of wounded or injured casualties returned to their units within one month of being wounded, while 45 per cent returned in the second month.[39] Casualties, therefore, were likely to be separated from their units for considerable periods of time, and certainly for the period of the battle in which they had been wounded.

A close analysis of casualty figures from some of the major engagements in the desert in 1941 and 1942 illustrates the extent of this problem. According to I. S. O. Playfair, the Crusader battles of November and December 1941 and January 1942 cost Eighth Army approximately 17,700 casualties (15 per cent of the force of 118,000 men that fought).[40] If we explore the casualty figures in greater depth, their effect on the ability of the primary group to act as a positive motivating factor becomes clearer.

---

[35] NA WO 277/7 McPherson, *Army: Discipline*, pp. 6–7.
[36] IWM Briggs Papers, Morale in Battle: Analysis by B. L. Montgomery, pp. 51–3.
[37] Ibid., p. 51.   [38] French, *Raising Churchill's Army*, p. 147.
[39] NA WO 32/10810 Proportions of Wounded Who Return to Duty within 1, 2, 3 or More Months, North Africa 1942–3.
[40] Playfair, *The Mediterranean and the Middle East*, vol. III, p. 97. The GHQ MEF figures are broadly similar to Playfair's (NA WO 201/2834 Middle East Command: Battle Casualties, Libya Campaign, AG Stats). They report 19,285 casualties from 18 November 1941 to 14 February 1942; so Playfair's figure of 17,700 for the Crusader battles is probably reasonably accurate.

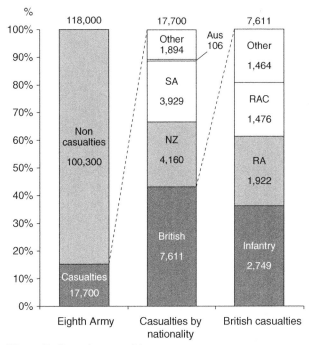

Figure 7 Crusader casualties

The GHQ MEF reports indicate that 43 per cent of the casualties were British and 36 per cent of these were infantry. Applying these percentages to Playfair's total of 17,700 casualties, it is probable that British casualties were about 7,611 and British infantry casualties were probably around 2,749 men (Figure 7).[41]

According to the official history, fifteen British infantry battalions plus a machine-gun company fought during Crusader.[42] Generally, the vast majority of casualties were suffered among the four rifle companies of a

---

[41] NA WO 201/2834 Middle East Command: Battle Casualties, Libya Campaign, AG Stats.
[42] These were 2nd York and Lancaster and 2nd Black Watch of the 14th Inf. Brigade, 2nd King's Own of the 16th Inf. Brigade, two battalions of the 23rd Infantry Brigade, 2nd Scots Guards of the 4th Armoured Brigade, 1st Kings Royal Rifle Corps and 2nd Battalion Rifle Brigade with the 7th Support Group, 1st Essex and a machine gun company of the Royal Northumberland Fusiliers with the 32nd Army Tank Brigade, 2nd Scots Guards, and 3rd Coldstream Guards with the 22nd Guards Brigade, 9th Battalion Rifle Brigade with the 22nd Armoured Brigade, 1st Royal Sussex of the 7th Indian Infantry Brigade, the 1st Buffs of the 5th Indian Brigade, and a British battalion under the 11th Indian Infantry Brigade.

battalion.[43] Each rifle company at this time was made up of 5 officers and 119 other ranks,[44] making a total establishment at the sharp end of 496 men to a rifle battalion (the total establishment of a rifle battalion at this time was 33 officers and 753 enlisted men). A motor battalion had about the same. A machine gun company had, at this time, about 146 men at the sharp end.[45] This meant that, in total, about 7,090 men carried the brunt of British infantry fighting during Crusader. If the casualties for these infantry units (2,749) are applied to the front-line infantry establishments as thus estimated (7,090), it suggests a casualty rate at the sharp end of about 39 per cent.[46]

A different estimate puts the total casualties for Crusader at 15,747, of which 5,403 were British.[47] These figures, however, do not break down the casualty statistics by arm of service. Nevertheless, it can be taken, as previously, that 36 per cent of British casualties were suffered by infantry battalions, which gives casualty figures for rifle, motor, and machine gun battalions of 1,945. This in turn suggests that the British front line infantry units that fought during Crusader suffered 27 per cent casualties. While there is some discrepancy between the two sets of casualty statistics, it is, nevertheless, very likely that between one-quarter and two-fifths of the British infantrymen who fought in the front line at Crusader were casualties.

New Zealand and South African infantry casualties were even more severe. The New Zealanders suffered about 4,160 casualties during Crusader. Most of these were likely to have come from their ten infantry battalions and one machine-gun battalion,[48] which made up around 5,106 front-line troops. This means that front-line New Zealand infantry casualties could have been as high as 81 per cent. However, the Crusader battle was a confused and fluid battle. Many New Zealand units, such as the 20th, 24th and 26th Infantry Battalions were overrun, meaning that 'non-front-line' units, such as support, HQ and divisional personnel, would have suffered casualties as well. Nevertheless, it is clear that the New Zealanders suffered debilitating casualties at Crusader, and that these casualties would have harmed the functioning of the primary group.

[43] Bungay, *Alamein*, pp. 198–9.
[44] IWM TM30/410 Handbook on the British Army, p. 25.   [45] Ibid., pp. 24–5.
[46] As this percentage is calculated on the basis of full establishments, it may underestimate the real casualty rate; front-line infantry units did not always enter battle with full complements.
[47] NA WO 201/2834 Middle East Command: Libyan Casualties, Part 2, app. A. These statistics were released by GHQ MEF a year later than those referred to in footnote 40.
[48] This includes the nine battalions of the 4th, 5th and 6th New Zealand Infantry brigades plus the 28th Maori Battalion and the divisional machine-gun battalion.

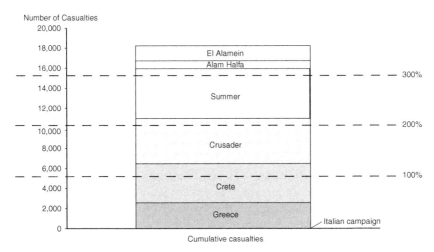

Figure 8 2nd New Zealand Division 'front-line' cumulative casualties, December 1940 to November 1942

In fact, if we use this front-line establishment estimate of 5,106 troops, and apply it to the total New Zealand casualties suffered between December 1940 and November 1942 (18,263 casualties), then, it is possible that the division could have suffered a casualty rate among its front-line infantry units, during this phase of the war, of as high as 300 per cent (Figure 8).[49] Again, as many non-front-line units were captured in the fluid battles of Crete, Greece and North Africa, this figure is likely to somewhat exaggerate front-line losses. However, it does illustrate the extent of the casualties suffered by the 2nd New Zealand Division in the Middle East.

The South Africans suffered 3,929 casualties[50] among the eighteen infantry battalions and two machine-gun battalions that fought at Crusader. That equates to a casualty rate of about 43 per cent among front-line infantry units.

Casualties were no less extreme for the armoured units engaged in Crusader. Playfair has estimated that Eighth Army began Crusader with 738 tanks[51] and lost about 600 by the end of the battle.[52] This means that around 81% of the tanks Eighth Army began the battle with were knocked out or suffered mechanical breakdown. A report by the Deputy Prime Minister, Clement Attlee, on the tank position in the Middle East in March 1942 showed that of forty-eight British tanks rendered

---

[49] W. G. Stevens, *Problems of 2nd NZEF*, p. 292.   [50] See Figure 7.
[51] Playfair, *The Mediterranean and the Middle East*, vol. III, p. 30.   [52] Ibid., p. 100.

unserviceable in action in operation Crusader and subsequently examined by GHQ Middle East Tank Directorate, twenty-four (50%) were knocked out by light weapons, mines or mechanical breakdown. That meant that the other 50% were likely to have been knocked out by 88 mm, 50 mm (either tank or anti-tank type) or 47 mm guns.[53] Another report, on 'The Comparative Performance of German Anti-Tank Weapons during World War II,' showed that about 12% of British tanks destroyed during Crusader were put out of action by mines.[54] The penetration or destruction of a tank by mines or large guns generally resulted in one or two casualties or fatalities among a tank crew; 40% of a crew became casualties if their tank was destroyed by an anti-tank gun, 46.4% if they were hit by a shell from another tank and 21.8% if they were incapacitated by a mine.[55] Such casualties required new crews or primary groups to form at short notice for the next day's battle. If it is the case that about 62% (those knocked out by mines and 88 mm, 50 mm or 47 mm guns) of the 600 tanks knocked out during Crusader suffered casualties, then the number of crews suffering disruption to their primary group would be in the order of around 372 out of the original 738, or roughly 50%.[56] Therefore it is possible to say that around half of the crews that fought during Crusader suffered some disruption to their primary group.

The casualties suffered during the summer battles of 1942 were even more damaging to the ability of the primary group to engender and support morale. Around 36% of the total forces engaged became casualties,[57] compared with 15% in Crusader. It is difficult, however, to break these figures down any further, due to the high turnover of battalions in the confused fighting of the summer months. At best it is possible to consider a few units. The losses suffered by both South African Divisions in the three

---

[53] NA WO 259/61 Enquiry by the Rt. Hon. C. R. Attlee MP into Tank Position in the Middle East, March 1942.

[54] NA WO 222/65 Army Operational Research Group, Memorandum no. A16, 'The Comparative Performance of German Anti-Tank Weapons during World War II', Prepared by H. G. Gee.

[55] NA WO 222/65 'Report of Casualties in Armoured Fighting Vehicles', Medical Research Section, GHQ, MEF, 20 July 42; NA WO 222/65 Army Operational Research Group, Memorandum no. A16, 'The Comparative Performance of German Anti-Tank Weapons during World War II', Prepared by H. G. Gee; Cyril Joly, *Take These Men* (London, 1955), p. 219.

[56] Eighth Army's various types of tanks during the North African campaign were crewed by between three and six men (depending on the model). Using the figures quoted (21.8 per cent of a crew were likely to be casualties if hit by a mine), it is statistically possible that in tanks such as the Crusader, which was manned by three men, a mine would not always cause a casualty among the crew.

[57] NA WO 163/51 The Army Council, Death Penalty in Relation to Offences Committed on Active Service, 11 August 1942.

weeks of heavy fighting before the fall of Tobruk amounted to 140 killed and died of wounds, and 1,945 wounded and missing, in all 2,085.[58] The casualty rate among the front-line infantry battalions for three weeks was therefore approximately 23%.[59] This figure would, of course, have rocketed on the capture of 2nd South African Division at Tobruk. Other units, such as the 4th East Yorks, the 9th King's Royal Rifle Corps, the 7th Green Howards and the 9th Battalion Rifle Brigade, had to be disbanded after the summer fighting due to high casualties.[60] By August 1942, only sixty-four men remained of the original establishment of the 9th Battalion Rifle Brigade that had sailed from England two years earlier.[61] The 4th Green Howards and the 2/5 Essex had been reduced to cadre strength. The 2nd Camerons had been reduced to 6 officers and 200 ordinary ranks, the 9th Durham Light Infantry to 11 officers and 200 ordinary ranks, the 1st Sherwood Foresters (Motor) to 6 officers and 130 ordinary ranks, the 1st Worcesters to 6 officers and 164 ordinary ranks, the 50 Recce Motor Battalion to 8 officers and 170 ordinary ranks, the 3rd Coldstream Guards to 21 officers and 250 ordinary ranks, while the 2nd Scots Guards had been reduced to 24 officers and 450 ordinary ranks.[62] These figures are all the more noteworthy when it is remembered that the total establishment of a rifle battalion at full strength at this time was about 33 officers and 753 enlisted men.[63]

The armoured regiments suffered catastrophic casualties as well. The 4th and 7th Royal Tank Regiments were lost at Tobruk and needed to be reconstituted in the UK. Almost all the rest of the RAC units involved in the summer battles needed re-forming.[64] Eighth Army began the Gazala battles with 849 tanks.[65] Niall Barr has suggested that, over the seventeen days of fighting, Eighth Army suffered 1,188 tanks damaged or destroyed.[66] The report on 'Comparative Performance of German

---

[58] SAMAD DCS – CGS, Box 51, Tobruk Recruiting Drive, appeal by PM, 26 June 1942.

[59] The 1st SA Division at this time was made up of the nine infantry battalions of 1st, 2nd, and 3rd Infantry brigades, plus one battalion, a machine-gun battalion, a machine-gun company and a reconnaissance battalion from the divisional troops. The 2nd SA Division was made up of the seven infantry battalions of the 4th and 6th Infantry brigades plus a machine-gun battalion and a reconnaissance battalion from the divisional troops.

[60] ANZ WAII/1/DA508/1 vol. 3, MEMCWS, no. XLIV (10 to 16 September 1942), p. 4. Accounts of the tank battles around Gazala, e.g. Joly, *Take These Men*, show that casualties were just as extreme in the tank and armoured units.

[61] ANZ WAII/1/DA508/1 vol. 3, MEMCWS, no. XLIII (3 to 9 September 1942), p. 5.

[62] LHCMA Adam (Box 2) C-in-C Middle East to War Office, 27 July 1942.

[63] IWM TM30/410 Handbook on the British Army, p. 25.

[64] LHCMA Adam (Box 2) C-in-C Middle East to War Office, 27 July 1942.

[65] Barr, *Pendulum of War*, p. 13.

[66] Ibid., p. 39. This would include replacements and those tanks that were quickly returned to battle after repair.

Anti-Tank Weapons during World War II' shows that about 42% of these tank losses (around 499 tanks) were due to mines.[67] If we once again apply Atlee's figures and assume that 50% of tanks lost (around 594 tanks) were knocked out by 88 mm, 50 mm or 47 mm guns,[68] that means that 1,093 tank crews (140% of the 849 tank crews Eighth Army began the battle with) would have suffered some kind of disruption to the primary group. It was quite usual for a crew to suffer casualties or the loss of a tank, jump into a new tank with some replacement men, and then re-enter combat, only to be 'knocked out' again.[69] In fact, the figures suggest that as many as 40% of crews may have suffered casualties on more than one occasion, disrupting whatever bonds might have developed over a short time in combat.[70] In addition, it must be noted, that these figures only include casualties from the seventeen days of fighting on the Gazala line and do not account for further attrition suffered during the July battles on the El Alamein line.

At El Alamein, during thirteen days of fighting in October and November 1942, there were 13,560 casualties, an average of 1,043 casualties a day. The total casualty figure of 13,560 made up about 6% of the army as a whole. The loss rate suffered by the front-line troops was far more severe, however. For example, the 51st Highland Division had the highest number of casualties during the battle. The Highlanders suffered 2,827 killed, wounded and missing (of whom 627 were on the opening night of the battle),[71] which was about 20% of its ration strength. However, the bulk of those casualties were suffered by its nine infantry battalions, which Stephen Bungay, in *Alamein*, numbers at roughly 6,750 men. That gives a casualty rate of about 40% for those units doing the fighting.[72] Bungay includes the nine battalions' HQ companies, each of roughly 8 officers and 248 enlisted men,[73] in his estimate. However, using

---

[67] NA WO 222/65 Army Operational Research Group, Memorandum no. A16, 'The Comparative Performance of German Anti-Tank Weapons During World War II', Prepared by H. G. Gee.

[68] NA WO 259/61 Enquiry by the Rt. Hon. C. R. Attlee MP into Tank Position in the Middle East, March 1942. It is likely that the figure for mechanical breakdown was much lower during the summer fighting as the reliability of Eighth Army's tanks had improved with the arrival of more American hardware, such as the Stuart and Grant tanks. The figures provided here suggest that mechanical breakdown might only have accounted for 8 per cent of casualties. The author was not able to find evidence to confirm or refute this estimate.

[69] Joly, *Take These Men*, p. 219.

[70] This figure would clearly be lower if replacement tanks with their own crews entered battle rather than depleted crews being given new tanks and replacements to help them continue fighting.

[71] IWM BLM 28 Diary Notes, 23 October to 7 November 1942. Saturday, 24 October.

[72] Bungay, *Alamein*, pp. 198–9.

[73] IWM TM30/410 Handbook on the British Army, p. 25.

Illustration 22   Casualties lie in the open on stretchers at a 51st Highland Division advanced dressing station, El Alamein, October 1942. High casualties could militate against the primary group operating as a positive motivating force in battle.

the same methodology used to assess front-line casualties in the Crusader and summer battles (i.e. excluding HQ companies from the category of 'front-line' troops), that figure could have been as high as 63%.

Two battalions of the 51st Highland Division can be examined in more detail to judge the effect of such high casualties. The 7th Black Watch, of the 154th Infantry Brigade, had 78 killed and 183 wounded at El Alamein, a total of 265, the highest figure for any of its individual engagements of the war.[74] Of those, 70 were killed and 140 wounded on the first night. Before

[74] *War History of the 7th Battalion, the Black Watch* (Fife, 1948), app. 4, p. 145.

the battle, 7th Black Watch had a strength of 781 officers and men, which meant that at El Alamein it suffered a casualty rate of 34%.[75] However, the battalion history makes it clear that the vast majority of these casualties were suffered among its four rifle companies. If most of the 265 casualties suffered by the 7th Black Watch were inflicted on these rifle companies (496 men), then that means that roughly up to 50% of those at the sharp end became casualties. If we take an even more tightly focused view of the battle, we see the range of casualties that the individual rifle companies suffered. 'A' and 'C' Companies of the 7th Black Watch each lost over 50% of their men. 'D' Company was still two platoons strong by the end of the battle while 'B' Company suffered most of all, reduced to the strength of one platoon by the end of the battle. That means 'B' Company suffered somewhere around 66% casualties at El Alamein.[76]

Another Scottish battalion, the 5th Seaforths, of the 152nd Infantry Brigade, also suffered heavy casualties at El Alamein. Twelve officers and 165 men of the battalion were killed or wounded, a total of 177.[77] The front-line units of 5th Seaforths, i.e. the men comprising the four infantry companies, had, therefore, a casualty rate of about 36%. However, the individual companies had very different experiences. 'A' and 'D' companies came out of El Alamein 'almost intact', while 'B' Company was reduced to half its strength. 'C' Company, on the other hand, 'which had started a hundred strong,' had only one officer and twelve men left by the end of the battle, a casualty rate of around 87%.[78]

The casualty rates of the 20th and 24th Australian Infantry Brigades show that they suffered similarly catastrophic casualties at El Alamein, producing a high turnover of men in the primary group (Tables 9 and 10).

Montgomery's diary for 24 October 1942 shows the extraordinarily high casualties that all the attacking divisions suffered on the first night of the battle (Table 11). These casualties would have substantially reduced the effect of primary group cohesion for the twelve days of battle that remained.

Montgomery noted in his diary three days later that 'it is clear from the casualty figures that we have got to be careful, especially as regards infantry'. The 1st South African Division had started low in strength and could therefore no longer undertake any major offensive operations, as no reinforcements were available. The New Zealand Division was capable of launching one more major offensive operation and would then be fit only for defensive tasks, as, again, no reinforcements were

---

[75] NA WO 169/4991 War Diary of 7th Battalion, the Black Watch.
[76] *War History of the 7th Battalion the Black Watch*, p. 18.
[77] Borthwick, *Battalion*, p. 43.   [78] Ibid., p. 39.

Table 9 *Casualties, 20th Australian Infantry Brigade, battle of El Alamein, 23 October to 4 November 1942*

	2/13 Battalion	2/15 Battalion	2/17 Battalion
Killed	66	30	59
Wounded	220	119	183
Missing	3	–	4
Evacuated Sick	60	25	58
Total removed from primary group	349	174	304
% removed from primary group	70%	35%	61%
Reinforcements	227	159	207

Percentage is derived from the 496 men that made up the four infantry companies that carried out the majority of the fighting in a battalion.
Source: AWM 54 526/6/10 20th Infantry Brigade Reports on Operation Lightfoot, October to November 1942, Statement of Casualties.

Table 10 *Casualties, 24th Australian Infantry Brigade, operations night of 31 October/1 November 1942*

	2/28 Battalion	2/32 Battalion	2/43 Battalion
Killed	13	21	43
Wounded	22	92	107
Missing	–	78	–
Missing believed killed	11	–	7
Total removed from primary group	46	191	157
% removed from primary group	9%	39%	32%

Percentage is derived from the 496 men that made up the four infantry companies that carried out the majority of the fighting in a battalion. Reinforcement figures were not available for the 24th Australian Infantry Brigade.
Source: AWM 54 526/6/12 24th Infantry Brigade, Operations 31 October to 1 November 1942, Casualties, Statement of Casualties.

available. The 9th Australian Division had suffered considerably but there were 4,000 reinforcements in the country. The 51st Highland Division had also endured heavy casualties, but had received 1,000 reinforcements to make up numbers.[79]

The armoured regiments did not suffer as badly at El Alamein as they did at Crusader or during the summer battles. Eighth Army started the battle with 1,029 tanks,[80] 332 of which became casualties.[81]

[79] Ibid.   [80] Barr, *Pendulum of War*, p. 276.   [81] Ibid., p. 404.

Table 11 *Casualties by division from night 23/24 October up to midnight 24 October 1942.*

Division	Officers	ORs	Total
1st South African	36	545	581
2nd New Zealand	n/a	651	651
4th Indian	4	40	44
9th Australian	29	551	580
51st Highland Division	23	604	627
Total	92	2391	2483

Source: IWM BLM 28 Diary Notes, 23 October to 7 November 1942. 'The Battle of Egypt, 23 October 1942 to 7 November 1942. Some Notes by Lieut.-Gen. B.L. Montgomery, Commander, Eighth Army', p. 8.

Therefore, using the same methodology as in the Gazala battle (i.e. that about 92 per cent of tank casualties were caused by mines, tanks or anti-tank guns), around 30 per cent (305 out of 1029) of the tanks that fought in the battle were likely to have suffered casualties among their crews. This represented considerably less disruption of the primary group amongst armoured units than in previous battles.

In assessing the effect of casualties on front-line units, J. H. A. Sparrow made it very clear that junior officers within the British Army were 'always handicapped' by 'heavy casualties, a rapid turnover of men, and reinforcements from strange units – which prevented [them] from getting to know [their] men'.[82] It can be safely concluded, therefore, that during those major battles of the North African campaign in which high casualties were the norm among front-line soldiers, the capacity of the primary group to function as a source of morale for the troops could be seriously undermined.

Where casualties were less extreme, such as in the three months of fighting against the Italians, from Sidi Barrani to Beda Fomm, under generals Wavell and O'Connor, the primary group was, in the main, less affected by disruption. British casualties in this phase of the war came to about 1,200 in dead, wounded and missing.[83] This, using the same methods of calculation and the same rationale as above, suggests a casualty rate for British front-line infantry troops of around 16 per cent suffered

---

[82] NA WO 277/16 Sparrow, *Army Morale*, p. 13.

[83] NA WO 201/2834 'Battle Casualties Reported by R. Casualties during Week Ending 8 February, 1941 and Totals since 25 November 1940 and Outbreak of War'. Playfair, *The Mediterranean and the Middle East*, vol. I, p. 362, quotes the total number of casualties in the campaign as 1,928 dead, wounded or missing.

over three months. For sure, the WDF was superior to the Italians in many ways. Nevertheless, one of the key reasons for their success was undoubtedly the morale of well-trained regular troops, who knew each other intimately, and were not subjected to the whittling away of that morale through high casualties.[84]

A second factor that might hinder the functioning of the primary group as a motivating force (and thereby lessen the applicability of primary group theory to the British, Commonwealth and Dominion forces in North Africa) is the impact on ordinary soldiers of the stress of the modern industrial battlefield. Fear could prevent men from acting as cohesive members of the unit, or, in extreme cases, cause men either to break down or to desert, thus absenting themselves from the primary group altogether. The bulk of the soldiers who made up the desert army after 1941 were conscripts, volunteers and Territorials. These men, unaccustomed to the sounds of battle, and unused to the threat of injury and death, were faced with a traumatic and unaccustomed environment. As the British general and theorist J. F. C. Fuller wrote, 'in an attack half the men on a firing line are in terror and the other half are unnerved'.[85] Many men found the extreme stress of battle too much and broke down. In the First World War this phenomenon was known as 'shellshock'. In the Second World War it came to be referred to as 'battle exhaustion'. 'The large majority of individuals diagnosed as suffering from battle exhaustion exhibited what the psychiatrists described as acute fear reactions and acute and chronic anxiety manifested through uncontrollable tremors, a pronounced startle reaction to war-related sounds and a profound loss of self-confidence.'[86]

Shils and Janowitz argued that the soldier's fear of death and injury tended to weaken primary group cohesion,[87] while Stouffer asserted that the real ambivalence in combat 'centred in the conflict between loyalty to one's outfit and buddies and the desire to escape from combat'.[88]

---

[84] It is difficult to gauge battle casualties for armoured units during this phase of the war. Barrie Pitt in *Wavell's Command*, p. 190, estimates that 80 per cent of the Western Desert Force's tracked and wheeled vehicles had either been destroyed or were worn out by the end of the operation. It is likely however that many of these 'casualties' were the result of breakdown due to wear and tear from the 500-mile advance.

[85] Atkinson, *An Army at Dawn*, p. 230.

[86] Copp, 'If this war isn't over, And pretty damn soon', in Addison and Calder, (eds.), *Time to Kill*, p. 149.

[87] Shils and Janowitz, 'Cohesion and Disintegration in the Wehrmacht in World War II', p. 291.

[88] Stouffer, *The American Soldier*, p. 139.

From the standpoint of the individual soldier, it is primarily the danger of death or injury which makes the combat situation so harassing an experience. The intense emotional strains of actual battle are to a large extent rooted in the inescapable fear and anxiety reactions continually aroused by ever-present stimuli which signify objective threats of danger. The threats of being maimed, of undergoing unbearable pain, and of being completely annihilated elicit intense fear reactions which may severely interfere with successful performance.[89]

Stouffer's studies demonstrated that a majority of men were willing to admit that they experienced fear and anxiety in combat.[90] In a survey carried out in the European theatre of operations in August 1944, 277 wounded combat veterans were asked about their experiences. The results were startling. Sixty-five per cent of the men questioned admitted having had at least one experience in combat in which they were unable to perform adequately because of intense fear. Forty-two per cent said that they had not been able to perform in combat 'once or twice' or 'a few times' because of fear. Twenty-three per cent reported that they had not been able to perform because of fear 'several times' or 'many times' in combat.[91] As Marshall put it, fear was 'ever present' on the battlefield, and 'uncontrolled fear' was ultimately the 'enemy of successful operations'.[92]

Sir Charles Wilson (later Lord Moran) built his own theory on morale and motivation on similar observations. He argued that each man had a finite stock of courage to carry him through in battle. The soldier did not become more battle hardened and immune to the horrors of war as his experience of combat increased. Instead, his reserves of courage were whittled away with each successive exposure to battle.[93] Terry Copp's statistics of breakdown, for British, American and Canadian units in the Mediterranean theatre of the Second World War, lend support to Wilson's argument. Copp showed that a ratio of 23 breakdowns for every 100 non-fatal battle casualties was normal for infantry divisions involved in intense combat in this theatre.[94] 'Every man had his breaking point,' and whether through sheer physical exhaustion, or the mental strain of combat, men eventually succumbed.[95] Stouffer's statistics showed that 23 per cent of wounded men in American military hospitals had not been able to perform in battle 'several times' or 'many times'

---

[89] Ibid., p. 192.   [90] Ibid., p. 200.

[91] Ibid., pp. 201–2. The sample taken was not a cross-section of all troops, but rather a random selection of wounded combat veterans in army hospitals.

[92] Marshall, *Men against Fire*, p. 37.

[93] Charles Wilson, *The Anatomy of Courage* (London 1945), p. x.

[94] Copp, 'If this war isn't over, And pretty damn soon', in Addison and Calder, (eds.), *Time to Kill*, p. 149.

[95] Ibid., p. 151; Linderman, *The World within War*, p. 355; Stouffer, *The American Soldier*, p. 191.

because of fear. Copp showed that 23 per cent of non-fatal battle casualties could be caused by breakdown. These remarkably symmetrical statistics cannot be ignored in assessing the impact of fear and breakdown on the primary group.

In 1942, battle schools were set up throughout Home Command and in the Middle East to improve training and accustom soldiers to the noise and fog of war by using maximum amounts of live ammunition and high explosive in exercises. It was realised by psychiatrists and soldiers alike that adequate preparation of this kind, if conducted along correct lines, might act to prevent breakdown under battle conditions. This process became known as 'battle inoculation'.[96] In the same year, exhaustion centres were also introduced by the War Office, in front-line areas, to combat breakdown and give fatigued soldiers some adequate rest. The War Office also attempted to limit the duration a man spent in combat without rest periods.[97] Brigadier G. W. B. James, the Consultant Psychiatrist Eighth Army, recommended, in the summer of 1942, that rest stations and camps be established, under divisional arrangement, between the Alexandria and El Alamein coast road and the sea. Thus, tired soldiers could get a few days away from battle and bathe in the Mediterranean.[98] However, with manpower shortages always a problem for front-line units, this did not always prove possible.

Battle exhaustion cases formed 7 to 10 per cent of the total sick and battle casualties in the forward areas of the El Alamein line in the summer of 1942.[99] In some units, notably the 2nd New Zealand Division and 1st South African Division, there was a ratio of over 25 such cases per 100 battle casualties.[100] By the time of El Alamein, however, when battle casualties were nearly as high as in July 1942, both divisions had a ratio of 1 to 2 battle exhaustion cases per 100 battle casualties.[101] The large number of battle exhaustion cases in Eighth Army in the summer of 1942 undoubtedly exacerbated the effect of high casualties on the primary group. Conversely, the remarkably low number of exhaustion cases during the battle of El Alamein aided primary group cohesion and somewhat offset the damaging effect of high casualties.

[96] NA WO CAB 21/914 'The Work of Army Psychiatrists in Relation to Morale', January 1944, p. 2.

[97] WO 277/16 Sparrow, 'Morale'.

[98] NA WO 177/324 Report on Tour of Eighth Army, 18 to 24 July 1942 by Consultant in Psychological Medicine (Brig. G. W. B. James), 28 July 1942.

[99] Ibid.; NA WO 177/324 Memo 'Sickness, Army Troops', by DDMS Eighth Army, 26 July 1942.

[100] ANZ WAII/8/Part 2/BBB Freyberg Papers, Morale.   [101] Ibid.

A third factor that might hinder the functioning of the primary group as a motivating force is the impact of 'misfits' on fighting units. Individuals who had problems in adjusting themselves to group life could damage primary group cohesion. These were the type of men who caused friction within groups or in more extreme circumstances deserted. Misfits, who were often men of very low intelligence, or men who had experienced psychological problems as civilians, were also likely to succumb to breakdown under the stresses of military life. Shils and Janowitz argued that

Among German deserters, who remained few until the close of the war, the failure to assimilate into the primary group life of the Wehrmacht was the most important factor, more important indeed than political dissidence. Deserters were on the whole men who had difficulty in personal adjustment, e.g., in the acceptance of affection or in the giving of affection. They were men who had shown these same difficulties in civilian life, having had difficulties with friends, work associates, and their own families, or having had criminal records.[102]

The British described the danger of 'misfits' in similar terms. As a circular to all medical officers entitled 'Morale Discipline and Mental Fitness' pointed out, 'misfits ... inevitably develop poor individual morale and hence affect group morale'.[103] The misfit tended to feel, and become, an 'outsider' in his unit. His loyalty to his unit was always doubtful and he was liable on slight cause to become openly resentful of authority,[104] or to abscond. Studies showed that in some parts of the UK one half of men under sentence for going AWOL 'had the intellectual capacity found in the least intelligent quarter of the population'.[105] Others demonstrated that nine out of ten men who reached a minimum level in intelligence tests were successful in training; below that minimum intelligence level, four out of five men either failed in training, or were reported as unsatisfactory by their field units.[106] A large body of such men in the army, as was the case for much of the desert war,[107] necessarily had a negative affect on the ability of the primary group to develop and maintain morale.

The difficulty of poor quality personnel applied just as much to officers as to ordinary recruits. The standard of regimental officers was of crucial

---

[102] Shils and Janowitz, 'Cohesion and Disintegration in the Wehrmacht in World War II', p. 285.

[103] NA WO 222/218 Circular to All Medical Officers, n.d., 'Morale, Discipline and Mental Fitness'.

[104] NA CAB 21/914 'The Work of Army Psychiatrists in Relation to Morale', The War Office Directorate of Army Psychiatry, January 1944.

[105] Ahrenfeldt, *Psychiatry in the British Army in the Second World War*, p. 78.

[106] NA WO 32/11972 Notes on the Use Now Being Made of Psychologists in the Army, 1942.

[107] See Chapter 3.

importance in maintaining morale.[108] Stouffer found that 'attitudes toward company officers were intimately associated with a group of attitudes which together were undoubtedly important to motivation in combat'.[109] Stouffer surveyed three different combat divisions in the Pacific and found that men who gave consistently favourable answers to questions concerning their feelings about their officers were more likely to show themselves to be relatively ready for further combat than were those who gave consistently unfavourable answers. Men who expressed intermediate attitudes toward their officers were also intermediate in expressed readiness for combat.[110] When unfavourable attitudes toward the unit officers developed, 'the formal, authoritative system of controls and the pattern of informal sanctions and values rooted in the men's attitudes would no longer merge in the person of the unit commander'. This meant that 'one source of the ties of individual to group w[as] ... impaired, and the soldier would be less likely to take extra risks or withstand extra stresses for the sake of his admired leader or in response to his support'.[111]

All the major combatants in the Second World War introduced various personnel assessment and selection systems in an attempt to allocate resources effectively and reduce the numbers of misfits and psychological defectives in combat units. The selection techniques, intelligence testing and psychological testing introduced by Adam, as Adjutant-General at the War Office, played a part in weeding out misfits and the psychologically defective men who proved incapable of integrating with the primary group. These initiatives helped to reduce instances of desertion and breakdown, problems that challenged primary group efficacy in Eighth Army. The case has been made in Chapter 3 that the Adjutant-General's initiatives had begun to produce dividends by the outbreak of the battle of El Alamein, in October 1942.

A fourth factor that might hinder the functioning of the primary group as a motivating force (and again lessen the applicability of primary group theory to the British, Commonwealth and Dominion forces in North Africa) is the effect of modern firepower on the battlefield. The use of high explosives and machine guns by an adversary requires units to disperse to survive. Marshall wrote that 'when an advancing infantry line suddenly encounters enemy fire and the men go to ground under circumstances where they cannot see one another, the moral disintegration of that line is for the moment complete. All organisational unity

---

[108] Gary Sheffield, 'Officer–Man Relations, Discipline and Morale in the British Army of the Great War', in Cecil and Liddle, *Facing Armageddon*, p. 421.
[109] Stouffer, *The American Soldier*, p. 127.   [110] Ibid., p. 126.   [111] Ibid., pp. 127–8.

vanishes temporarily. What has been a force becomes a scattering of individuals.'[112]

The effect of firepower certainly played a role in undermining primary group cohesion in the desert, especially during the mobile operations of 1941 and the first half of 1942. The reality of the desert environment forced units to 'dig or die'. The lack of cover also compelled units to disperse to ensure protection from artillery and air attack. Montgomery therefore, on taking over command, made a point of insisting that units gathered together from time to time to develop bonds and listen to their commanders.[113] The more concentrated dispositions dictated by the geography of the El Alamein line also facilitated the creation of unit cohesion.

A fifth factor that might hinder the functioning of the primary group as a positive motivating force is the tendency for primary groups, in abnormal situations of stress, to act in a negative fashion, encouraging the group to disobey orders, refuse to fight, mutiny, or surrender. This can be especially dangerous in circumstances where the primary group divorces itself from 'the collective goals of the higher organization which the group is designed to serve'.[114] For instance, John Helmer claimed that in Vietnam, 'where primary-group solidarity existed, more often than not it served to foster and reinforce *dissent* from the goals of military organisation and to organize *refusal* to perform according to institutional norms'.[115]

The issue of whether the primary group acted as a negative influence on combat performance in the desert certainly deserves consideration. The astonishingly high missing/surrender rate of 88 per cent (as Auchinleck reported), or 85 per cent (as the 'hot spot' casualty figures indicate),[116] suggests that the primary group may have acted as a negative motivational influence during the summer months of 1942. Groups of soldiers isolated in the desert and outgunned by the *Panzerarmee Afrika*[117] may have found it in their collective best interests to surrender.

Having identified and explored five factors that may reduce the ability of the primary group to act as a positive force for morale, it seems reasonable to conclude that, at least in the context of the war in the desert, primary group theory, on its own, is not a sufficient explanation of morale and motivation among combat troops.

---

[112] Marshall, *Men against Fire*, p. 129.
[113] NA WO 32/10810 Army Commander's Personal Memorandum, 20 August 1942.
[114] Strachan, 'Training, Morale and Modern War', *Journal of Contemporary History*, p. 213.
[115] Quoted in Stephen D. Wesbrook, 'The Potential for Military Disintegration', in Sarkessian (ed.), *Combat Effectiveness*, p. 257.
[116] See Chapter 1.   [117] See Chapter 2.

Illustration 23 British infantry advance in open formation towards German positions, El Alamein, October 1942. Modern firepower required units to disperse in battle. This could limit the positive effects of the primary group on morale.

There are, however, a number of other theories that attempt to explain combat morale and motivation. One such approach focuses on the use of discipline to coerce troops to fight. Coercion, Hew Strachan has argued, is not always given enough recognition as a motivational tool.[118] Soldiers had to accept 'the basic philosophy governing human relationships within an army',[119] according to Marshall, or take what Stouffer referred to as 'the institutionally sanctioned consequences'.[120]

[118] Hew Strachan, 'The Soldier's Experience in Two World Wars: Some Historiographical Comparisons', in Addison and Calder (eds.), *Time to Kill*, pp. 374–5.
[119] Marshall, *Men against Fire*, p. 165.   [120] Stouffer, *The American Soldier*, p. 101.

John Erickson has illustrated how coercion was used in the Russian Army in the Second World War.

> Stalin's Order No. 270, dated 16 August 1941, prescribed ruthless punishment for desertion, panic-mongering and surrender. The families of commanders and commissars who ... deserted would be arrested. The families of those taken prisoner would be deprived of state support and benefits. In divisions those regiment and battalion commanders who 'cowered in slit trenches' and did not lead from the front were to be reduced to the ranks, or if necessary shot on the spot and replaced by 'brave and steadfast' junior officers or outstanding soldiers.[121]

The Red Army gave its men a stark choice. 'Ahead of the Soviet soldier lay German guns and tanks, behind him the NKVD machine-gunners of the "holding detachments" (*zagradotryadyi*).' If the Russian soldier failed to achieve his objective and retreated, he was as likely to be shot by his own countrymen as by the enemy. Stalin was reported to have said that it took a brave soldier to be a coward in the Red Army.[122] During the battle of Stalingrad, General Chuikov, the commander of the Soviet forces fighting within the city, reportedly felled 13,500 of his own men by firing squad. This was the equivalent of more than a whole division of troops, an enormous number for any army. Antony Beevor argued that the barely believable ruthlessness of the Red Army at Stalingrad largely accounted for the 50,000 Soviet citizens that fought for von Paulus's Sixth Army.[123] Nevertheless, the result of Chuikov's disciplinary measures was that the Russian soldier had little choice but to fight, and as Erickson has drily remarked, 'Stalingrad did not fall.'[124]

Germany's disciplinary profile in two world wars resonates with Russian experiences on the eastern front. During the 1914–18 war, Germany executed forty-eight of its own soldiers for desertion or coward-ice in the field. Between 1939 and 1945, by comparison, it is estimated that over 15,000 German soldiers were executed.[125] By the end of the First World War, desertion and indiscipline were widespread throughout the German Army.[126] Alexander Watson has argued that the German Army had broken down by the summer of 1918.

[121] John Erickson, 'Red Army Battlefield Performance, 1941–45: The System and the Soldier', in Addison and Calder (eds.), *Time to Kill*, p. 242.

[122] Ibid., p. 247.   [123] Antony Beevor, *Stalingrad* (London, 1999), p. xiv.

[124] Erickson, 'Red Army Battlefield Performance', in Addison and Calder (eds.), *Time to Kill*, p. 244.

[125] Strachan, 'The Soldier's Experience in Two World Wars', in Addison and Calder (eds.), *Time to Kill*, p. 375.

[126] Wilhelm Deist, 'The Military Collapse of the German Empire: The Reality Behind the Stab-in-the-Back Myth', *War in History*, 3(2) (1996), p. 202. See Watson, *Enduring the Great War*, pp. 206–11 for a critique of Deist's argument.

Although some troops continued to fight bravely, the willingness and ability of most to resist the Allied offensive disappeared. While, in the estimation of . . . Haig, the German army possessed enough material resources to prolong the war into 1919, its men lacked both the inclination and energy to do so. Matters of morale, which had been decisive in determining the conflict's longevity, were also pivotal in bringing about its termination. As Ludendorff himself acknowledged two and a half weeks before the armistice, at the end of the war it was not primarily the number (*die Zahl*) but rather the spirit of the troops (*Geist der Truppe*) which was decisive.[127]

The German Army 'may have claimed that it still stood intact on enemy soil in November 1918, but many of its elements had ceased fighting long before the Armistice'.[128]

In the Second World War, the German Wehrmacht fought, comparatively, to the bitter end. Shils and Janowitz acknowledged the key role played by discipline in motivating the German soldier to fight with such tenacity.[129] They remarked that

The belief in the efficacy and moral worth of discipline . . . was expressed in the jettisoning of the German Army Psychiatric Selection Services in 1942. When the manpower shortage became stringent and superfluities had to be scrapped, the personnel selection system based on personality analyses was one of those activities which was thought to be dispensable.

Instead, with the need for manpower at a premium, it was hoped that hard, soldierly discipline would maintain cohesion in the Wehrmacht after 1942.[130] It is impossible to prove that discipline was the key factor in the Wehrmacht's fanatical resistance into the summer of 1945. But the comparison between the disciplinary measures in force during the two wars is instructive.

Brigadier A. B. McPherson, who, in 1950, compiled the War Office monograph on discipline, remarked that 'in the inculcation of "morale" discipline is an indispensable factor. Self-respect, self-control and obedience to authority, which go hand in hand in training in discipline, are sturdy elements also in the foundation of morale.'[131] Whereas Britain executed 346 men in the First World War, it executed none in the Second World War.[132] The War Office believed that a disciplined soldier was

---

[127] Watson, *Enduring the Great War*, p. 184.
[128] Strachan, 'The Soldier's Experience in Two World Wars', in Addison and Calder (eds.), *Time to Kill*, p. 375.
[129] Shils and Janowitz, 'Cohesion and Disintegration in the Wehrmacht in World War II', p. 291.
[130] Ibid., p. 293. [131] NA WO 277/7 McPherson, *Army: Discipline*, p. 2.
[132] Strachan, 'Training, Morale and Modern War', *The Journal of Contemporary History*, p. 215.

created more efficiently and rapidly by 'intelligent and persuasive means than by rigid methods of force and punishment'. With the death penalty for cowardice and desertion in the field abolished in 1930, the British Army could not rely on coercion along Soviet and German lines. Instead the War Office believed that a system which 'appealed to a man's honour, sense of duty and patriotism', would prove deeper and more lasting in effect than one based upon repression or threat of punishment'. A coercive system, it believed, was in any case 'liable to collapse as soon as the threat of punishment was removed'.[133] For this reason, the quality of British officers was of the highest importance (a problem which beset Eighth Army for much of the conflict), as it was their job to develop pride in their unit and to persuade their men to fight. The evidence from the desert is that coercive measures played a negligible role in motivating troops to fight. This led Auchinleck to seek the reintroduction of the death penalty for desertion and for cowardice. In any event, Auchinleck's suggestion was rejected by the Cabinet and the disciplinary measures then in force, as a South African report on 'Desertion and Absence without Leave from Front Lines', written in August 1942, pointed out,[134] clearly did not restrain soldiers from deserting in large numbers during the summer of 1942.

Another explanation for combat morale and motivation is ideology or 'cause'. Hew Strachan has argued that military factors alone do not suffice to explain combat motivation.[135] This viewpoint, it has been suggested, is 'grounded in the belief that the ways and ideals of the combatants, rather than purely internal military logic, often better explain how war is fought'. This approach has been characterised as the 'cultural' study of war by some authors.[136] Marshall's own definition of morale shows that he recognised this inherent complexity.

Morale is the thinking of an army. It is the whole complex body of an army's thought: The way it feels about the soil and about the people from which it springs. The way that it feels about their cause and their politics as compared with other causes and other politics. The way that it feels about its friends and allies, as well as its enemies. About its commanders and goldbricks. About food and shelter. Duty and leisure. Payday and sex. Militarism and civilianism. Freedom and slavery.

[133] NA WO 277/7 McPherson, *Army: Discipline*, p. 3.
[134] SAMAD Div Docs, Box 119, Desertion and Absence without Leave from Front Lines, Main HQ 1 SA Division, 23 August 1942.
[135] Strachan, 'The Soldier's Experience in Two World Wars', in Addison and Calder (eds.), *Time to Kill*, p. 375.
[136] J. E. Lendon, *Soldiers and Ghosts: A History of Battle in Classical Antiquity* (London, 2004), p. 393.

Work and want. Weapons and comradeship. Bunk fatigue and drill. Discipline and disorder. Life and death. God and the devil.[137]

'Above and beyond any symbol', in Marshall's view, 'whether it be the individual life or a pillbox commanding a wadi in [the] Sahara – are all of the ideas and ideals which press upon men, causing them to accept a discipline and to hold to the line even though death may be at hand ... If any man doubts that these values have a place in hardening the resolve of an army, let him answer the question: What happens when an army loses faith in its cause? It is in fact defeated and wholly submissive to the enemy. Its will is defeated. If it can expect to receive quarter, the last reason for resistance has disappeared.'[138] The collapse of France in 1940 was the perfect example for Marshall to prove his point, while Bataan, Stalingrad, El Alamein and Bastogne were battles where belief in ultimate victory did more than all else to rally tactical troops and to persuade them to sell their lives dearly.[139]

Stouffer disagreed with Marshall. He disregarded motivational factors that could be grouped under the generic title of 'cause'. He said that attitudes toward the war showed a consistent, but statistically not reliable, relationship to combat performance ratings.[140] Officers and enlisted men alike, he contended, attached little importance to idealistic motives such as patriotism and concern about war aims.[141]

While Stouffer listed a number of examples to support his argument on 'cause', two of his own surveys offered more support to Marshall's point of view. In April and May 1944, Stouffer questioned veterans and replacements in line infantry companies of two veteran infantry divisions. He also questioned men in line infantry companies of three inexperienced divisions (Table 12). He asked, 'how much do the things that this war is being fought over mean to you personally?' The answers clearly show that a substantial majority of the front-line soldiers questioned reported that the cause for which they were fighting was significant for them personally.

In another study, enlisted infantrymen, in a veteran division that saw action in the Mediterranean campaign, were surveyed. Officers in divisions in both the European and Pacific theatres of action were also questioned (Table 13). Enlisted men were asked, 'generally from your combat experience what was most important to you in making you want to keep going and do as well as you could?' Officers were asked, 'when the

---

[137] Marshall, *Men against Fire*, p. 158.   [138] Ibid., pp. 161–2.
[139] Ibid., p. 169.   [140] Stouffer, *The American Soldier*, p. 39.   [141] Ibid., p. 111.

Table 12 *'How much do the things that this war is being fought over mean to you personally?'*

	Number of cases	Percentage making favourable responses
All enlisted men		
Veteran Division A		
Veterans	605	62%
Replacements	427	71%
Veteran Division B		
Veterans	2,227	67%
Replacements	983	75%
Inexperienced divisions	9,850	74%

Source: Stouffer, *The American Soldier*, p. 262.

Table 13 *Enlisted men's motivations for keeping fighting: officers' and enlisted men's perceptions*

Incentives	Percentage of comments naming each incentive among:	
	Enlisted men	Officers
Ending the task	39%	14%
Solidarity with the group	14%	15%
Sense of duty and self-respect	9%	15%
Thoughts of home and loved ones	10%	3%
Self-preservation	6%	9%
Idealistic reasons	5%	2%
Vindictiveness	2%	12%
Leadership and discipline	1%	19%
Miscellaneous	14%	11%

Source: Stouffer, *The American Soldier*, p. 108.

going is tough for your men, what do you think are the incentives which keep them fighting?'[142]

Stouffer concluded from these results that idealistic motives, like patriotism and concern about war aims, were insignificant in motivating front-line soldiers.[143] The incentive of 'idealistic reasons' only received a

[142] Ibid., p. 108.   [143] Ibid., p. 111.

response of 5% for enlisted men and 2% for officers. However, if 'ending the task', 'sense of duty and self respect', 'thoughts of home and loved ones', 'idealistic reasons' and 'vindictiveness' are grouped together under the generic title of 'ideology' or 'cause', a very different picture emerges. These factors, counted together, give the enlisted men a response of 65% and officers 46% for cause-related incentives; this comes a good deal closer to the findings in Table 12. It might be noted that the methodology employed does not allow for multiple responses, and therefore assumes 'one only' incentive or 'one only' most important factor. This is perhaps a serious flaw when studying such a complex motivational area, but understandable in the context of a time when considerable effort was being expended on discovering how to explain why a given motive might be dominant at a given time.[144]

Shils and Janowitz did not give much credence to arguments relating to ideology in explaining combat motivation.[145] For them, the Nazi Party's propagandistic preoccupation with political ideology was only a 'secondary aspect' of morale,[146] and was relevant only so far as it affected the workings of the primary group.[147] They did, however, recognise the presence in the German Army of a 'hard core' of believers in the cause. This 'hard core' made up approximately 10 to 15 per cent of the total enlisted men (the percentage was higher for non-commissioned officers and was very much higher among junior officers). These men, according to Shils and Janowitz, were responsible to a large measure for the stability and military effectiveness of the primary group. 'These were, on the whole, young men between 24 and 28 years of age who had had a gratifying adolescence in the most rewarding period of National Socialism. They were imbued with the ideology of *Gemeinschaft* (community solidarity), were enthusiasts for the military life ... and ... placed a very high value on "toughness", manly comradeliness, and group solidarity.'[148] The presence of a few such men in the group, zealous, energetic and unsparing of themselves, provided models for weaker men, and facilitated the process of identification with the primary group.[149] Nevertheless, Shils and Janowitz maintained that there was 'little inclination to discuss political matters' at the front, and that belief in the 'cause' of itself was of minor value to German soldiers' morale.[150]

---

[144] Abraham Maslow's influential article 'A Theory of Human Motivation' had been published in 1943 (in *Psychological Review* 50, pp. 370–6); he suggested that a hierarchy of prepotency explained how dominant motivations changed as individuals matured psychologically.

[145] Shils and Janowitz, 'Cohesion and Disintegration in the Wehrmacht in World War II', pp. 284 and 303.

[146] Ibid., p. 297.   [147] Ibid., p. 281.   [148] Ibid., p. 286.   [149] Ibid.   [150] Ibid., p. 287.

Omer Bartov, however, in his study of the Wehrmacht on the eastern front in the Second World War, has argued that ideology did play a role in motivating German soldiers to fight. He focused his research on three divisions, examining the effects of acute physical hardship and extremely high casualty rates on the functioning of the primary group. He argued that, due to the extraordinary number of casualties experienced between 1941 and 1945, primary group theory could only feature as part of the explanation for German soldiers' resilience. Instead, he postulated that their officers had to rely heavily on political indoctrination in order to maintain the fighting capability of the German troops. Furthermore, he argued that the indoctrination of troops in the National Socialist ideology by the officers of the Wehrmacht, especially the junior officers, facilitated the barbarisation of warfare on the eastern front. This was because Nazi ideology preached the destruction and enslavement of *Untermenschen* such as the Russian people.[151]

John Dower has argued that ideology was also a primary factor in motivating the troops of both Japan and the United States in the Pacific theatre of operations in the Second World War. The American soldier, according to Dower, viewed his Japanese enemy as a creature closer to apes and monkeys than man. They were a childlike race, bent on domination of the world, who had to be stopped to save civilisation. The Japanese, on the other hand, aimed to liberate East Asia from white invasion and oppression. Eight hundred thousand whites, the tally went, controlled 450 million Asians.[152] Dower has suggested that, as a result of these beliefs, no rules complicated the encounter with the enemy. J. E. Lendon has stated that 'restraints are grounded in shared belief . . . Where such beliefs are not shared, as in the Pacific theatre in World War II, for example, fighting achieves a singular brutality.'[153] The conflict in the Pacific, therefore, just like the war on the eastern front, took on an ideological dimension that facilitated its slide into barbarism.

Other authors, such as Mark Johnston, Gerald F. Linderman and John Ellis, corroborate Dower's argument.[154] Ellis has remarked that

In the war against Japan . . . it is possible to speak of a real loathing for the whole race . . . Neither the British, the Indians nor the Americans really regarded the Japanese as human beings. Their fantastic bravery and spirit of self-sacrifice was seen merely as a dangerous form of insanity, and one killed them as one might exterminate a particularly intransigent pest.[155]

---

[151] Bartov, *The Eastern Front* and *Hitler's Army*.
[152] Dower, *War without Mercy*, p. 24.   [153] Lendon, *Soldiers and Ghosts*, p. 4.
[154] Johnston, *Australian Soldiers and their Adversaries in World War II*, chap. 6; Linderman, *The World within War*, chap. 4.
[155] Ellis, *The Sharp End*, p. 319.

As regards the war in the desert, the legend that both sides took part in a 'war without hate' suggests that ideological motivations were of no great importance to combat morale. The remarkable respect that Eighth Army held for its German enemy during much of the desert fighting was a matter the censorship summaries commented upon widely and led, according to the censors, to increased rates of surrender among the troops.[156]

The War Office made considerable efforts to inculcate ideological fervour amongst the men in the desert. 'Middle East Training Pamphlet no. 10', which dealt with the lessons from Operation Compass (December 1940 to February 1941), stated clearly that

The maintenance of discipline on active service was difficult enough when troops fought and moved in close order. In modern war under Eastern conditions, wide frontages and great dispersion prevent close control of individuals by their superiors. Instead, the individual must discipline himself and this is only possible where the individual has learnt to understand and respect the cause for which he fights and to take pride in his army, his unit and himself. Where these incentives are lacking, lamentable things happen which bring disgrace on our cause and may expose the Army to a dangerous reverse.[157]

The introduction of army education and ABCA in the run-up to El Alamein certainly played a role in motivating soldiers to fight. By the second half of 1942, education officers and information officers were integral parts of units in Eighth Army. Both personal diaries and mail show that the men were interested in current affairs and were concerned about their future following the war.[158] As Montgomery postulated, in an argument that was subsequently echoed by Shils and Janowitz, it was not always necessary for large numbers of troops to be ideologically charged. It was more important for officers, who played a vital role in developing troop morale, to believe in the cause they were fighting for. In this way, they would be more determined and efficient, thus passing on their enthusiasm and spirit to the troops.[159] Chapter 5 has suggested that many of the educational initiatives introduced in the run up to El Alamein played a significant role in inculcating morale among the front line troops.

The remarkable connection that existed between front line combatants and the people at home also shows the importance of cause-related motives to

---

[156] ANZ WAII/1/DA508 vol. 1, MEMCWS, no. XXXVIII (29 July to 4 August 1942), p. 2; ANZ WAII/1/DA508 vol. 1, MEMCWS, no. XL (12 to 18 August 1942), p. 2.

[157] NA WO 201/2586 'Middle East Training Pamphlet no. 10'. Lessons of Cyrenaica Campaign: Training Pamphlet, December 1940 to February 1941, p. 60.

[158] NA WO 193/453 Draft Morale Report, May to July 1942; AWM 54 883/2/97 British Troops in Egypt no. 92 Field Censorship Report Week Ending 31 July 1941, p. 4.

[159] IWM Brigg Papers, Morale in Battle: Analysis by B. L. Montgomery, p. 54.

morale.[160] Recent studies on the First World War have demonstrated the extent of this link. Stephane Audoin-Rouzeau has argued that

Even after several years in the trenches, the soldiers remained civilians in uniform: they still belonged to the civilian society they had left and hoped to rejoin. Hence the front was not an island but a peninsula with solid links to the rest of the community. The soldiers remained attached to it through every fibre in their bodies, whatever feelings of resentment they might harbour ... The postal censorship service for 1916 proves that the main news items concerning the war were known in the trenches and that morale varied in direct proportion to whether the information received was judged to be favourable or ominous.[161]

Postal statistics for the British Army during the First World War show that 12.5 million letters were sent weekly to the front and for every one that was sent there was nearly one in return.[162] In the Second World War, the volume of post could be similarly huge. By June 1943, 'an additional weekly allotment of 3,000 lbs for carriage of troops' air mail to and from North Africa and the Middle East and beyond ha[d] been arranged, making a total weekly allotment of 15,000 lbs'.[163]

David Fraser, in his study of the British Army in the Second World War, argued that a 'factor of great importance to the morale of the army was the connection with family and home'. A man could be away for a very long time; a regular soldier might serve seven, eight, even nine years abroad, a conscripted man four. 'During this time the bombing of the United Kingdom created anxiety and, often, hardship. Families were uprooted and bereaved. The high incidence of unfaithfulness of wives and sweethearts ... caused great suffering among soldiers ... Time and distance exacerbated suspicion, and, with loneliness and anxiety, were potent factors working against high morale.'[164]

Shils and Janowitz noted that German prisoners of war during the Second World War often reported that they had planned to desert because of their families and not from any dissatisfaction with the strategic situation or National Socialist ideology. 'The recollection of concrete family experiences' by soldiers, they argued, 'reactivated sentiments of

---

[160] Stephane Audoin-Rouzeau, 'The French Soldier in the Trenches', in Cecil and Liddle, *Facing Armageddon*; Strachan, 'The Soldier's Experience in Two World Wars', in Addison and Calder (eds.), *Time to Kill*.

[161] Audoin-Rouzeau, 'The French Soldier in the Trenches', in Cecil and Liddle, *Facing Armageddon*, p. 226. See also Richard C. Hall, '"The Enemy Is behind Us": The Morale Crisis in the Bulgarian Army during the Summer of 1918', *War in History*, 11(2) (April 2004).

[162] David Englander, 'Soldiering and Identity: Reflections on the Great War', *War in History*, 1(3) (1994), p. 304.

[163] NA WO 165/52 War Office Progress Report, June 1943.

[164] Fraser, *And We Shall Shock Them*, p. 105.

dependence on the family for psychological support.' This, correspondingly, weakened the hold of the military primary group. It was in such contexts, as the German Army retreated westwards from Russia, that German soldiers were willing to discuss group surrender.[165]

Citizen-soldiers left families, businesses and farms at home. Nevertheless, they fought to preserve these bastions of peaceful existence from the enemy. As Hew Strachan has pointed out,

> If soldiers expressed their alienation from home, they did so with regret – they were giving voice to the hope that the gulf between them and their families would not remain forever fixed … The soldier may excoriate the politician and the war profiteer, but he still fights for home and hearth – for mother, wife, and children. Because historians have looked for flag-waving patriotism they have failed to detect more subtly expressed loyalties.[166]

Stouffer, nevertheless, believed quite the contrary. He argued that the isolation of the front-line unit made the soldier feel completely set apart from the home front. This reinforced his arguments in favour of the primary group. In his words,

> The unit … lived and died apart from that other great world of the rear … In a thousand ways, great and small, the soldier coming into the line had defined for him a world that felt itself to be and was, in fact, removed physically and psychologically from all that lay behind it. Behind the front the great military machine inexorably continued to send forward supplies and men – and the orders that sent men into attack. But the rifleman's world shrank to the tremendous immediacies of staying alive and destroying the enemy.[167]

As regards North Africa, the evidence outlined in Chapter 5 certainly suggests that the link between home and front was extremely strong. Morale was influenced as much by news from home as any other factor. The War Office, realising this fact, made considerable efforts to ensure that the troops' means of communicating with their loved ones ran as smoothly and efficiently as possible. Although they could not control the content of such communications, they hoped in this way to maintain and encourage morale as well as possible.

More recently, Strachan has also argued that training should be considered a key factor in maintaining morale in combat. Marshall's own work, he has pointed out, deals more with the importance of training than with

---

[165] Shils and Janowitz, 'Cohesion and Disintegration in the Wehrmacht in World War II', pp. 289–90.
[166] Strachan, 'The Soldier's Experience in Two World Wars', in Addison and Calder (eds.), *Time to Kill*, p. 376.
[167] Stouffer, *The American Soldier*, pp. 99–100.

the dynamics of the primary group.[168] In Marshall's words, 'fear is ever present, but it is uncontrolled fear that is the enemy of successful operation, and the control of fear depends upon the extent to which all dangers and distractions may be correctly anticipated and therefore understood' through training.[169]

There is no doubt that Eighth Army was better trained for the El Alamein offensive than at any other period of the desert war. Throughout the summer of 1942, numerous reports listed the problem of exposing untrained troops to battle. Much of the confidence that pervaded Eighth Army on the eve of El Alamein was derived from the heavy and practical training the troops underwent, in battle schools and on mock battlefields, prior to combat. Montgomery's reputation as a trainer of men remains intact and this element of his approach prior to El Alamein must be considered a vital influence on the morale of Eighth Army.

In addition to the roles played by the primary group, coercion, cause and training in explaining combat motivation and morale in the desert, a number of other explanatory factors have emerged in the course of researching this book.

The first is the effect of weapons on morale. Marshall argued that 'a careful study of past military history and particularly of the "little picture" of our own infantry operations in the past war leads to the conclusion that weapons when correctly handled in battle seldom fail to gain victory. There is no other touchstone to tactical success, and it is a highly proper doctrine which seeks to ingrain in the infantry soldier a confidence that superior use of superior weapons is his surest protection.'[170] Marshall did not believe in technological determinism, or that firepower would defeat an enemy all on its own. The importance of firepower, in his view, was its effect on the psychology of the fighting soldier.[171]

Marshall pointed out that 'unwilling riflemen' could often be 'switched to heavier and more decisive one-man weapons' with great effect.

This sounds like a paradox – to expect greater response to come from increased responsibility. But it works. I have seen many cases where men who had funked it badly with a rifle responded heroically when given a flame-thrower or BAR. Self-pride and the ego are the touchstone of most of these remarkable conversions. A

[168] Strachan, 'Training, Morale and Modern War', *Journal of Contemporary History*, pp. 215–6.
[169] Marshall, *Men against Fire*, p. 37.   [170] Ibid., pp. 39–40.
[171] Hew Strachan, 'Training, Morale and Modern War', *Journal of Contemporary History*, p. 217.

man may fail with the rifle because he feels anonymous and believes that nothing important is being asked of him.[172]

It has been argued in Chapter 2 that technology was a crucial factor in deciding the outcome of the desert war. However, superior numbers and quality of weapons did not guarantee victory in North Africa. Instead, technology, in addition to providing necessary firepower capability also played a vital role in developing combat morale and motivation among the troops. Throughout the summer of 1942, the influx of more and better equipment boosted Eighth Army's morale. However, it was not until the battle of El Alamein that the performance of these new weapons matched expectations and thus played a decisive role in motivating troops to fight.

The impact of the environment and provisions on morale has also been shown to be hugely important. The morale of the soldier is affected by the conditions he experiences as much as any other factor. Some conditions arise from the 'normal' exigencies of industrial level war (such as the supply of food and water) and some are attributable to the particular difficulties that are special to any climate or location. In North Africa soldiers had to contend with the morale sapping factors of sun, sand and flies (among many others). The case has been made in Chapter 4 that an army's ability to prepare the soldier for such trials and its capacity to mitigate their affects on the soldiers' health (both mental and physical) play a crucial role in maintaining morale.

Chapters 3 and 5 of this book dealt with the importance of the quality of manpower, welfare and education in the maintenance of morale. As has already been suggested in this chapter, personnel selection played a crucial role in ensuring that men were allocated to the right group and to the correct job within the army. Efforts to remove misfits and those with psychological problems from fighting units proved equally important. These initiatives played a vital role in aiding the functioning of the primary group, thus helping morale. Welfare has similarly been shown to be a key aspect in developing a strong relationship between leader and led and between soldiers and the people 'back home'. In this way, welfare played a vital role in promoting the smooth functioning of the primary group as well as the ideological motivations for soldiers to fight.

Marshall contended that in battle it was the 'touch of human nature', or welfare, that gave men courage and enabled them to make proper use of their weapons.

One [man], patting another on the back, may turn a mouse into a lion; an unexpected GI can of chocolate, brought forward in a decisive moment, may

---

[172] Marshall, *Men against Fire*, p. 76.

rally a stricken battalion. By the same token, it is the loss of this touch which freezes men and impairs all action. Deprive it of this vitalizing spark and no man would go forward against the enemy.[173]

He also argued that the soldier's belief in his cause was nourished by the manner in which he was treated by those who were in authority over him.

Though belief in the nation is the foundation of [the soldier's] personal discipline, the superstructure is raised by human hands which toil within his sight. There is nothing more soulless than a religion without good works unless it be a patriotism which does not concern itself with the welfare and dignity of the individual.[174]

Stouffer's surveys certainly identified the importance of welfare and other issues of man-management to morale. One study asked veteran enlisted infantry men to characterise one of the best combat officers they had known. Fifty-six per cent of men listed 'leadership ability and practices',[175] or what could be referred to as 'man-management', as their most important characteristic. This may be compared with 43 per cent who identified issues directly relating to combat performance as important.[176] Another survey asked men, 'can you recall a case in your experience in which an officer did a particularly good job of helping his men to feel more confident in a tough or frightening situation?' Again, about 54 per cent of respondents chose issues such as 'showed active concern for welfare and safety of men', 'encouraged men; gave pep talks, joked, passed on information' or 'showed informal, friendly attitude; worked along with men' as the most important. Only 31 per cent of respondents gave examples directly related to combat performance, such as 'led by example; did dangerous things himself', or 'displayed personal courage and coolness' as the most important characteristic.[177] Stouffer also recognised welfare issues such as mail as critical determinants of morale and performance. In a survey carried out on new replacements in the Pacific theatre of operations, 'complaints about mail' were acknowledged to be 'more frequent than any other aspect of living conditions and facilities'.[178]

---

[173] Ibid., p. 41.   [174] Ibid., p. 162.
[175] This was broken down into 'leadership ability and miscellaneous leadership practices', 'helped other men; took personal interest in them and their problems', 'led by personal example; always with men in combat' and 'cheered men by humorous remarks'.
[176] Stouffer, *The American Soldier*, p. 134. This was broken down into 'fearless, brave, cool', '"had guts"', 'disregarded personal safety', 'displayed aggressiveness and initiative', 'knew what to do and did job well', 'observant; alert; excellent on scouting and patrol work', 'carried out orders to the letter', and 'used good judgment, common sense; good planner'.
[177] Ibid., p. 125.   [178] Ibid., p. 273.

Shils and Janowitz made similar arguments for the Wehrmacht in the Second World War. They pointed out that German officers were clearly directed to pay attention to the subjects of welfare and man-management.

Special orders were issued and particular attention was paid in the training of officers to fatherly and considerate behaviour in relations with their men; the combination of sternness and benevolence was strongly counselled. Numerous small indications of affection such as congratulations on birthdays and on anniversaries, and fatherly modes of address, e.g. '*Kinder*' (children), were recommended as helping to build the proper relations between officers and men.[179]

The role of leadership and command in inculcating morale and motivating troops to fight in the desert has also been addressed. In war, just as in any other form of collective human activity, it is necessary to organise, enthuse and energise individuals. Effective leadership is paramount in this process. According to Alan Hawley, 'it is axiomatic in a military population that fighting power requires appropriate leadership. Indeed, armies throughout history have greatly prized leaders and leadership.'[180]

Marshall believed that one of the essentials of combat morale was 'confidence in leadership and ... an acceptance of the basic philosophy governing human relationships within an army'.[181] He described the art of leading as 'the art of dealing with humanity, of working diligently on behalf of men, of being sympathetic with them, but equally, of insisting that they make a square facing toward their own problems'.[182] It was important to morale, in Marshall's view, that a commander should have a relationship with his troops; 'the values which derive from inspection and personal reconnaissance are in direct ratio to the difficulties of the situation'.[183]

According to Marshall, the soldier with a positive attitude towards his commanders would 'stand iron rations and the misery of outdoor living in foul weather for indefinite periods, provided that his tactical experience ma[de] sense and he remain[ed] convinced of the general soundness of operations'. Once he lost that faith, however, it became very difficult to restore his confidence. The combat soldier lost his faith in his commanders once he saw that casualties were wasted on useless operations or when he began to feel that he was in any respect the victim of bad planning or faulty concepts.[184]

---

[179] Shils and Janowitz, 'Cohesion and Disintegration in the Wehrmacht in World War II', pp. 297–8.
[180] Alan Hawley, 'People Not Personnel: The Human Dimension of Fighting Power', in Hew Strachan (ed.), *The British Army, Manpower and Society into the Twenty-First Century* (London 2000), p. 213.
[181] Marshall, *Men against Fire*, p. 165.   [182] Ibid., p. 160.
[183] Ibid., p. 105.   [184] Ibid., pp. 105–6.

Neither Shils and Janowitz nor Stouffer saw leadership and command, in the sense being discussed here, as being overly important to morale. Stouffer did, however, accept that 'such factors as the existence of personally dramatic commanders in particular high headquarters may have had an effect on the extent to which the higher headquarters impressed themselves on the men'.[185]

Shils and Janowitz were more concerned with the leadership role of Adolf Hitler rather than specific army commanders. They argued that, for German soldiers, Hitler personified the concept of leadership and the strong identification with the Führer was one of the prime motivational factors in the Wehrmacht's stoic resistance to the very end.[186] According to Guy Sajer, German soldiers believed so fanatically in Hitler's leadership abilities that they thought, right up to 1945, that victory could be grasped from the jaws of defeat.[187]

For the British Army, command carried an importance arguably greater than in other armies in the Second World War. This was because it adopted a master-plan approach to controlling battles and the chaos that ensued from contact with the enemy. British doctrine required the senior officer in command to issue precise orders to his subordinates, who were expected to carry them out unwaveringly. 'Co-operation', the Field Service Regulations of 1924 asserted, 'can be ensured only by unity of control.'[188]

This meant that the British Army tended to prefer set-piece rehearsed battles, such as those in the First World War, to the 'encounter' type battles that were more frequent in the vast open spaces of the desert. O'Connor had planned his successful campaign against the Italians, in 1940/41, a month before the start date. As a result, much like Montgomery before El Alamein, he was able to carry out a precise rehearsal a few days before the operation began to give his troops confidence and experience. Because the British Army relied on a preconceived master plan, it was particularly vulnerable if events did not go according to the script. Hence it was essential to have a good plan and a commander who could create such a plan. The ingenuity and unpredictable nature of Rommel made the issue even more pertinent in the desert.

The remarkable effect Montgomery's leadership style had on the troops has been discussed in Chapter 6. The improvement in officer selection

---

[185] Stouffer, *The American Soldier*, p. 315.
[186] Shils and Janowitz, 'Cohesion and Disintegration in the Wehrmacht in World War II', p. 302.
[187] Guy Sajer, *The Forgotten Soldier: War on the Russian Front – A True Story* (London, 1999).
[188] French, *Raising Churchill's Army*, p. 19.

and education (Chapter 3) also played a role in ensuring that primary group leadership had improved by the time of El Alamein. This combined improvement in leadership and command in Eighth Army played a dramatic and important role in the turn around in morale that was a decisive factor in victory at El Alamein.

Another factor addressed in this book is the effect of success in battle on morale. Field Marshal Bill Slim, who commanded the British Fourteenth Army against the Japanese in Burma, believed that the most important effect of any successful offensive was its impact on the morale of the troops.[189] Strategic and tactical reverses, on the other hand, were damaging to morale.[190]

Shils and Janowitz, having studied the German retreats in North Africa in 1943, and in France and Germany in September and October 1944 and March 1945, echoed these sentiments.

As long as a retreat is orderly and the structure of the component units of an army is maintained, strategic difficulties do not break up the army. An army in retreat breaks up only when the retreat is poorly organized, when command is lost over the men, so that they become separated from their units and become stragglers, or when enemy penetrations isolate larger or smaller formations from the main group.[191]

Marshall succinctly summed up the relationship between success and morale thus. 'In combat nothing succeeds like success. The knowledge of victory is the beginning of a conviction of superiority. Just as truly, the savor of one small triumph will wholly drive out the bitter taste of any number of demoralizing defeats.'[192]

Montgomery understood the relevance of this aspect of morale. 'High morale', in his opinion, 'was a pearl of great price' and a sure way to obtain it was 'success in battle'.[193] Eighth Army's lack of success was one of the main reasons for the morale problems that developed in the summer of 1942. He wrote, following the war, that 'high morale is possible in defeat but not during a long period of defeat. On such occasions confidence in the leaders will inevitably wane and ... be undermined. Success will aid good morale by creating confidence in the leader and in the Command.'[194]

---

[189] Slim, *Defeat into Victory*, p. 150.
[190] NA WO 193/453 Draft Morale Report, May to July 1942.
[191] Shils and Janowitz, 'Cohesion and Disintegration in the Wehrmacht in World War II', p. 289.
[192] Marshall, *Men against Fire*, p. 122.
[193] NA WO 277/7 McPherson, *Army: Discipline*, p. 13.
[194] IWM Briggs Papers, Morale in Battle: Analysis by Montgomery, April 1946.

Montgomery only asked of his troops what they were capable of and trained to do. He fought a limited and successful battle at Alam Halfa that was a masterpiece in managing the human factor in warfare. The confidence derived from Alam Halfa catapulted Eighth Army out of the doldrums of the summer months, reinvigorated morale, and prepared the troops for the great battle to come.

Since 1945, a number of theories have been adduced to explain what maintains morale in modern war. The most dominant of these explanations has been primary group theory. Primary group theory, however, has been shown to contain serious defects as a catch-all explanation for combat morale and motivation. Marshall stated that 'it should be well recognized that everything which touches the circumference of tactics bears sooner or later on the heart of the fighting man – his will to win, his courage to act and to endure'.[195] Stouffer commented that 'the motivation of combat behaviour was so complex that at most it c[ould] be hoped that few major factors have been entirely neglected'.[196]

In the final analysis, it is clear that no one factor can explain the causes of good and poor morale in the desert. Factors such as technology, environment and provisions, manpower, welfare, education, leadership and command, training, the primary group, discipline/coercion, belief in a cause and success in battle, all played a role in developing morale. Any morale theory should, therefore, incorporate the impacts of all of these factors. Morale would seem to be multidimensional and any attempt to understand and influence it must acknowledge that reality.

[195] Marshall, *Men against Fire*, pp. 157–8.   [196] Stouffer, *The American Soldier*, p. 106.

Conclusion

Let me then assure you, soldiers and airmen, that your fellow-countrymen regard your joint work with admiration and gratitude, and that after the war when a man is asked what he did it will be quite sufficient for him to say, 'I marched and fought with the Desert Army.' And when history is written and all the facts are known, your feats will gleam and glow and will be a source of song and story long after we who are gathered here have passed away.[1]

(Winston Churchill)

The consistent narrative that emerges from the research presented in this book is that success in battle is significantly influenced by morale, the soldier's willingness, engendered by desire or discipline, to prepare for and engage in the actions required by the military. However, morale is fragile and fluid, and needs to be nurtured and developed for armies to prevail. This book has examined the North African campaign of the Second World War through the lens of morale and has shown how the morale of the troops was reflected in the performance of Eighth Army on the battlefield, from the WDF's victory over the Italians in 1940/41, to the crisis in the summer of 1942 that nearly cost Eighth Army the desert war, to the resurgence that ultimately led to victory at El Alamein.

This perspective on war is not a new one; military theorists and practitioners, from Xenophon to Clausewitz to Rupert Smith, have argued for the primacy of morale and psychological factors in war. During the Second World War, the highest ranking officers in the British Army recognised the significance of morale in deciding defeat and victory. Nevertheless, morale is not the generally accepted explanation for the outcomes of the major engagements of the desert war.[2]

---

[1] Winston S. Churchill (ed.), *Never Give In! The Best of Winston Churchill's Speeches* (London, 2003), p. 348.
[2] See for example, Barnett, *The Desert Generals*; Connell, *Auchinleck*; Pitt, *Auchinleck's Command*; Pitt, *Montgomery and Alamein*; Young, *Rommel;* Bungay, *Alamein;* Latimer, *Alamein;* Barr, *Pendulum of War*; Johnston and Stanley, *Alamein*; Kitchen, *Rommel's Desert War*.

There is an intricate web of factors that can be considered when studying morale. Some of these are primarily outcomes or correlates of morale; desertion, sickness, battle exhaustion and missing/surrender rates, for example, fall into this category. Others, such as weapons, quality of manpower and the primary group, are influencers or determinants of morale. All of these factors are amenable to qualitative analysis; some, however, are also readily assessable by more quantitative approaches. The integrated presentation of qualitative and quantitative analyses of the sources gives added texture to the picture of morale that has emerged.

This book has focused on Eighth Army's path to the decisive engagement of the North African campaign, the battle of El Alamein (23 October to 5 November 1942). In so doing it has analysed, in particular, the causes of Eighth Army's defeats in the immediate run up to that critical battle, at Gazala and Tobruk in May and June 1942, and the factors that led to stalemate on the El Alamein line in July 1942. It has argued that these failures were influenced significantly by a morale crisis that reached a peak in the first two weeks of August 1942. The censorship summary for that period stated categorically that the troops' mail showed 'little or no traces of the offensive spirit, and an almost complete absence of any reference to forcing the enemy to give up the ground gained in the last two months'.[3] Eighth Army also exhibited a number of measurable outcomes of poor morale that confirmed that morale was indeed at an all time low. For example, Eighth Army suffered a 73% increase in sickness between March and August 1942.[4] In July, battle exhaustion cases caused between 7 to 10% of the total sick and battle casualties.[5] More specifically, they caused around 26% of South African battle casualties.[6] They caused 28% of New Zealand battle casualties in August.[7] The situation as regards desertion was so serious that, in July 1942, the Commander-in-Chief, Claude Auchinleck, with the unanimous agreement of his army commanders, sought the reintroduction of the death penalty for desertion and cowardice in the field. Auchinleck presented figures to the War Office to support his request showing that around 88% of casualties during the summer fighting could be classified as missing or having surrendered.[8]

---

[3] ANZ WAII/1/DA/508/1 vol. 1, MEMCWS, no. XXXIX (5 to 11 August 1942), p. 1.
[4] NA WO 177/324 Monthly Report on Health Eighth Army, March, July, August 1942.
[5] NA WO 177/324 Memo 'Sickness, Army Troops', by DDMS Eighth Army, 26 July 1942; Report on Tour of Eighth Army, 18 to 24 July 1942 by Consultant in Psychological Medicine (Brig. G. W. B. James), 28 July 1942.
[6] NA WO 177/324 Monthly Statistical Report on Health Eighth Army, July 1942.
[7] ANZ WAII/8/Part 2/BBB Freyberg Papers, Morale.
[8] NA WO 163/89 ECAC, The Death Penalty for Offences Committed on Active Service, 21 July 1942.

It is clear that this situation was rectified, and that a dramatic turnaround in the fortunes of Eighth Army took place in September and October 1942. This turnaround, it is argued, was driven by a resurgence of morale. The censorship summary for 21 October to 3 November reported that 'morale displayed in correspondence from forward ... troops' had 'never reached a higher level'.[9] The incidence of battle exhaustion during the thirteen days of fighting at El Alamein was remarkably low, especially for an attritional infantry battle.[10] The monthly statistical reports on the health of Eighth Army for October and November 1942 stated that the incidence of exhaustion was much smaller during the offensive than it had been in previous battles, the total number of cases for the two months combined being 209. The number for the July battles alone had been 557.[11] The 2nd New Zealand Division suffered only fifty-seven instances of battle exhaustion at El Alamein. This represented a ratio of 1 to 100 battle casualties, the lowest New Zealand ratio of the war.[12] The South Africans suffered a rate of 2 exhaustion cases per 100 battle casualties. The rate during the summer battles had been 26 cases per 100 battle casualties.[13] The daily sick admission rate was also remarkably low. By November, the rate was 1.6 per 1,000 (a monthly rate of 47.7 per 1,000), a 33 per cent drop from 2.4 (a monthly rate of 75 per 1,000) in August. The incidence of surrender and desertion also dramatically decreased. At El Alamein, those who were missing or captured made up only 17 per cent of casualties. This morale turnaround decisively influenced the performance of Eighth Army at El Alamein, and thus played a crucial role in deciding the outcome of the battle.

This book has also questioned a number of accepted explanations for defeat and victory in North Africa. In particular, it has rejected the contention that Allied success in the desert war was a function of technological and numerical superiority.[14] It has been argued, instead, that a key contribution made by weapons was their effect in both building and impairing morale. Eighth Army possessed a numerical advantage in weapons and manpower throughout 1942 that rarely converted into strategic or tactical success. Instead, the confidence, or lack of it, that soldiers had in

[9] AWM 54 423/11/43 MEMCFS, no. XLIX (21 October to 3 November 1942), p. 27.
[10] Shephard, *A War Of Nerves*, p. 217; Harrison, *Medicine and Victory*, p. 123.
[11] NA WO 177/324 Monthly Statistical Report on Health of Eighth Army, October and November 1942.
[12] ANZ WAII/8/Part 2/BBB Freyberg Papers, Morale.
[13] NA WO 177/324 Monthly Statistical Report on Health Eighth Army, July 1942.
[14] Warlimont, 'The Decision in the Mediterranean 1942' in Jacobsen and Rohwer (eds.), *The Decisive Battles of World War II*, p. 203; ANZ WAII/11/20 German–Italian Forces in Africa 23 October 1942 to 23 February 1943. German War Narrative, 2 November 1942.

their own weapons, as compared with those of their enemy, played a fundamentally important role in convincing them whether to risk their lives or not. Many of the Axis victories of 1941 and 1942 were influenced by the perceived inferiority of Eighth Army's weapons. This had a profound effect on the morale of the troops, and thus a considerable effect on Eighth Army's combat performance.

Furthermore, the creation of brigade groups and Jock columns led to dispersal instead of concentration and prevented Eighth Army from amassing sufficient firepower at the decisive point of engagement, meaning that units, in spite of their superior numbers, were normally outgunned when they met the *Panzerarmee*. This, in turn, had a detrimental effect on morale as tank units, anti-tank detachments and infantry battalions lost confidence in their ability to defend themselves and attack effectively.

Montgomery, on his arrival as Commander Eighth Army, made a number of decisions that considerably offset the disadvantages under which Eighth Army laboured. He announced that divisions would fight as divisions and he put a firm end to the use of brigade groups and Jock columns, a policy that Auchinleck had begun to revise during the summer battles on the El Alamein line. He devised a defensive plan at Alam Halfa and a plan of attack at El Alamein that focused on achieving the possible rather than what might have been ideally desired with the quality and quantity of the weapons at his disposal. At Alam Halfa, Montgomery refused to 'let loose' his armoured brigades, who had lost their confidence, to take on the German panzers. Instead, he fought an entirely defensive battle, in which he used his concentrated artillery to bombard and destroy the attacking *Panzerarmee*'s morale. At El Alamein, Montgomery reversed the normal plan of attack in desert warfare. His offensive utilised his best forces, his infantry and his artillery, rather than the armoured brigades, whose morale was less sound, to break into the Axis positions.

Montgomery realised that his technological and numerical advantage did not guarantee him victory any more than it had guaranteed Auchinleck success in the summer battles. His infantry only had a two-to-one numerical advantage, instead of the three-to-one advantage usually considered necessary for a frontal attack to succeed. El Alamein, therefore, involved a hard and bloody infantry battle that required the highest levels of morale and determination from the troops. The lessons from operations derived from the battle acknowledged that 'considering the density of the artillery support during the various attacks, the number of enemy dead and wounded found by the leading troops was surprisingly light, and that enemy automatic weapons quickly opened up when the barrage or concentration ... passed'.[15] The superiority in firepower enjoyed by Eighth Army over the Axis, it is argued, functioned primarily as a tool to encourage the troops and demoralise the enemy rather than as a battle-winning factor all of its own.

A deficiency in the quality of its manpower was another cause for concern in Eighth Army. On the outbreak of war in September 1939, the British Army was forced to admit into its ranks large numbers of men of inferior intellectual and psychological outlook. Such men tended to experience particular problems in integrating into the primary group. Throughout 1941 and 1942, psychologists such as Brigadier G. W. B. James and Major H. B. Craigie who worked in the desert highlighted the effect such large numbers of 'problem characters' were having on the efficiency of Eighth Army. The incidence of neuroses and desertion throughout June, July and August 1942 was undoubtedly influenced, to a degree, by the presence of high numbers of intellectually deficient and psychologically defective men.

The appointment of Ronald Adam as Adjutant-General in the War Office marked a turning point in the army's use of manpower during the Second World War. Adam introduced selection procedures, through the Directorate of Selection of Personnel, that were designed both to classify and to allocate soldiers depending on their intellectual and psychological capacities. The directorate was also given the role of 'weeding out' many misplaced individuals (misfits) who had been incorrectly allocated within the army during the first years of the war.

Adam's initiatives began to bear fruit by August and September 1942.[16] Improved selection techniques and screening of overseas drafts dramatically reduced the number of unsuitable men sent overseas. The fact that selection procedures, such as the Matrix test, were sent to, and put into practice in, the Middle East, also allowed psychologists in the theatre to weed out 'problem cases' from front-line units.

In addition, Adam introduced measures to improve the quality of officers in the army. J. H. A Sparrow, the compiler of the army morale reports during the war, admitted after the war that creating 'a sufficient number of first-class officers – whatever pains were spent on perfecting the methods of selection and of training – was an impossible task'. Sparrow wrote that 'the shortage of good officer material was perhaps the gravest of all the enemies to military morale, and "man-management" was the

---

[15] NA WO 201/2596 Lessons from Operations: Training. Preliminary Draft Lessons from Operations, October and November 1942 (referring to the battle of El Alamein), p. 24.

[16] NA WO 32/11972 Correspondence between the Army Council Secretariat and the DAG, Letter from DAG to ACS, 7 August 1942.

lesson that a large proportion of officers found it hardest to learn'.[17] The evidence from the censorship summaries suggests that, although poor man-management techniques played a significant role in negatively affecting morale during the summer months of 1942, by the autumn man-management and officer–man relations were better than they had ever been in Eighth Army. Improved selection and allocation, in both the UK and Middle East, combined with a concerted effort to educate officers in the need for and methods of man-management, made a difference to the morale of Eighth Army by the crucial battle of El Alamein.

The ordeal of fighting in an inhospitable and alien environment was almost constant throughout the desert war. Whether in advance or in retreat, the flies were intolerable, the sand was unbearable and hunger and thirst were inevitable. However, it was noticeable that Eighth Army tended to perform better in the winter months of 1940, 1941 and 1942 when the heat of the desert sun and all the problems that accompanied it were less extreme. The rout of the Italians, Crusader and El Alamein all occurred in the months of October, November, December and January. Conversely, the serious setbacks suffered by the Western Desert Force and Eighth Army were mainly in the summer months of 1941 and 1942. Although conditions were still extraordinarily difficult during the battle of El Alamein, it is fair to say that their effect on morale was reduced by the cooler days that arrived with the coming of winter. The field censorship summaries also reveal that throughout 1942, and noticeably towards its second half, problems arising from rations and water and other supplies all ameliorated. The men in the desert undoubtedly 'had it better' in the lead-up to El Alamein than they did a few months earlier, with a consequent rise in morale.

Although the men of Eighth Army were physically 'imprisoned' in the desert, they were psychologically and emotionally still resident in Britain, Australia, New Zealand or South Africa. The ability of the army to help bridge the emotional gap between the desert and their homes and loved ones, through welfare policies and practices, was, therefore, key to morale.

The introduction of a central welfare organisation in the first year of the war marked a step forward from the First World War, when no comparable organisation had existed, and signified the seriousness with which the War Office viewed the subject. The new Directorate of Army Welfare and Education, controlled by Major-General H. Willans, and closely tied to Adam as Adjutant-General, oversaw and encouraged a number of schemes that both centrally supported the soldiers' welfare and educated regimental officers in welfare matters.

[17] NA WO 277/4 Morgan, *Army Welfare*, p. 21.

News from home and about the war generally was especially important. Major efforts were made, throughout the war, to improve the regularity of mail and the tone and tenor of the BBC's war coverage. Of perhaps greatest significance was the part welfare played in maintaining the soldiers' relationships with their women. The length of separation, combined with the irregularity and slowness of mails, put tremendous strain on many relationships. No news or bad news could cause misunderstandings or jealousies, which were a real and substantial danger to morale. These trends were exacerbated by the presence of large numbers of foreign Allied troops in the British, New Zealand, Australian and South African homelands. Concern about these men drove the soldiers of Eighth Army to such levels of jealousy and worry about the fidelity of their loved ones that the problem almost became an epidemic. To counteract such worries Adam and Willans put in place a sophisticated and compassionate scheme of initiatives, using the aid of the SSAFA to patch up misunderstandings, or, if the need was there, to initiate legal proceedings for divorce. These schemes reassured the soldier that he was part of a benevolent organisation that cared for his needs and understood his psychology.

These improvements brought the soldier emotionally closer to home and made him feel like a recognised and valued member of the war effort, with a consequent effect on morale. The introduction of army education built on these changes. Education, through the Army Education Corps and Army Bureau of Current Affairs, reinforced the soldier's connection with the causes for which he was fighting, and, therefore, with his homeland. Education also informed the soldier of what he could expect from a post-war world. These enlightened measures affected combat motivation from El Alamein onwards and proved so successful that they were requested for the invasion of Sicily in 1943.

Due attention has also been given to the quality of leadership and command provided at army level in the desert. Notwithstanding Auchinleck's many positive attributes, his policies, personality and tactical approach to warfare did play a part in causing the morale crisis of June, July and August 1942. Montgomery differentiated himself from his predecessor by introducing innovative policies that placed the human factor first and foremost. He concentrated on four critical elements of leadership and command that directly impinged on morale: clarity of direction, communication with the troops, the commander's image and the handling of formations. His contribution undoubtedly helped to build the morale of Eighth Army and shape it into a successful fighting force. The legend of Montgomery's impact on the morale of Eighth Army was, in fact, a reality.

The attention given to training was also affected by the style and character of Eighth Army's leaders. The Soldiers of Eighth Army, all too often, were thrown into battle without adequate training in the tactics or weapons they were provided with. While this was a problem repeatedly highlighted by commanders, it was one that was not adequately addressed until Montgomery arrived on the scene. Montgomery, like Auchinleck before him, recognised the fact that Eighth Army was insufficiently trained. However, unlike Auchinleck, he developed a style of warfare that catered for this undertrained army. His strategy at Alam Halfa, and beyond, was shaped by the need to develop confidence and maintain morale by only asking of the troops what they were capable of doing. Montgomery, whose reputation as a trainer of men has remained intact, developed his training programme along three clear lines: further toughening and hardening of the troops, developing battle drills suited to the operation, and making training so similar to the initial attack that every man and officer would become familiar with the part he was to play. His clearly thought out preparation of the troops before El Alamein played a crucial role in convincing them that they were ready, this time, to defeat Rommel.

This book suggests that a re-evaluation is necessary of the relevance of primary group theory to the war in the desert and to its ability to provide an all-encompassing explanation of battle morale and motivation. It is clear that the high number of casualties, cases of battle exhaustion and misfits in fighting units must have severely hampered the functioning of primary groups as positive motivating influences in the prevailing battle conditions. The dispersion of forces due to the destructive effect of modern firepower, and the possible negative influence of primary groups, which could inculcate behaviours contrary to the best interests of the army (such as surrender), may also have reduced the ability of the primary group to act as a positive motivating force. Other factors, as well as the primary group, played a part in developing and sustaining morale in Eighth Army. These include discipline/coercion, ideology, training, confidence in weapons, management of the impact of the environment and provisions, welfare and education, success in battle, and leadership and command. It can be concluded that, at least in the context of the war in the desert, primary group theory, on its own, is not a sufficient explanation of morale and motivation among combat troops and that any such theory should take account of the many factors that are influences on or correlates of morale. Morale is multidimensional and any attempt to understand and influence it must acknowledge that reality.

It has not been the purpose of this study to bring the courage of any of the men who fought in the desert into question. Men are as much a product of their environment as they are a function of their own innate nature and character. The army that fought in the desert in the summer of 1942 was inadequately trained, poorly equipped and averagely led. It is testament to the soldiers of Eighth Army that, once these handicaps had been removed, they fought with determination and resilience at El Alamein and beyond.

Nor has this book been conceived as an explanation for, or a defence of, Montgomery's record as a commander in the Second World War. Montgomery's failings, both as a commander and as a man, have been well documented. However, this study does clearly show that Montgomery played a vital role in turning a defeated army into a victorious one in the desert. His subsequent failings should not detract from his unquestionable contribution to reinvigorating and sustaining Eighth Army's morale at a crucial moment of the war.

With a new commander, better training, better weapons and a more enlightened War Office approach to the human problems of war, a more confident citizen army emerged victorious at El Alamein. The many key elements that engendered and maintained morale were all deflated in the summer months of 1942. This in turn affected combat performance. Many of these factors had recovered and reached a peak by October 1942, just in time for the crucial battle of El Alamein. This morale turnaround should be considered as key to the success of Eighth Army, and given its proper place by historians among the causes of victory and defeat in the desert war.

Appendix: Battle maps

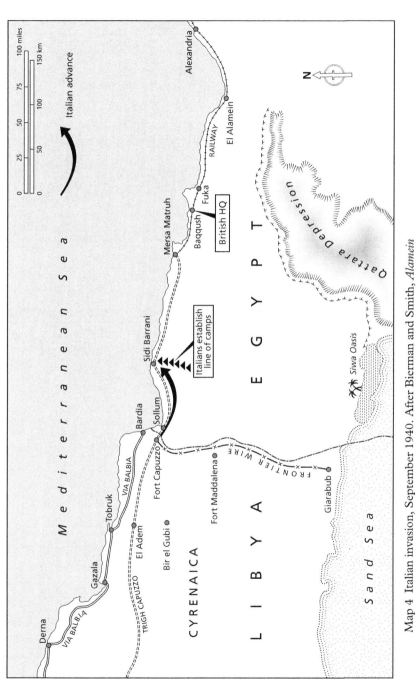

Map 4 Italian invasion, September 1940. After Bierman and Smith, *Alamein*

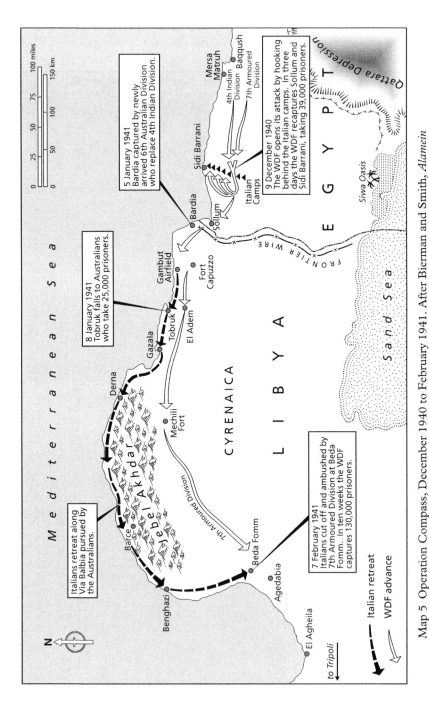

Map 5 Operation Compass, December 1940 to February 1941. After Bierman and Smith, *Alamein*

Mediterranean Sea

100 miles
150 km

0   25   50   75   100 miles
0   50   100   150 km

N

5 January 1941
Bardia captured by newly arrived 6th Australian Division who replace 4th Indian Division.

8 January 1941
Tobruk falls to Australians who take 25,000 prisoners.

9 December 1940
The WDF opens its attack by hooking behind the Italian camps. In three days the WDF recaptures Sollum and Sidi Barrani, taking 39,000 prisoners.

Italians retreat along Via Balbia pursued by the Australians.

7 February 1941
Italians cut off and ambushed by 7th Armoured Division at Beda Fomm. In ten weeks the WDF captures 130,000 prisoners.

Mersa Matruh

4th Indian Division   Baqqush   7th Armoured Division

Sidi Barrani

Italian Camps

Bardia

Sollum

Gambut Airfield

Fort Capuzzo

Tobruk

El Adem

Gazala

Derna

Mechili Fort

7th Armoured Division

Barce

Benghazi

Beda Fomm

Agedabia

El Agheila

to Tripoli

Jebel Akhdar

CYRENAICA

LIBYA

EGYPT

Qattara Depression

Siwa Oasis

Sand Sea

FRONTIER WIRE

Italian retreat
WDF advance

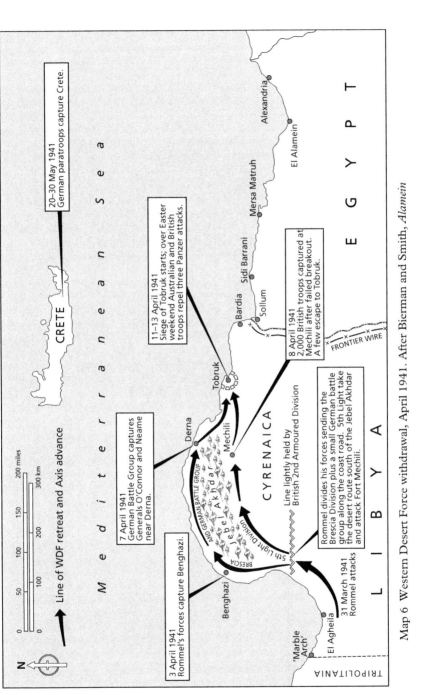

N

| 0 | 50 | 100 | 150 | 200 miles |
| 0 | 100 | 200 | 300 km |

→ Line of WDF retreat and Axis advance

20–30 May 1941
German paratroops capture Crete.

CRETE

M e d i t e r r a n e a n   S e a

11–13 April 1941
Siege of Tobruk starts; over Easter
weekend Australian and British
troops repel three Panzer attacks.

7 April 1941
German Battle Group captures
Generals O'Connor and Neame
near Derna.

3 April 1941
Rommel's forces capture Benghazi.

Tobruk

Derna

Mechili

Benghazi

BRESCIA

J e b e l   A k h d a r

AND GERMAN BATTLE GROUP

5th Light Division

CYRENAICA

L I B Y A

'Marble Arch'

El Agheila

31 March 1941
Rommel attacks

Rommel divides his forces sending the
Brescia Division plus a small German battle
group along the coast road. 5th Light take
the desert route south of the Jebel Akhdar
and attack Fort Mechili.

Line lightly held by
British 2nd Armoured Division

8 April 1941
2,000 British troops captured at
Mechili after failed breakout.
A few escape to Tobruk.

Bardia

Sidi Barrani

Sollum

FRONTIER WIRE

Mersa Matruh

E G Y P T

Alexandria

El Alamein

TRIPOLITANIA

Map 6 Western Desert Force withdrawal, April 1941. After Bierman and Smith, *Alamein*

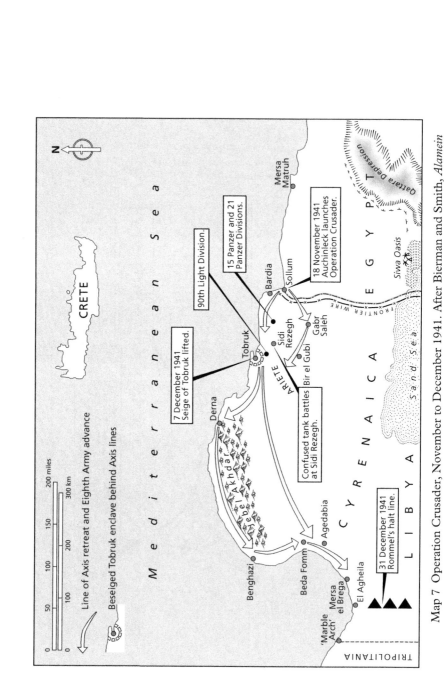

Map 7 Operation Crusader, November to December 1941. After Bierman and Smith, *Alamein*

Map labels

N

Line of Axis retreat and Eighth Army advance

Beseiged Tobruk enclave behind Axis lines

0 50 100 150 200 miles
0 100 200 300 km

CRETE

Mediterranean Sea

90th Light Division.

15 Panzer and 21 Panzer Divisions.

18 November 1941 Auchinleck launches Operation Crusader.

7 December 1941 Seige of Tobruk lifted.

Confused tank battles at Sidi Rezegh.

31 December 1941 Rommel's halt line.

Mersa Matruh

Bardia

Sollum

Gabr Saleh

Sidi Rezegh

Bir el Gubi

ARIETE

Tobruk

Derna

Jebel Akhdar

Benghazi

Agedabia

Beda Fomm

El Agheila

Mersa el Brega

'Marble Arch'

FRONTIER WIRE

Siwa Oasis

Sand Sea

Qattara Depression

E G Y P T

C Y R E N A I C A

L I B Y A

TRIPOLITANIA

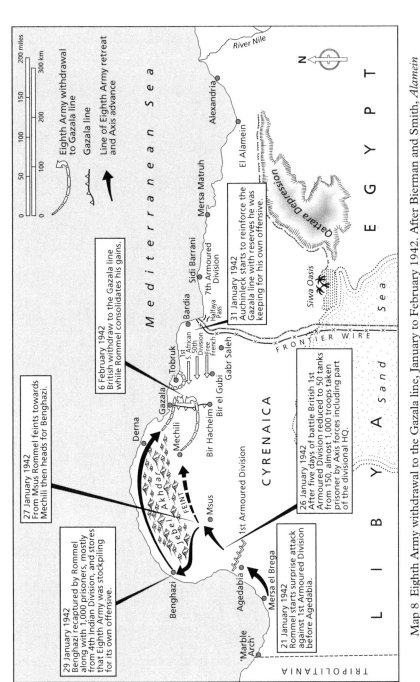

27 January 1942
From Msus Rommel feints towards Mechili then heads for Benghazi.

6 February 1942
British withdraw to the Gazala line while Rommel consolidates his gains.

29 January 1942
Benghazi recaptured by Rommel along with 1,000 prisoners, mostly from 4th Indian Division, and stores that Eighth Army was stockpiling for its own offensive.

31 January 1942
Auchinleck starts to reinforce the Gazala line with reserves he was keeping for his own offensive.

26 January 1942
After five days of battle British 1st Armoured Division reduced to 50 tanks from 150, almost 1,000 troops taken prisoner by Axis forces including part of the divisional HQ.

21 January 1942
Rommel starts surprise attack against 1st Armoured Division before Agedabia.

Eighth Army withdrawal to Gazala line

Gazala line

Line of Eighth Army retreat and Axis advance

Map 8 Eighth Army withdrawal to the Gazala line, January to February 1942. After Bierman and Smith, *Alamein*

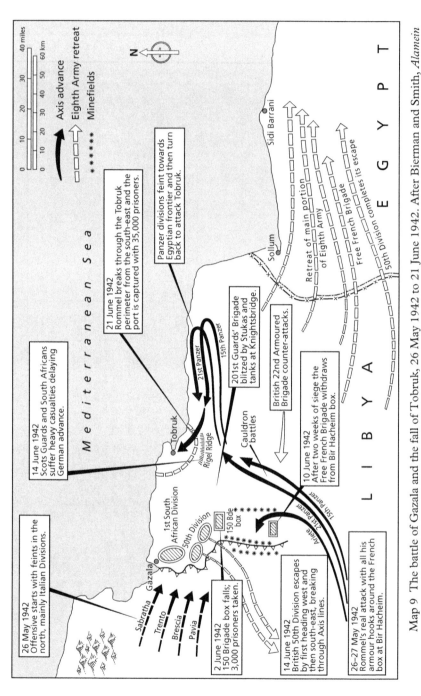

Map 9 The battle of Gazala and the fall of Tobruk, 26 May 1942 to 21 June 1942. After Bierman and Smith, *Alamein*

Map labels and annotations:

40 miles
60 km

Axis advance
Eighth Army retreat
Minefields

N

Mediterranean Sea

14 June 1942
Scots Guards and South Africans suffer heavy casualties delaying German advance.

21 June 1942
Rommel breaks through the Tobruk perimeter from the south-east and the port is captured with 35,000 prisoners.

Panzer divisions feint towards Egyptian frontier and then turn back to attack Tobruk.

Sidi Barrani

Sollum

Tobruk

21st Panzer
15th Panzer

Rigel Ridge

201st Guards' Brigade blitzed by Stukas and tanks at Knightsbridge.

British 22nd Armoured Brigade counter-attacks.

Cauldron battles

10 June 1942
After two weeks of siege the Free French Brigade withdraws from Bir Hacheim box.

Retreat of main portion of Eighth Army

Free French Brigade's escape

50th Division completes its escape

L I B Y A

E G Y P T

26 May 1942
Offensive starts with feints in the north, mainly Italian Divisions.

1st South African Division

50th Division

150 Bde box

Sabratha
Trento
Brescia
Pavia

Gazala

2 June 1942
150 Brigade box falls; 3,000 prisoners taken.

14 June 1942
British 50th Division escapes by first heading west and then south-east, breaking through Axis lines.

Ariete
21st Panzer
15th Panzer

26–27 May 1942
Rommel's real attack with all his armour hooks around the French box at Bir Hacheim.

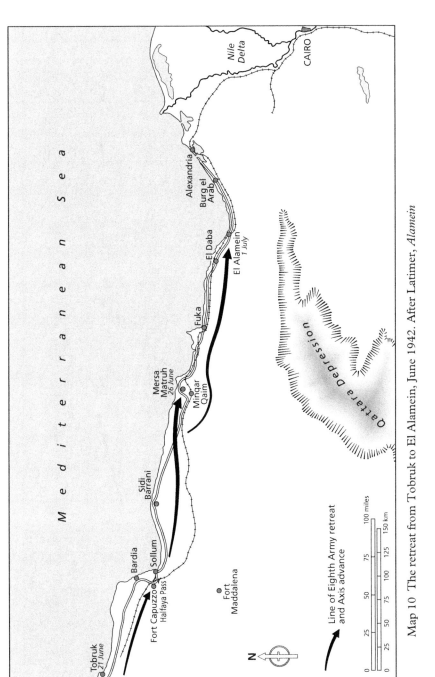

Map 10 The retreat from Tobruk to El Alamein, June 1942. After Latimer, *Alamein*

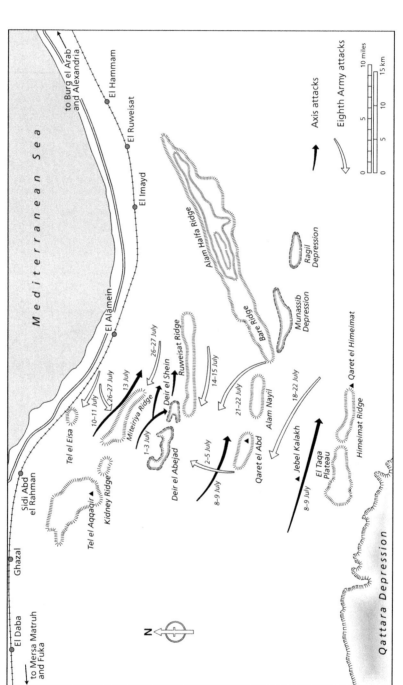

Map 11 The July battles, 1942. After Liddell Hart (ed.), *the Rommel Papers*

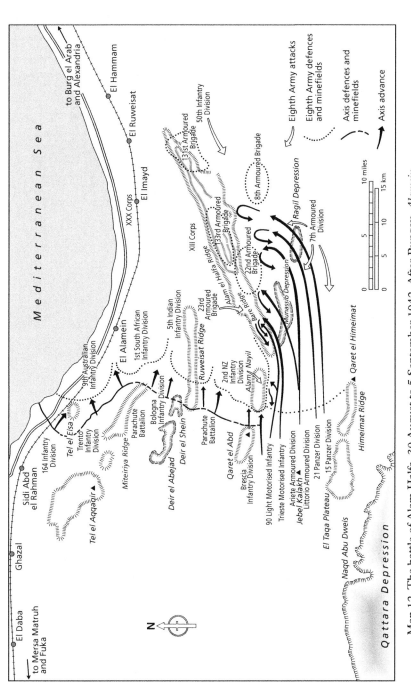

Map 12 The battle of Alam Halfa, 30 August to 5 September 1942. After Bungay, *Alamein*

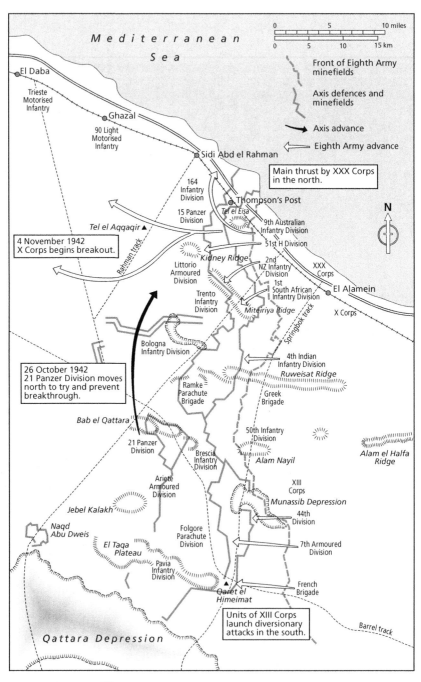

Map 13 The battle of El Alamein, 23 October to 5 November 1942.
After Neillands, *Eighth Army*

Bibliography

Primary Sources

AUSTRALIA

AUSTRALIAN WAR MEMORIAL

Printed Material

Casualties, the official magazine of 2/3 CCS.

Khamseen Kronicle, 3DRL 6338 Troopship and Unit Serials Folder 115.

Observation Post, the journal of the 2/11th Field Regiment, RAA, 8th Division, AIF.

The Observer, journal of the 2 Australian Flash Spotting Battery RAA (AIF).

The Wagflagger, AWM 077594.

Official Documents

AWM 52 11/12/12 2/3rd Field Ambulance War Diary.

AWM 54 52/2/19 Australian Army Education Service, Some Aspects of Its Functions, Group Discussion Courses, Pastime and Hobby Activities, Unit Libraries, 1942.

AWM 54 52/2/38 Army Education Service: Minutes of Conference of Deputy Assistant Adjutant General (Education) Held in Melbourne, 14, 15, 16 and 17 July 1942.

AWM 54 171/2/32 Casualties 9th Division Western Desert, 1941 to 1942.

AWM 54 171/21/43 El Alamein Battle Casualties for the Whole Period, Australian Imperial Forces.

AWM 54 175/2/1 Appointment of Capt. A. N. Cooper to LHQ Censorship.

AWM 54 265/2/4 Esprit de Corps and Discipline. The Officer's Task. Army Discipline, Dress, Saluting, Drill and Physical Fitness.

AWM 54 265/3/6 Reports re Undisciplined Acts Involving Australian Troops in Cairo and Syria, 1941 to 1942.

AWM 54 267/4/5 Disease Groups, AIF Middle East. Statistical Breakdown of Diseases and Disabilities in Their Categories – (Numbers and Period of Treatment), October to December 1941.

AWM 54 335/10/11 'Mines by the Million', by Lieut.-Col. Paul W. Thompson – from the *Infantry Journal*, December 1942.

AWM 54 421/1/2 The Toll of Accidents in the AIF Middle East, 1942.

AWM 54 423/11/43 Middle East Military Censorship Fortnightly Summary, November/December 1942.

AWM 54 481/7/48 Detailed Statistics over Short Period Middle East.

AWM 54 481/12/59 Medical Aspects of the Alamein Battle, Report by Colonel H. G. Furnell ADMS 9th Australian Division, 1942.

AWM 54 481/12/73 Correspondence and Reports Dealing with Scheme for Occupational Therapy for Men Suffering from Neuroses.

AWM 54 481/12/120 'War Neurosis at Tobruk' by E. L. Cooper, Lieut.-Col., and A. J. M. Sinclair, Capt., AAMC, AIF.

AWM 54 492/4/34 War History of the Australian Army Education Service, 1939 to 1945.

AWM 54 492/4/76 War History Branch, Department of Internal Affairs, Wellington New Zealand. German–Italian Forces in Africa, 20 June to 27 July 1942. Translation of Appendices to German War Narrative.

AWM 54 423/4/103 *Panzerarmee* War Diary, 3 July 1942.

AWM 54 423/11/18 Part 5 App. 'A' to 9th Australian Division Intelligence Summary no. 356. Diary of Gnr. Alfred Zeigler.

AWM 54 519/3/7 The Last Campaign in North Africa 1942 to 1943. Operations as Affecting the Medical Services, 1941 to 1942.

AWM 519/6/15 Précis of an Appreciation by the Commander-in-Chief Middle East at Eighth Army at 0800 hrs, 1 August 1942.

AWM 54 519/7/26 Lessons of Second Libyan Campaign, 9th Division Training Instruction.

AWM 54 522/1/2 Lieut.-Gen. Morshead Letter, and 3 Pages of Comments on the Fighting in Tobruk and at El Alamein, to Colonel Rasmussen DGPR, August 1944.

AWM 54 524/7/1 Summary of the AIF's First Year Abroad.

AWM 54 526/1/1 Statement by OX 3840 Pte. W. C. Lloyd, Captured Alamein, 17 July 1942.

AWM 54 526/1/2 Statement by OX 7393 Pte. L. E. Casey, Captured Alamein, 17 July 1942.

AWM 54 526/3 Statement by OX 3841 Pte. W. H. Lloyd, Captured Alamein, 17 July 1942.

AWM 54 526/1/4 Statement by OX 7480 Pte. J. M. Welsh, Captured Alamein, 17 July 1942.

AWM 54 526/4/22 30 Corps Operation Orders. 9th Australian Division nos. 57 to 94, July to November 1942.

AWM 54 526/6/2 Libya, Day by Day, and the Battle for Egypt. Report on Withdrawal from Libya to El Alamein, 27 May 1942 to 1 August 1942.

AWM 54 526/6/4 9th Division Various Units Reports on Operations Alamein, Lightfoot, 23 October to 6 November 1942.

AWM 54 526/6/5 HQ 9th Division Report on Operations 24th Brigade, 3 to 29 July and to 6 November 1942.

AWM 54 526/6/6 Reference Notes, Memoranda, Orders and Correspondence in Connection with Lightfoot. El Alamein Operations, October/November 1942.

AWM 54 526/6/9 El Alamein, Reports on Operations, 10 to 29 July 1942. AA and QMG Branch 9th Australian Division.

AWM 54 526/6/10 20th Infantry Brigade Reports on Operation Lightfoot, October to November 1942.

AWM 54 526/6/12 24 Australian Infantry Brigade Operations, 31 October to 1 November 1942.

AWM 54 526/6/13 Battle of El Alamein, Article in *Izvestia* by Maj.-Gen. Galaktionev, 10 January 1947.

AWM 54 526/6/17 Report on Operations by 24 Australian Infantry Brigade Group on Night 26/27 July 1942.

AWM 54 526/6/19 The Crisis at El Alamein, 30 June to 4 July 1942.

AWM 54 527/1/2 Statement by OX7333 Cpl. H. C. Ellis, Captured Alamein, 31 October 1942.

AWM 54 527/1/3 Statement by Pte. R. J. Sharp, Captured Alamein, 27 July 1942.

AWM 54 527/1/4 Statement by OX 17905 Pte. L. Jackson, Captured Alamein, 29 October 1942.

AWM 54 527/6/3 LHQ Tactical School, Lessons Western Desert, in Particular El Alamein Operations, 1942.

AWM 54 527/6/9 26 Australian Infantry Brigade, Report on Operation 'Lightfoot', 23 October to 5 November 1942.

AWM 54 529/1/1 Statement by Sgt. Loney. Captured Alamein, 31 October 1942.

AWM 54 703/5/113 Order of Battle for 'Egypt Corps'.

AWM 54 805/2/1 Papers in Connection with Printing and Distribution of Army Journal *SALT*.

AWM 54 805/3/1 Current Affairs Bulletin, Responsibility for Weekly Distribution, 1942.

AWM 54 805/5/1 Australian Army Publication. Soldiering in the Tropics, Army Training Memorandum, 1942.

AWM 54 805/5/3 Verse Written by Troops.

AWM 54 805/7/1 Articles Submitted for Publication in *SALT*.

AWM 54 805/7/2 AIF News. Copy of Final Report and Supporting Details, February 1943.

AWM 54 805/7/4 Proposal for Issue of Daily Bulletin to AIF, 1941.

AWM 54 805/7/5 Publication and Distribution of AIF News, Cairo 1942.

AWM 54 805/8/1 Contributions to AIF Christmas Book 1942.

AWM 54 829/2/1 Scheme for Rationing and Messing, Working Parties at Scattered Localities, 1942.

AWM 54 839/1/2 Liaison Officer Reports on Officer Reinforcements, Reinforcements Generally and Standard of Training of Other Ranks Arriving in the Middle East, July 1941.

AWM 839/3/2 Notes on the AIF (ME) Reinforcement Depot, 1941.

AWM 54 865/3/1 Instructions Regarding Rum Issues – Special Hospital Diets – and Issue Rum, 1940 to 1943 and 1946.

AWM 54 877/4/3 Tank Destruction School Middle East AIF, 'Tank Hunting and Destruction', 1942.

AWM 54 883/2/97 'Middle East Field Censorship: Part 1, Summary of British Troops in Egypt and Libya 1941; Part 2: Weekly Summary, British Troops in Egypt and Libya, January to June 1942'.

AWM 54 903/2/3 Parts 1, 2 and 3.

AWM 54 903/3/2 Australian Imperial Forces. Census Taken in the Middle East, with the Object of A: Enabling the Man-Power of the AIF to be Utilised to the Best Advantage. B: Planning for Post War Problems Involving the Re-absorption of the Army into Civil Life, February 1942.

AWM 54 963/23/19 Middle East, Reinforcement Position by Arms, November 1941.

AWM 67 3/220E Long, Gavin, Articles Published as Defence Correspondent of the *Sydney Morning Herald*, 1942 to 1943.

AWM 72 Item no. 22 Barton Maughan, 'Tobruk and El Alamein': chap. 15, 'The Dog Fight', October to December 1942.

AWM 72 Item no. 28 Barton Maughan, 'Tobruk and El Alamein': Notes July to October 1942.

Private Records

Butler, Papers of Lance-Corporal J. M., 2/23 Battalion 2 AIF, 3 DRL 3825.

Carleton, F. L., 2/23 Battalion, PR 91/10033.

Clothier, Sgt. L., 2/13 Battalion, PR 00588.

Cumpston, J. S., PR 87/147.

Derrick, Lt. T., 2/48 Battalion, AIF, PR 82/190.

MacArther, Sgt. K. B., 2/15 Battalion, PR 86/121.

Mears, Cpl. C. W., 2/17 Battalion, PR 84/379.

Perversi, Sgt. F. G., MSS 1605.

Plank, D. L., 2/2 MG Battalion, Wartime Letters, PR 90/182.

Watkins, Leslie W., 2/13 Battalion, MSS 1587.

Morshead, Lieutenant General Sir L., Letter to Douglas L. Dowdell on 12 November 1942, 3DRL 2562 419/28/10.

Papers of Lieut.-Gen. Sir L. Morshead

3DRL 2632 Items 46–47 Summary of 24 Australian Infantry Brigade Operation 17 July, Supplied by LO to TAC 9 Australian Division 18 July 1942.

3DRL 2632 Items 53–54 Secret and Personal Messages Sent to General Sir Thomas Blamey LHQ Melbourne from Tactical HQ 9 Australian Division, July to November 1942.

3DRL 2632 Series 2: Official Correspondence, 1916 to 1947.

3DRL 2632 Series 6: Operational Papers, Middle East, 1939 to 1945.

3DRL 2632 Series 11: Printed Material, 1941 to 1947.

3DRL 2632 Series 13: Miscellaneous, 1941 to 1947.

Blamey Papers

3DRL 6643 2/23.81 Correspondence between Blamey and Ministry of Defence.

3DRL 6643 2/31.4 Future Employment of 9th Division AIF, Report by Chiefs of Staff.

3DRL 6643 2/170.5 Correspondence between Blamey and Morshead.

Sound Archives

James Bruce.

Jack Hawkes.

Douglas LeFevre.

Stan Morton.

Georgy Pomeroy.

NATIONAL ARCHIVES OF AUSTRALIA

A2684/3 894 Future Employment of 9th Division, April 1942.
A5954/1 323/14 'Criticism of Middle East Command', by Chester Wilmot.
A5954/1 843/4 Movements of 9th Division AIF, July 1942.
A5954 574/1 Future Employment of AIF, May 1942.
A5954 574/2 Future Employment of AIF, June/July 1942.
A5954 574/3 Future Employment of AIF, October 1942 to March 1943.
A5954 762/6 Temporary Retention of 9th Division in Middle East, 1942.
A5954/69 529/9 Operations in the Middle East.
SP109/3 323/14 'Active Service' Book and 'Soldiering On'.
SP300/4 Item 145 'Discipline and Morale', by Chester Wilmot.
A5954 649/9 Eligibility of Dominion Commanders for Commands in Middle East.
A2421 G953 Self-Inflicted Wounds, Breaches of Discipline.

MARK JOHNSTON COLLECTION

Castle, Cpl. Jack, 2/32 Battalion.
Kennedy, Pte. T. J., 2/43 Battalion.
Murphy, Pte. T. L., 2/23 Battalion.
O'Dea, Pte. C. J., 2/28 Battalion.

NEW ZEALAND

ARCHIVES NEW ZEALAND

PACB 7385 W4809/1 The Disposal of Waste Material and Fly Prevention with
    Special Reference to the Middle East, 1942.

WAII/1
WAII/1/DA21.1/9/G4/11 Part 1, 2 NZ Division Field Censor Reports.
WAII/1/DA21.1/9/G4/11 Part 2, 2 NZ Division Field Censor Reports.
WAII/1/DA21.1/9/G4/12 Part 1, 2 NZ Division Field Censor Reports.
WAII/1/DA21.1/9/G4/12 Part 2, 2 NZ Division Field Censor Reports.
WAII/1/DA21.1/9/G4/12 Part 3, 2 NZ Division Field Censor Reports.
WAII/1/DA21.1/10/9 L. Inglis, Comments of Ruweisat.
WAII/1/DA156/9/G8/3 Morale, Maadi Camp.
WAII/1/DA302/15/10 2 NZ Division – Reports.
WAII/1/DA359.01/10/1 Major T. H. Bevan, the Attack on Munassib Depression
    by 132 Brigade, 4 September 1942.
WAII/1/DA407.2/12 Official List of Casualties.
WAII/1/DA407.23/1 Battle Casualties.
WAII/1/DA407.24/1 Battle Casualties.
WAII/1/DA441.23/5 Inglis, Brig. L. M., Private Diary Covering the Period
    27 June to 7 August 1942, while GOC 2 NZEF.
WAII/1/DA457 Box 15 *NZEF Times* January to December 1942.
WAII/1/DA508/1 vol. 1 and 2 Censorship Summaries.
WAII/1/DA508/1 vol. 3 Censorship Summaries.

WAII/1/DA508/1 vol. 4 Censorship Summaries.
WAII/1/DA516.23/1 Narrative of the Assault on Point 63.

WAII/2
WAII/2 Box 58 WAII/2/44 Crusader Campaign Casualties.
WAII/2 Accession W3281, Box 1, 101b part 1 The New Zealand Division in Cyrenaica and Lessons of the Campaign, part 1, Narrative and Lessons.
WAII/2 Accession W3281, Box 1, 101d part 1 The New Zealand Division in Egypt and Libya, Operations 'Lightfoot' and 'Supercharge', part 1, Narrative and Lessons.
WAII/2 Box 58 2/44 Middle East Field Censorship Weekly Summaries 1941 to 1942.

WAII/8
WAII/8/26 Freyberg General Correspondence, February to October 1942.

WAII/11
WAII/11/20 German–Italian Forces in Africa, 23 October 1942 to 23 February 1943. German War Narrative.
WAII/11/23 German–Italian Forces in Africa, 21 Panzer Division, 135 AA Regiment, 10 Panzer Division, 19 AA Division, 24 British Armoured Brigade, Translations by W. D. Dawson from German Official War Records.

TURNBULL LIBRARY MANUSCRIPT COLLECTION

Bates, Peter, Collection.
Dawson, William Denham: Diary Describing Fighting in North Africa and Italy, 1945.
Jenkin, J. M.
Little Family.
MacClean, J. N.
McClean, A. A.
Miller, L. L.

SOUTH AFRICA
SOUTH AFRICAN MILITARY ARCHIVES DEPOT
Adjutant-General
AG Group 4, Box 61
Intelligence, Security, Censorship.
Release of Casualty Information through Private Correspondence, Letter 20 March 1942.

Chief of the General Staff
Chief of the General Staff (War), Medical Services, Box 93
Annual Reports SAMC

Chief of the General Staff (War), Box 94
Middle East Notes on Intelligence in the Field.

Chief of the General Staff (War), Box 142
Personal CGS and Brooke.
CGS Personal Correspondence with Generals Wavell and Auchinleck.

Chief of the General Staff (War), Box 151
Deserters and Illegal Absentees.
Discharges.
Discipline.

Chief of the General Staff (War), Box 155
Morale of Troops in the Field.
Apathy towards the War, Morale Training.

Chief of the General Staff (War), Propaganda, Publications and Publicity, Box 201
UDF Journals and Publications.
Broadcasts by CGS.
Issues of *Kommando* (All 1950s).

Chief of the General Staff (War), Box 248
Summaries of Intelligence Summaries for CGS.

Chief of the General Staff (War), Box 267
Censorship Reports by SAAF, CMF.

Chief of the General Staff, Gp 2, Box 588
Training Memorandum, 'Morale'.

Chief of the General Staff, Gp 2, Box 643
Discipline.
Army Cooperation.

Chief of the General Staff, Gp 2, Box 651
All Training Memoranda.
Training Memoranda, Anti-Aircraft.
Training Memoranda, Artillery.
Training Memoranda, Engineers.
Training Memoranda, AFV.
Training Memoranda, Infantry.

Chief of the General Staff, Gp 2, Box 654
Training Memoranda, Lessons from Battle of Egypt – Questionnaire HQ 1
    Armoured Division, MEF, March 1943.
Middle East Military Vocabulary.
GHQ ME Tactical Discussion on New Model Infantry and Armoured Divisions,
    24 to 26 November 1942.
Smoke, Use of and Training Memoranda, vol. II.

Deputy Chief of Staff – Chief of the General Staff
DCS – CGS, Box 50
Cyrenaica – Land Operations.

DCS – CGS, Box 51
Tobruk Casualties.
Prime Minister's Appeal for Recruitment Post Tobruk.
South African Units in Tobruk.
Units in Tobruk.

Divisional Documents
Divisional Documents, Gp 1, Box 1 File no. 1
1 SA Division Artillery Equipment, February to October 1942.
General Officer Commanding, Morale.
Report on Lessons of the Operations in the Western Desert, December 1940.
Eighth Army Routine Orders, October 1941 to May 1942.

Divisional Documents, Gp 1, Box 5
1 SA Infantry Brigade Group, Report on Operations in Cyrenaica, November to
    December 1941.
1 SA Division (Operational).

Divisional Documents, Gp 1, Box 6 File no. 8
Miscellaneous Reports from Operations.
Battle Reports 5 SA Infantry Brigade, 13 November to 13 December 1941.
Operations Reports and Lessons, April to July 1942.
Operations Reports, October to December 1941.
AQ'T' Branch Reports 1st SA Division HQ, November to December 1941.

Divisional Documents, Gp 1, Box 49
1 SA Division Information Officer.
FSW Weekly Report, May to August 1941.
Field Security Service, Reports.
UWH, 1st SA Division File IS/G55.

Divisional Documents, Gp 1, Box 50 File no. 46
Censorship, June 1941 to September 1942.
Enemy Tactics, Training and Campaigns, May 1940 to May 1941.

Divisional Documents, Gp 1, Box 51 File no. 48
Censorship Correspondence, Officers and Others, February to December
    1942
1 SA Division FSS, January 1942.
Stragglers – Lists of Statements and Reports, February to May 1942.
Interrogation Reports Prisoners of War, June to October 1942.
Prisoners of War, Policy and General Correspondence, March 1942 to January
    1943.

Divisional Documents, Box 53
13 Corps I Summaries.

Divisional Documents, Box 54
Siwa Medical and Hygiene, July to September 1941.
Patrol Reports Siwa, July to September 1941.
Siwa Security, August 1941.
Matruh, July to September 1942.
1 SA Division Special ROs, Matruh Fortress Orders.
Appreciation.

Divisional Documents, Box 62
1 SA Division History (ME), CRA.
The Story of the 1 SA Division HQ and 1 SA Divisional Troops in Operations in
    Cyrenaica, 18 November to 2 December 1941.
Operations Reports, December 1941.
1 SA Division Operations Report Cyrenaica, 18 November to 2 December 1941.

Divisional Documents, Box 119
Discipline, Policy and Standing Instructions.
Discipline, June 1941 to January 1942.
Illegal Absentees, 1942.
Discipline, Illegal Absentees, January to December 1942.
Disciplinary Matters.

Divisional Documents, Box 120
Discipline, Illegal Absentees, October 1942 to January 1943.

Divisional Documents, Box 122
UDF Unit Publications.

Divisional Documents, Gp 1, Box 124 File no. 111
Morale, August to October 1942
Greetings, Congratulatory Messages.
Correspondence – Appreciations, Congratulations etc., December 1941 to June
    1942.

Divisional Documents, Box 248
Security Orders and Other Correspondence.

Union Defence Forces
UDF Box 42
Reports Neurosis Board and Disposal of Personnel so Reported on.

Union War Histories
Union War Histories, Foreign Documents, Box 184
Battle Report 1a on the Operations of Panzerarmee Afrika, 18 November 1941 to
    6 February 1942 (a), 18 November 1941 to 24 December 1941.

Union War Histories, Foreign Documents, Box 203
Der Feldzug in Nord-Afrika, Kriebel, Various Translations.
History of the Campaign in North Africa, vol. 1 part 2 by Rainer Kriebel. Up to
and Including 23 November 1941.
Geschichte Des Feldzugs in Nordafrika, 1941 to 1943 (Edited by General
Walther Nehring), vol. 1 part 2 by Rainer Kriebel Oberst (iG). From 24
November 1941 to 4 December 1941, Die Zerschlagung der 2 Neuseeland
Div.
Geschichte Des Feldzugs in Nordafrika, 1941 to 1943 (Edited by General Walther
Nehring) vol. 1 part 2 by Rainer Kriebel Oberst (iG). From 5 December 1941
to 7 February 1942.

Union War Histories, Foreign Documents, Box 205
Cavallero's Diary, 'Commando Supremo', 2 November 1941 to 31 March
1942.
UWH Translation no. 13, Ministero della Difesa, Stato Maggiore Esercito –
'Ufficio Storico, Seconda Controffensiva Italo–Tedesca in Africa
Settentrionale da El Agheila a El Alamein, (Gennaio–Settembre 1942)',
pp. 9–82.
UWH Translation no. 5, 'Seconda Controffensiva Italo–Tedesca in Africa
Settentrionale da El Agheila a El Alamein, (Gennaio–Maggio 1942)'.

Union War Histories, Civil Section Documents, Box 264
Confidential Telegrams.
Intelligence Reports.
Censorship.

Union War Histories, Civil Section Documents, Box 276
Soldiers' Riots.

Union War Histories, Draft Narratives, Box 316
Fifteenth Panzer Division Report on the Battle of Alamein and the Retreat to
Marsa El Brega, 23 October to 20 November 1942.
Twenty-first Panzer Division Report on the Battle of Alamein and the Retreat to
Marsa El Brega, 23 October to 20 November 1942.
War Diary of Panzer Army Africa, 28 July to 23 October 1942.
War Diary of Panzer Army Africa, 24 April 1942 to 25 May 1942.
War Diary of the German Africa Corps, June 1942.
War Diary of the German Africa Corps, July 1942.
War Diary of the German Africa Corps, 3 August to 22 November 1942.

Union War Histories, Box 322
The German Assault on the Gazala Position and the Fall of Tobruk, 26 May 1942
to 21 June 1942, book I, Brig. C. J. C. Molony.
The German Assault on the Gazala Position and the Fall of Tobruk, 26 May 1942
to 21 June 1942, book II, Brig. C. J. C. Molony.

Union War Histories, Box 343
Lessons from Operations Middle East and East Africa.

Union War Histories, Published Books, Box 364
Tobruk, Narrative.
Tobruk, Press and BBC Reports, Extracts from Books.
Tobruk, Enemy Reports on Capture of Tobruk.
Tobruk, Tactical Problems.
Tobruk, Accounts from British Sources.
Tobruk, Miscellaneous.
Tobruk, 4 SA Infantry Brigade.

Union War Histories, Published Books, Box 368
Court of Inquiry, Tobruk.
Court of Inquiry, Tobruk, Correspondence.
The Book of Scandals.
See-Saw in the Desert, Retreats and Recoveries, The Desert Ebb and Flow.

Union War Histories, Narratives, Box 376
Crisis in the Desert, May to July 1942, part 3 – El Alamein.
The Crisis at El Alamein, 30 June to 4 July 1942.

War Records
War Records, Box 166
Deserters, Standing Court of Inquiry.
Deserters, Returns of.
Deserters, Members of SA Police.

War Records, Box 82
Imperial Forces, Discharges from and Admissions to Union Hospitals.
Imperial Forces, Illegal Absentees.

UNITED KINGDOM

Published Primary Sources
War Office, *Field Service Regulations*, vol. II *Operations* (1929).
War Office, *Field Service Regulations*, vol. II (1935).
War Office, *Report of the War Office Committee of Enquiry into 'Shell-Shock'* (London, 1922).
IWM TM 30–410, *Technical Manual, Handbook on the British Army with Supplements on the Royal Air Force and Civilian Defence Organizations* (Washington, 1943).

BRITISH LIBRARY

India Office Papers
L/MIL/17/5 Indian Army.
L/WS War Staff.

IMPERIAL WAR MUSEUM

Memoirs/Diaries/Letters
Abrams, G. H. C., 89/13/1.
Allen, Sir George, 67/324/1.
Allnut, G., 80/46/1.
Anderson Smith, Lieut.-Col. J., Con Shelf.
Angel, Capt. R. L., MBE, MM, 88/46/1.
Arderne, Brig. E. A., DSO, OBE, 97/7/1.
Ashworth, H., 01/32/1.
Awdry, Lieut.-Col. R. J., Con Shelf.
Barrington, Maj. P. M., 03/22/1.
Beech, C. G., 90/18/1.
Belsey, Lieut. H. J., 92/11/2.
Bennet, F. T., 88/12/1.
Bone, Lieut. H. T., 87/31/1.
Bowden, K. J., 91/26/1.
Briggs, Maj.-Gen. Raymond, 99/1/2.
Brogan, Professor Sir Denis, 2066 92/25/1.
Brooks, J. E., 84/13/1.
Browne, Lieut.-Col. A. T. A., MSS 86/4/1.
Buckle, H., 81/10/1.
Bunn, L., 94/8/1.
Butt, Maj. C. H., 02/19/1.
Caffell, Lieut. E. W., P 469.
Candler, Capt. J. H., 94/47/1.
Carracher, E., P100.
Challoner, L., 10851 P479 Private Papers.
Charles, H. W. F., 02/19/1.
Cleere, Paddy, 67/279/1.
Codling, E. A., MSS 88/4/1.
Cope, E. W., 80/37/1 & 1A.
Crimp, R. L., 96/50/1 and PP/MCR/245.
Crocket, A. R. R., PP/MCR/314.
Danger, E. P., MSS 82/37/1.
Dunn, Sir Robin, 2848 94/41/1.
Elkington, H.
Fisher, H. G., 01/13/1.
Framp, C. T., 85/18/1.
Garrett, W. R., 93/19/1.
Gaskin, A. R., MSS 87/44/1.
Gladman, R., MSS 92/1/1.
Gutteridge, contained in Morrison, D. E., 05/34/1.
Harris, A. S., 96/35/1.
Harris, J. R., 86/5/1.
Harris, T. R., 83/48/1.
Higgins, R. I., 86/49/1.

Hughes, A. E., 87/6/1.
Jones, Lieut.-Col. E., 94/4/1.
Kerans, E., 86/61/1.
Lee, H., 04/15/1.
Lewis, W. A., 88/60/1.
Liddell Davison, Joseph, 93/19/1.
Lock, Hugh, contained in Morrison, D. E., 05/34/1.
Mackay, Ian, 94/8/1.
Main, Lieut. D. A., 87/35/1.
McClure, Lieut.-Col. W. D., 94/47/1.
Miles, Capt. B. E., 86/25/1.
Montgomery, Field-Marshal B. L. Papers.
Morris, K. W., 87/44/1.
Morrison, D. E., 05/34/1.
Morrison, Lieut. G. F., DS/Misc/63.
Parish, J. S., 04/31/1.
Parker, A., 87/44/1.
Philips, Maj. D. A., 95/33/1.
Philips, K. L.
Quinn, Rev. J. E. G., 10509 P247.
Sheppard, Capt. E. N., 86/72/1.
Slaney, W. H., 96/51/1.
Stewart, A. B., 87/34/1.
Stratton, Lieut.-Gen. W. H., 71/5/1.
Sutton, Lieut. R., 6729 78/1/1.
Symes, Maj.-Gen. G. W., 82/15/1.
Thompson, Rev. Canon A., MBE, 218 90/40/1.
Tilly, G., MSS PP/MCR/326.
Tutt, L. E., 85/35/1.
Wagner, Maj., MS 411 90/18/1.
Waller, Len, 87/42/1.
Wimberley, Maj.-Gen. D. N., 430 PP/MCR/182.
Windeatt, Lieut.-Col. J. K., OBE, 305 90/20/1.
Witte, J. H., 1279 87/12/1.
Wood, W., 86/35/1.
Wray, N., 9365 99/85/1.

Miscellaneous
'Tactical Handling of Anti-Tank Regiments, Military Training Pamphlet no.19',
April 1939.
Artillery Training, Vol. I, Pamphlet no. 9, 1942. 'Employment and Tactical
Handling of the Anti-Tank Regiment, part I, the 64-Gun Regiment', the
War Office, 21 February 1942.
Misc 62 (960) Letter Describing Operations in the Western Desert in March
1942.
Misc 74 (1110) Personal Messages from Montgomery to the Officers and Men of
the Eighth Army, 1942 to 1943.

Misc 123 (1908) Special Order of the Day, Alexander Relaying King's Message to the Troops, 2 September 1942. Personal Christmas Message from the C-in-C, 1944.

Misc 146 (2298) Two-Page Poem Entitled 'Eighth Army', Author POW in Italian Camp.

Misc 154 (2392) One-Page Poem, 'Western Desert', by Charles Barker.

Misc 169 (2613) Experience in Greece and Training in N. Africa, 1941 and 1942.

Misc 225 (3233) Grenadier Guards Newsletter no. 4, April 1943, around the Time of the Battle of Mareth.

Strong Room (Special Misc L5) Draft of Montgomery's Personal Message on the Eve of the Battle of Medenine, March 1943.

'Psychiatric Casualties, Hints to Medical Officers', Cairo, March 1941.

LIDDELL HART CENTRE FOR MILITARY ARCHIVES

Adam, General Sir R.
Alanbrooke, Field Marshal Lord.
Crick, Alan John Pitts.
Darlow, Brigadier Eric William Townsend.
Pyman, General Sir Harold.

NATIONAL ARCHIVES

Records of the Air Ministry
AIR 16 Fighter Command: Registered Files
AIR 16/378 Demonstration Flights by Fighters to Raise Morale.

Records of the Cabinet Office
CAB 21 Registered Files (1916 to 1965)
CAB 21/ 914 (annex) Committee on the Work of Psychologists and Psychiatrists in the Services, 1940 to 1942, 'Parts of the Body with a Morale Significance', 'Battle Inoculation' and 'Summary of Lectures on Psychological Aspects of War'.

CAB 21/914 Committee on the Work of Psychologists and Psychiatrists in the Services, 1940 to 1942.

CAB 66 Memoranda
CAB 66/17 War Cabinet Memoranda, Papers nos 128(41) to 177(41), 1941.

CAB 98 Miscellaneous Committees: Minutes and Papers
CAB 98/25 Expert Committee on the Work of Psychologists and Psychiatrists in the Services, 1942.

CAB 101 Official Histories: e.g. of Operations
CAB 101/346 Mediterranean and Middle East: Vol. VI, 'Human Interest', Extracts from Public and Private Records Collected by D. F. Butler, 1971.

CAB 106 Historical Section: Archivist and Librarian Files
CAB 106/565 Tobruk, Extract from Draft History of the 3rd Coldstream Guards, 20 to 21 June 1942, by Lt.-Col. J. H. A. Sparrow.
CAB 106/703 Field Marshal Montgomery's Address to Officers of Eighth Army, 13 August 1942, Address on Taking Command.

CAB 121 Special Secret Information Centre: Files
CAB 121/320 Training and Morale of the Fighting Services, June 1941 to July 1946.
CAB 121/636 Reinforcements for the Middle East, November 1941 to April 1943.

CAB 123 Office of the Lord President of the Council: Registered Files, Correspondence and Papers
CAB 123/273 Correspondence. Sir John Anderson and Others on the Oxford Group for Moral Rearmament, 1941.

Records of the Foreign Office
FO 371 Political Departments: General Correspondence from 1906
FO 371/30878 Allied Morale, 1942.
FO 371/32329 Censorship File no. 140, 1942.
FO 371/32826 Morale in Norway, 1942.

FO 898 Political Warfare Executive and Foreign Office, Political Intelligence Department: Papers
FO 898/190 Research into German Morale and Propaganda: Organisation and Procedure, 1942 to 1943.

Records of the Home Office
HO 192 Research and Experiments Department: Registered Papers
HO 192/1210 Morale, Surveys of Damage in Great Britain, Birmingham.

Records of Government Communications Headquarters
HW 1 Government Code and Cipher School: Signals Intelligence Passed to the Prime Minister, Messages and Correspondence
HW 1/636 North Africa: German Report on British Morale, Training Supplies and Intentions, 4 June with Note by C that He Is Satisfied that US Ciphers in Cairo Are Compromised, 1942.

Records of the Central Office of Information
INF 1 Files of Correspondence, 1936 to 1950
INF 1/252 Planning Committee, Miscellaneous Papers Dealing with Morale, 1940 to 1942.

Records of the Ministry of Pensions
PIN 15 War Pensions: Registered Files
PIN 15/2401 Report of Conference on Compensation in Cases of Neurasthenia and Psychosis, Held on 3 to 7 July 1939.

Records of the Prime Minister's Office
PREM 3 Operations Correspondence and Papers
PREM 3/439/20B Report on Morale of Allied Forces in North West Africa, 1942.
PREM 3/504 Sir Charles Wilson's Enquiry into Forces Morale, August to September 1941.

PREM 4 Confidential Correspondence and Papers
PREM 4/6/2 ABCA, September 1941 to August 1943.

Records of the War Office
WO 32 War Office and Successors: Registered Files (General Series)
WO 32/4453 Abolition of Bayonets in Various Arms of the Service, 1936 to 1937.
WO 32/9362 Military Discipline of United Kingdom and Dominion Troops in South Africa, 1940 to 1944.
WO 32/9429 Education in the Army in War Time, 1940.
WO 32/9447 Report of the Committee on Personal Rations and Ration Allowance (Evans Committee), 1936 to 1940.
WO 32/9735 Army Bureau of Current Affairs: Formation, 1941 to 1946.
WO 32/10400 Infantry Battalion: Reorganisation, 1942 to 1944.
WO 32/10455 Compulsory Education in the Army in Winter months, 1942 to 1944.
WO 32/10462 Education in the Army: Policy, 1943.
WO 32/10810 Battle Casualties All Theatres, 1943 to 1952.
WO 32/10924 Status of Infantry Soldiers, 1944 to 1945.
WO 32/11194 Inter-Service Committee Report on Morale, 1944 to 1945.
WO 32/11550 Psychiatry in Forward Areas, 1945.
WO 32/11972 Use of Psychologists and Psychiatrists in the Service: Inquiry by Lord Privy Seal, 1942 to 1946.
WO 32/11974 Work of Psychologists and Psychiatrists in the Services, 1946 to 1947.
WO 32/15178 Infantry Weapon Development: Progress Report, 1952 to 1953.
WO 32/15492 Committee on Disciplinary Amendments, 1924 to 1925.
WO 32/15494 Death Penalty, 1927 to 1928.
WO 32/15495 Abolition of Death Sentence, 1930 to 1931.
WO 32/15496 Death Penalty in Relation to Offences Committed on Active Service, 1940.
WO 32/15772 War Office Morale Committee Reports, 1942 to 1948.
WO 32/15773 Death Penalty for Desertion in Field: Reintroduction, 1942.
WO 32/15774 Death Penalty for Desertion in Field: Reintroduction, 1942.

WO 33 Reports, Memoranda and Papers (O and A Series)
WO 33/1297 Report of the Committee on the Lessons of the Great War, the War Office, October 1932.

WO 71 Judge Advocate General's Office: Courts Martial Proceedings
WO 71/807 Court Martial of Pt. A Sparrow, 1943.

WO 106 War Office: Directorate of Military Operations and Military Intelligence
WO 106/1024 Ratio of Officer to Other Rank Casualties in the Infantry.
WO 106/2186 Lessons of 'Crusader', March 1942.
WO 106/2223 Notes from Theatres of War, Cyrenaica, November 1941 to June 1942.

WO 162 Adjutant-General's Papers
WO 162/132 Battle Casualties: Statistical Returns. Libya 1st to 9th Campaigns, May 1942 to March 1943.
WO 162/133 Battle Casualties: Statistical Returns, Libya 8th Campaign, January to February 1943.
WO 162/160 Battle Casualties: Statistical Returns, Summary of British/UK Army Casualities, September 1939 to October 1945.
WO 162/305 Battle Casualties: Correspondence and miscellaneous analyses.
WO 162/318 Indian and Dominion Forces, Strengths and Casualties as Reported to Central Statistics Office.

WO 163 War Office Council
WO 163/48 Army Council: Meetings 1–31, October 1939 to December 1940.
WO 163/50 Army Council: Meetings 1–11, January to December 1941.
WO 163/51 Army Council: Meetings 12–19, January to December 1942.
WO 163/52 Army Council: Meetings 20–44, January to December 1943.
WO 163/66 War Committee Meetings 51–87, January to May 1940.
WO 163/72 ECAC: January to December 1941.
WO 163/73 ECAC: January to December 1942.
WO 163/88 ECAC: Meetings 52–63, March to June 1942.
WO 163/89 ECAC: Meetings 64–90, June to December 1942.
WO 163/123 Major-General H. Willans, Army Welfare and Education.
WO 163/183 Organisation and Weapons Policy Committee, July 1942 to December 1944.
WO 163/402 Haining Report.
WO 163/403 Report of the Committee to Consider the Amalgamation of the Royal Military Academy and the Royal Military College, March 1939.

WO 165 Directorates (Various): War Diaries, Second World War
WO 165/85 War Diaries, Second World War, Education, September 1940 to December 1943.
WO 165/101 War Diary of Directorate of Selection of Personnel, June 1941 to December 1942.

WO 169 British Forces, Middle East: War Diaries, Second World War
WO 169/13405 301–303 British Field Censor Unit PAIFORCE.
WO 169/13904 No 1 ME Officer Selection Board, War Diary, 1943.

WO 175 Unit War Diaries, British North Africa Forces
WO 175/491 War Diaries of the 8th Argyll and Sutherland Highlanders, November 1942 to June 1943.

WO 177 Army Medical Services: War Diaries, Second World War
WO 177/27 Medical Diaries, DMS GHQ, June to July 1942.
WO 177/324 Medical Diaries DDMS 8th Army, October 1941 to December 1942.

WO 193 Directorate of Military Operations and Plans
WO 193/423 Miscellaneous, December 1939 to July 1942, Maintenance of British Morale.
WO 193/452 Morale Committee: Agenda and Minutes, March 1942 to February 1946.
WO 193/453 Miscellaneous, Morale Committee Papers, 25 February 1942 to 25 October 1945.
WO 193/456 Miscellaneous, Morale: Sundry Papers, June 1941 to July 1945.

WO 199 Home Forces: Military Headquarters Papers, Second World War
WO 199/799 'Psychological Aspects of Training', January 1942 to October 1943.
WO 199/839 'The Principles of Basic Training', April 1944 to April 1945.
WO 199/840 'Home Forces Training', April to July 1945.
WO 199/872B 'Notes from Theatres of War', May 1940 to July 1944.
WO 199/725 Demi-official Correspondence Chief of Staff Home Forces, July 1941 to March 1942.
WO 199/1644 GOC-in-C Conference at HQ, Southern Command, February to April 1940.
WO 199/1656 C-in-C Conference: Notes for inclusion in Agenda and Extract from Minutes, April to June 1942.

WO 201 Middle East Forces Headquarters Papers
WO 201/352 Operations in the Western Desert: Lessons Learned, December 1940 to September 1941.
WO 201/357 Operation 'Battleaxe', Lessons of the Campaign, June to November 1941.
WO 201/378 Eighth Army Commander's Report on Operations, November 1941 to June 1942.
WO 201/431 RA Notes on the Offensive by Eighth Army from 23 October to 4 November 1942 on the El Alamein Position.
WO 201/444 AG Casualty Returns Extracted from 'Lightfoot', 28 October 1942 to 6 December 1942, vols. 1, 2, 3.
WO 201/455 Eighth Army Operations: Situation Reports, December 1942 to February 1943.
WO 201/527 Armoured Formations: Tactical Handling of Armoured Forces, December 1941 to March 1942.
WO 201/538 Lessons from Operations, 14 September 1941 to 25 August 1942.
WO 201/666 Water Supply Western Desert, October 1941 to April 1942.
WO 201/678 Western Desert Pipeline, December 1941 to August 1942.
WO 201/2140 DMI's Weekly Desert Review, August/September 1942.
WO 201/2215 Moves to and from the Western Desert and Cyrenaica, June, July 1942.
WO 201/2339 Manpower Situation in the ME, June 1941 to September 1942.

WO 201/2586 Lessons of Cyrenaica Campaign: Training Pamphlets, December 1940 to February 1941.

WO 201/2590 Training: Miscellaneous, January to October 1942.

WO 201/2591 Training: Miscellaneous, May 1942 to January 1943.

WO 201/2596 Lessons from Operations: Training, March to November 1943.

WO 201/2834 Middle East Command: Battle Casualties, AG Stats, January 1942 to December 1944.

WO 201/2870 General Martel's Report on His Visit to the Middle East, 26 January 1942.

WO 202 British Military Missions in Liaison with Allied Forces; Military Headquarters Papers, Second World War

WO 202/33 Spears Mission, Western Desert, Notes on Desert Warfare, December 1941 to March 1942.

WO 203 Military Headquarters Far East

WO 203/4537 SEAC: Morale Reports July 1944 to February 1945.

WO 203/4538 Allied Land Forces South East Asia: Morale Reports, August to November 1944.

WO 203/5184 General Correspondence and Reports Including the Morale Effect of Bombing in Burma, October 1943 to April 1946.

WO 204 Allied Forces Mediterranean Theatre, Military Headquarters Papers, Second World War

WO 204/257 Censorship, Security and Reports, North African, Sicilian and Italian Operations, 2 February to 31 October 1943.

WO 204/3900 Censorship of Military and Civilian Mail in the Mediterranean Theatre: Morale Reports Adjutant-General's Record Branch, January 1943.

WO 204/3901 Censorship of Military and Civilian Mail in the Mediterranean Theatre: Morale Reports, February 1943.

WO 204/4769 Rations.

WO 204/6702 Publication, 'Morale and the Officer', August/September 1944.

WO 204/6862 Administrative Sitreps in Eighth Army Showing Accumulative Casualties, August 1943.

WO 208 Directorate of Military Operations and Intelligence, and Directorate of Military Intelligence; Ministry of Defence, Defence Intelligence Staff: Files

WO 208/763 Indian Army Morale, Mutinies and Cases of Indiscipline, January 1940 to August 1941.

WO 208/774 Army Fighting Capacity, India, April 1940 to November 1945.

WO 208/959 Miscellaneous Information on the Army: Morale, Suicide Lists, Strengths, Logistics etc. JAPAN, October 1943 to July 1945.

WO 208/1354 Japan, Discipline, Interior Economy and Welfare and Morale Generally, January 1941 to October 1942.

WO 216 Office of the Chief of the Imperial General Staff: Papers

WO 216/3 Middle East: Tank Strengths and Comparison of Performance with Enemy Equipment; Summary of Defects, April 1941 to April 1942.

WO 216/15 Appreciation on Tobruk, September 1941.

WO 216/61 Officer Selection and Training: Report of a Meeting Called by the Secretary of State for War, and memoranda, January 1941.

WO 216/85 Middle East: Notes on Operations, July/August 1942.

WO 217 Private War Diaries of Various Army Personnel, WW2
WO 217/33 Private Diary of Capt. K. M. Oliphant, 2/3 Field Regt. RA.

WO 222 Medical Historians' Papers: First and Second World Wars
WO 222/28 German Psychological Warfare Survey and Bibliography, Edited by Ladislas Farago, Committee for National Morale, New York, 1941.

WO 222/65 Casualties in AFVs, Middle East, Major A. L. Chute RCAMC, 1942.

WO 222/66 Psychological Questions Relating to AA Personnel, Major E. T. C. Spooner RAMC, 1942.

WO 222/103 Return of Psychiatric Patients Seen in All Commands During 1942.

WO 222/124 The Moral Effect of Weapons, Investigation into Reactions of Group of 300 Wounded Men in North Africa, 1943.

WO 222/129 Desert Sores, Summary of Situation as to Incidence, Aetiology, Prevention, Consulting Physician, Middle East, February 1943.

WO 222/218 Circular to All Medical Officers, n.d. but Second World War, 'Morale Discipline and Mental Fitness'.

WO 222/266 Estimated Casualties for Operation Torch, September 1942.

WO 222/1584 Command Specialist Reports on Psychological Medicine, 1940 to 1941.

WO 227 Office of the Engineer-in-Chief: Papers
WO 227/22 Western Desert Pipe Line, January 1942.

WO 231 Directorate of Military Training
WO 231/10 Lessons from Tunisian Campaign, 1942 to 1943.

WO 231/14 Operations in Sicily: Notes and Reports on the Campaign, August to December 1943.

WO 231/16 El Alamein to Messina: Lessons Learned by 152 Infantry Brigade during the Years of Fighting, November 1943.

WO 231/17 Extracts from the Report of a Visit by the Director-General, Army Medical Services, to North Africa and Italy, November 1943.

WO 232 Directorate of Tactical Investigation: Papers
WO 232/21 Army Operations Research Report: The West Kapelle Assault on Walcheren, June 1944 to January 1947.

WO 236 General Sir George Erskine: Papers
WO 236/1 Mersa Matruh and Tobruk: Semi-official Correspondence with Cabinet Office, September 1939 to September 1950.

WO 258 Department of the Permanent Under Secretary of State: Private Office Papers
WO 258/25 Army and Public Morale Reports, April to June 1942.

WO 259 Department of the Secretary of State for War: Private Office Papers
WO 259/38 Cables between PM and Auchinleck, June to September 1941.
WO 259/44 'Army Morale', Paper by Adjutant-General, May 1944.
WO 259/61 Enquiry by the Rt. Hon. C. R. Attlee MP into Tank Position in the Middle East, March 1942.
WO 259/62 Morale in the Army: Press Criticism, October 1941 to January 1942.
WO 259/64 Press Meetings and Reports, February to April 1942.

WO 277 Historical Monographs
WO 277/4 Army Welfare.
WO 277/7 Discipline.
WO 277/12 Manpower Problems.
WO 277/16 Morale.
WO 277/19 Personnel Selection.
WO 277/35 History of Army Education.

WO 279 War Office and Ministry of Defence: Confidential Print
WO 279/57 Report on the Staff Conference held at the Staff College Camberley, 17 to 20 January 1927.
WO 279/74 Report on the Staff Conference held at the Staff College, Camberley 9 to 11 January 1933.

WO 291 Military Operational Research Unit
WO 291/904 Morale Effect of Bombardment, 1945.
WO 291/1186 Army Operational Research Group, Memorandum no. 16. 'The Comparative Performance of German Anti-Tank Weapons in World War II', 1950.
WO 291/1327 Bombardment to Break Morale, 1944.
WO 291/1299 Report on Tour of Armoured Formations in North Africa, April to June 1943, General HQ MEF.

WO 365 War Office: Department of the Adjutant-General, Statistics Branch
WO 365/39 British Army, Religious Denominations AG Stats (War Office), 1942 to 1944.
WO 365/47 AG Stats., Casualties from Enemy Action in the UK, 1941 to 1944.
WO 365/79 Forces under British Empire Control, Battle Casualties, 1943.

WO 366 Department of the Permanent Under Secretary of State
WO 366/21 'Morale', by Lieut.-Col. J. H. A. Sparrow, Production and Printing 1945 to 1949.

Secondary Sources

Addison, Paul, *The Road to 1945: British Politics and the Second World War* (London, 1975).
Addison, Paul and Calder, Angus (eds.), *Time to Kill: The Soldier's Experience of War in the West 1939–1945* (London, 1997).

Agar-Hamilton, J. A. I. and Turner, L. C. F., *Crisis in the Desert May–July 1942* (Oxford, 1952).
The Sidi Rezeg Battles 1941 (Oxford, 1957).
Ahrenfeldt, Robert H., *Psychiatry in the British Army in the Second World War* (London, 1958).
Allen, Louis, *Burma: The Longest War 1941–1945* (London, 2000).
Allmand, Christopher, *The Hundred Years War: England and France at War c.1300–c.1450* (Cambridge, 1989).
Alpert, Michael, 'The Clash of Spanish Armies: Contrasting Ways of War in Spain, 1936–1939', *War in History*, 6(3) (1999).
Ambrose, Stephen E., *Crazy Horse and Custer: The Epic Clash of Two Great Warriors at the Little Bighorn* (London, 1975).
Ambrose, Stephen E. and Brinkley, Douglas G., *Rise to Globalism: American Foreign Policy since 1938* (London, 1997).
Arthur, Max, *Forgotten Voices of the Great War* (London, 2002).
Ashley Hart, Stephen, *Colossal Cracks: Montgomery's 21st Army Group in Northwest Europe, 1944–45* (Westport, CT, 2000).
Ashworth, Tony, *Trench Warfare: The Live and Let Live System* (London, 1980).
Atkinson, Rick, *An Army at Dawn: The War in North Africa, 1942–1943* (London, 2003).
Balfour, Michael, *Propaganda in War, 1939–1945: Organisations, Policies and Publics in Britain and Germany* (Boston, 1979).
Barbusse, Henri, *Under Fire* (London, 1926).
Barkawi, Tarak, 'Culture and Combat in the Colonies: The Indian Army in the Second World War', *Journal of Contemporary History*, 41(2) (2006).
Barnett, Correlli, *The Desert Generals* (London, 1983).
Barr, Niall, *Pendulum of War: The Three Battles of El Alamein* (London, 2005).
Bartov, Omer, *The Eastern Front, 1941–45: German Troops and the Barbarisation of Warfare* (Oxford, 1985).
Hitler's Army: Soldiers, Nazis, and War in the Third Reich (Oxford, 1992).
Bates, Peter, *Dance of War: The Story of the Battle of Egypt* (London, 1992).
Baylis, John and Smith, John (eds.), *The Globalization of World Politics: An Introduction to International Relations* (Oxford, 2005).
Baylis, John, Wirtz, James, Cohen, Eliot and Gray, Colin S. (eds.), *Strategy in the Contemporary World: An Introduction to Strategic Studies* (Oxford, 2002).
Baynes, John, *Morale: A Study of Men and Courage* (London, 1967).
Beddington, Major-General W. R., *A History of the Queen's Bays (The 2nd Dragoon Guards) 1929–1945* (Winchester, 1954).
Beevor, Antony, *Berlin: The Downfall 1945* (London, 2003).
The Spanish Civil War (London, 1982).
Stalingrad (London, 1999).
Berger, Peter and Luckmann, Thomas, *The Social Construction of Reality: A Treatise in the Sociology of Knowledge* (London, 1991).
Bernstein, Douglas A., Clarke-Stewart, Alison, Roy, Edward J., Wickens, Christopher D., *Psychology* (Boston, 1997).
Bessonov, Evgeni, *Tank Rider: Into the Reich with the Red Army* (London, 2005).
Beveridge, William, *Social Insurance and Allied Services* (London, 1942).

Bharucha, Major P. C., *Official History of the Indian Armed Forces in the Second World War 1939–45, Campaigns in the Western Theatre, The North African Campaign 1940–43* (London, 1956).

Bidwell, Shelford, *Modern Warfare: A Study of Men, Weapons and Theories* (London, 1973).

The Royal Horse Artillery (London, 1973).

Bidwell, Shelford and Graham, Dominick, *Firepower: British Army Weapons and Theories of War 1904–1945* (London, 1982).

Bierman, John and Smith, Colin, *Alamein: War without Hate* (London, 2003).

Bogacz, Ted, 'War Neurosis and Cultural Change in England, 1914–22: The Work of the War Office Committee of Enquiry into "Shell Shock"', *Journal of Contemporary History*, 24(2) (April 1989).

Bond, Brian, *British Military Policy between the Two World Wars* (Oxford, 1980).

Borthwick, Alastair, *Battalion: A British Infantry Unit's Actions from El Alamein to the Elbe, 1942–1945* (London, 1994).

Bourgogne, Sergeant, *Memoirs of Sergeant Bourgogne, 1812–1813* (London, 1996).

Bourke, Joanna, *Dismembering the Male: Men's Bodies, Britain and the Great War* (London, 1996).

An Intimate History of Killing: Face-to-Face Killing in Twentieth-Century Warfare (London, 2000).

Bowlby, Alex, *The Recollections of Rifleman Bowlby* (London, 1999).

Bowman, Timothy, *Irish Regiments in the Great War: Discipline and Morale* (Manchester, 2003).

Bradley, Omar N., *A Soldier's Story* (New York, 1999).

Bramson, Leon and Goethals, George W. (eds.), *War: Studies from Psychology, Sociology, Anthropology* (London, 1968).

British Way and Purpose: Consolidated Edition of BWP Booklets 1–18, with Appendices of Documents of Post-war Reconstruction (London, 1944).

Brown, A. T. A., 'A Study of the Anatomy of Fear and Courage in War', *The Army Quarterly and Defence Journal*, 106(3) (July 1976).

Brumwell, Steve, '"A Service Truly Critical": The British Army and Warfare with the North American Indians, 1755–1764', *War in History*, 5(2) (1998).

Bucholz, Arden, *Moltke, Schlieffen, and Prussian War Planning* (Oxford, 1991).

Budiansky, Stephen, *Air Power: The Men, Machines, and Ideas That Revolutionized War, from Kitty Hawk to Gulf War II* (London, 2004).

Bullock, Alan, *Hitler and Stalin: Parallel Lives* (London, 1993).

Bungay, Stephen, *Alamein* (London, 2002).

Caesar, *The Gallic War* (Oxford, 1996).

Calder, Angus, *The People's War: Britain 1939–45* (London, 1992).

Callahan, Raymond, *Churchill and His Generals* (Lawrence, KS, 2007).

Camfield, Thomas M., '"Will to Win" – The U.S. Army Troop Morale Program of World War I', *Military Affairs*, 41(3) (October 1977).

Canadian Defence Academy, Canadian Forces Leadership Institute, *Leadership in the Canadian Forces: Doctrine* (Kingston, ON, 2005).

Carver, Field Marshal Michael, *Britain's Army in the 20th Century* (London, 1999).

Dilemmas of the Desert War: A New Look at the Libyan Campaign 1940–1942 (London, 1986).

El Alamein (London, 1962).

Tobruk (London, 1964).

Cecil, Hugh and Liddle, Peter H., *Facing Armageddon: The First World War Experienced* (London, 1996).

Chaplin, H. D., *The Queen's Own Royal West Kent Regiment 1920–1950* (London, 1954).

Churchill, Winston, *Never Give In! The Best of Winston Churchill's Speeches* (London, 2003).

The Second World War (London, 2002).

Citino, Robert M., *Death of the Wehrmacht: The German Campaigns of 1942* (Lawrence, KS, 2007).

Clausewitz, Carl von, *On War* (London, 1993).

Condell, Bruce and Zabecki, David T., *On the German Art of War: Truppenführung* (London, 2001).

Connell, John, *Auchinleck: A Biography of Field-Marshal Sir Claude Auchinleck* (London, 1959).

Connelly, Mark and Miller, Walter, 'The BEF and the Issue of Surrender on the Western Front in 1940', *War in History*, 11(4) (2004).

Copeland, Norman, *Psychology and the Soldier: The Art of Leadership* (London, 1944).

Copp, Terry J., 'Battle Exhaustion and the Canadian Soldier in Normandy', in *British Army Review*, 85 (1987).

Copp, Terry and McAndrew, Bill, *Battle Exhaustion: Soldiers and Psychiatrists in the Canadian Army, 1939–1945* (London, 1990).

Corum, James S., *The Luftwaffe: Creating the Operational Air War, 1918–1940* (Lawrence, KS, 1997).

The Roots of Blitzkrieg (Lawrence, KS, 1992).

Cowley, Robert (ed.), *No End Save Victory* (London, 2002).

Cox, S. and Gray, P. (eds.), *Air Power History: Turning Points from Kitty Hawk to Kosovo* (London, 2002).

Craig, Norman, *The Broken Plume: A Platoon Commander's Story, 1940–45* (London, 1982).

Crang, Jeremy A., *The British Army and the People's War, 1939–1945* (Manchester, 2000).

Crew, F. (ed.), *History of the Second World War: United Kingdom Medical Services – Army Medical Services*, vol. I, *Campaigns* (London, 1957).

Daly, Lieutenant-Colonel C. D., 'A Psychological Analysis of Military Morale', *Army Quarterly*, 32(1) (April 1936).

Danchev, Alex and Todman, Daniel (eds.), *War Diaries 1939–1945, Field Marshal Lord Alanbrooke* (London, 2002).

De Guingand, Major-General Sir F., *Operation Victory* (London, 1947).

Deist, Wilhelm, 'The Military Collapse of the German Empire: The Reality Behind the Stab-in-the-Back Myth', in *War in History*, 3(2) (1996).

Dennis, Peter, *The Territorial Army, 1906–1940* (Woodbridge, 1987).

D'Este, Carlo, *Decision in Normandy: The Unwritten Story of Montgomery and the Allied Campaign* (London, 1983).

Doherty, Richard, *The Sound of History: El Alamein, 1942* (London, 2002).

Douglas, Keith, *Alamein to Zem Zem* (London, 1992).

Dower, John W., *War without Mercy: Race and Power in the Pacific War* (London, 1986).

Droz, Bernard and Lever, Evelyne, *Histoire de la guerre d'Algérie 1954–1962* (éditions du seuil, 1982).

Du Picq, Colonel Ardant, 'Battle Studies: Ancient and Modern Battle', in *Roots of Strategy, Book Two: Three Military Classics* (Mechanicsburg, PA, 1987).

Ellis, Chris and Chamberlain, Peter (eds.), *Handbook on the British Army 1943* (Military Book Society, 1975).

Ellis, John, *Brute Force: Allied Strategy and Tactics in the Second World War* (London, 1990).

The Sharp End: The Fighting Man in World War II (London, 1993).

The World War II Databook: The Essential Facts and Figures for All the Combatants (London, 1993).

Englander, David, 'Soldiering and Identity: Reflections on the Great War', *War in History*, 1(3) (1994).

Erskine, David, *The Scots Guards, 1919–1955* (London, 1956).

Falvey, Denis, *A Well-Known Excellence: British Artillery and an Artilleryman in World War Two* (London, 2002).

Fancher, Raymond E., *Pioneers of Psychology* (London, 1996).

Fanke, Dick (ed.), *Mud and Blood in the Field* (Hughesdale, 1984).

Ferguson, Niall, *The Pity of War* (London, 1999).

'Prisoner Taking and Prisoner Killing in the Age of Total War: Towards a Political Economy of Military Defeat', *War in History*, 11(2) (2004).

The War of the World: History's Age of Hatred (London, 2006).

Foch, Ferdinand, *The Principles of War* (London, 1918).

Ford, Ken, *Battleaxe Division: From North Africa to Italy with the 78th Division 1942–45* (Stroud, 1999).

Forsdyke, C. D., 'The Diary of a Corporal: North Africa to Austria, 1942–1946', unpublished war diary, in author's possession.

Förster, Jürgen, 'Ludendorff and Hitler in Perspective: The Battle for the German Soldier's Mind, 1917–1944', *War in History*, 10(3) (2003).

Forty, George, *British Army Handbook 1939–1945* (Stroud, 2002).

Forty, George (ed.) *Leakey's Luck: A Tank Commander with Nine Lives* (Stroud, 2002).

Tanks across the Desert: The War Diary of Jake Wardrop (Stroud, 2003).

France, John, *Western Warfare in the Age of the Crusades 1000–1300* (London, 1999).

Fraser, David, *And We Shall Shock Them: The British Army in the Second World War* (London, 1999).

French, David, 'Discipline and the Death Penalty in the British Army in the War against Germany during the Second World War', in *The Journal of Contemporary History*, 33(4) (October 1998).

'The Mechanization of the British Cavalry between the World Wars', in *War in History*, 10(3) (2003).

Raising Churchill's Army: The British Army and the War against Germany 1919–1945 (Oxford, 2000).

Fritz, Steven G., *Frontsoldaten: The German Soldier in World War II* (Lexington, KY, 1995).

'"We Are Trying … to Change the Face of the World" – Ideology and Motivation in the Wehrmacht on the Eastern Front: The View from Below', in *The Journal of Military History*, 60(4) (October 1996).

Fussell, Paul, *The Great War and Modern Memory* (London, 1981).

Gatt, Azar, *War in Human Civilization* (Oxford, 2006).

Gill, Douglas and Dallas, Gloden, 'Mutiny at Étaples Base in 1917', *Past and Present*, 69 (November 1975).

Glantz, David M. and House, Jonathan M., *When Titans Clashed: How the Red Army Stopped Hitler* (Kansas, 1995).

Goldsworthy, Adrian, *Roman Warfare* (London, 2002).

Graves, Robert, *Goodbye to All That* (London, 1960).

Grayling, A. C., *Among the Dead Cities: The History and Moral Legacy of the WWII Bombing of Civilians in Germany and Japan* (New York, 2006).

Hall, Richard C., '"The Enemy Is Behind Us": The Morale Crisis in the Bulgarian Army during the Summer of 1918', *War in History*, 11(2) (April 2004).

Hallion, Richard P., *Storm over Iraq: Air Power and the Gulf War* (London, 1992).

Hamilton, Nigel, *The Full Monty: Montgomery of Alamein 1887–1942* (London, 2002).

Master of the Battlefield: Monty's War Years 1942–1944 (London, 1983).

Monty: The Making of a General 1887–1942 (London, 1982).

Monty: The Man behind the Legend (London, 1988).

Handy, Charles, *Understanding Organisations* (London, 1993).

Harper, Glyn and Hayward, Joel (eds.), *Born to Lead?: Portraits of New Zealand Commanders* (Titirangi, 2003).

Harris, J. P., *Men, Ideas and Tanks* (Manchester, 1995).

Harrison, Mark, *Medicine and Victory: British Military Medicine in the Second World War* (Oxford, 2004).

Harrison Place, Timothy, 'Lionel Wigram: Battle Drill and the British Army in the Second World War', in *War in History*, 7(4) (2000).

Military Training in the British Army 1940–1944: From Dunkirk to D-Day (London, 2000).

Hastings, Major R. H. W. S., *The Rifle Brigade in the Second World War* (Aldershot, 1950).

Hastings, Max, *Armageddon: The Battle For Germany 1944–45* (London, 2004).

Overlord: D-Day and the Battle for Normandy (London, 1984).

Hawkins, Major T. H. and Brimble, L. J. F., *Adult Education: the Record of the British Army* (London, 1947).

Herr, Michael, *Dispatches* (London, 1978).

Heuser, Beatrice, *Reading Clausewitz* (London, 2002).

Hildyard, Myles, *It Is Bliss Here: Letters Home 1939–1945* (London, 2005).

Holland, James, *Together We Stand: Turning the Tide in the West: North Africa 1942–1943* (London, 2006).

Holmes, Richard, *Acts of War: The Behaviour of Men in Battle* (London, 2004).

Dusty Warriors: Modern Soldiers at War (London, 2006).

Horne, John (ed.), *State, Society and Mobilization in Europe during the First World War* (London, 1997).

Horne, John and Kramer, Alan, *German Atrocities, 1914: A History of Denial* (London, 2001)

Horrocks, Brian, *A Full Life* (London, 1960).

Howard, Michael, *War in European History* (Oxford, 2001).

Hughes, Daniel J., *Moltke on the Art of War: Selected Writings* (Novato, CA, 1993).

Hutchinson, Godfrey, *Xenophon and the Art of Command* (London, 2000).

Jacobsen, Hans-Adolf and Rohwer, Jürgen (eds.), *The Decisive Battles of World War II: The German View* (London, 1965).

James, G. W. B., 'Psychiatric Lessons from Active Service', *The Lancet* (1945).

Johnston, Mark, *At the Front Line: Experiences of Australian Soldiers in World War II* (Cambridge, 1996).

Australian Soldiers and Their Adversaries in World War II (Cambridge, 2000).

Johnston, Mark and Stanley, Peter, *Alamein: The Australian Story* (Oxford, 2002).

Joly, Cyril, *Take These Men* (London, 1955).

Jomini, Antoine-Henri, *The Art of War* (New York, 2007).

Joslen, Lieutenant-Colonel H. F., *Orders of Battle: Second World War 1939–1945*, vol. I (London, 1960).

Journal of Military History, 57(5), Special Issue: Proceedings of the Symposium on 'The History of War as Part of General History' at the Institute for Advanced Studies, Princeton, New Jersey (October 1993).

Jünger, Ernst, *Storm of Steel* (London, 2003).

Kassimeris, George (ed.), *The Barbarisation of Warfare* (London, 2006).

Keegan, John, *The Face of Battle* (London, 1991).

The Second World War (London, 1997).

Keegan, John (ed.), *The Penguin Book of War: Great Military Writings* (London, 2000).

Kippenberger, Howard, *Infantry Brigadier* (London, 1949).

Kitchen, Martin, *Rommel's Desert War: Waging World War II in North Africa, 1941–1943* (Cambridge, 2009).

Kolb, Eberhard, *The Weimer Republic* (London, 2001).

Latimer, Jon, *Alamein* (London, 2002).

Leach, Barry A., *German Strategy against Russia, 1939–1941* (Oxford, 1973).

Lendon, J. E., *Soldiers and Ghosts: A History of Battle in Classical Antiquity* (New Haven, CT, 2005).

Lewin, Ronald, *The Chief: Field Marshal Lord Wavell, Commander-in-Chief and Viceroy, 1939–1947* (London, 1980).

Liddell Hart, B. H., *The British Way in Warfare* (London, 1932).

The Decisive Wars of History: A Study in Strategy (London, 1929).

The Future of Infantry (London, 1933).

A History of the World War, 1914–1918 (London, 1934).

Strategy: The Indirect Approach (London, 1967).

Liddell Hart, B. H. (ed.), *The Rommel Papers* (New York, 1953).

Linderman, Gerald F., *The World within War: America's Combat Experience in World War II* (London, 1997).

Litvin, Nikolai, *800 Days on the Eastern Front: A Russian Soldier Remembers World War II* (Lawrence, KS, 2007).

Lock, Hugh, *War Was a Cross to Bear* (self-published, 1998).

Lowe, John, *The Warden: A Portrait of John Sparrow* (London, 1998).

Lucas Phillips, C. E., *Alamein* (London, 1962).

Lynn, John A., *Battle: A History of Combat and Culture* (Oxford, 2003).

MacCurdy, J. T., *The Structure of Morale* (Cambridge, 1943).

Machiavelli, Niccolò, *The Discourses* (London, 1998).

MacKenzie, S. P., *British War Films, 1939–1945* (London, 2001).

    Politics and Military Morale: Current Affairs and Citizenship Education in the British Army, 1914–1950 (Oxford, 1992).

    'The Treatment of Prisoners of War in World War II', *Journal of Modern History*, 66(3) (September 1994).

    'Vox Populi: British Army Newspapers in the Second World War', *Journal of Contemporary History*, 24(4) (October 1989).

Maclear, Michael, *Vietnam: The Ten Thousand Day War* (London, 1982).

MacNalty, Arthur S. (ed.), *Medical Services in War: The Principal Medical Lessons of the Second World War Based on the Official Medical Histories of the United Kingdom, Canada, Australia, New Zealand and India* (London, 1968).

Mahan, A. T., *The Influence of Sea Power upon History, 1660–1783* (Gretna, LA, 2003).

Mainwaring, Hugh S. K., *Three Score Years and Ten with Never a Dull Moment* (privately printed, 1976).

Man, John, *The Penguin Atlas of D-Day and The Normandy Campaign* (London, 1994).

Margiotta, Franklin D. (ed.), *Brassey's Encyclopaedia of Military History and Biography* (London, 1994).

Marshall, S. L. A., *Men against Fire: The Problem of Battle Command in Future War* (New York, 1966).

Marston, Daniel P., *Phoenix from the Ashes: The Indian Army in the Burma Campaign* (Westport, CN, 2003).

McGuin, Keith Q., 'Leadership Training', *Infantry* (Summer 2002).

McIntyre, Allister and Davis, Karen D. (eds.), *Dimensions of Military Leadership* (Kingston, ON, 2006).

McLaine, Ian, *Ministry of Morale: Home Front Morale and the Ministry of Information in World War II* (London, 1979).

McLeod, John, *Myth and Reality: The New Zealand Soldier in World War II* (Auckland, 1986).

McManners, John, *Fusilier: Recollections and Reflections 1939–1945* (Norwich, 2002).

McPherson, James, *For Cause and Comrades: Why Men Fought in the Civil War* (Oxford, 1997).

Mellor, W. Franklin (ed.), *Casualties and Medical Statistics, History of the Second World War* (London, 1972).

Merridale, Catherine, 'Culture, Ideology and Combat in the Red Army, 1939–45', in *The Journal of Contemporary History*, 41(2) (2006).

    Ivan's War: The Red Army 1939–45 (London, 2005).

Messinger, Gary S., *British Propaganda and the State in the First World War* (Manchester, 1992).

Montgomery, B. L., *The Memoirs of Field-Marshal Montgomery of Alamein* (London, 1958).

Moorehead, Alan, *African Trilogy: The Desert War 1940–1943* (London, 2000). *The Desert War* (London, 1984).

Murray, Williamson and Millett, Allan R., *A War to Be Won: Fighting the Second World War* (London, 2000).

Nagl, John A., *Learning to Eat Soup with a Knife: Counterinsurgency Lessons from Malaya and Vietnam* (Chicago, 2005).

Neillands, Robin, *Eighth Army: From the Western Desert to the Alps, 1939–1945* (London, 2004).

North, John (ed.), *Field-Marshal Earl Alexander of Tunis: The Alexander Memoirs 1940–1945* (London, 1962).

Oram, Gerard, 'Pious Perjury: Discipline and Morale in the British Force in Italy, 1917–1918', *War in History*, 9(4) (2002).

Overy, Richard, *Why the Allies Won* (London, 1995).

Owen, James, and Walters, Guy, *The Voice of War: The Second World War Told by Those Who Fought It* (London, 2004).

Panichas, George, *Promise of Greatness: The War of 1914–1918* (London, 1968).

Paret, Peter (ed.), *Makers of Modern Strategy from Machiavelli to the Nuclear Age* (Oxford, 1986).

Parker, Matthew, *Monte Cassino: The Story of the Hardest-Fought Battle of World War Two* (London, 2003).

Peukert, Detlev J. K., *The Weimar Republic: The Crisis of Classical Modernity* (London, 1991).

Pitt, Barrie, *The Crucible of War: Wavell's Command: The Definitive History of the Desert War*, vol. I (London, 2001).

The Crucible of War: Auchinleck's Command: The Definitive History of the Desert War, vol. II (London, 2001).

The Crucible of War: Montgomery and Alamein: The Definitive History of the Desert War, vol. III (London, 2001).

Playfair, I. S. O., Stitt, G. M. S., Molony, C. J. C. and Toomer, S. E., *The Mediterranean and Middle East*, vol. I, *The Early Success against Italy. History of the Second World War* (London, 1954).

Playfair, I. S. O., Flynn, F. C., Molony, C. J. C. and Toomer, S. E., *The Mediterranean and Middle East*, vol. II, *The Germans Come to the Help of Their Ally. History of the Second World War* (London, 1956).

Playfair, I. S. O., Molony, C. J. C., Flynn, F. C. and Gleave, T. P., *The Mediterranean and Middle East*, vol. III, *British Fortunes Reach their Lowest Ebb. History of the Second World War* (London, 1960).

The Mediterranean and Middle East, vol. IV, *The Destruction of the Axis Forces in Africa. History of the Second World War* (London, 1966).

Porch, Douglas, *Hitler's Mediterranean Gamble: The North African and Mediterranean Campaigns in World War II* (London, 2004).

Prysor, Glyn, 'The "Fifth Column" and the British Experience of Retreat, 1940', *War in History*, 12(4) (2005).

Quilter, D. C., *No Dishonourable Name: The 2nd and 3rd Battalions Coldstream Guards 1939–1946* (London, 1972).

Raudzens, George, 'War-Winning Weapons: The Measurement of Technological Determinism in Military History', *Journal of Military History*, 54(4) (October 1990).

Reid, Brian Holden, *Studies in British Military Thought: Debates with Fuller and Liddell Hart* (Lincoln, NE, 1998).

Reiter, Dan and Stam, Allan C. III, 'Democracy and Battlefield Military Effectiveness', *Journal of Conflict Resolution*, 42(3) (June 1998).

Reynolds, David, *In Command of History: Churchill Fighting and Writing the Second World War* (London, 2004).

Richardson, Major-General F. M., *Fighting Spirit: A Study of Psychological Factors in War* (London, 1978).

Rissik, David, *The DLI at War: The History of the Durham Light Infantry 1939–1945* (Brancepeth, 1954).

Sajer, Guy, *The Forgotten Soldier* (London, 1999).

Salmond, J. B., *The History of the 51st Highland Division 1939–1945* (Durham, 1994).

Sandes, E. W. C., *From Pyramid to Pagoda: The Story of the West Yorkshire Regiment (The Prince of Wales's Own) in the War 1939–45 and Afterwards* (London, 1952).

Sarkessian, Sam C. (ed.), *Combat Effectiveness: Cohesion, Stress, and the Volunteer Military* (London, 1980).

Schrijvers, Peter, *The Crash of Ruin: American Combat Soldiers in Europe during World War II* (London, 1998).

Scoullar, J. L., *Battle for Egypt: The Summer of 1942. Official History of New Zealand in the Second World War 1939–1945* (Wellington, 1955).

Semmler, Clement (ed.), *The War Diaries of Kenneth Slessor, Official Australian Correspondent 1940–1944* (St Lucia, 1985).

Sheffield, G. D., *Leadership in the Trenches: Officer–Man Relations, Morale and Discipline in the British Army in the Era of the First World War* (London, 2000).

Shephard, Ben, '"Pitiless Psychology": the Role of Prevention in British Military Psychiatry in the Second World War', *History of Psychiatry*, 10 (1999).

   A War of Nerves: Soldiers and Psychiatrists 1914–1994 (London, 2002).

Shils, Edward A. and Janowitz, Morris, 'Cohesion and Disintegration in the Wehrmacht in World War II', *Public Opinion Quarterly*, 12 (Summer 1948).

Short, Captain E. W., *The Story of the Durham Light Infantry*, (Newcastle, ND).

Sillman, Leonard R., 'Morale', *War Medicine*, 3(5) (May 1943).

Simpkins, Major B. G., *Rand Light Infantry* (Cape Town, 1965).

Slim, Field-Marshal Viscount, *Defeat into Victory* (London, 1999).

Smith, Leonard V., *Between Mutiny and Obedience: The Case of the French Fifth Infantry Division during World War I* (Princeton, 1994).

Smith, General Sir Rupert, *The Utility of Force: The Art of War in the Modern World* (London, 2005).

Snyder, Jack, *The Ideology of the Offensive: Military Decision Making and the Disaster of 1914* (London, 1984).

Spiller, Roger J., 'S. L. A. Marshall and the Ratio of Fire', *RUSI Journal*, 133 (Winter 1988).

Stevens, William George, *Problems of 2 NZEF: Official History of New Zealand in the Second World War 1939–45* (Wellington, 1958).

Stewart, Adrian, *North African Victory: The Eighth Army from Alam Halfa to Tunis 1942–1943* (London, 2002).

Stora, Benjamin, *Histoire de la Guerre d'Algérie (1954–1962)* (Paris, 1995).

Stouffer, Samuel A. et al., *The American Soldier: Combat and Its Aftermath* (New York, 1965).

Strachan, Hew, *Carl von Clausewitz's On War: A Biography* (London, 2007).

European Armies and the Conduct of War (London, 1983).

The First World War, vol. I, *To Arms* (London, 2001).

'Training, Morale and Modern War', *Journal of Contemporary History*, 41(2) (London, 2006).

The British Army, Manpower and Society into the Twenty-First Century (London, 2000).

Military Lives: Intimate Biographies of the Famous by the Famous (Oxford, 2002).

The Oxford Illustrated History of the First World War (Oxford, 1998).

Sun Tzu, *The Art of War* (Oxford, 1963).

Swaab, Jack, *Field of Fire: Diary of a Gunner Officer* (Stroud, 2005).

Tooze, Adam, *The Wages of Destruction: The Making and Breaking of the Nazi Economy* (London, 2006).

Trachtenberg, Marc, *The Craft of International History: A Guide to Method* (Oxford, 2006).

Valentine, C. W., *The Human Factor in the Army: Some Applications of Psychology to Training, Selection, Morale and Discipline* (Aldershot, 1943).

Van Creveld, Martin, *Supplying War: Logistics from Wallenstein to Patton* (Cambridge, 1977).

Von Luck, Hans, *Panzer Commander: The Memoirs of Colonel Hans Von Luck* (London, 1989).

Walker, Allan S., *Clinical Problems of War. Australia in the War of 1939–1945*, vol. I (Canberra, 1952).

Middle East and Far East. Australia in the War of 1939–1945, vol. II (Canberra, 1953).

Wanke, Paul, 'American Military Psychiatry and Its Role among Ground Forces in World War II', in *The Journal of Military History*, 63(1) (January 1999).

War History of the 7th Battalion The Black Watch (R.H.R.), 1939–45 (Fife, 1948).

Washburn, Stanley, 'What Makes Morale?', *Public Opinion Quarterly*, 5(4) (Winter 1941).

Watson, Alexander, *Enduring the Great War: Combat, Morale and Collapse in the German and British Armies, 1914–1918* (Cambridge, 2008).

Weeks, John, *Men against Tanks: A History of Anti-Tank Warfare* (Newton Abbot, 1975).

Weinberg, Gerhard L., 'Unexplored Questions about the German Military during World War II', *Journal of Military History*, 62(2) (April 1998).

A World At Arms: A Global History of World War II (Cambridge, 2005).

Wessely, Simon, 'Twentieth-Century Theories on Combat Motivation and Breakdown', *Journal of Contemporary History*, 41(2) (2006).

White, Lorraine, 'The Experience of Spain's Early Modern Soldiers: Combat, Welfare and Violence', *War in History*, 9(1) (2002).

White, Peter, *With the Jocks* (Stroud, 2002).

Wilson, Charles, *The Anatomy of Courage* (London, 1945).

Winter, Denis, *Death's Men: Soldiers of the Great War* (London, 1979).

Young, Desmond, *Rommel* (London, 1950).

Zetterling, Niklas, *Normandy 1944: German Military Organization, Combat Power and Organizational Effectiveness* (Winnipeg, MB, 2000).

Zinn, Howard, *A People's History of the United States, 1492-Present* (New York, 1995).

UNPUBLISHED THESIS

Pratten, Garth M., 'The "Old Man": Australian Battalion Commanders in the Second World War' (Ph.D. thesis, Deakin University, Melbourne, 2005).

WEBSITES

www.remuseum.org.uk/specialism/rem_spec_pcsww2.htm. The Royal Engineers Museum. Second World War Army Postal Services, 1939–45.

www.queensu.ca/sarc/Conference/1940s/Roos.htm. Neil Roos, 'The Second World War, the Army Education Scheme and the 'Discipline' of the White Poor in South Africa', Workshop on South Africa in the 1940s, Southern African Research Centre, Kingston, September, 2003.

Index

Printed in Great Britain
by Amazon